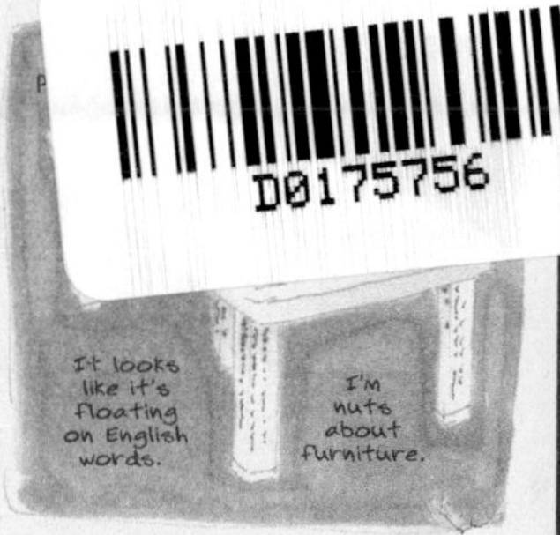
It looks like it's floating on English words.
I'm nuts about furniture.

...oving at the end of ... In other words, by the ...his volume comes out in ... I should be in my new ...

Hey!
Will I be?!
I will be, right?!

-Tite Kubo

Bleach is author Tite Kubo's second title. Kubo made his debut with *ZOMBIEPOWDER.*, a four-volume series for *Weekly Shonen Jump*. To date, *Bleach* has been translated into numerous languages and has also inspired an animated TV series that began airing in the U.S. in 2006. Beginning its serialization in 2001, *Bleach* is still a mainstay in the pages of *Weekly Shonen Jump*. In 2005, *Bleach* was awarded the prestigious Shogakukan Manga Award in the *shonen* (boys) category.

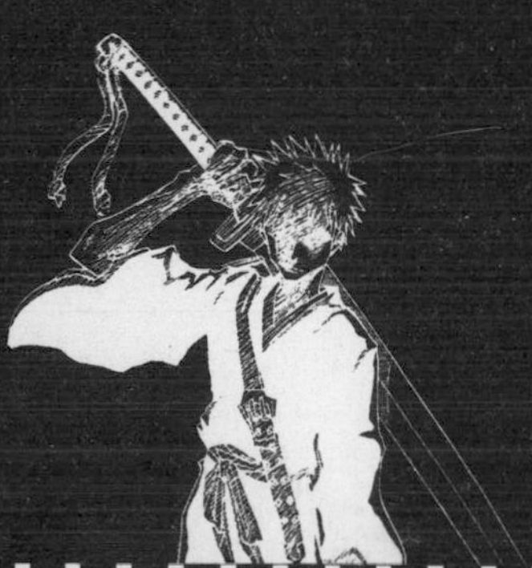

BLEACH
Vol. 44: VICE IT
SHONEN JUMP Manga Edition

STORY AND ART BY
TITE KUBO

English Adaptation/Lance Caselman
Translation/Joe Yamazaki
Touch-up Art & Lettering/Mark McMurray
Design/Yukiko Whitley, Kam Li
Editor/Alexis Kirsch

Printed in the U.S.A.

Published by VIZ Media, LLC
P.O. Box 77010
San Francisco, CA 94107

10 9 8 7 6 5 4 3 2 1
First printing, August 2012

People are all evil.
In order to falsely believe yourself to be just
You must inevitably falsely believe
That someone else is more evil than you.

BLEACH 44 VICE IT

STARS AND

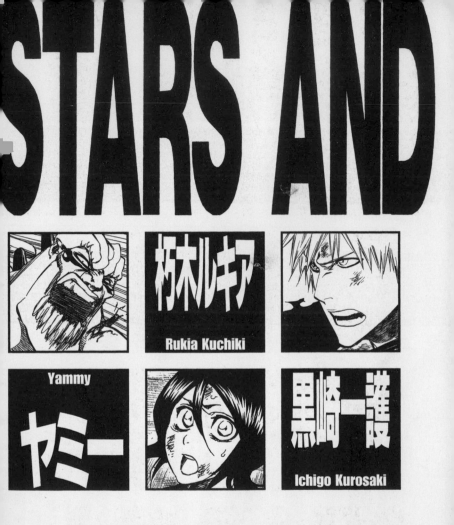

Rukia Kuchiki

Yammy

Ichigo Kurosaki

plot

When high school student Ichigo Kurosaki meets Soul Reaper Rukia Kuchiki his life is changed forever. Soon Ichigo is a soul-cleansing Soul Reaper too, and he finds himself having adventures, as well as problems, that he never would have imagined. Now Ichigo and his friends must stop renegade Soul Reaper Aizen and his army of Arrancars from destroying the Soul Society and wiping out Karakura as well.

Ichigo reveals a new side of himself when he defeats Ulquiorra to rescue Orihime, and Rukia faces a Yammy who has transformed into a huge monster! Meanwhile, the Thirteen Court Guard Companies and the Visoreds face the Espadas in mortal combat. But will the tide of battle turn with the appearance of Aizen himself?

BLEACH ALL

檜佐木修兵

Shuhei Hisagi

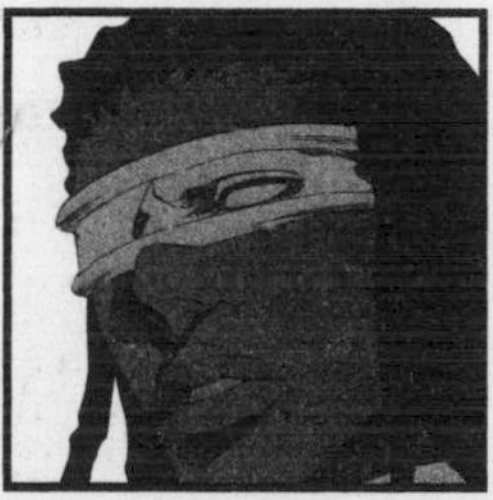

狛村左陣

Sajin Komamura

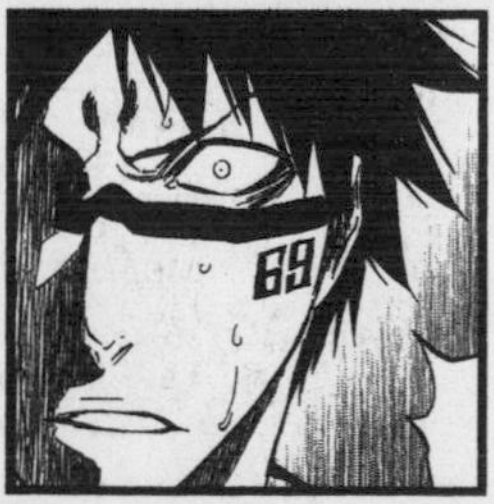

Kaname Tôsen

東仙要

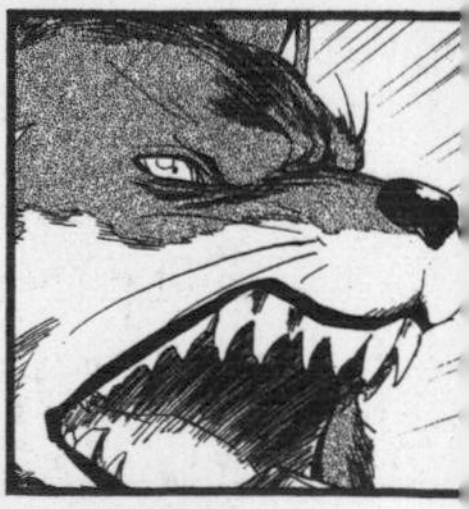

STORIES

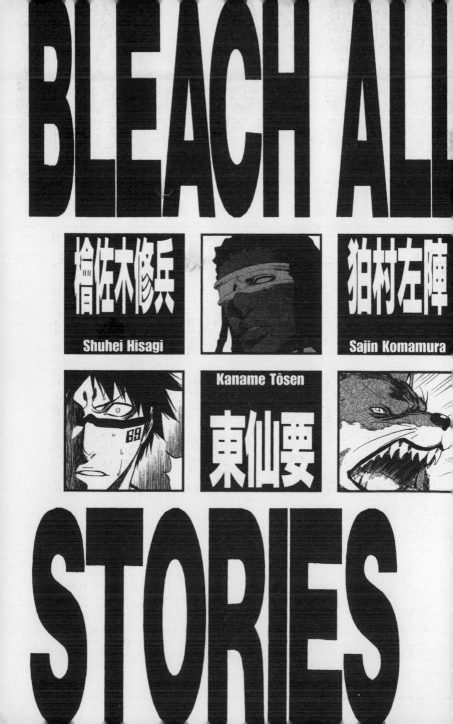

BLEACH 44

VICE IT

Contents

378. Eyes of the Victor

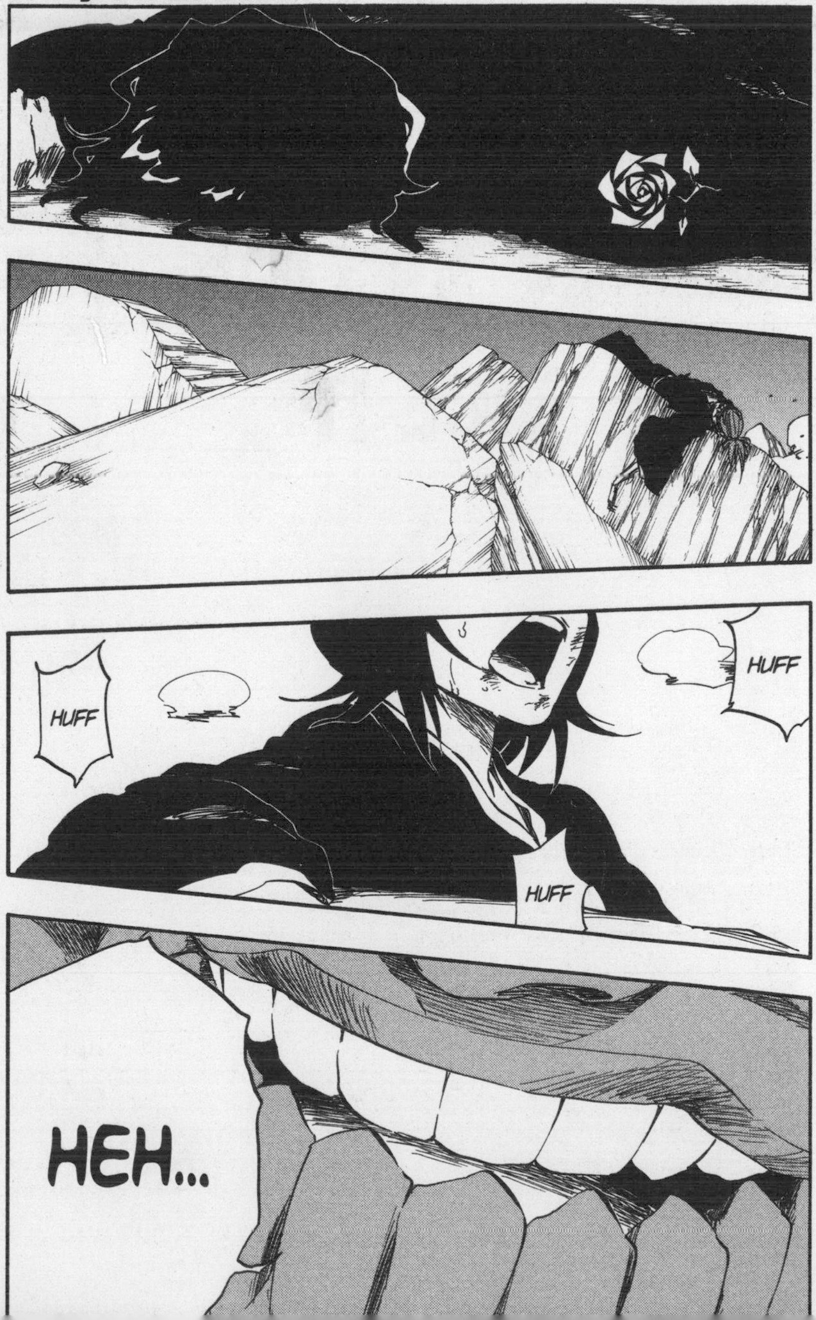
HUFF
HUFF
HUFF
HEH...

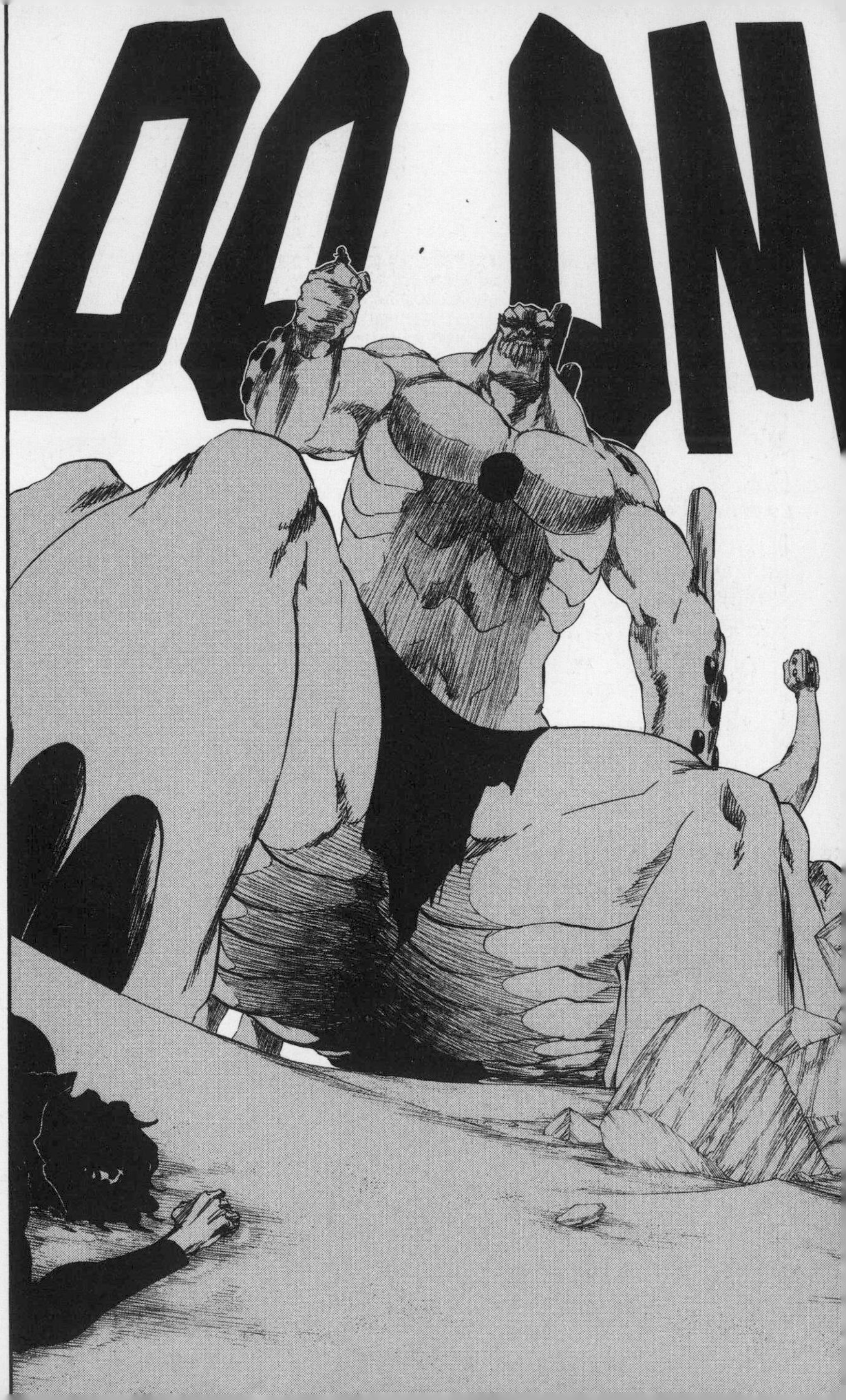
DOOM

READ THIS WAY

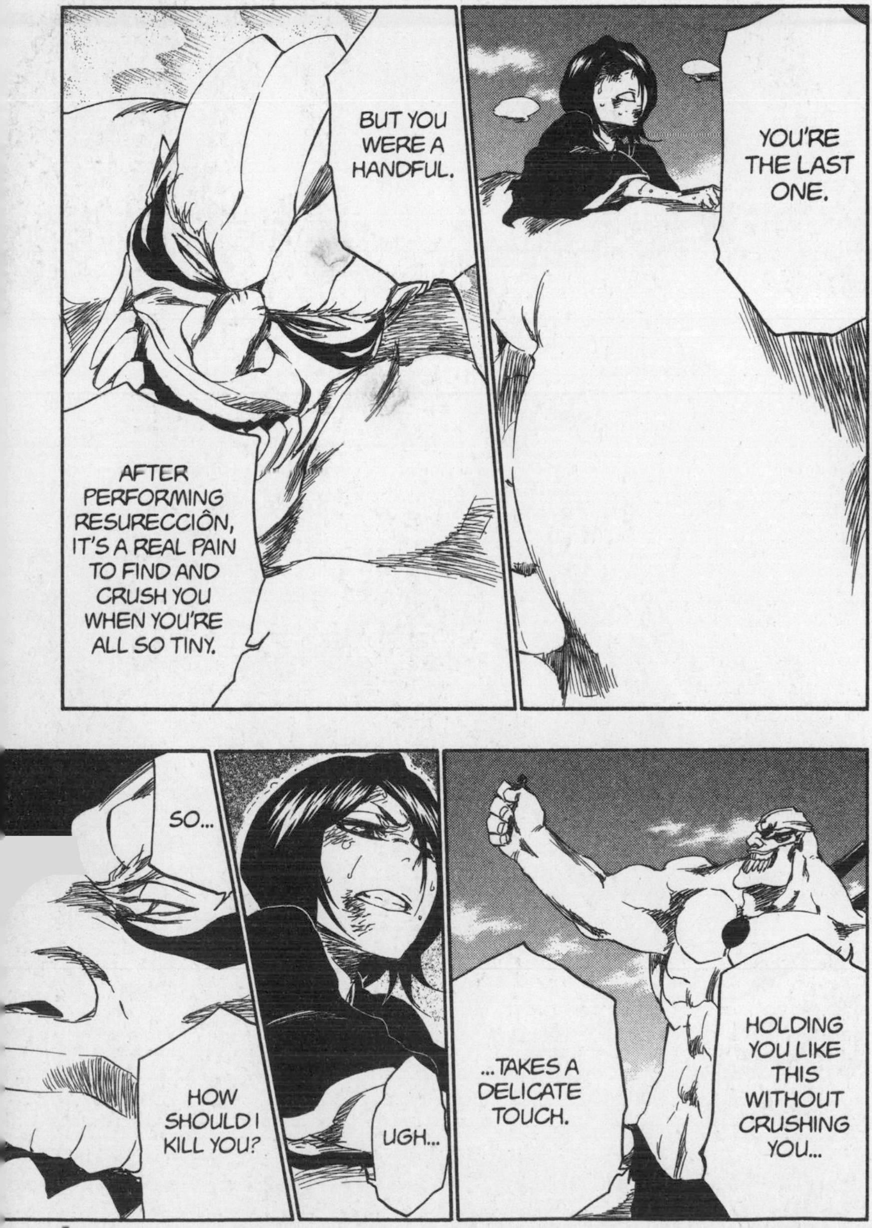
YOU'RE THE LAST ONE.
BUT YOU WERE A HANDFUL.
AFTER PERFORMING RESURECCIÔN, IT'S A REAL PAIN TO FIND AND CRUSH YOU WHEN YOU'RE ALL SO TINY.
HOLDING YOU LIKE THIS WITHOUT CRUSHING YOU...
...TAKES A DELICATE TOUCH.
UGH...
SO...
HOW SHOULD I KILL YOU?

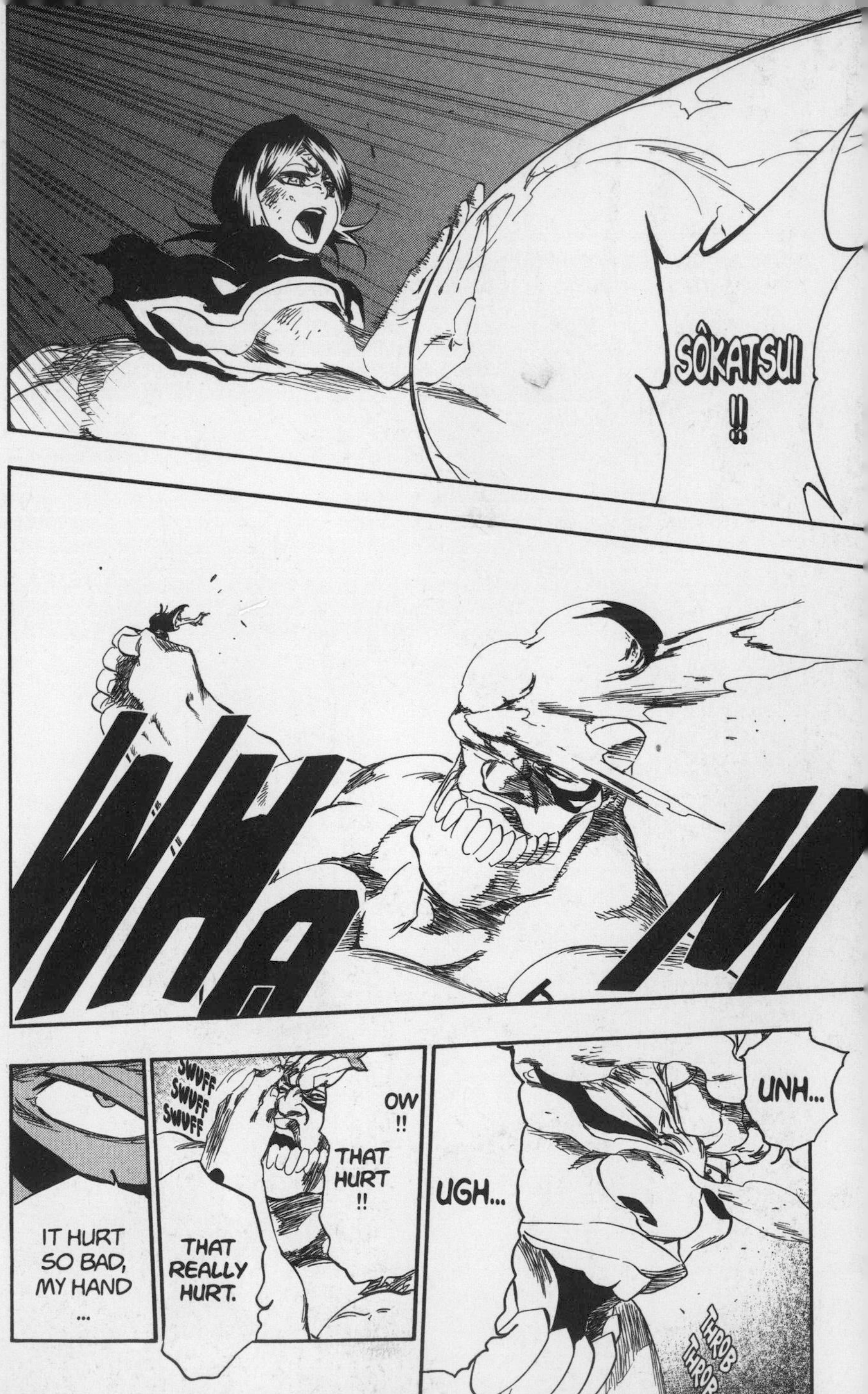
SÔKATSUI!!
WHAM
UNH...
UGH...
THROB THROB
OW!!
THAT HURT!!
SWUFF SWUFF SWUFF
THAT REALLY HURT.
IT HURT SO BAD, MY HAND...

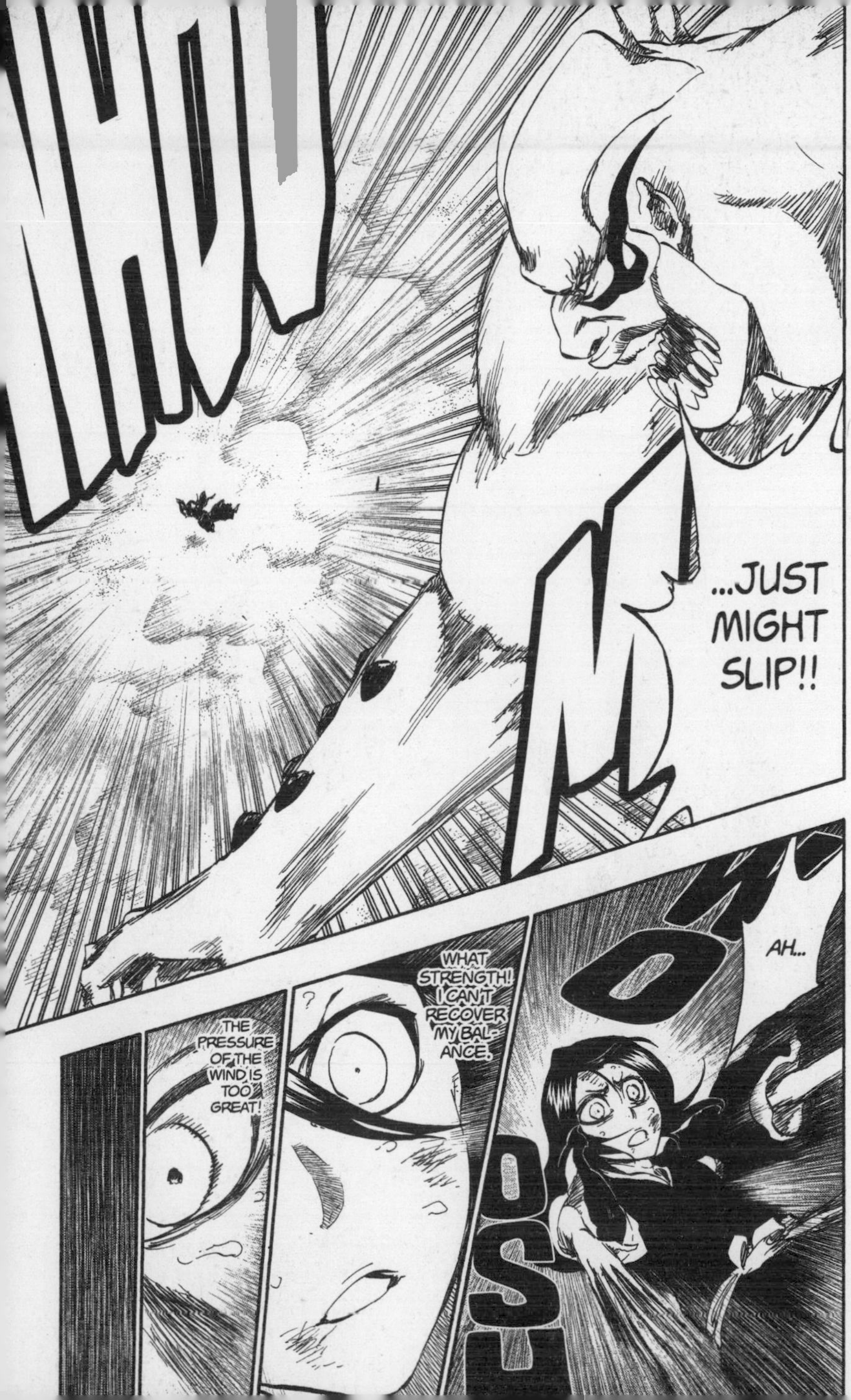
...JUST MIGHT SLIP!!
AH...
WHAT STRENGTH! I CAN'T RECOVER MY BALANCE.
THE PRESSURE OF THE WIND IS TOO GREAT!

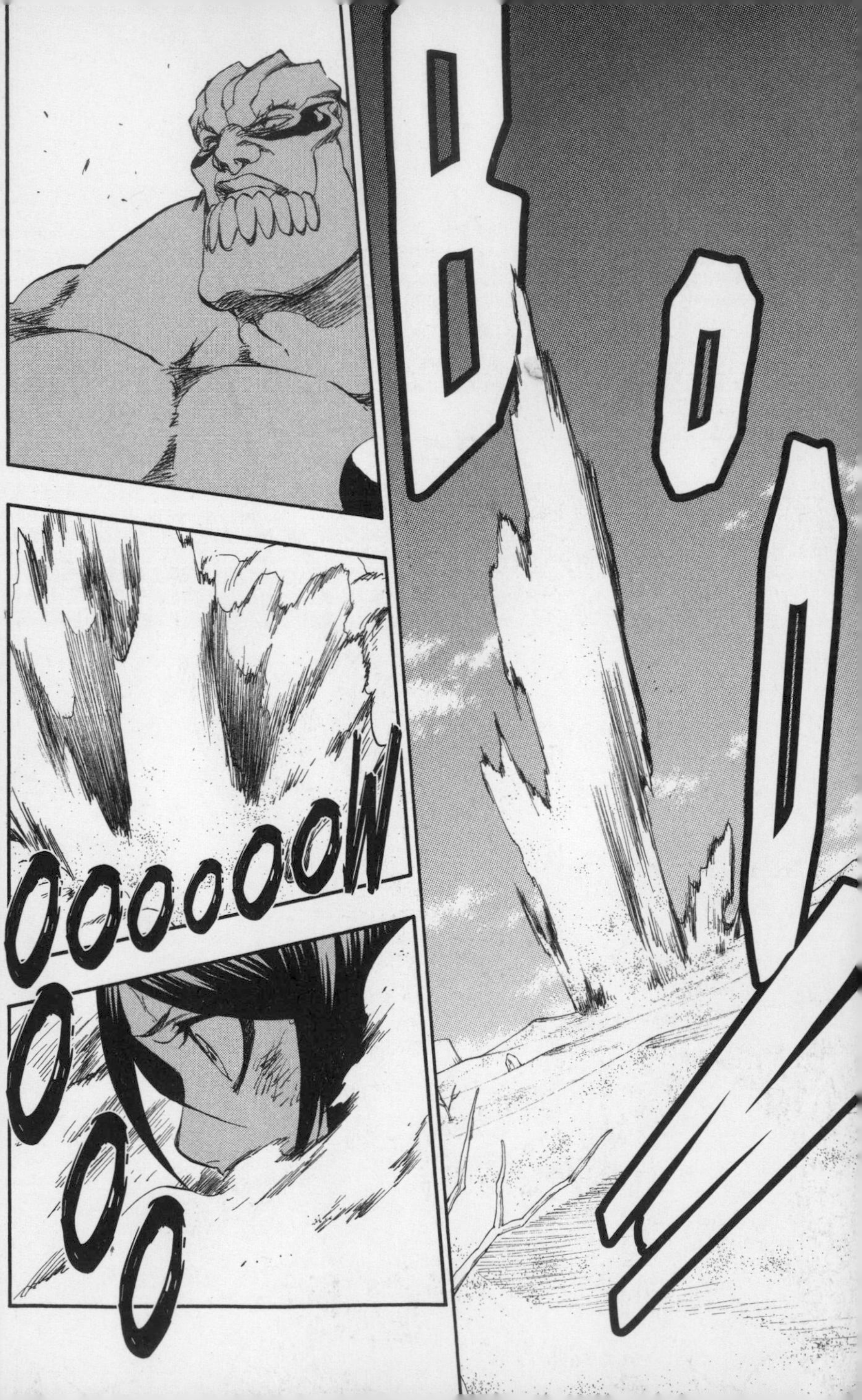
BOOM
OOOOOOW

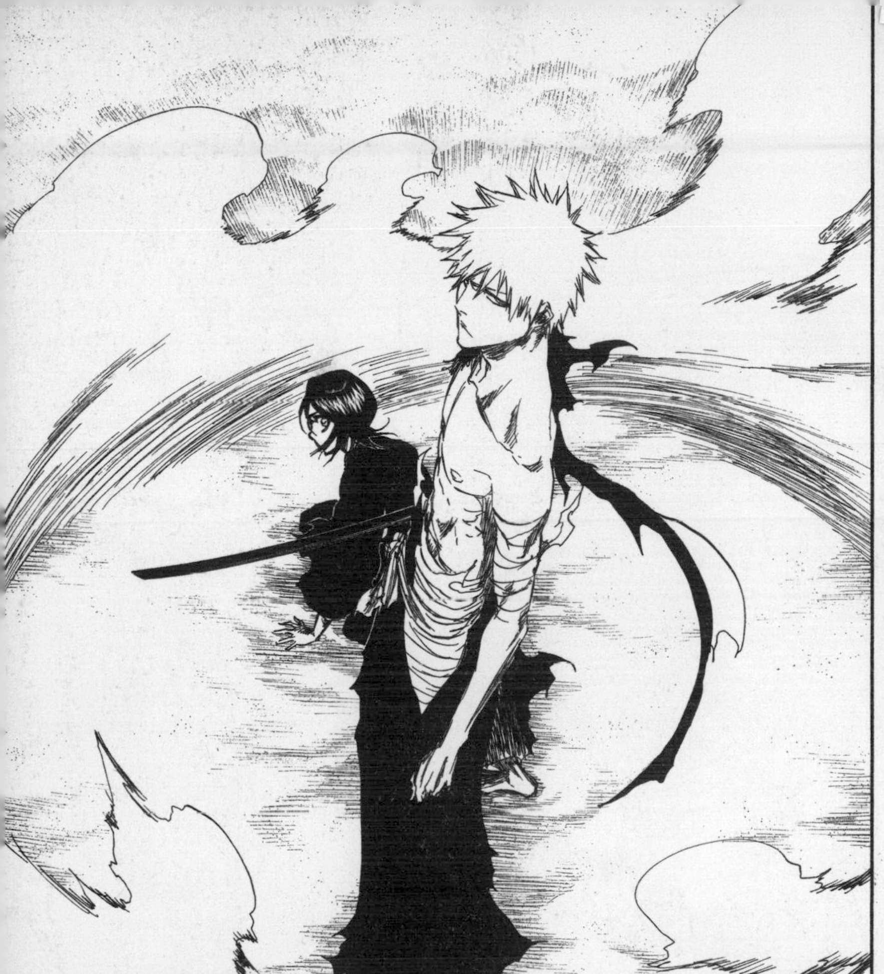
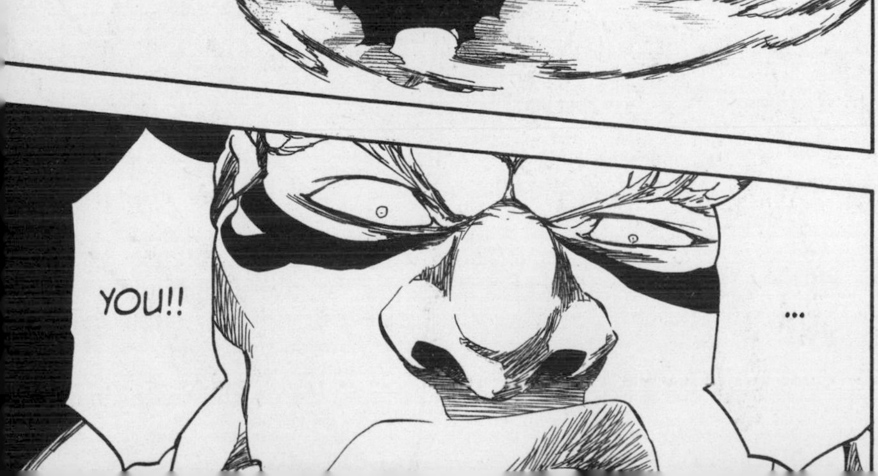
...
YOU!!

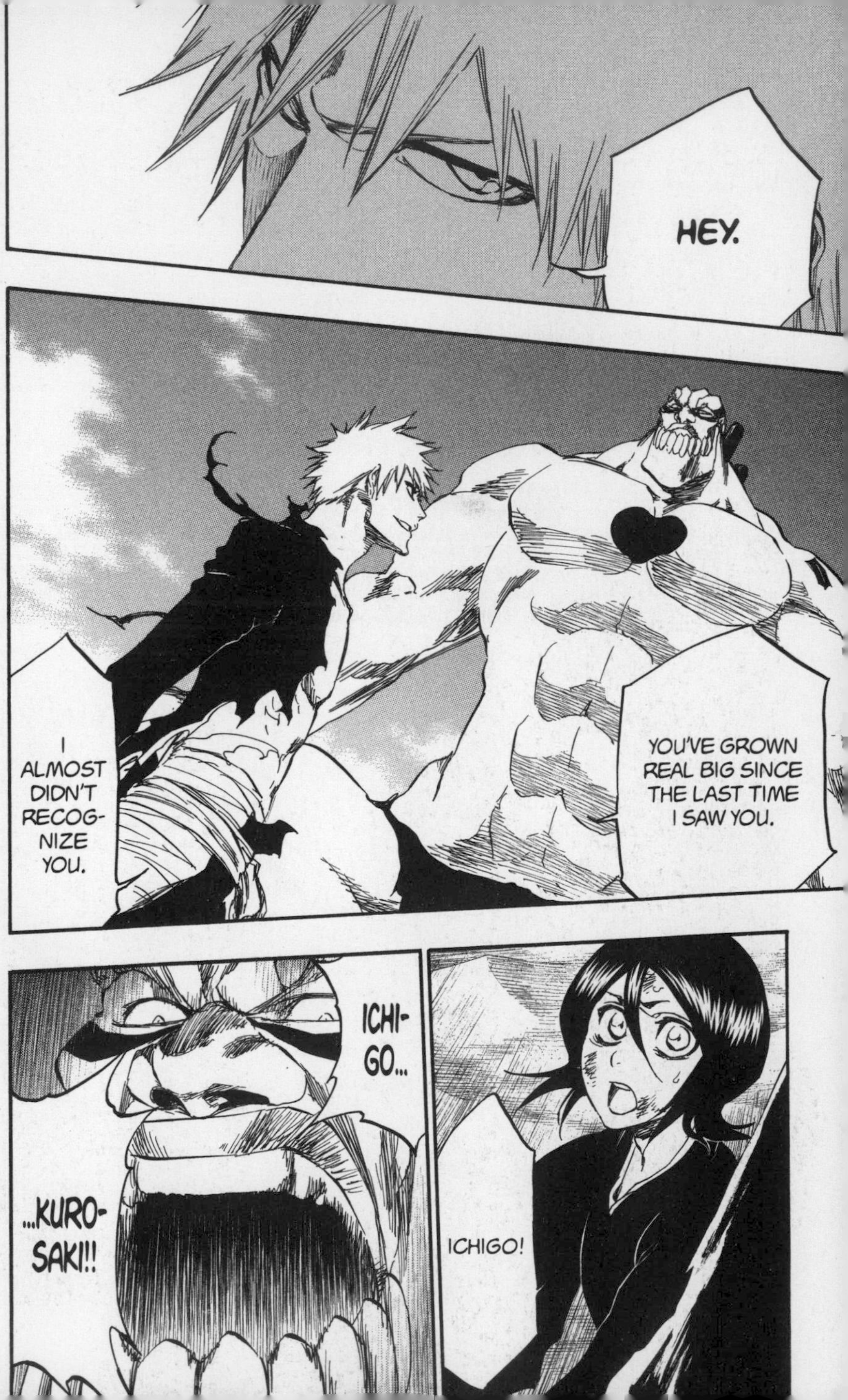
HEY.
YOU'VE GROWN REAL BIG SINCE THE LAST TIME I SAW YOU.
I ALMOST DIDN'T RECOG-NIZE YOU.
ICHIGO!
ICHI-GO...
...KURO-SAKI!!

BLEACH378. Eyes of the Victor

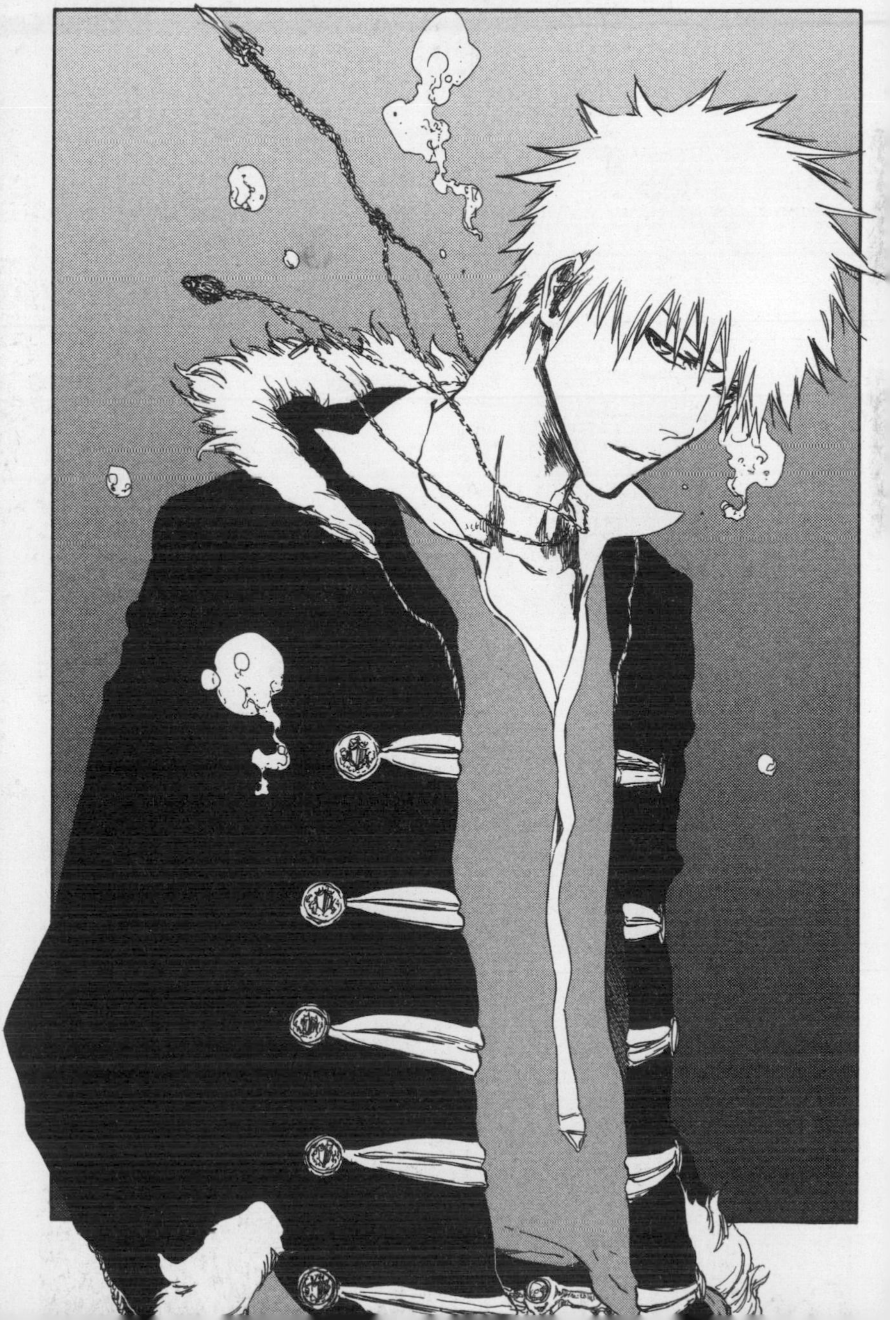

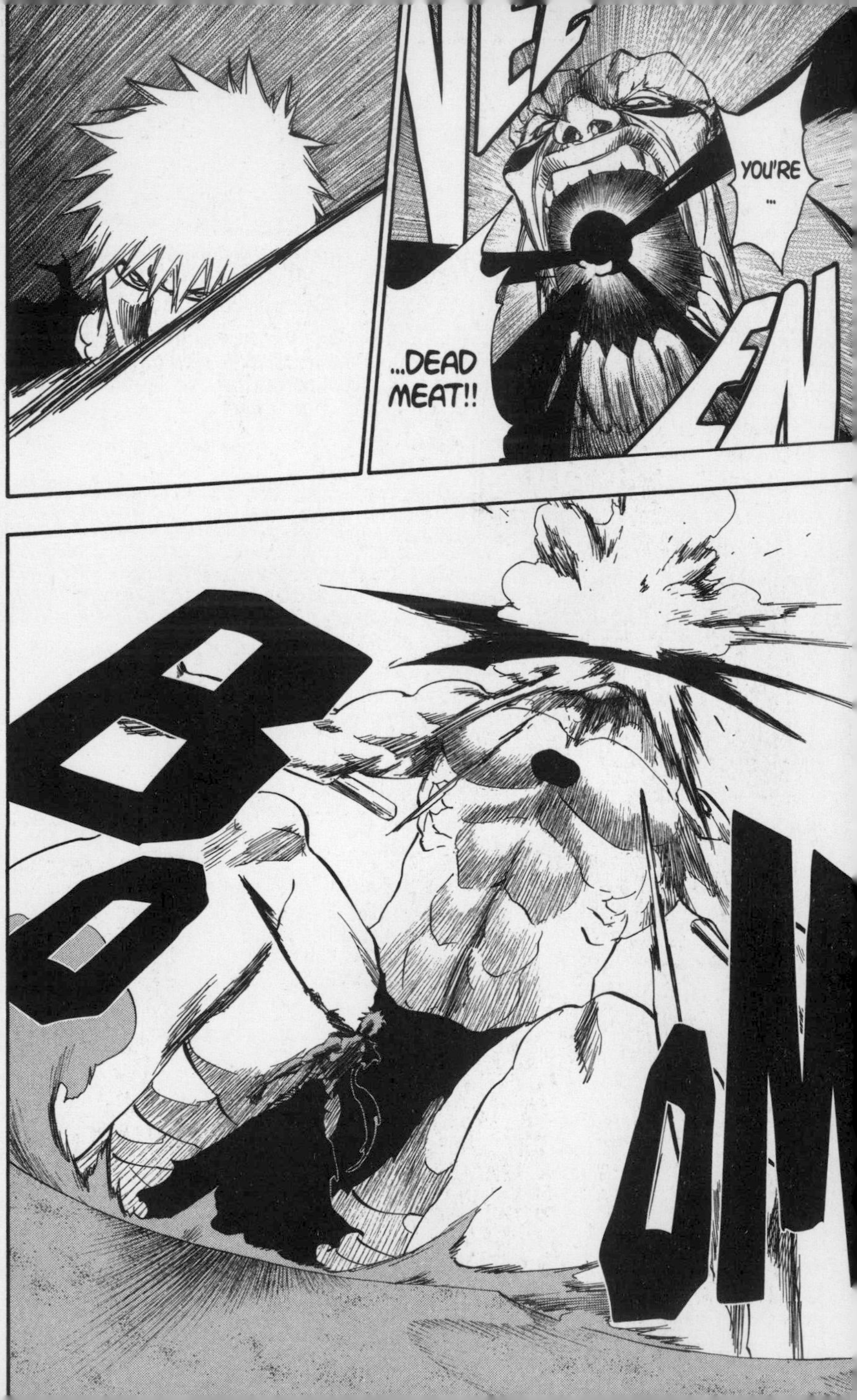
YOU'RE ...
...DEAD MEAT!!

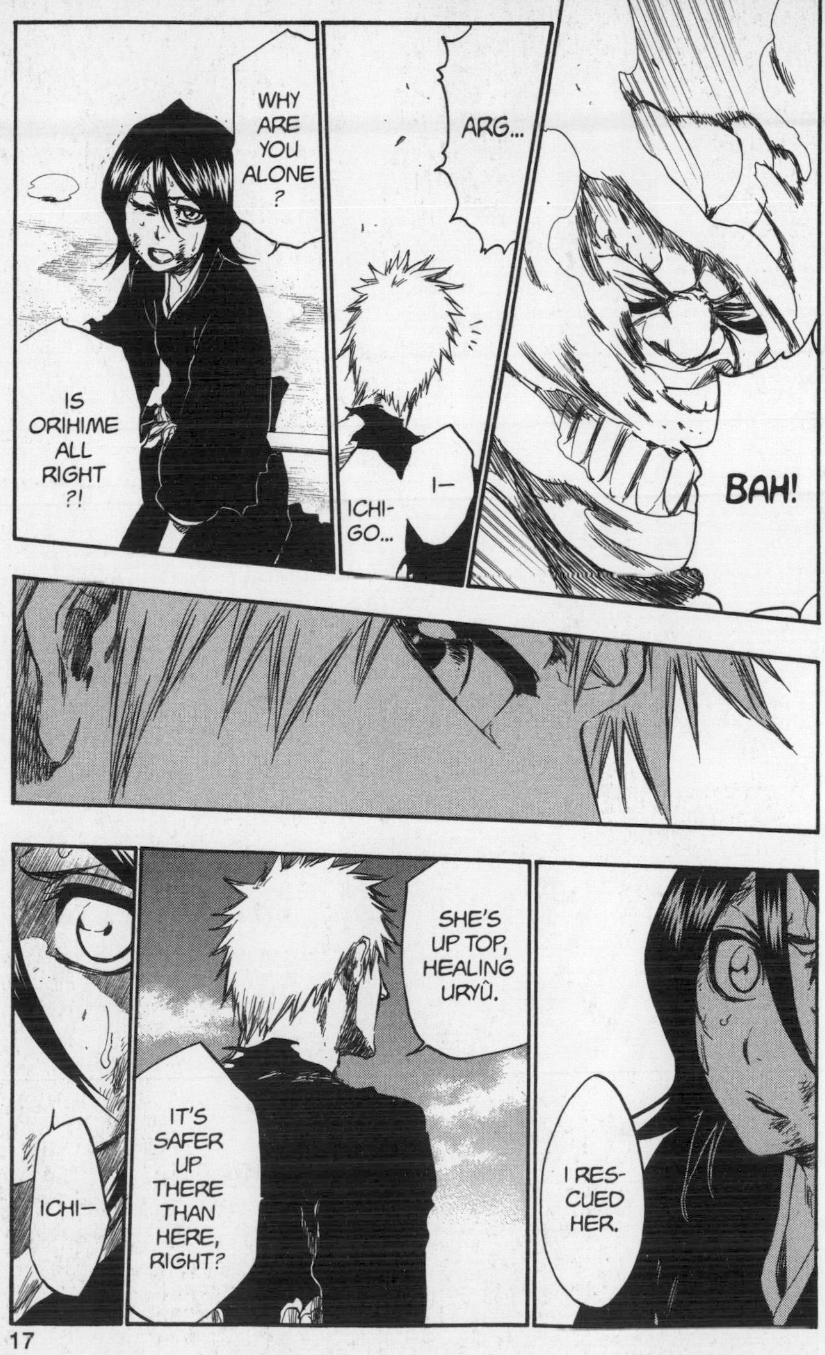
BAH!
ARG...
I—
ICHI-GO...
WHY ARE YOU ALONE?
IS ORIHIME ALL RIGHT?!
I RES-CUED HER.
SHE'S UP TOP, HEALING URYÛ.
IT'S SAFER UP THERE THAN HERE, RIGHT?
ICHI—

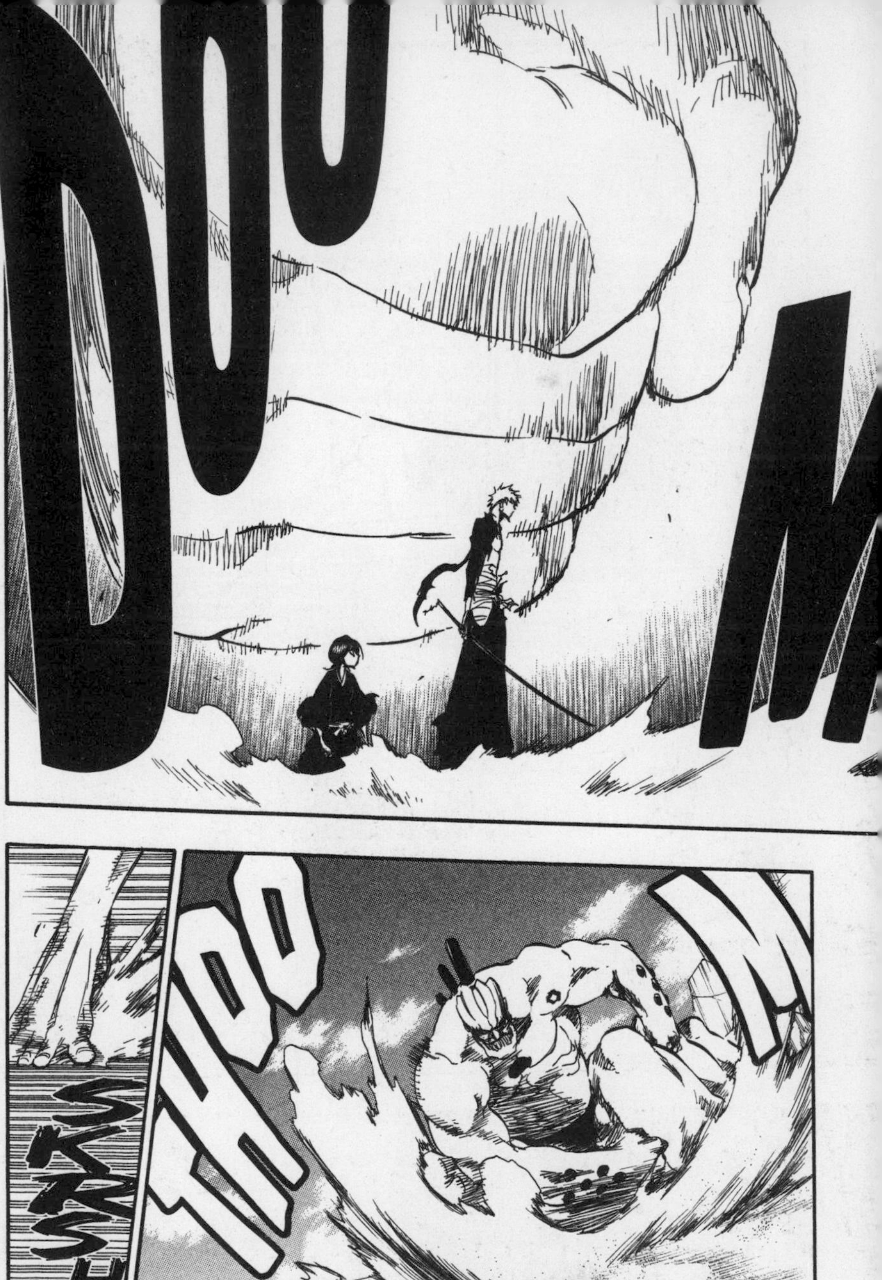
DOOM
THOOM
SWISH

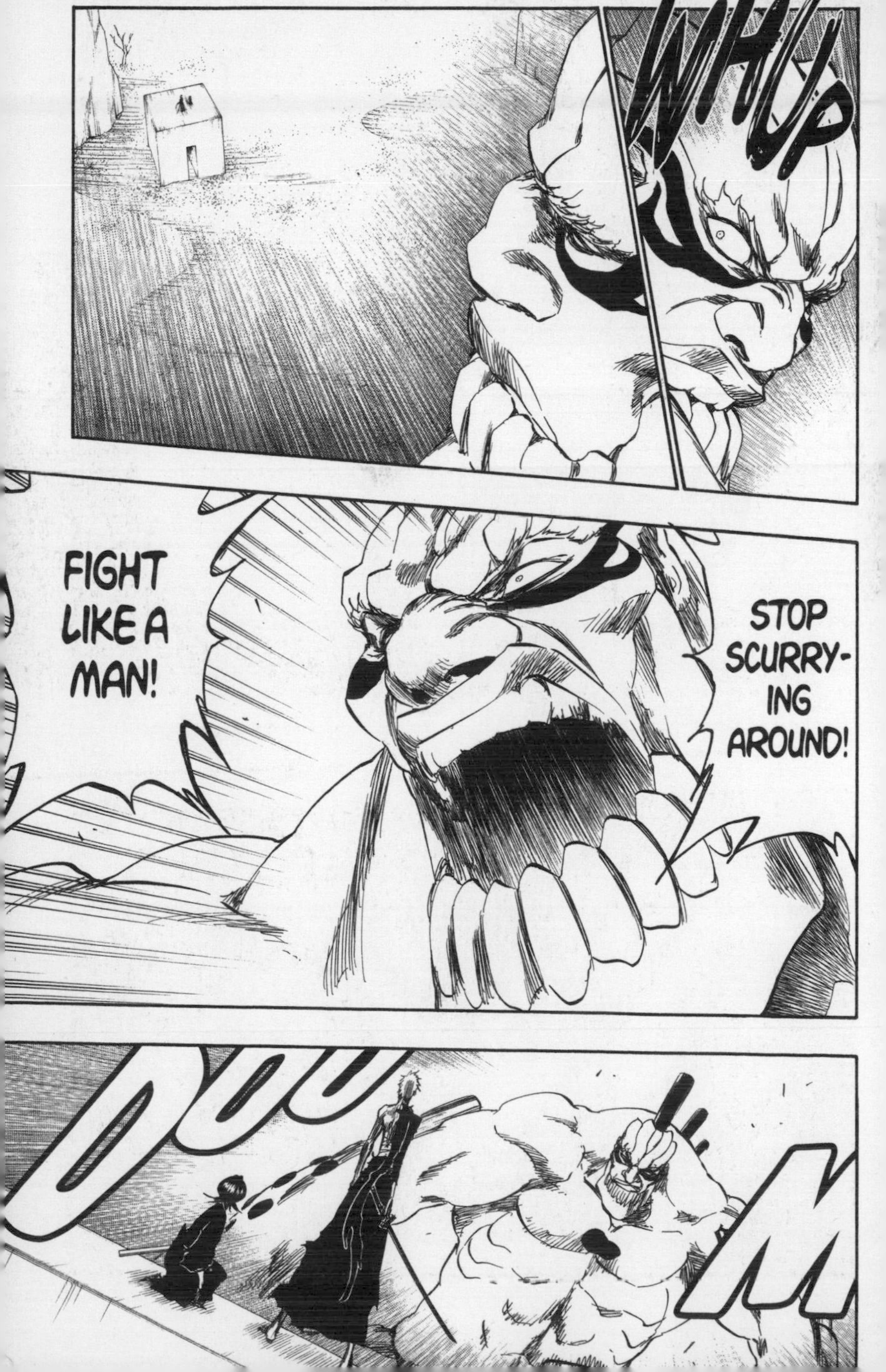
WHUP
STOP SCURRYING AROUND!
FIGHT LIKE A MAN!

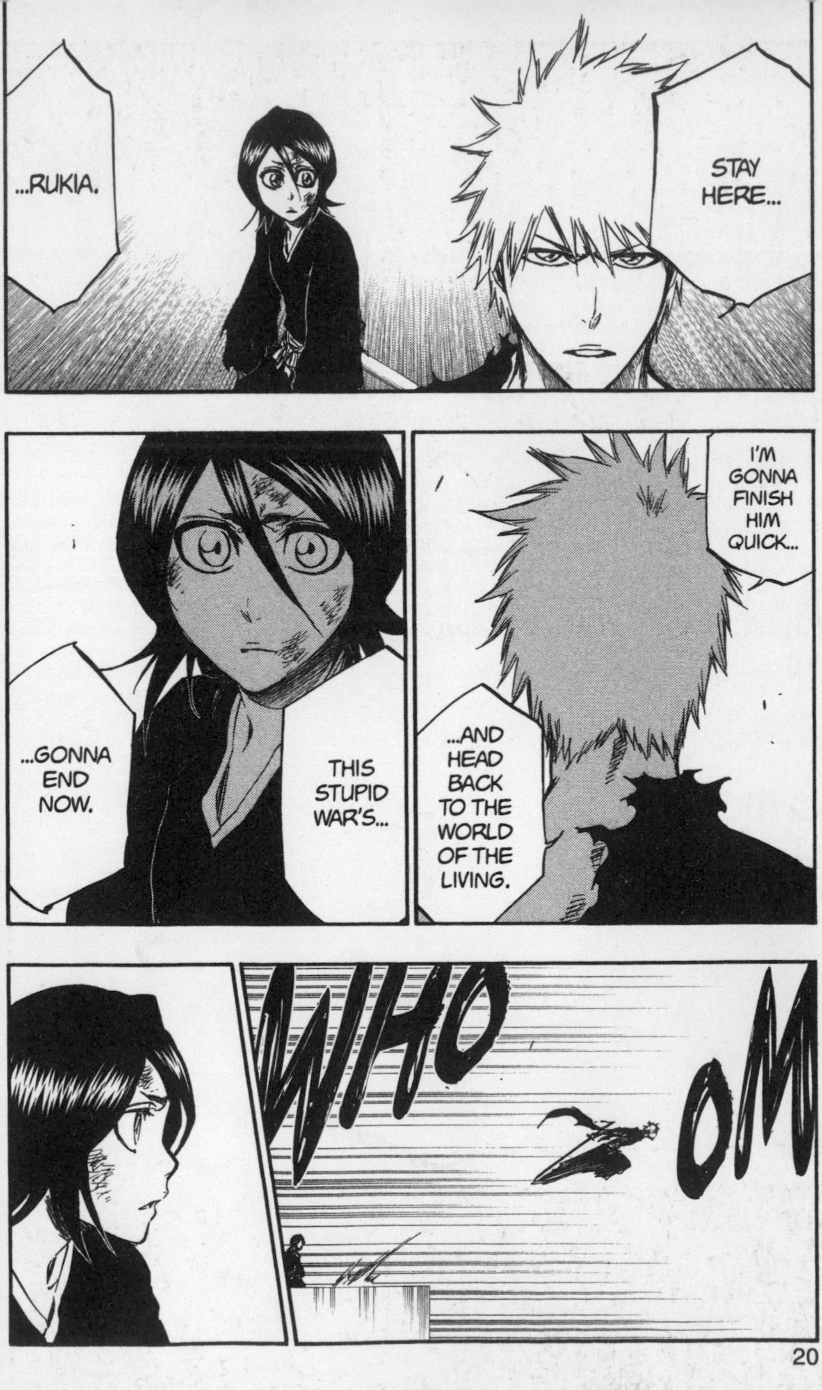
STAY HERE...
...RUKIA.
I'M GONNA FINISH HIM QUICK...
...AND HEAD BACK TO THE WORLD OF THE LIVING.
THIS STUPID WAR'S...
...GONNA END NOW.
WHO OM

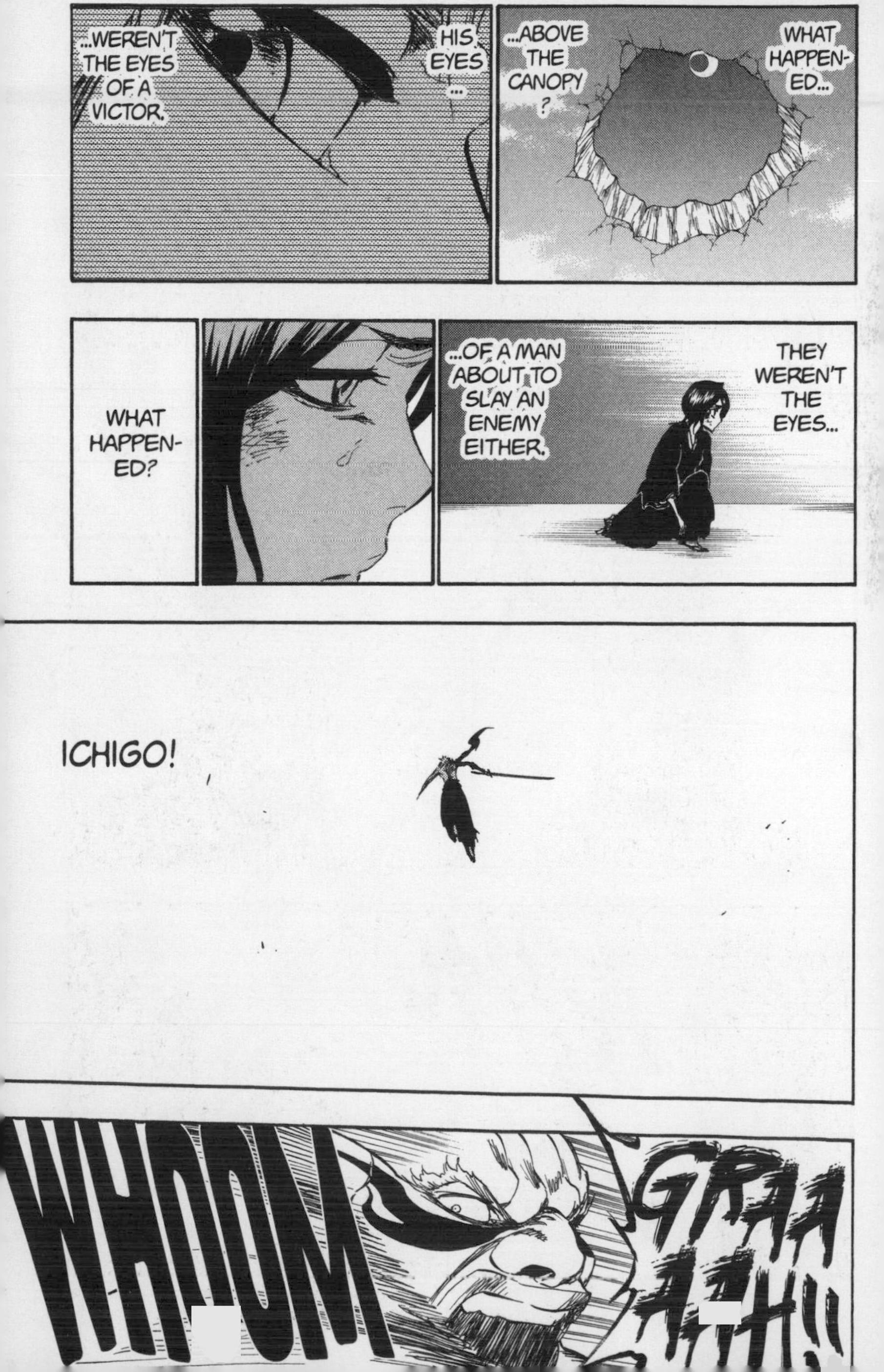
WHAT HAPPENED...
...ABOVE THE CANOPY?
HIS EYES...
...WEREN'T THE EYES OF A VICTOR.
THEY WEREN'T THE EYES...
...OF A MAN ABOUT TO SLAY AN ENEMY EITHER.
WHAT HAPPENED?
ICHIGO!
GRAAAAH!!
WHOOM

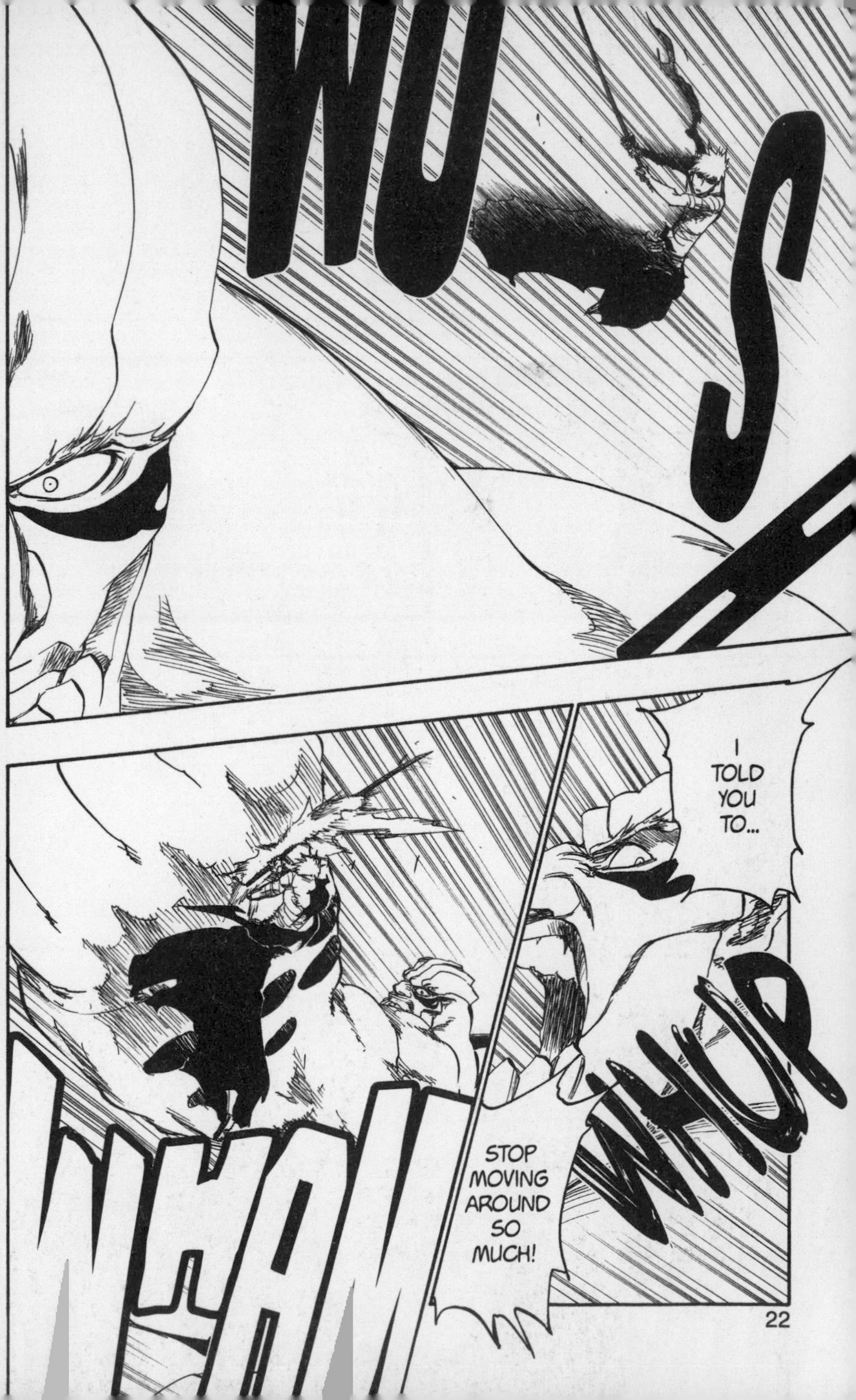
WUSH
I TOLD YOU TO...
WHUP
STOP MOVING AROUND SO MUCH!
WHAM

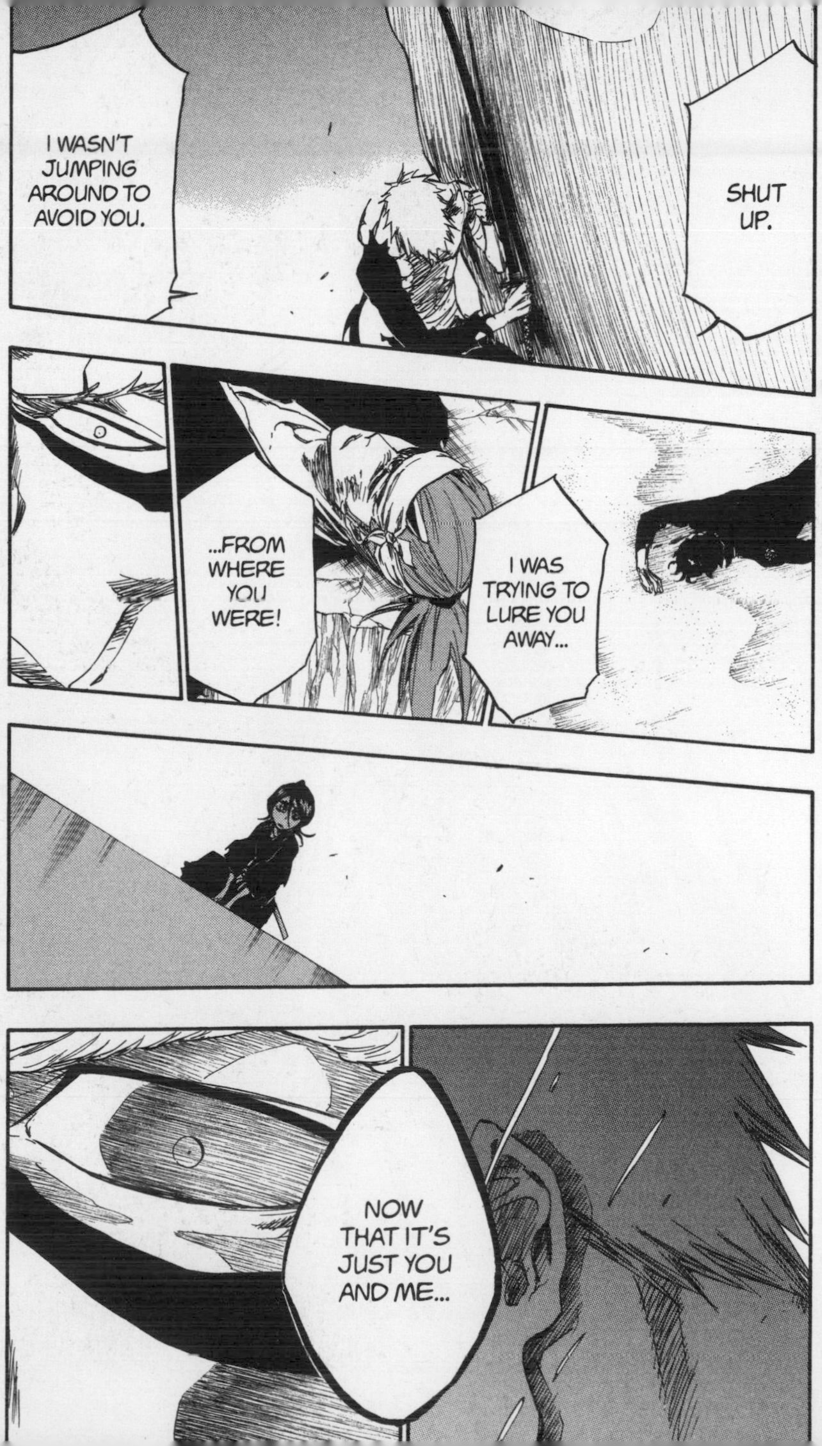
SHUT UP.
I WASN'T JUMPING AROUND TO AVOID YOU.
I WAS TRYING TO LURE YOU AWAY...
...FROM WHERE YOU WERE!
NOW THAT IT'S JUST YOU AND ME...

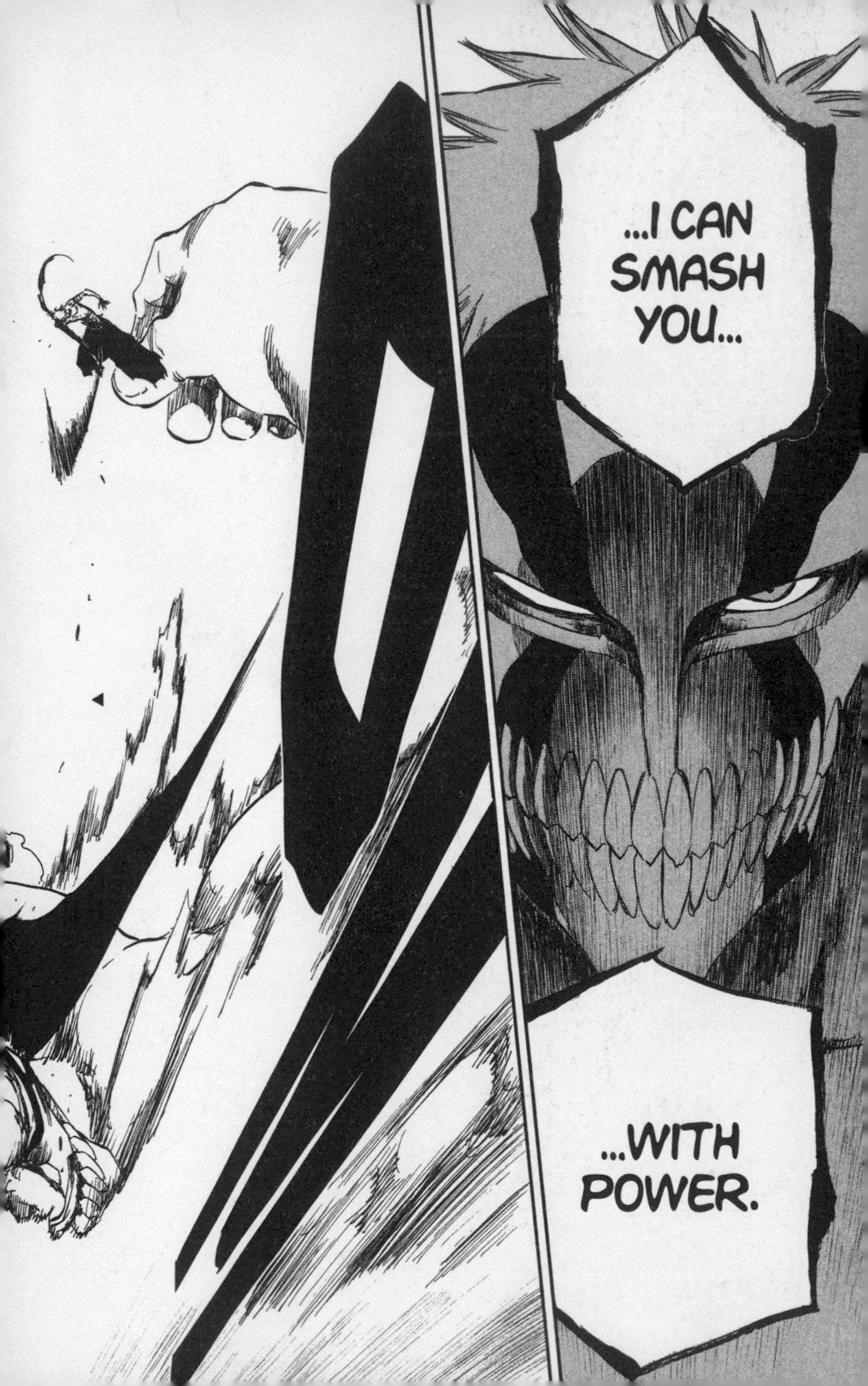
...I CAN SMASH YOU...
...WITH POWER.

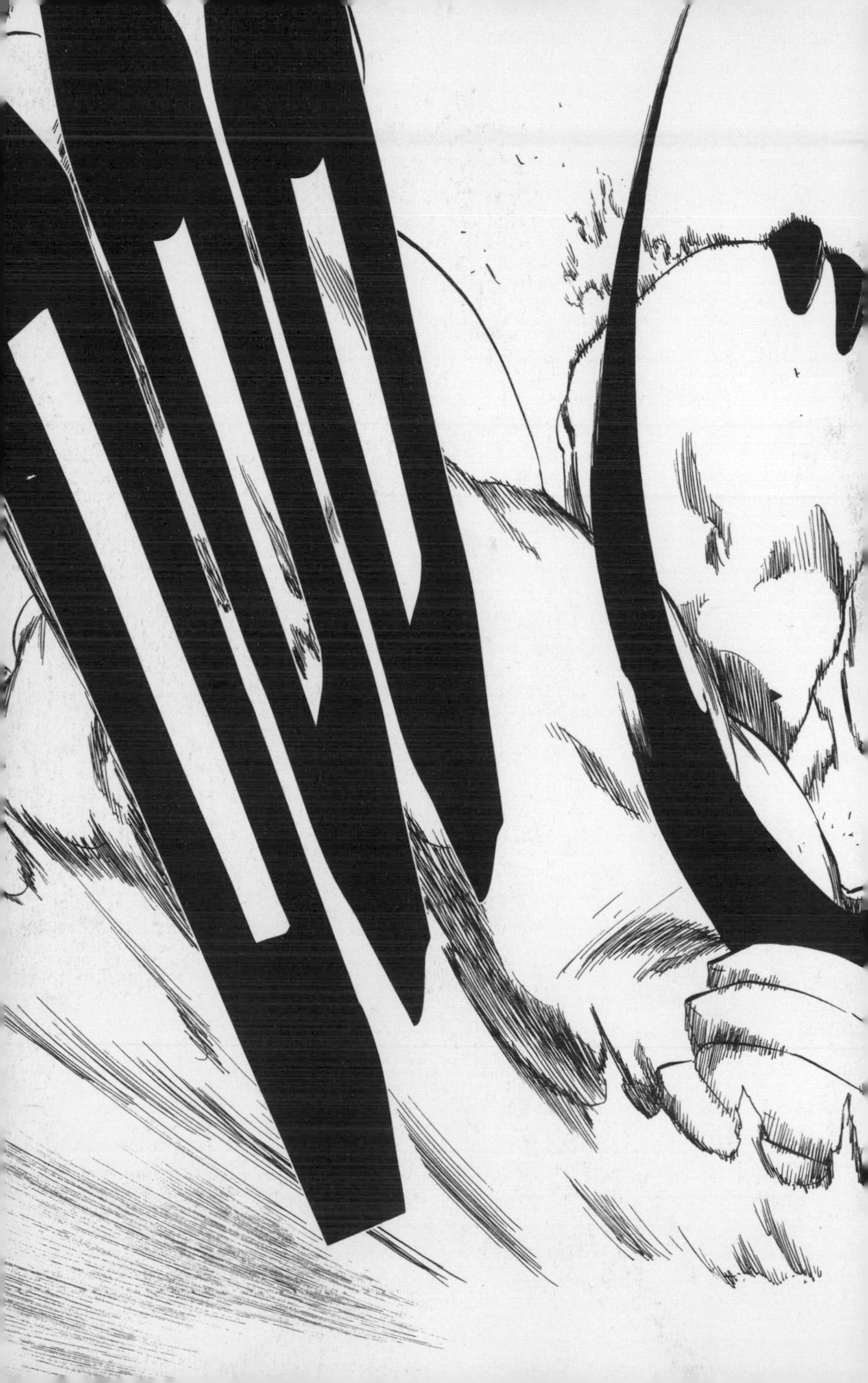

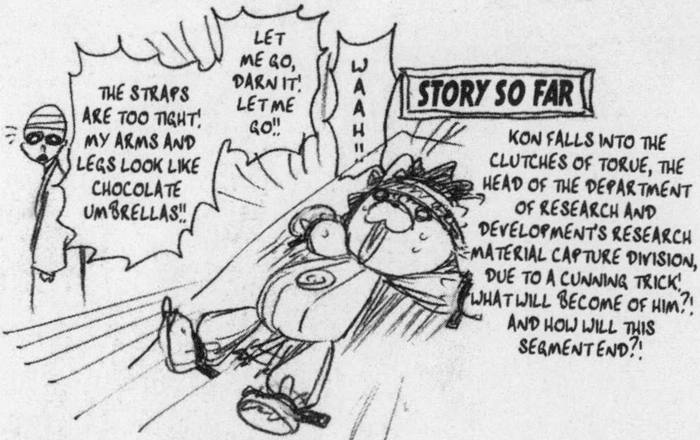
STORY SO FAR
KON FALLS INTO THE CLUTCHES OF TORUE, THE HEAD OF THE DEPARTMENT OF RESEARCH AND DEVELOPMENT'S RESEARCH MATERIAL CAPTURE DIVISION, DUE TO A CUNNING TRICK! WHAT WILL BECOME OF HIM?! AND HOW WILL THIS SEGMENT END?!
WAAAH!!
LET ME GO, DARN IT! LET ME GO!!
THE STRAPS ARE TOO TIGHT! MY ARMS AND LEGS LOOK LIKE CHOCOLATE UMBRELLAS!!

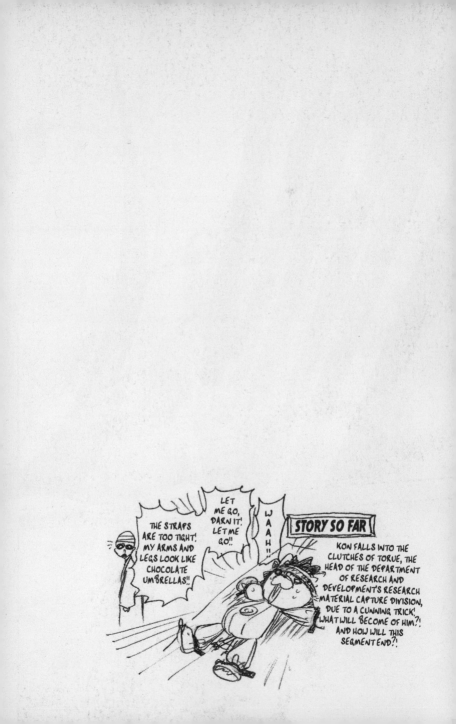

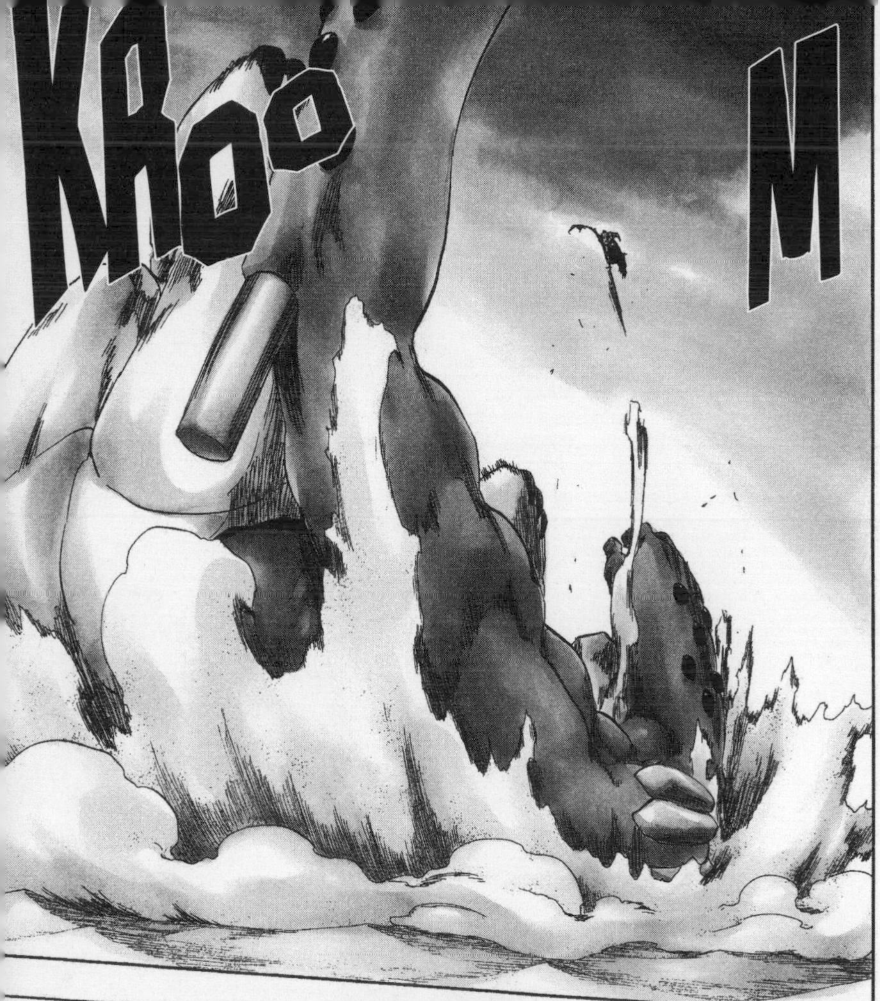
KABOOM

379. Falta de Armonia

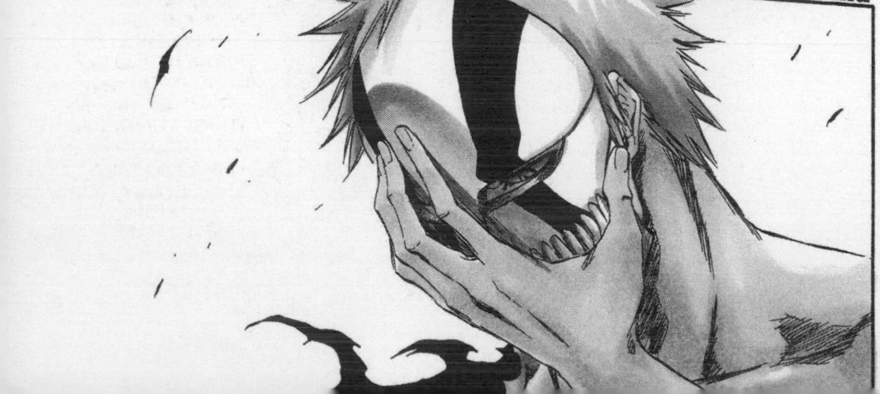

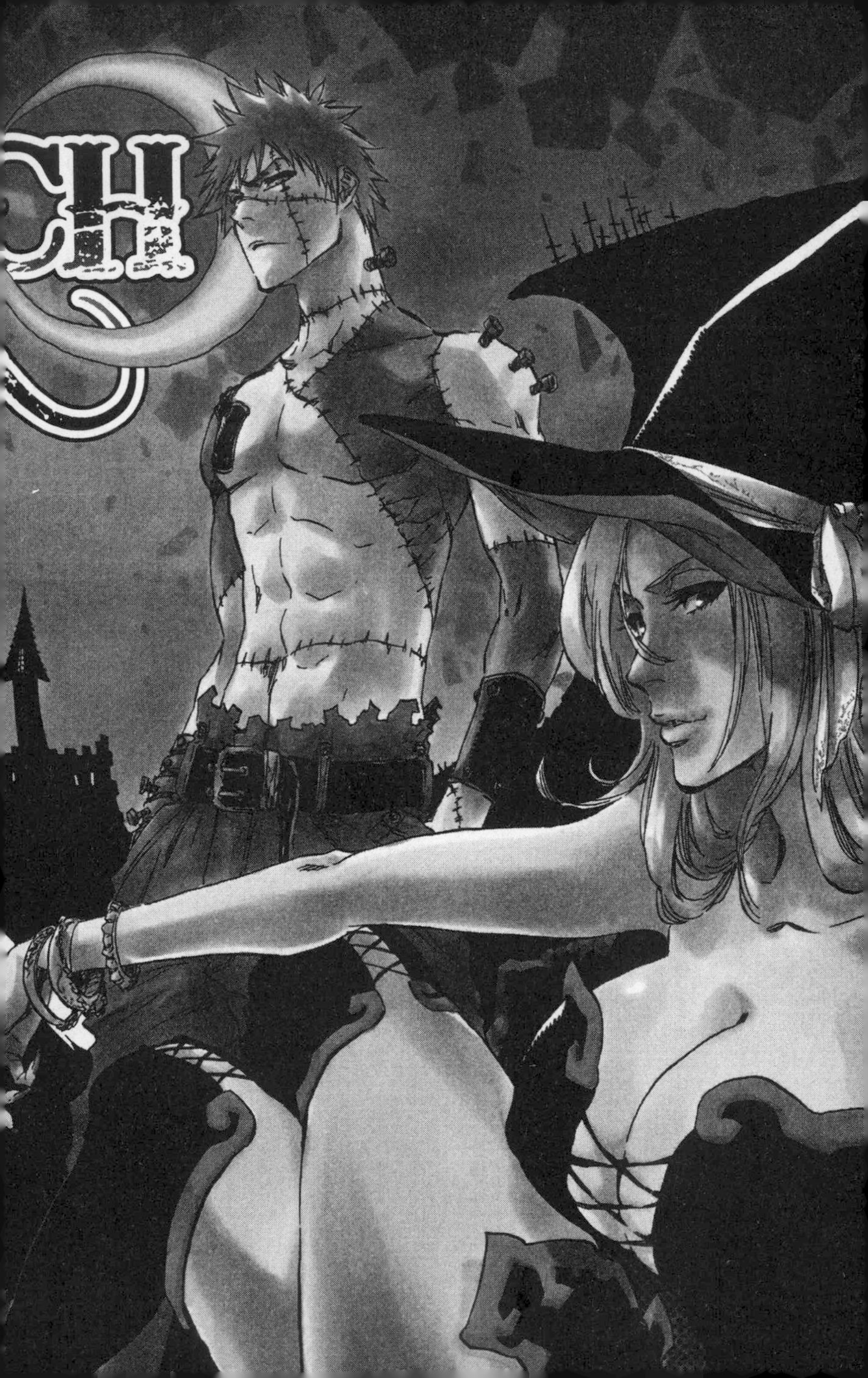
CH

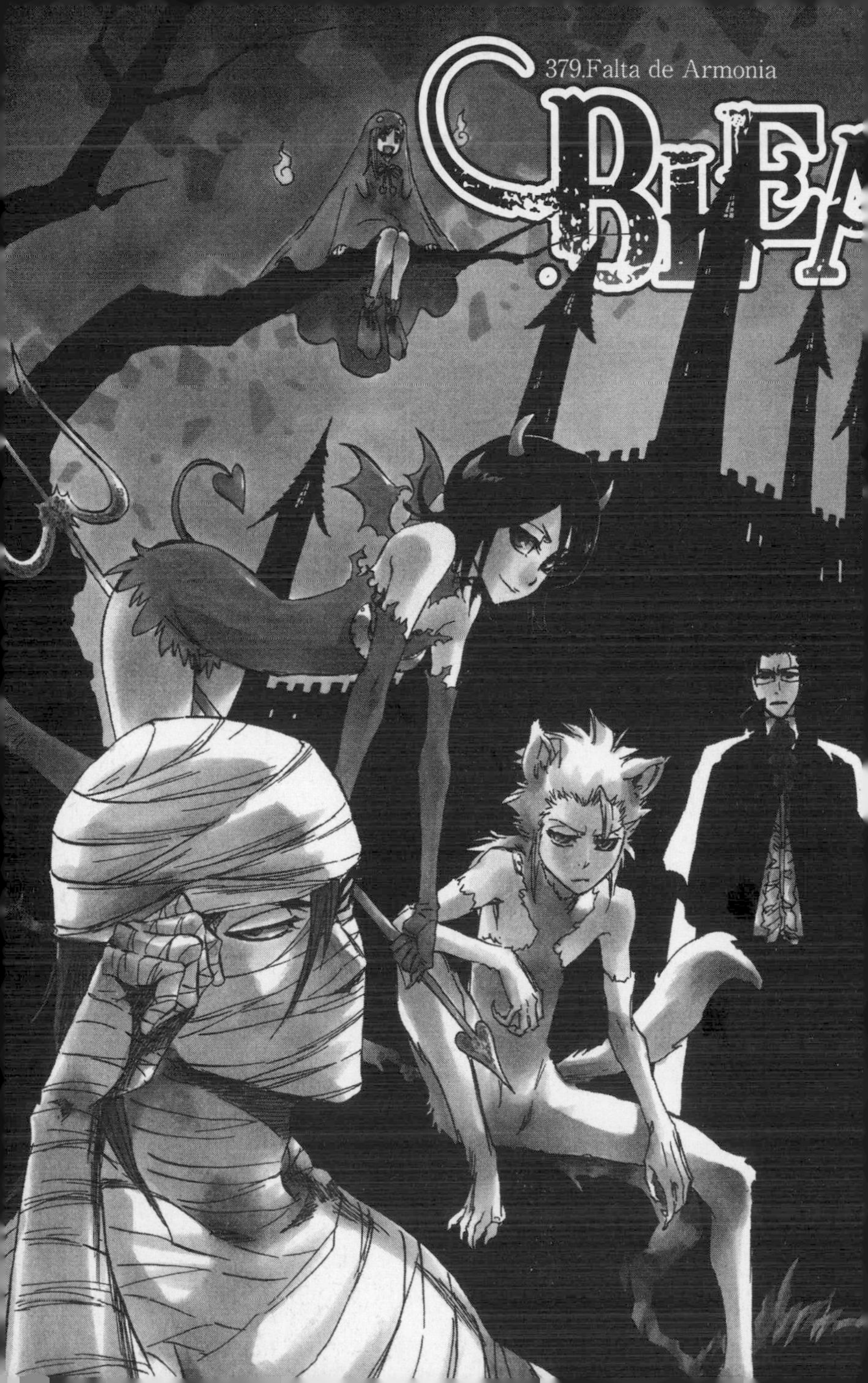
379.Falta de Armonia
BLEA

BLEACH
ブリーチ

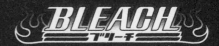

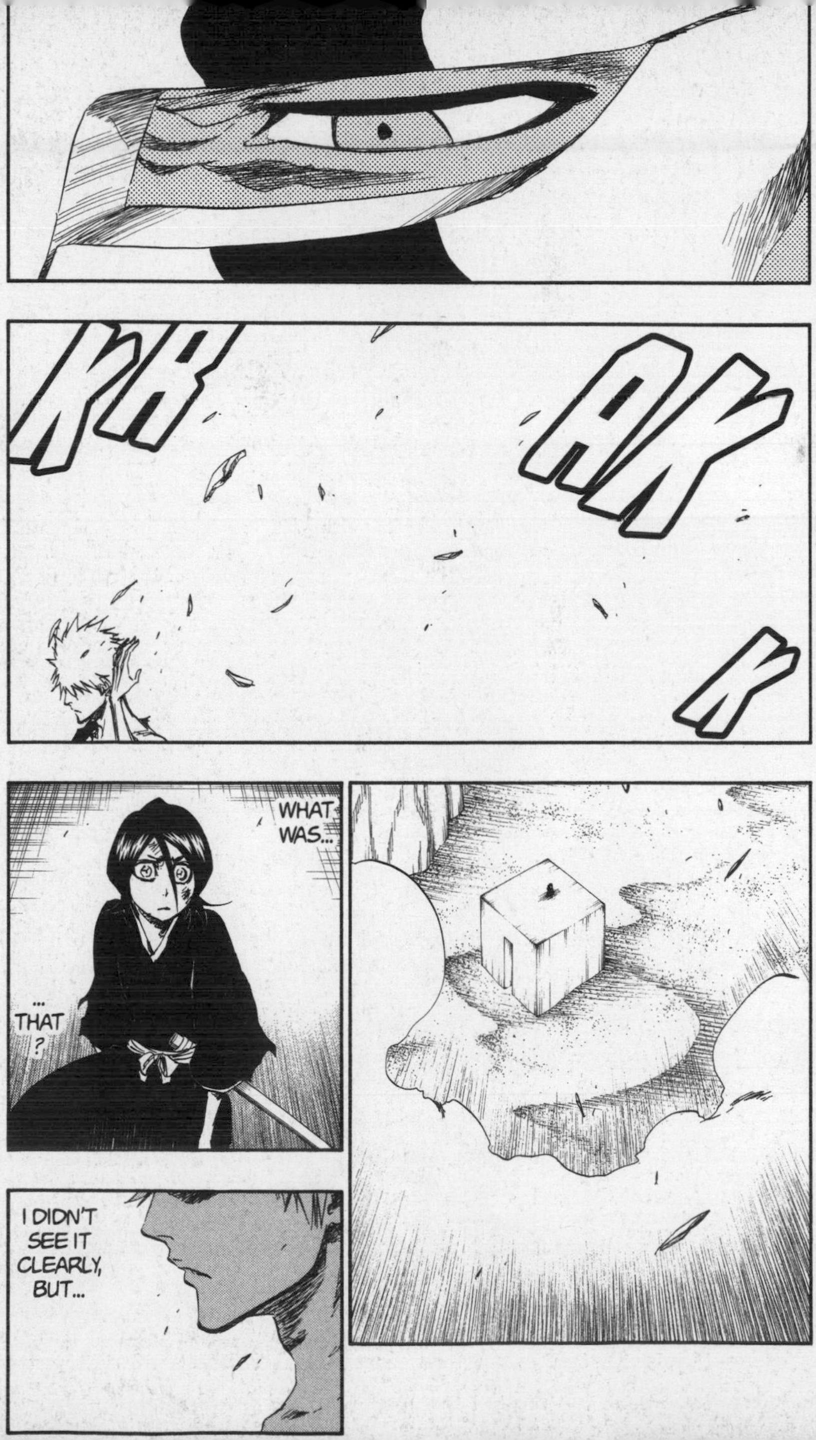
KR
AK
K
WHAT WAS...
...THAT?
I DIDN'T SEE IT CLEARLY, BUT...

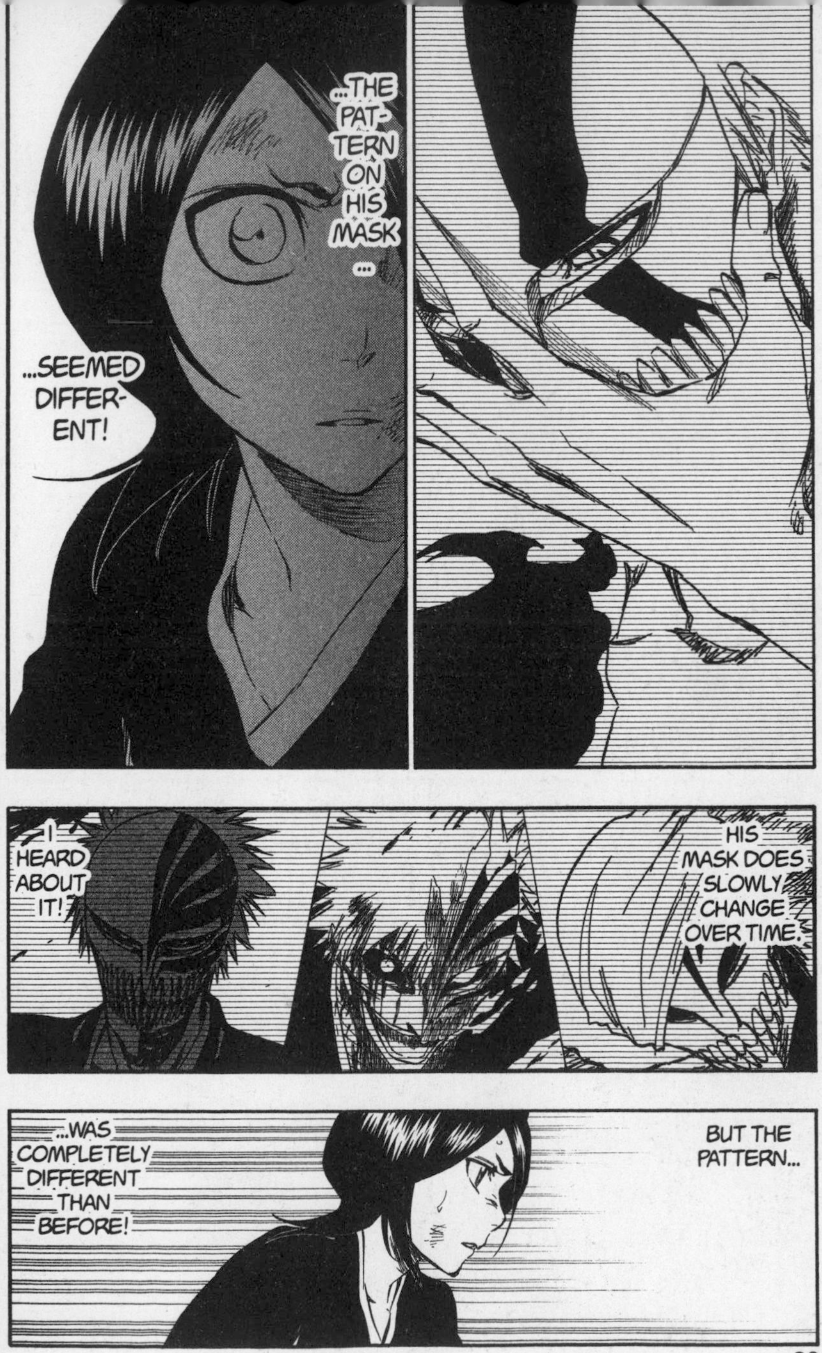
...THE PAT-TERN ON HIS MASK ...
...SEEMED DIFFER-ENT!
HIS MASK DOES SLOWLY CHANGE OVER TIME.
I HEARD ABOUT IT!
BUT THE PATTERN...
...WAS COMPLETELY DIFFERENT THAN BEFORE!

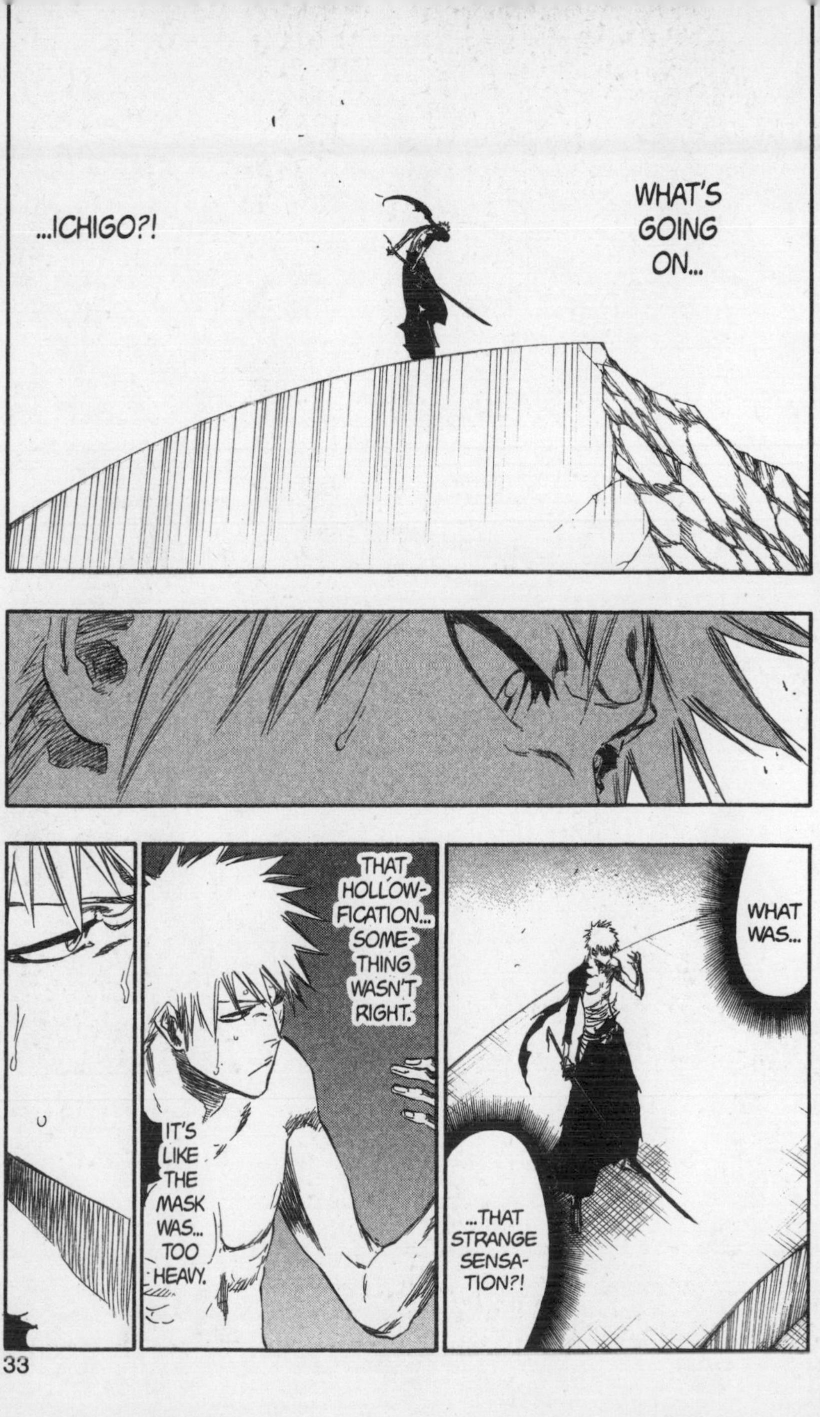
WHAT'S GOING ON...
...ICHIGO?!
WHAT WAS...
...THAT STRANGE SENSATION?!
THAT HOLLOWFICATION... SOMETHING WASN'T RIGHT.
IT'S LIKE THE MASK WAS... TOO HEAVY.

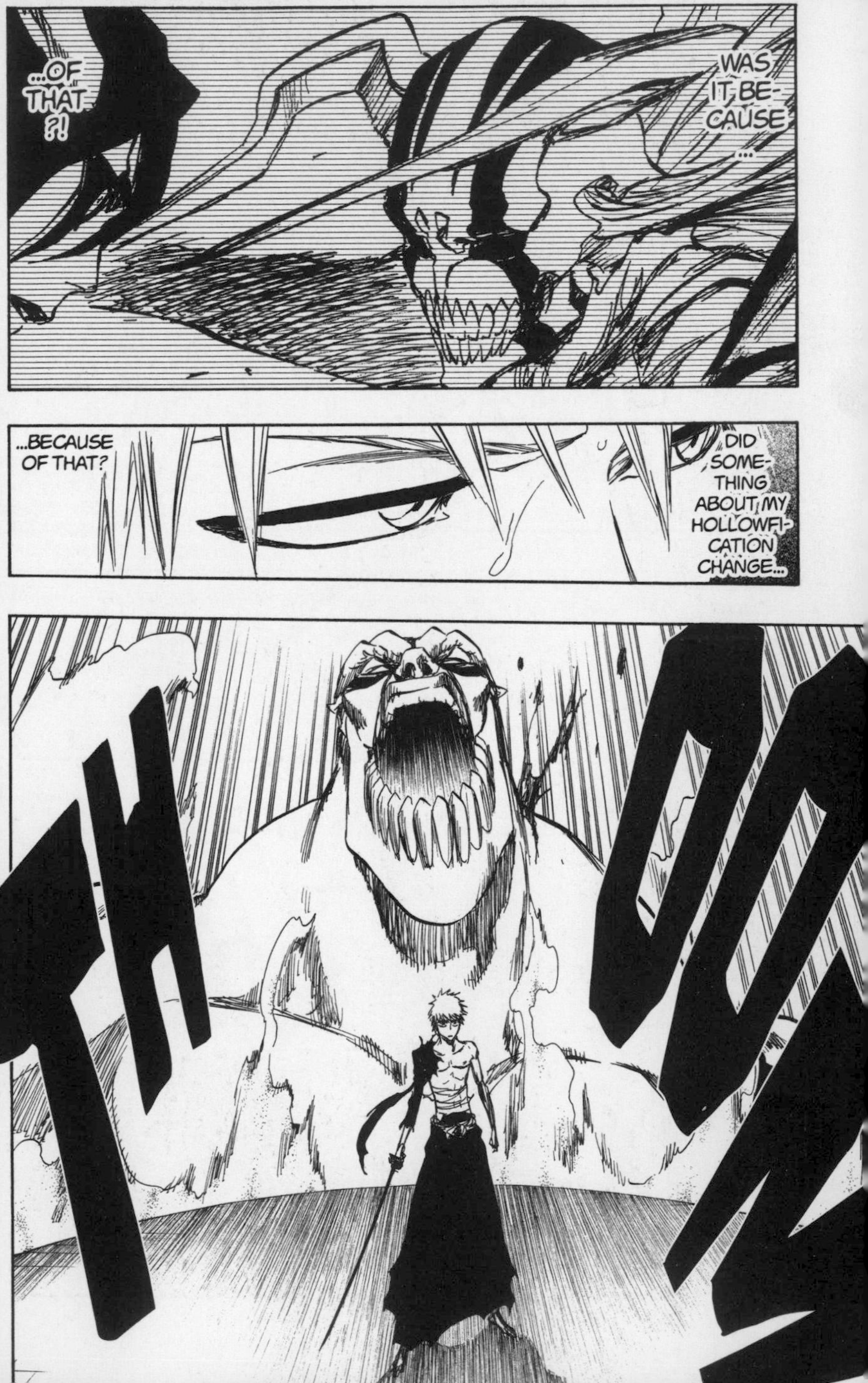
WAS IT BE-CAUSE...
...OF THAT?!
DID SOME-THING ABOUT MY HOLLOWFI-CATION CHANGE...
...BECAUSE OF THAT?

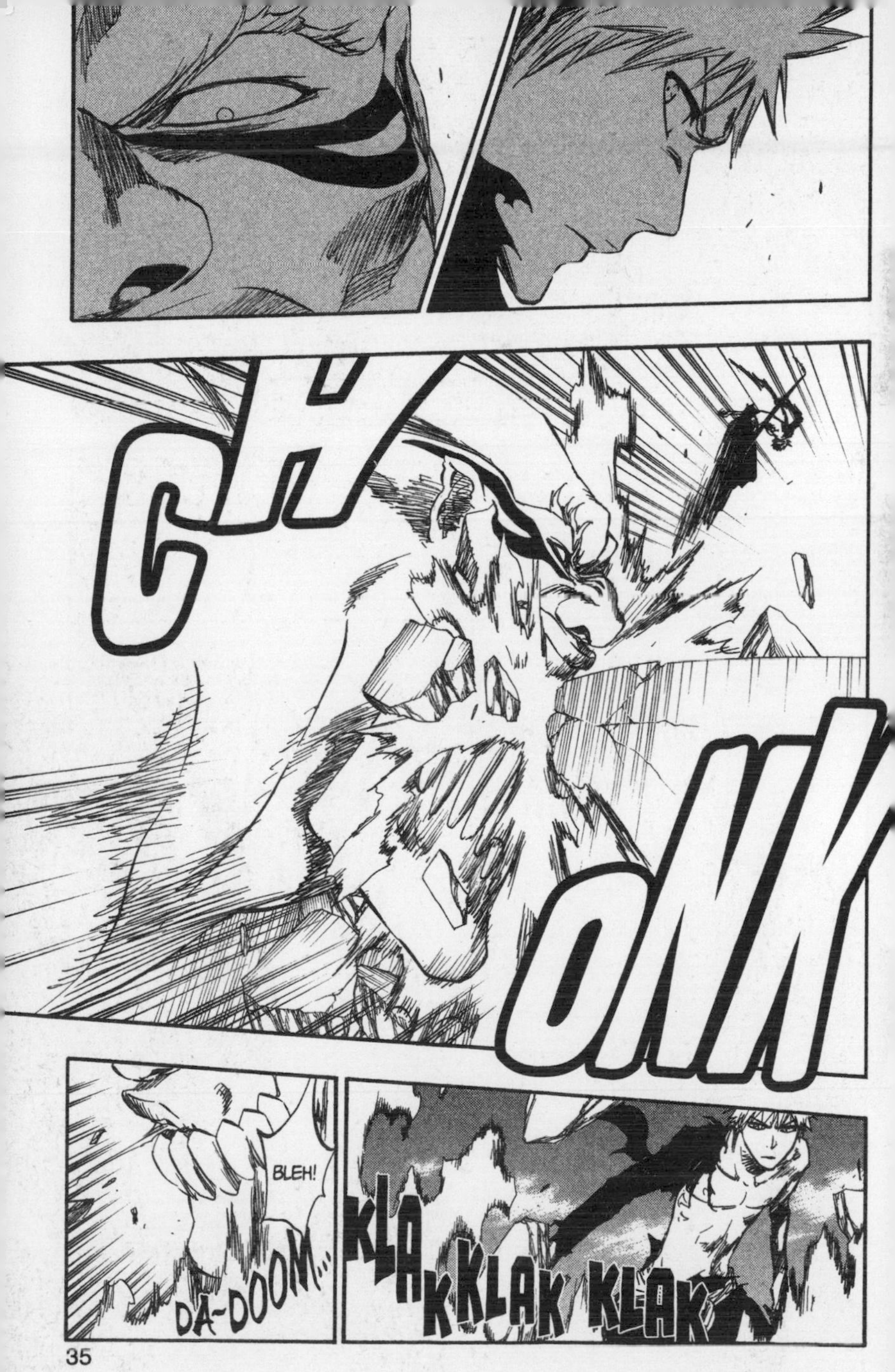
CH
ANK
KLAK KLAK KLAK
BLEH!
DA-DOOM...

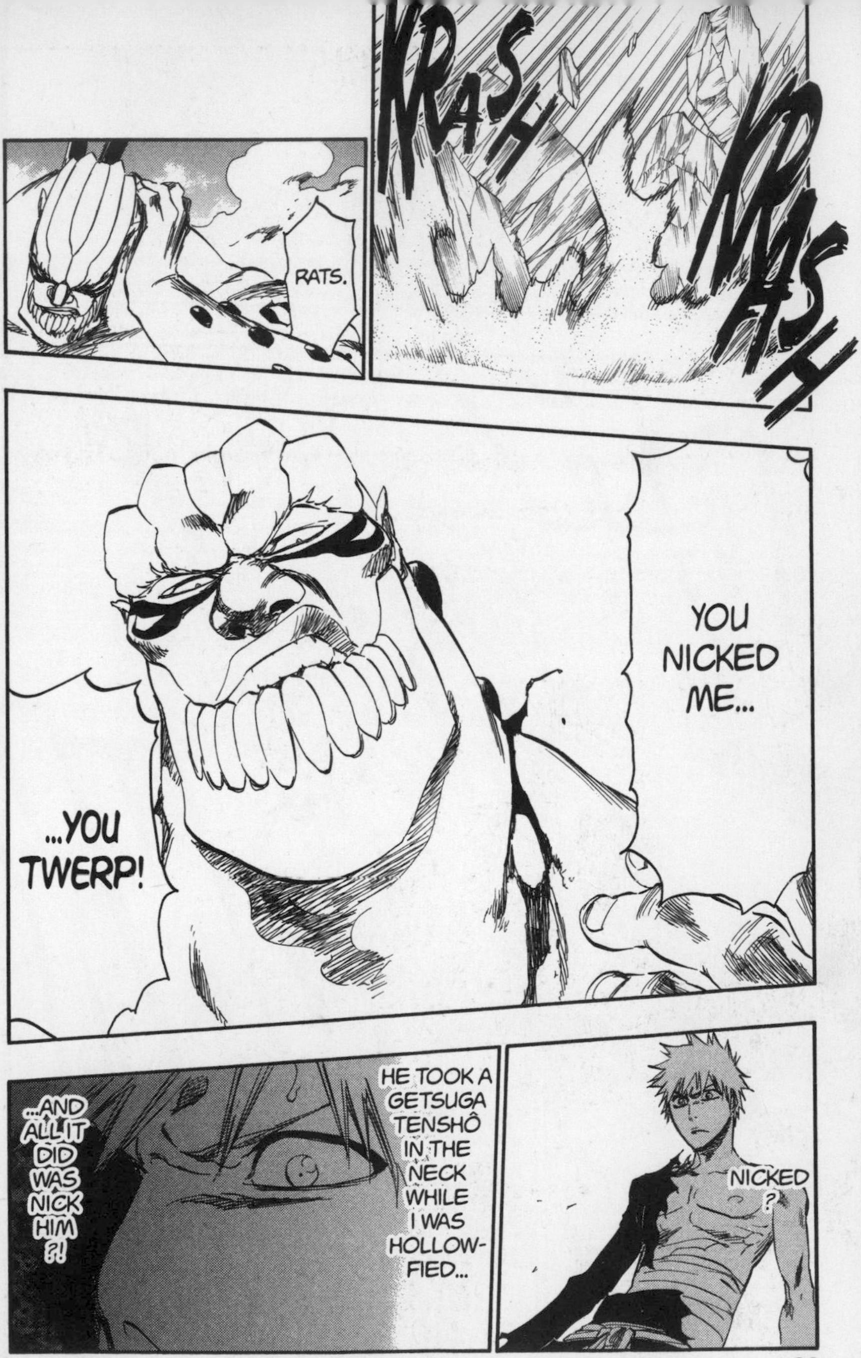
KRASH
KRASH
RATS.
YOU NICKED ME...
...YOU TWERP!
NICKED?
HE TOOK A GETSUGA TENSHÔ IN THE NECK WHILE I WAS HOLLOW-FIED...
...AND ALL IT DID WAS NICK HIM?!

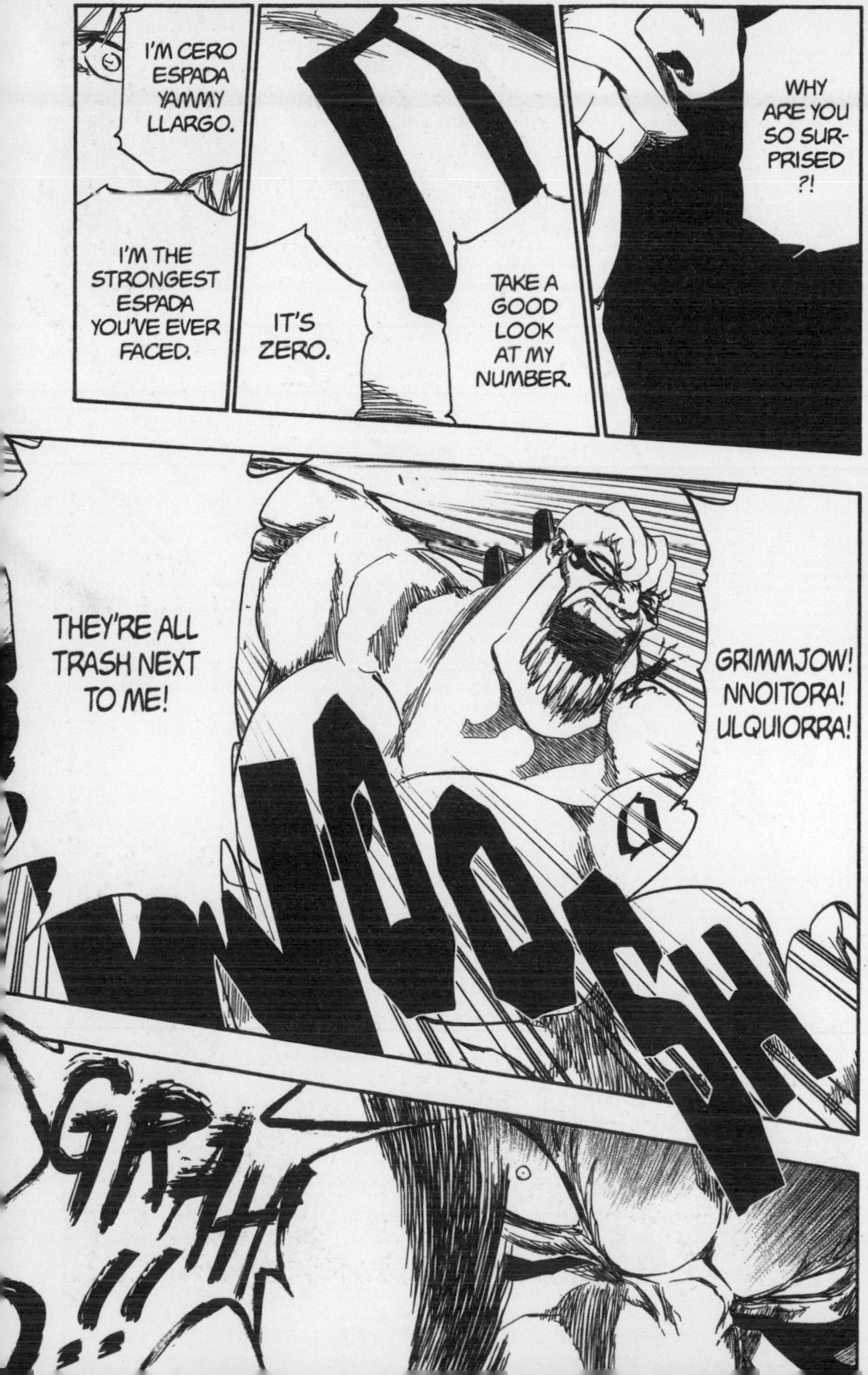
WHY ARE YOU SO SURPRISED?!
TAKE A GOOD LOOK AT MY NUMBER.
IT'S ZERO.
I'M CERO ESPADA YAMMY LLARGO.
I'M THE STRONGEST ESPADA YOU'VE EVER FACED.
GRIMMJOW! NNOITORA! ULQUIORRA!
THEY'RE ALL TRASH NEXT TO ME!
WHOOSH
GRAH

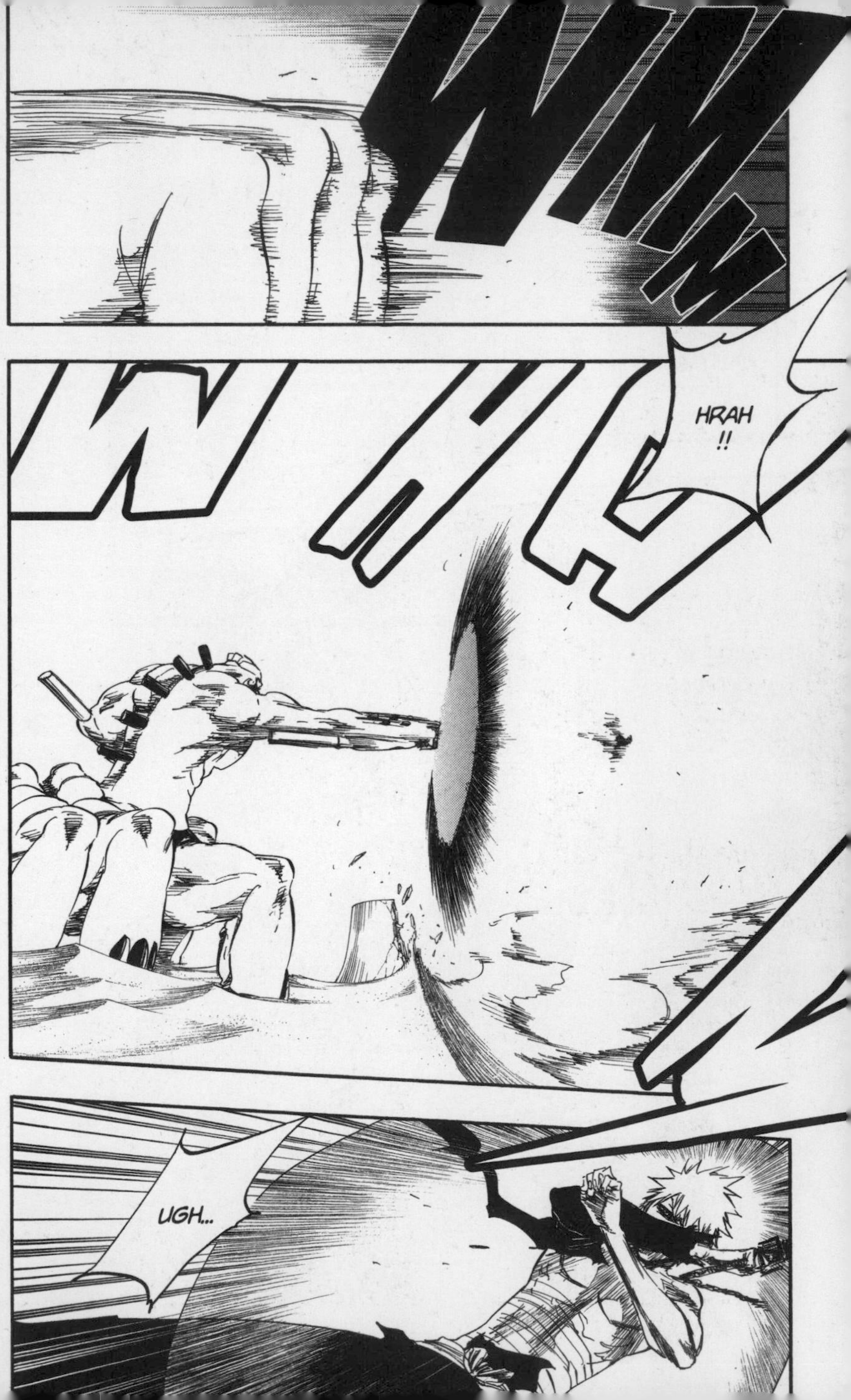
HRAH !!
UGH...

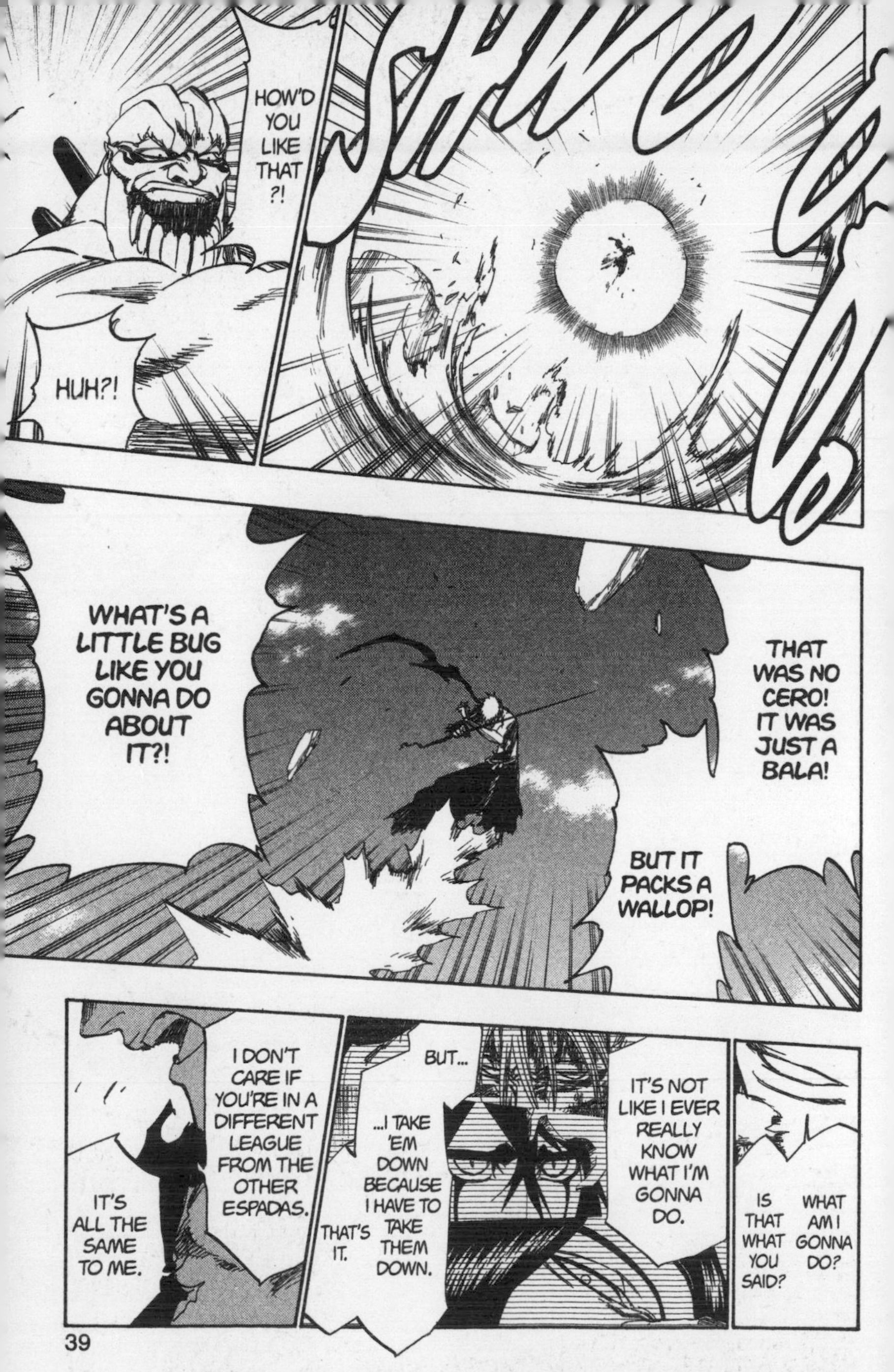
HOW'D YOU LIKE THAT?!
HUH?!
THAT WAS NO CERO! IT WAS JUST A BALA!
BUT IT PACKS A WALLOP!
WHAT'S A LITTLE BUG LIKE YOU GONNA DO ABOUT IT?!
WHAT AM I GONNA DO?
IS THAT WHAT YOU SAID?
IT'S NOT LIKE I EVER REALLY KNOW WHAT I'M GONNA DO.
BUT...
...I TAKE 'EM DOWN BECAUSE I HAVE TO TAKE THEM DOWN.
THAT'S IT.
I DON'T CARE IF YOU'RE IN A DIFFERENT LEAGUE FROM THE OTHER ESPADAS.
IT'S ALL THE SAME TO ME.

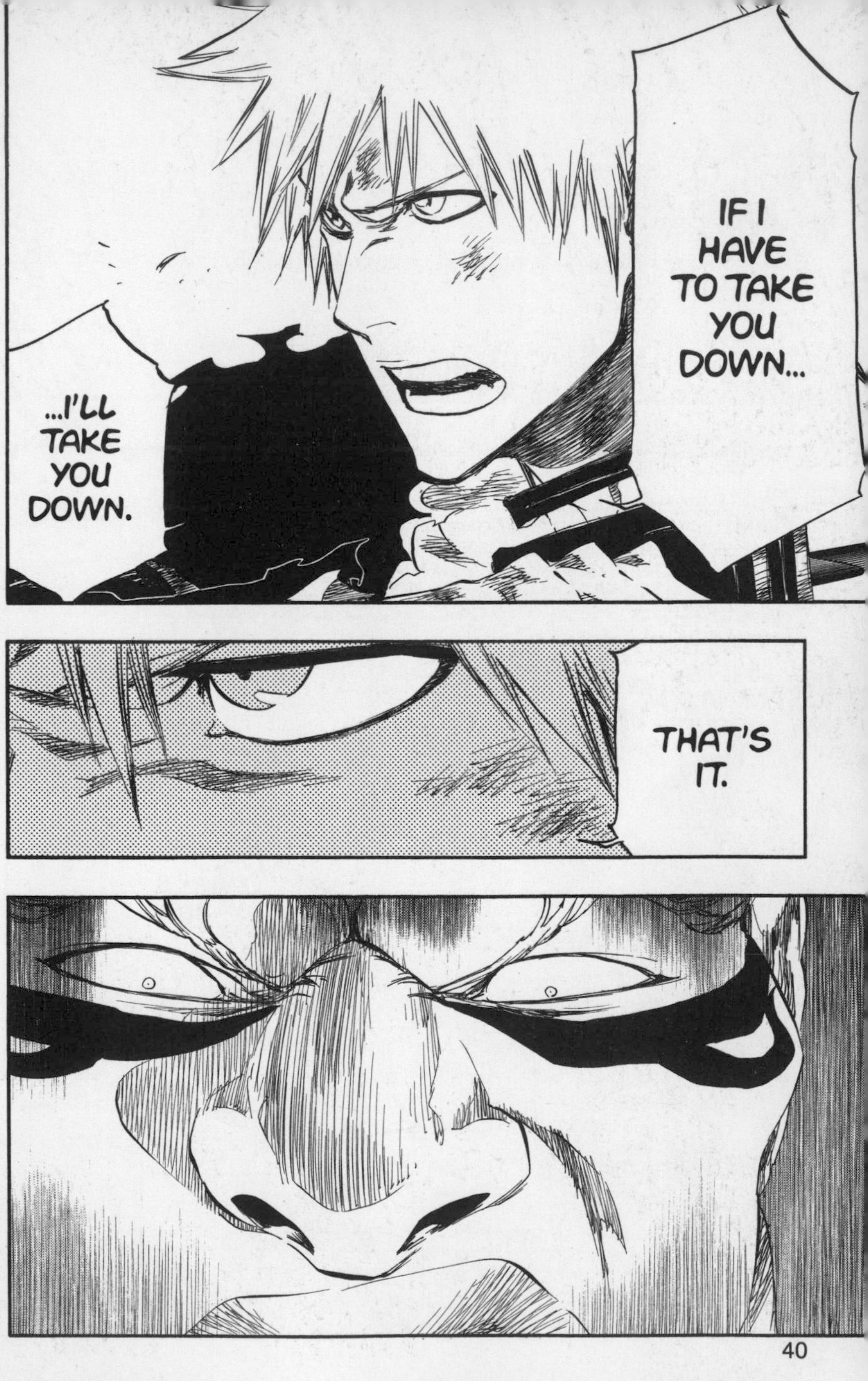
IF I HAVE TO TAKE YOU DOWN...
...I'LL TAKE YOU DOWN.
THAT'S IT.

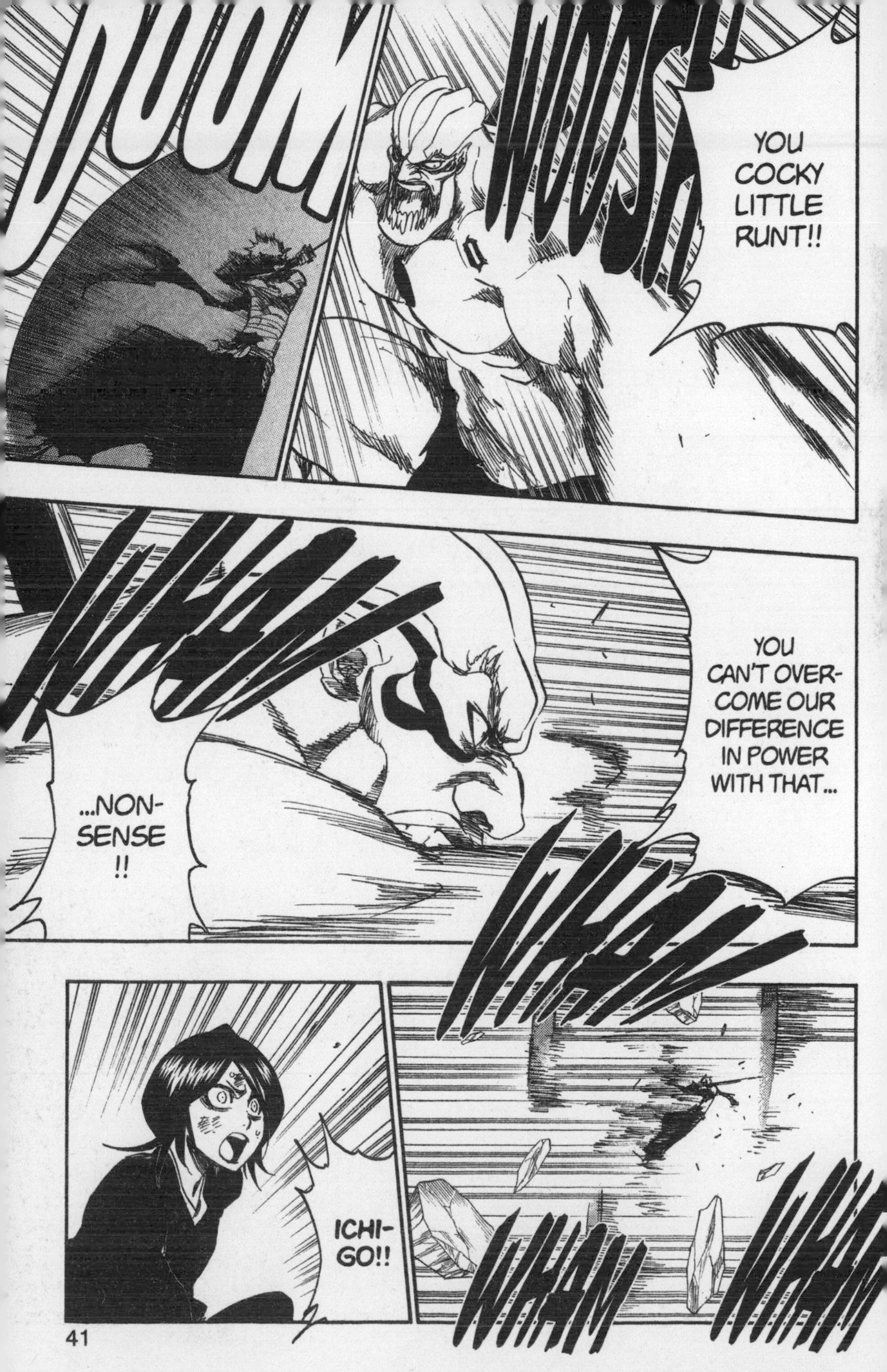
WOOSH
YOU COCKY LITTLE RUNT!!
YOU CAN'T OVER-COME OUR DIFFERENCE IN POWER WITH THAT...
...NON-SENSE !!
WHAM
WHAM
WHAM
WHAM
ICHI-GO!!

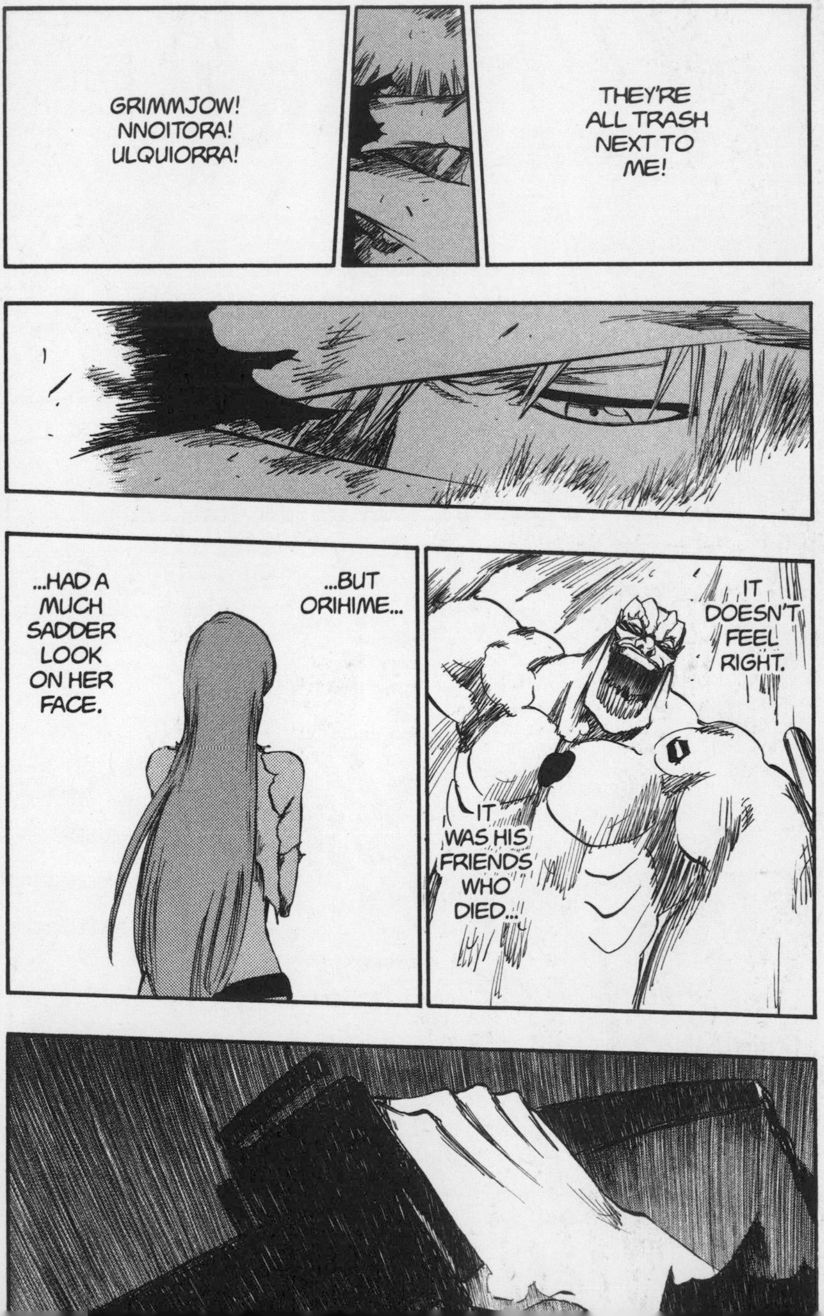
THEY'RE ALL TRASH NEXT TO ME!
GRIMMJOW! NNOITORA! ULQUIORRA!
IT DOESN'T FEEL RIGHT.
IT WAS HIS FRIENDS WHO DIED...
...BUT ORIHIME...
...HAD A MUCH SADDER LOOK ON HER FACE.

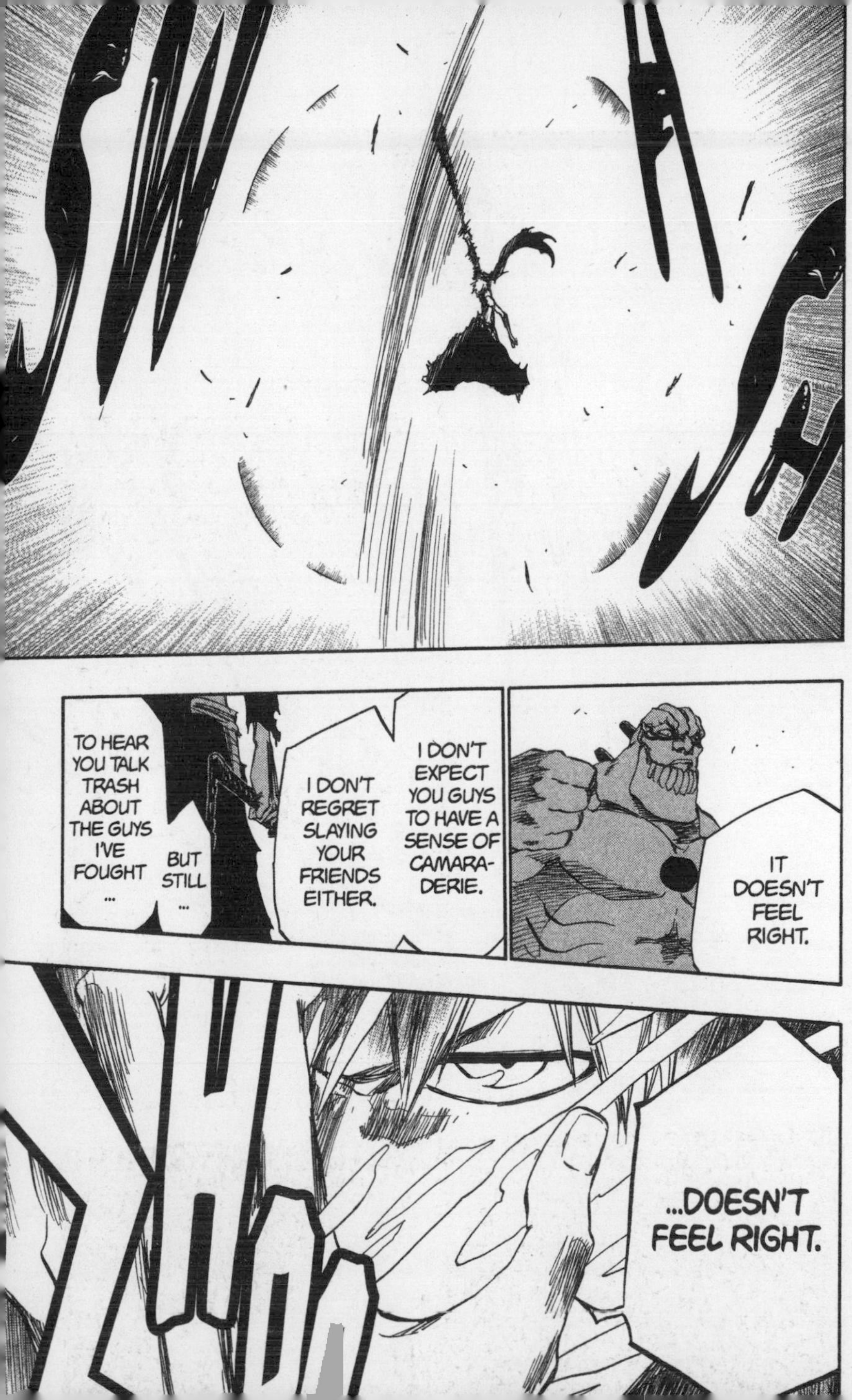
IT DOESN'T FEEL RIGHT.
I DON'T EXPECT YOU GUYS TO HAVE A SENSE OF CAMARA-DERIE.
I DON'T REGRET SLAYING YOUR FRIENDS EITHER.
BUT STILL ...
TO HEAR YOU TALK TRASH ABOUT THE GUYS I'VE FOUGHT ...
...DOESN'T FEEL RIGHT.

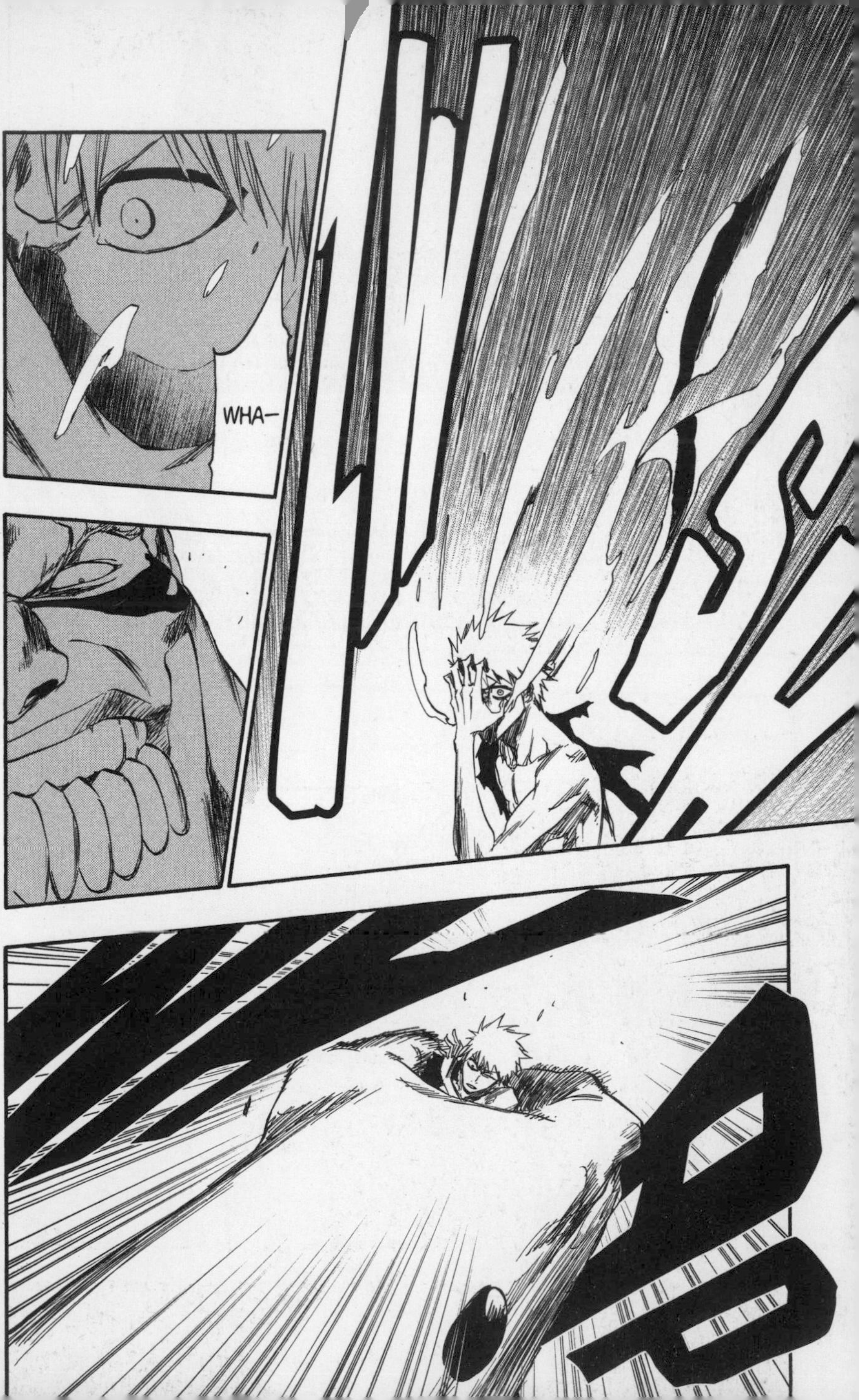
WHA–

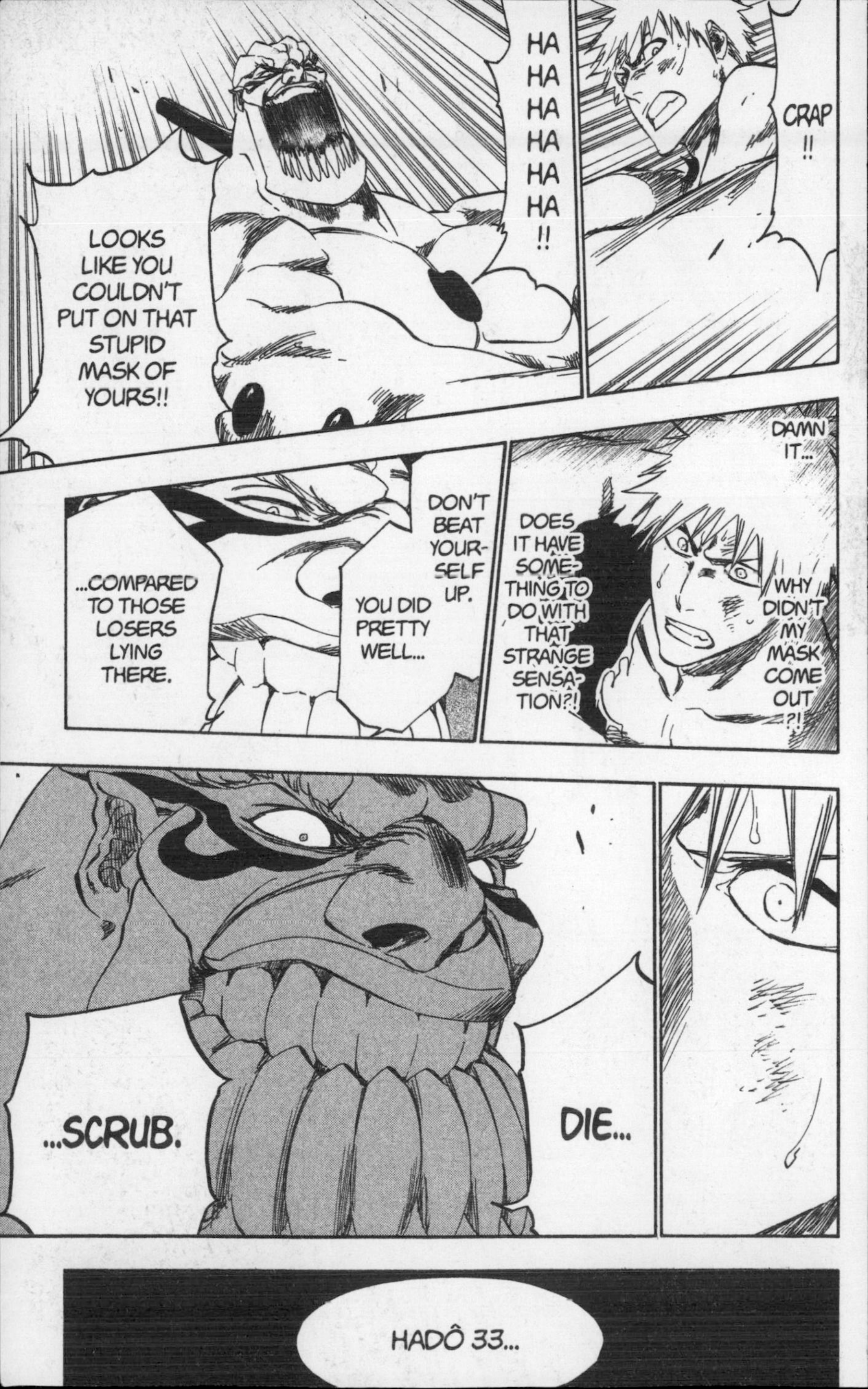
CRAP !!
HA HA HA HA HA HA !!
LOOKS LIKE YOU COULDN'T PUT ON THAT STUPID MASK OF YOURS!!
DAMN IT...
WHY DIDN'T MY MASK COME OUT?!
DOES IT HAVE SOMETHING TO DO WITH THAT STRANGE SENSATION?!
DON'T BEAT YOURSELF UP.
YOU DID PRETTY WELL...
...COMPARED TO THOSE LOSERS LYING THERE.
DIE...
...SCRUB.
HADÔ 33...

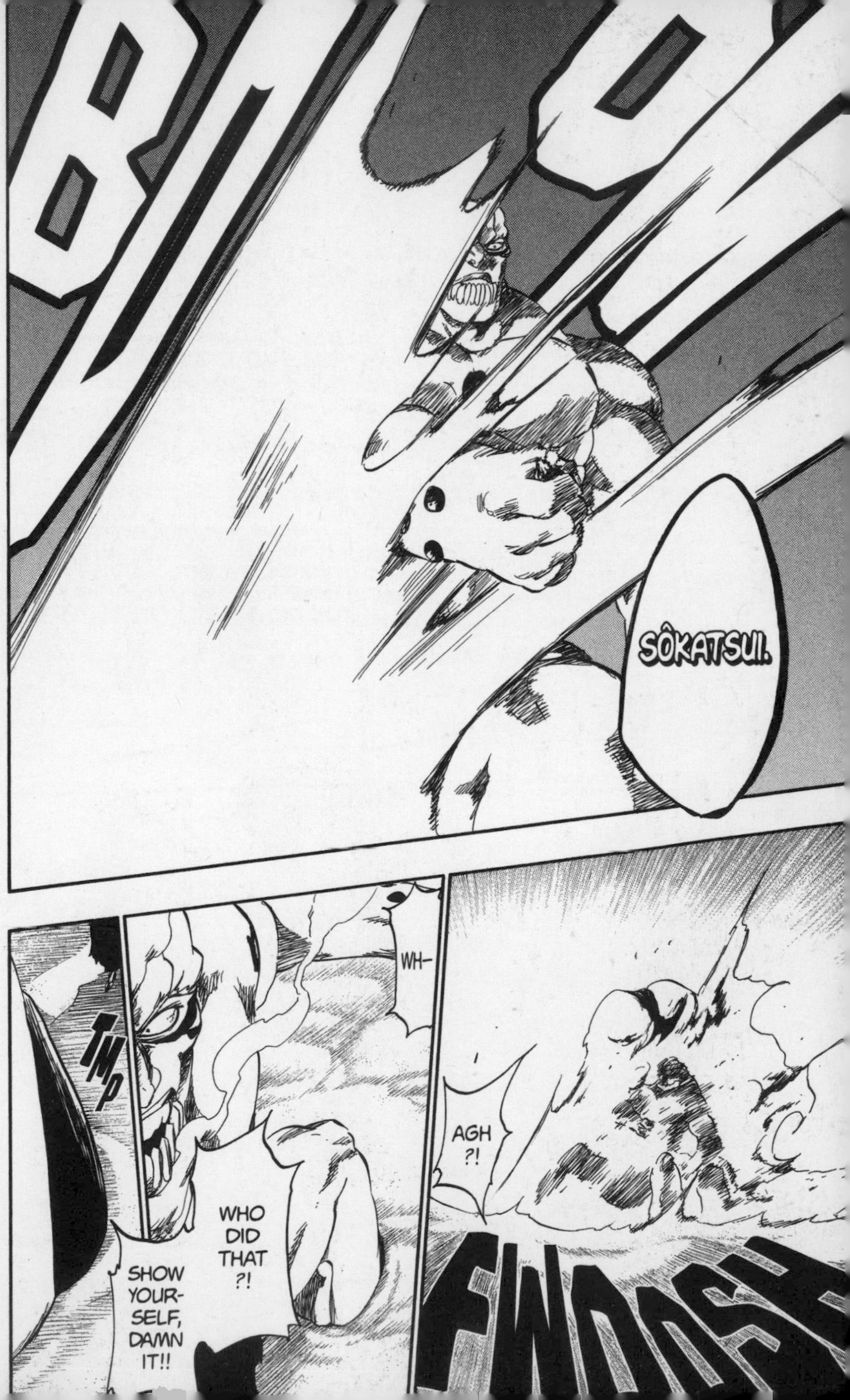
SÔKATSUI.
AGH ?!
FWOOSH
WH-
WHO DID THAT ?!
TMP
SHOW YOUR-SELF, DAMN IT!!

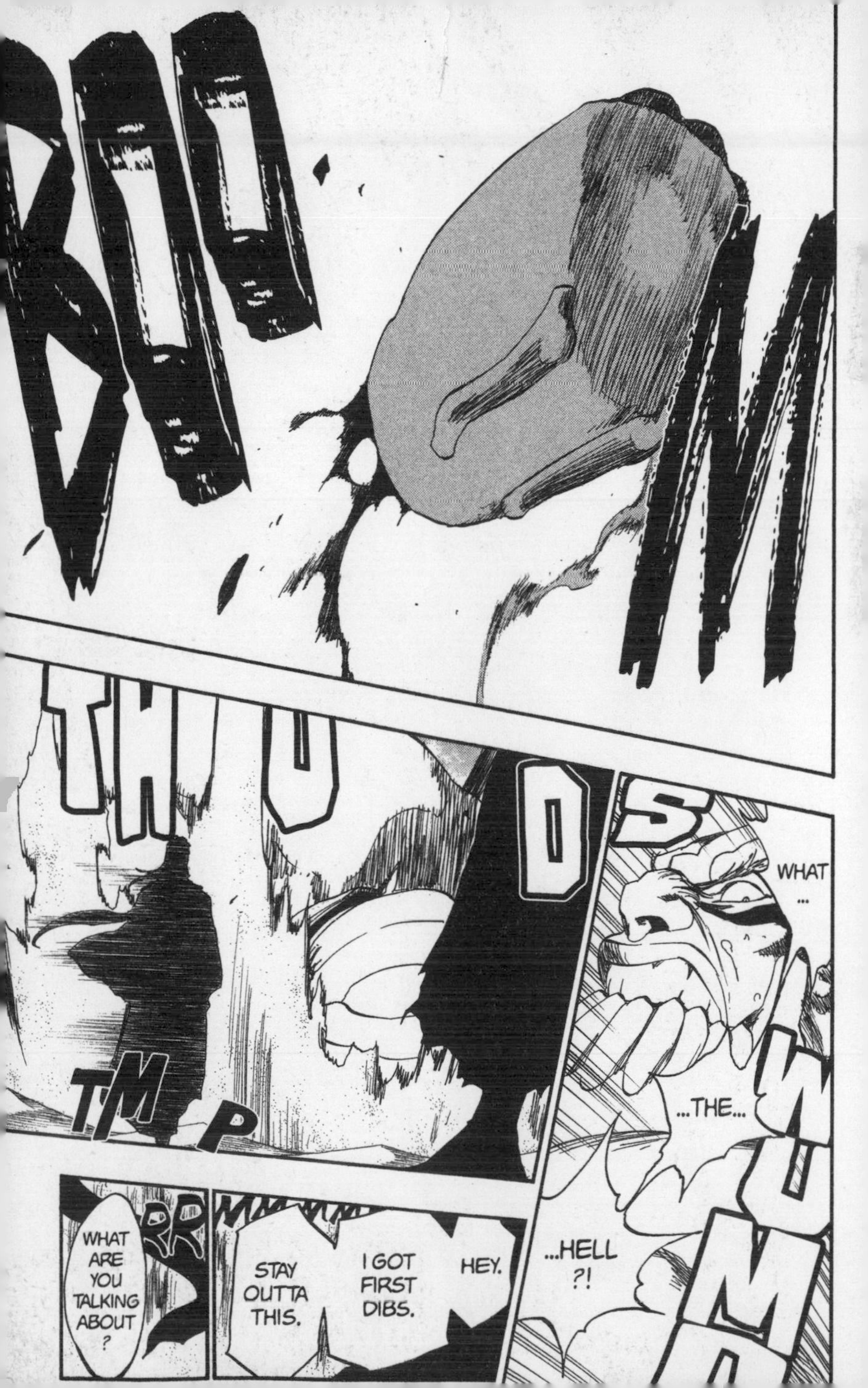
BOOM
WHAT ...
...THE...
...HELL ?!
THUDS
TMP
HEY.
I GOT FIRST DIBS.
STAY OUTTA THIS.
WHAT ARE YOU TALKING ABOUT ?

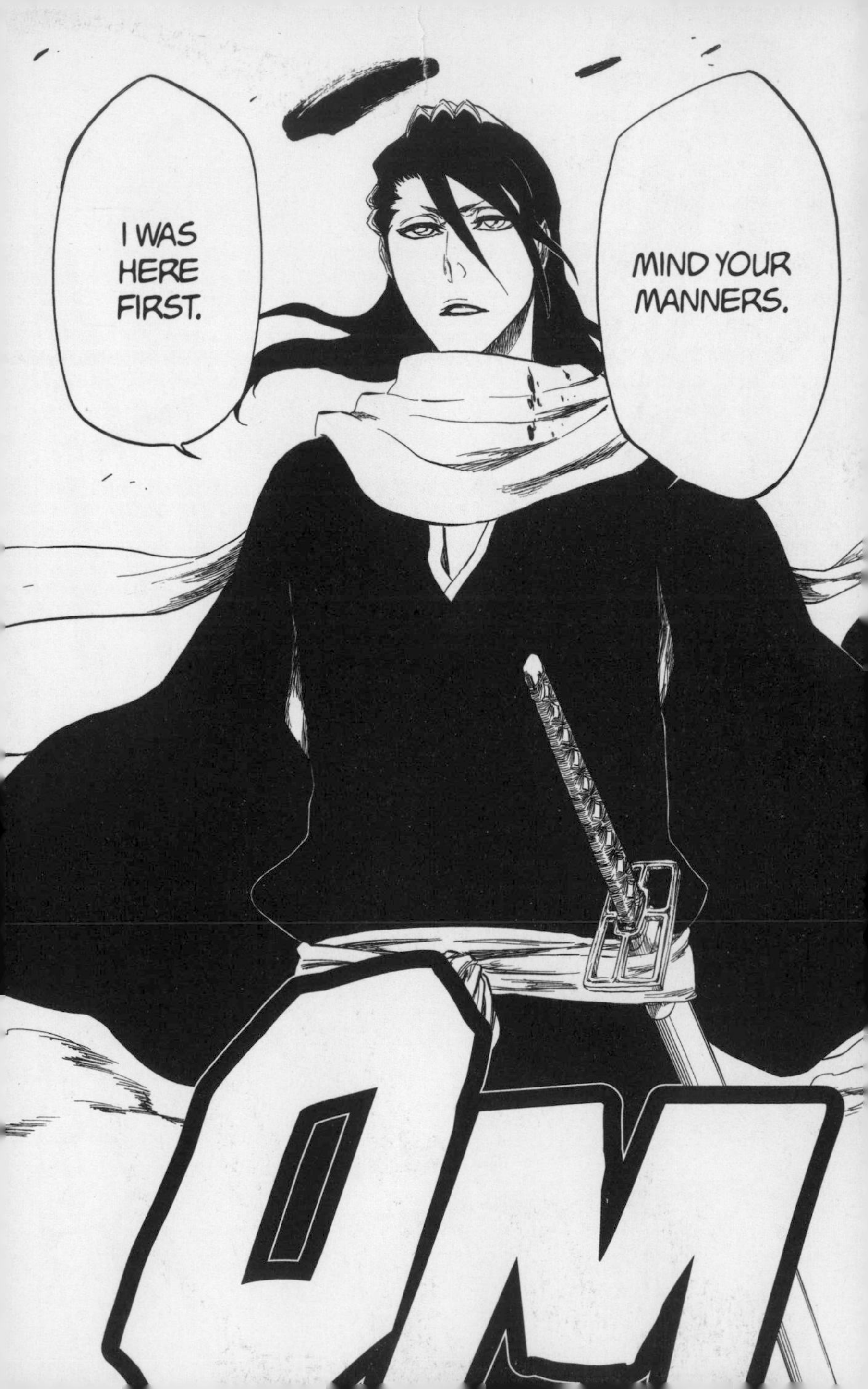
MIND YOUR MANNERS.
I WAS HERE FIRST.

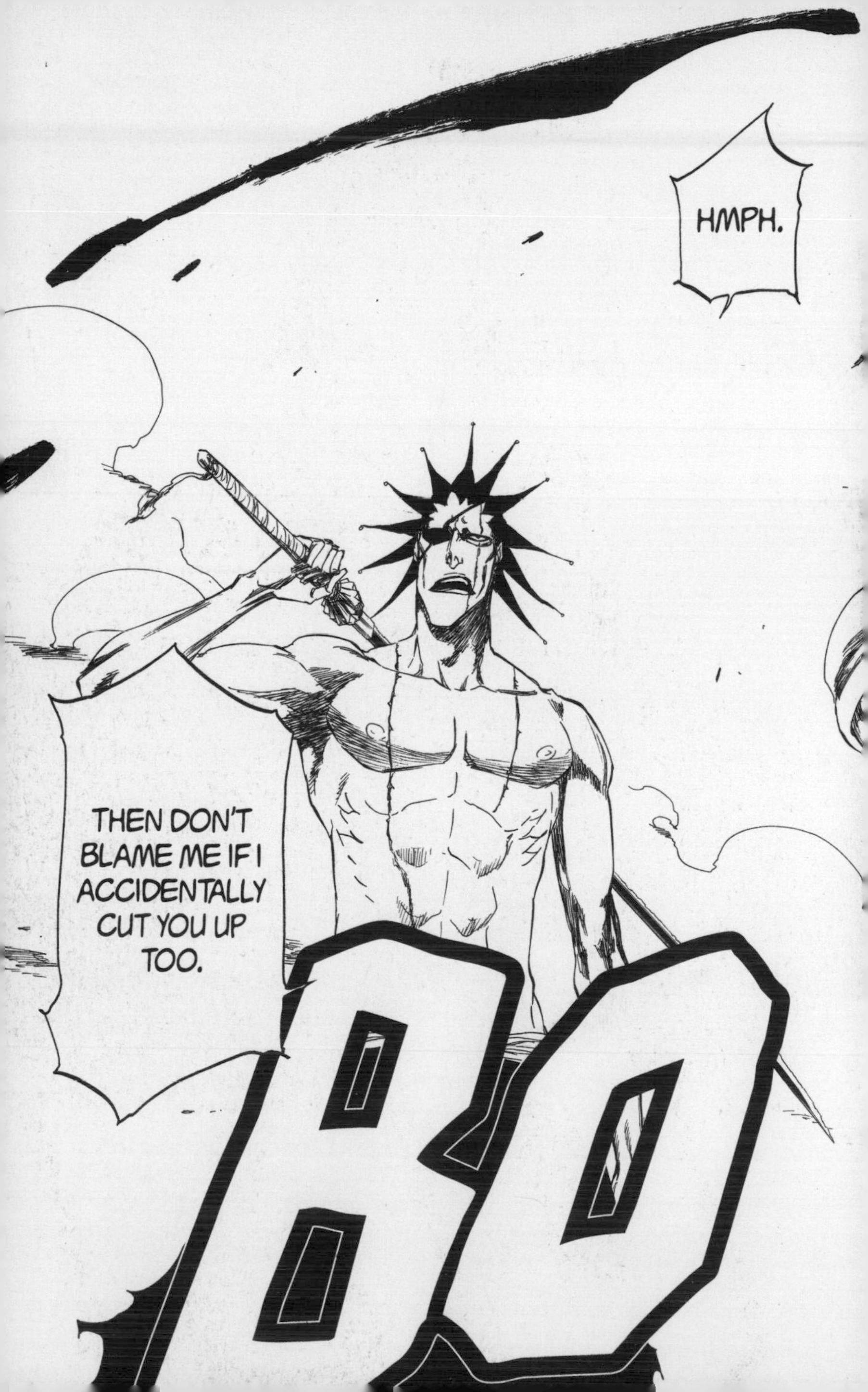
HMPH.
THEN DON'T BLAME ME IF I ACCIDENTALLY CUT YOU UP TOO.
BO

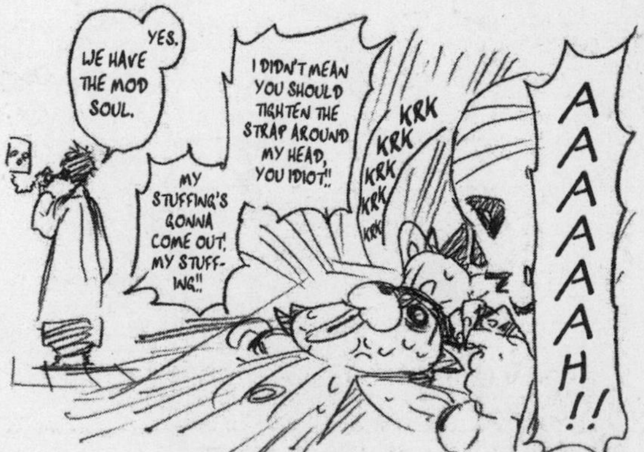
AAAAAAH!!
KRK KRK KRK KRK KRK
I DIDN'T MEAN YOU SHOULD TIGHTEN THE STRAP AROUND MY HEAD, YOU IDIOT!!
YES. WE HAVE THE MOD SOUL.
MY STUFFING'S GONNA COME OUT! MY STUFF-ING!!

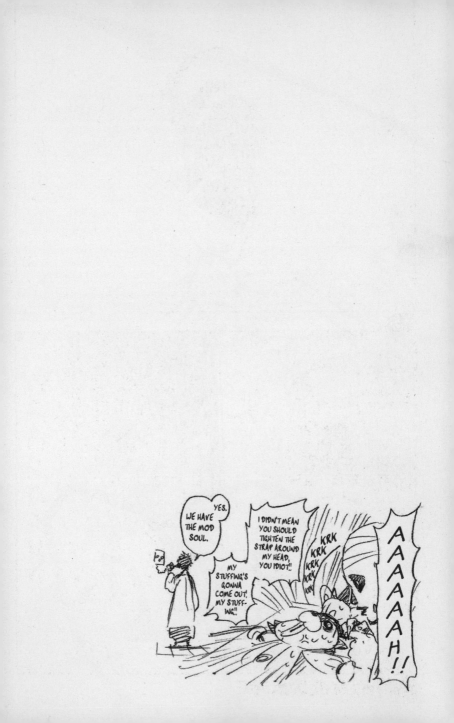

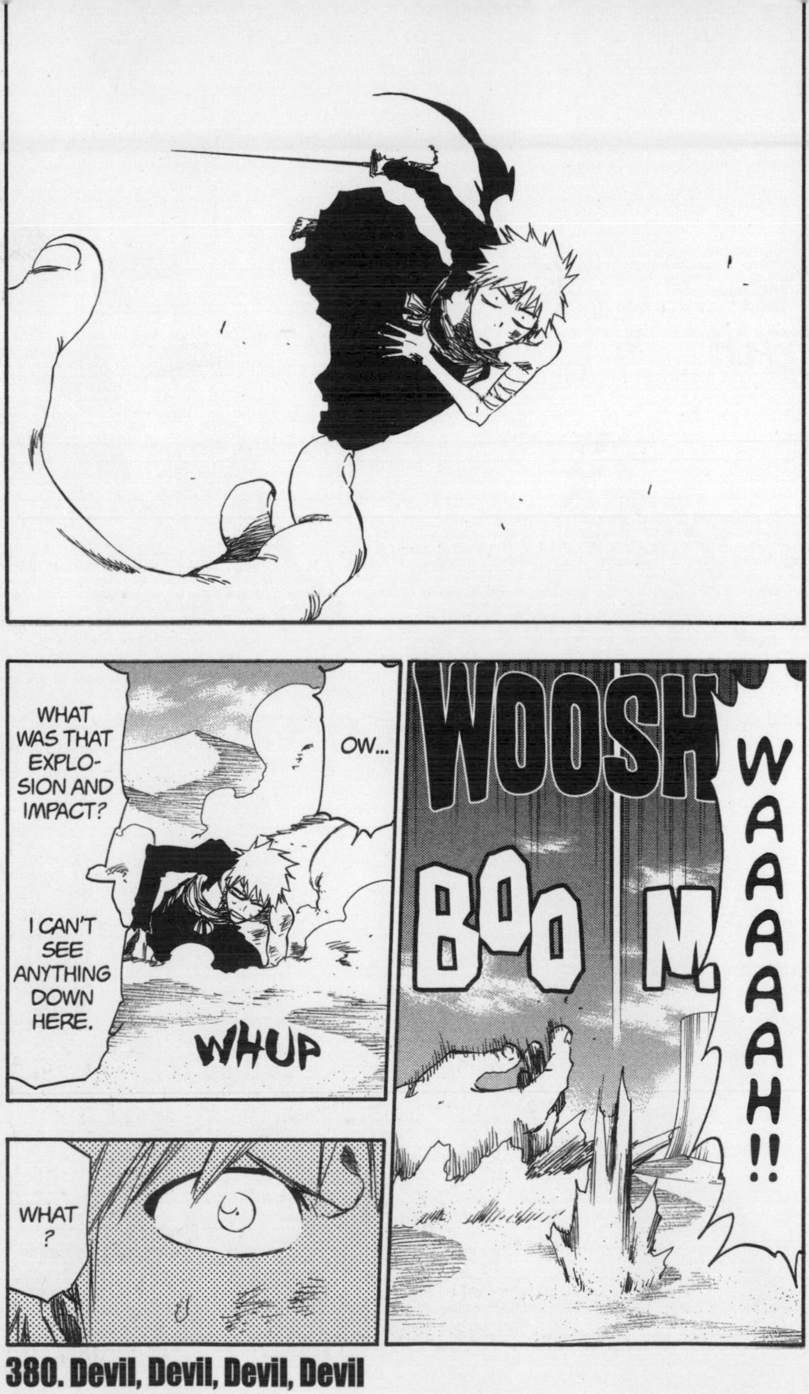
WOOSH
BOOM.
WAAAAAH!!
OW...
WHAT WAS THAT EXPLOSION AND IMPACT?
I CAN'T SEE ANYTHING DOWN HERE.
WHUP
WHAT?

380. Devil, Devil, Devil, Devil

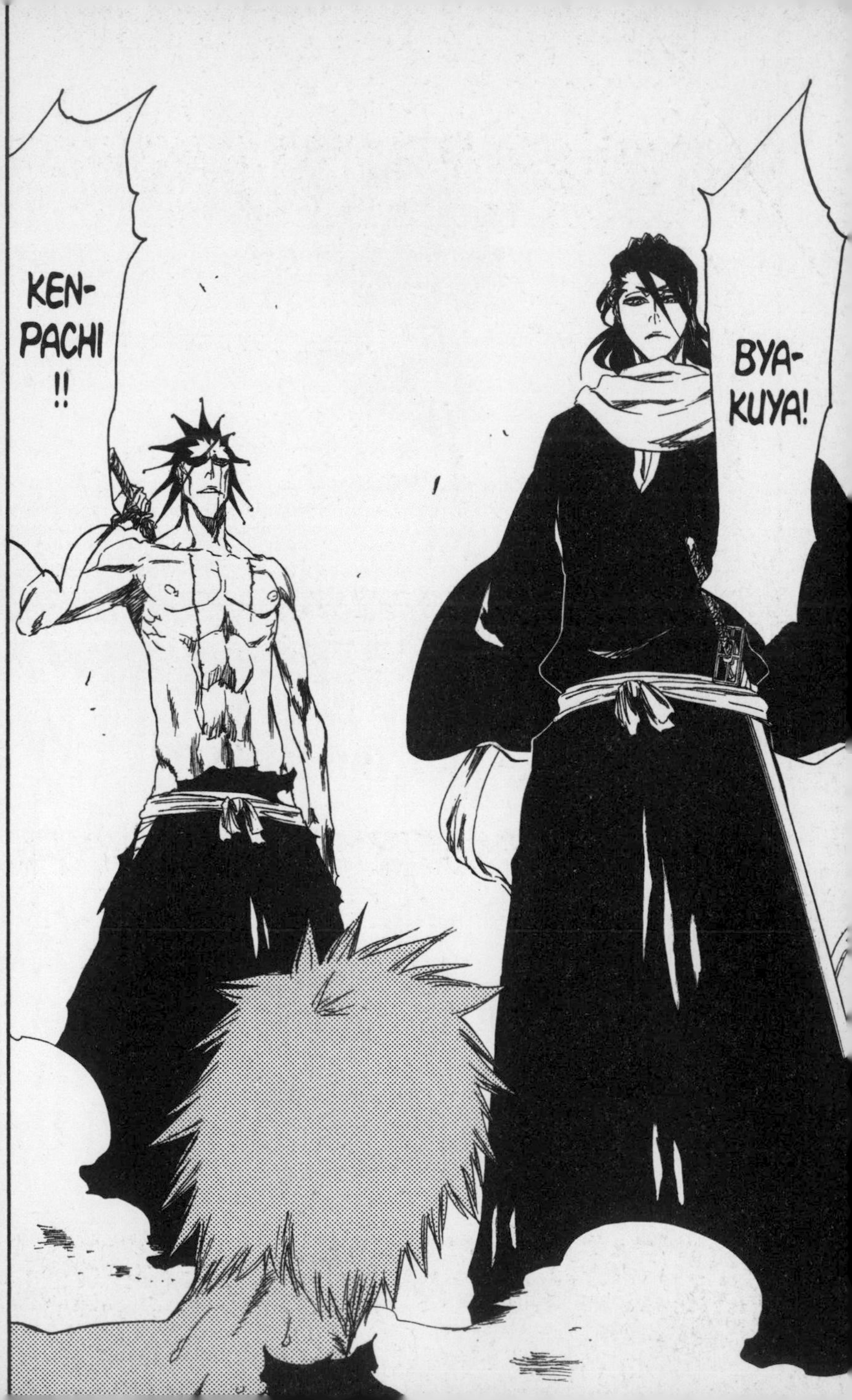
BYA-KUYA!
KEN-PACHI!!

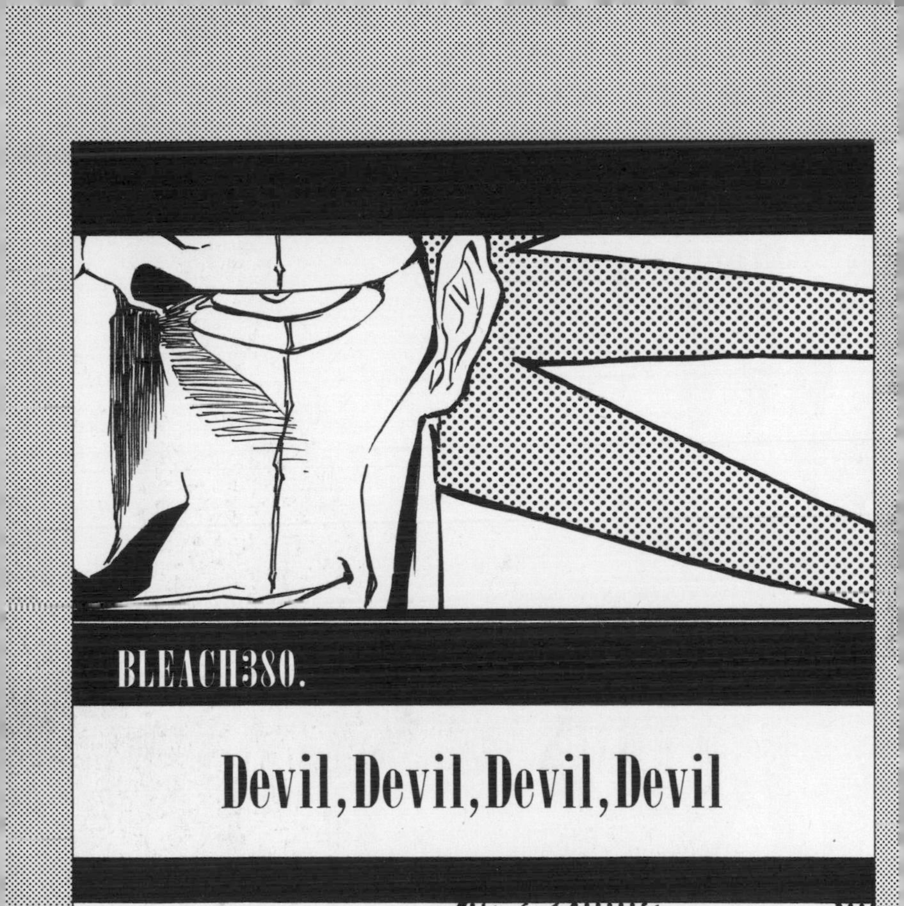

BLEACH380.

Devil, Devil, Devil, Devil

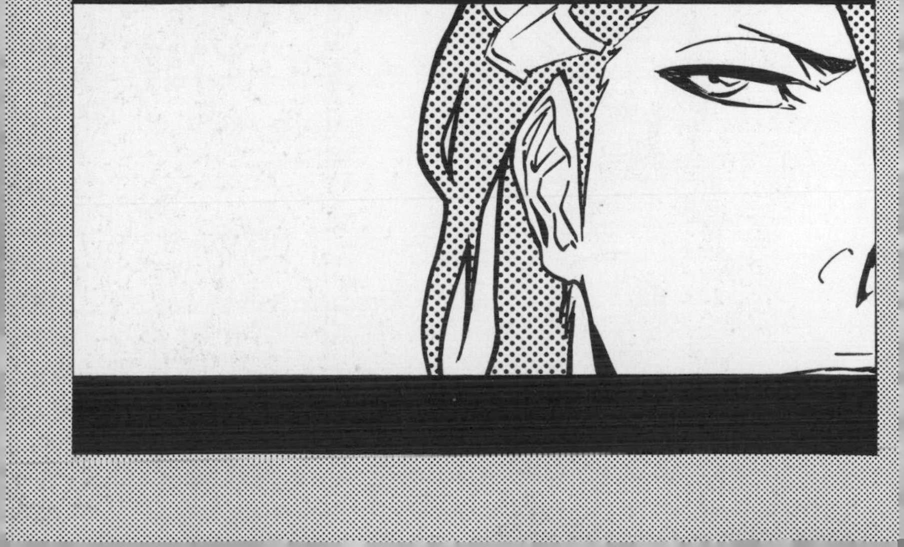

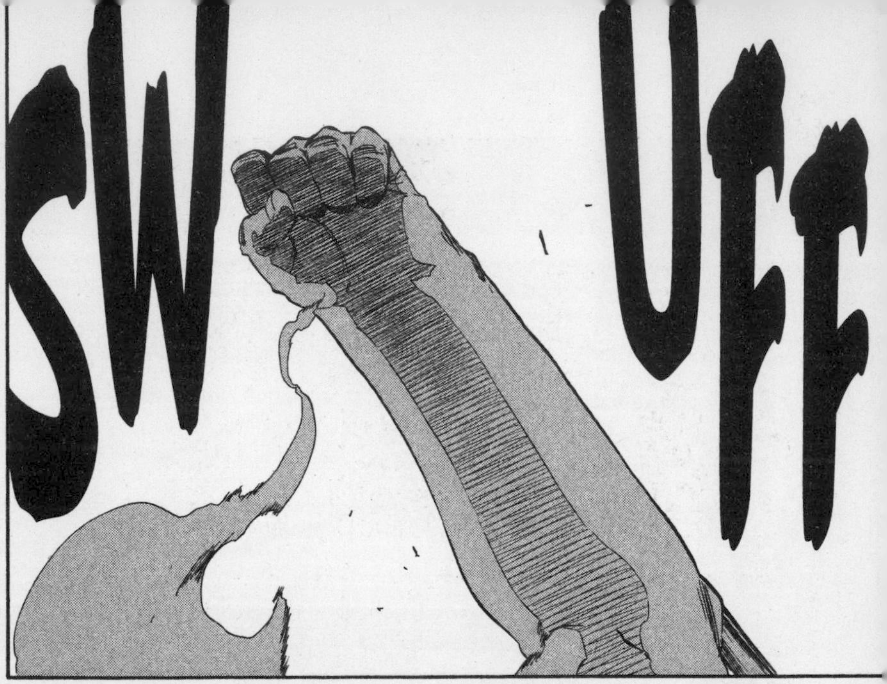
SWUFF
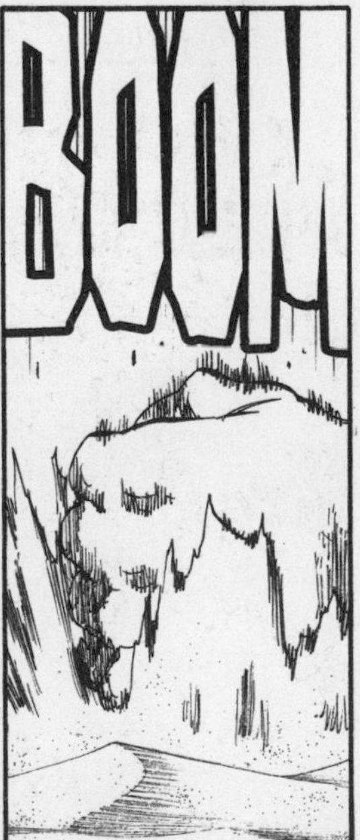
BOOM
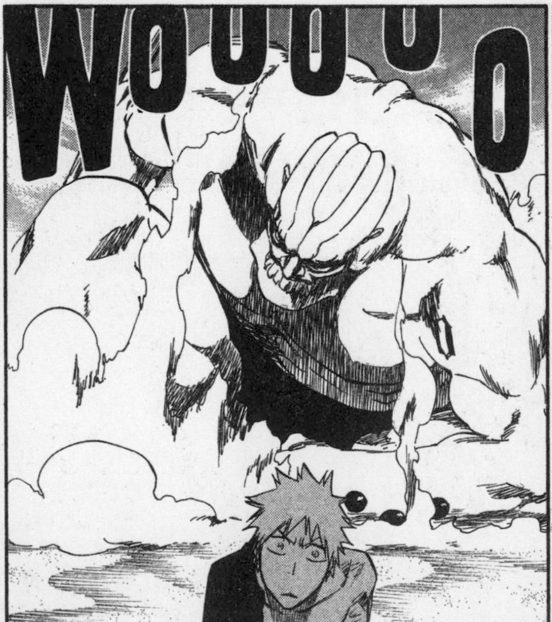
WOOOOO

READ THIS WAY

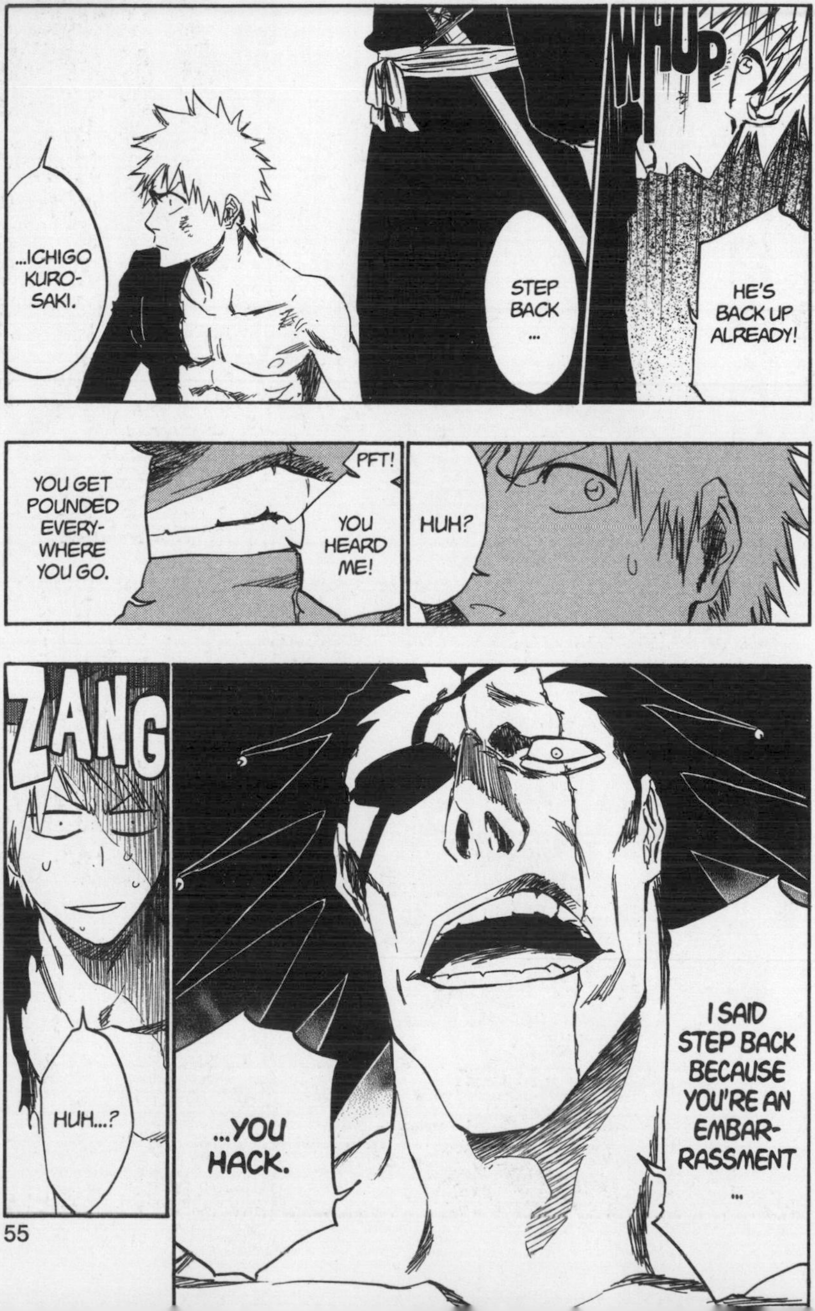
WHUP
HE'S BACK UP ALREADY!
STEP BACK ...
...ICHIGO KURO-SAKI.
HUH?
PFT!
YOU HEARD ME!
YOU GET POUNDED EVERY-WHERE YOU GO.
I SAID STEP BACK BECAUSE YOU'RE AN EMBAR-RASSMENT ...
...YOU HACK.
ZANG
HUH...?

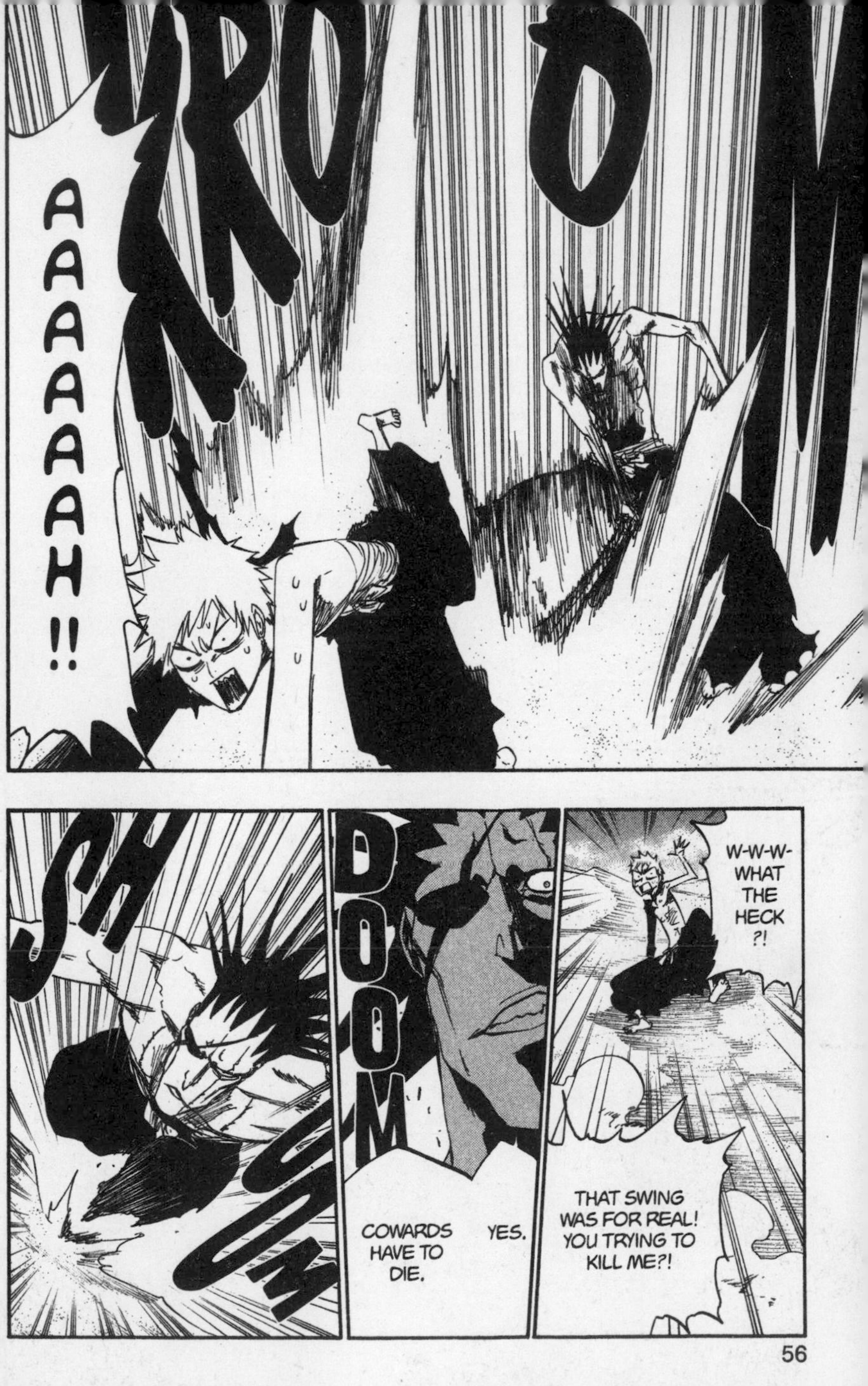
AAAAAAH!!
W-W-W-WHAT THE HECK?!
THAT SWING WAS FOR REAL! YOU TRYING TO KILL ME?!
DOOOM
YES.
COWARDS HAVE TO DIE.
SHUUM

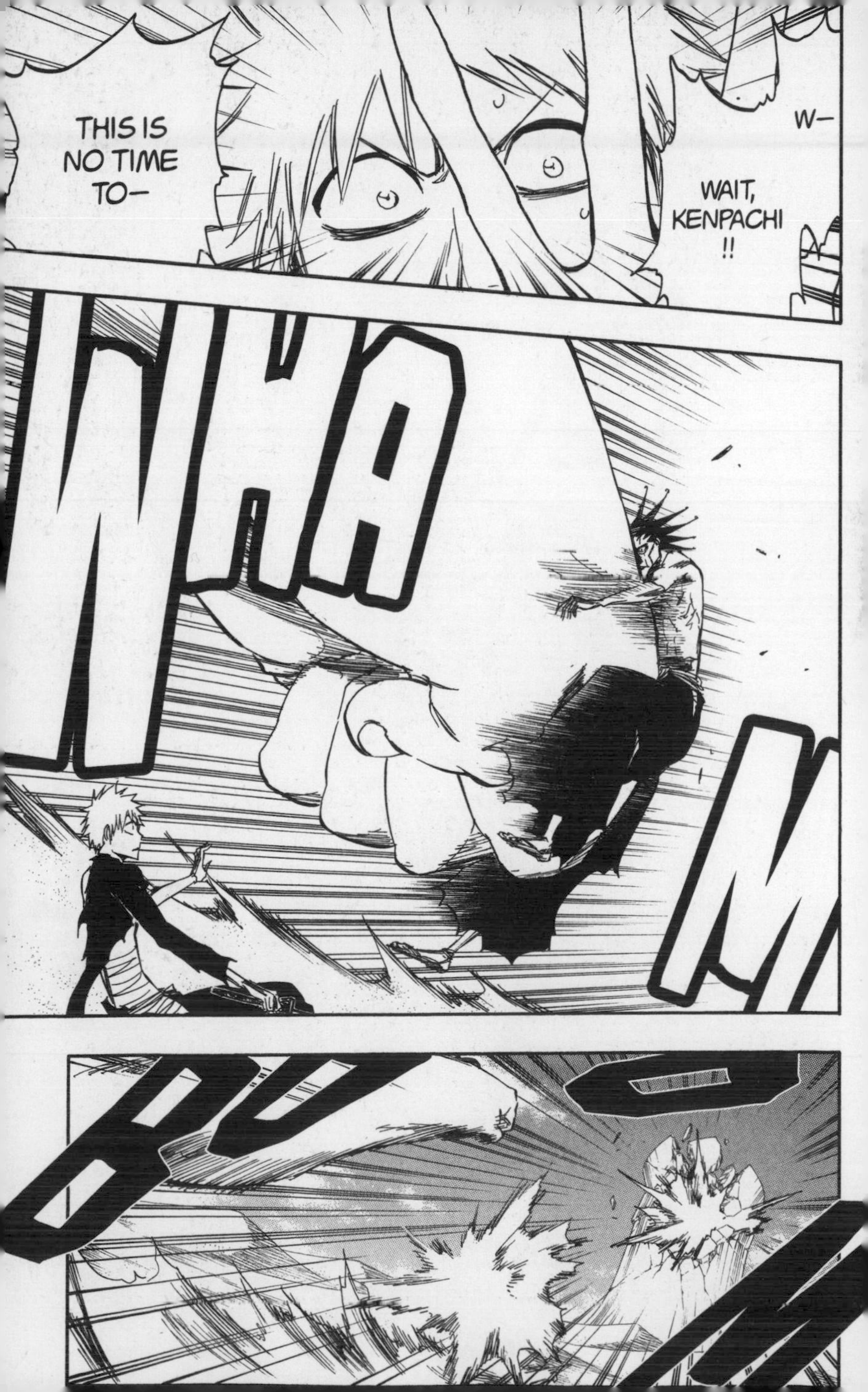
W—
WAIT, KENPACHI !!
THIS IS NO TIME TO—
WHAM

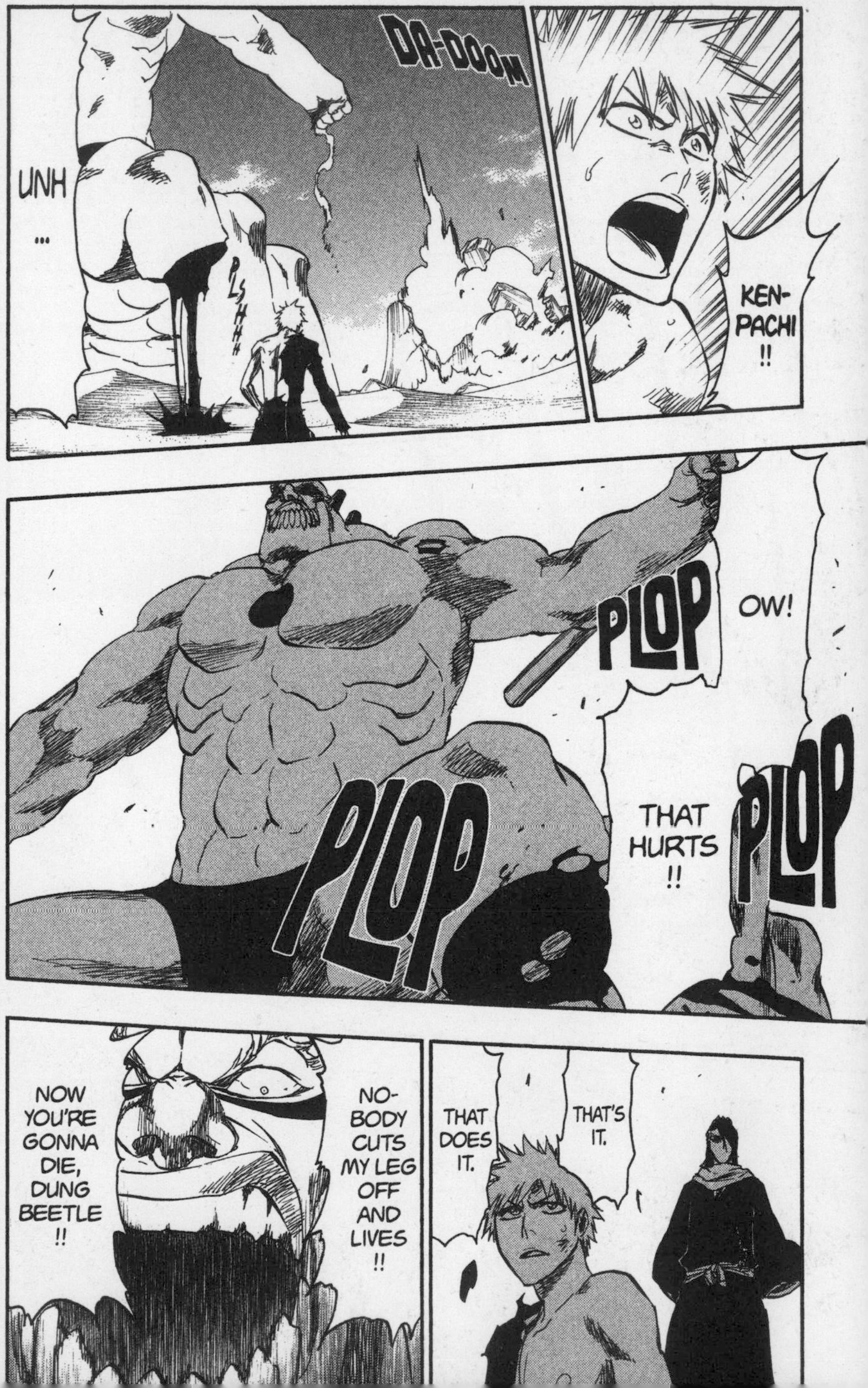
KEN-PACHI!!
DA-DOOM
PLSHHH
UNH...
OW!
PLOP
PLOP
THAT HURTS!!
PLOP
THAT'S IT.
THAT DOES IT.
NO-BODY CUTS MY LEG OFF AND LIVES!!
NOW YOU'RE GONNA DIE, DUNG BEETLE!!

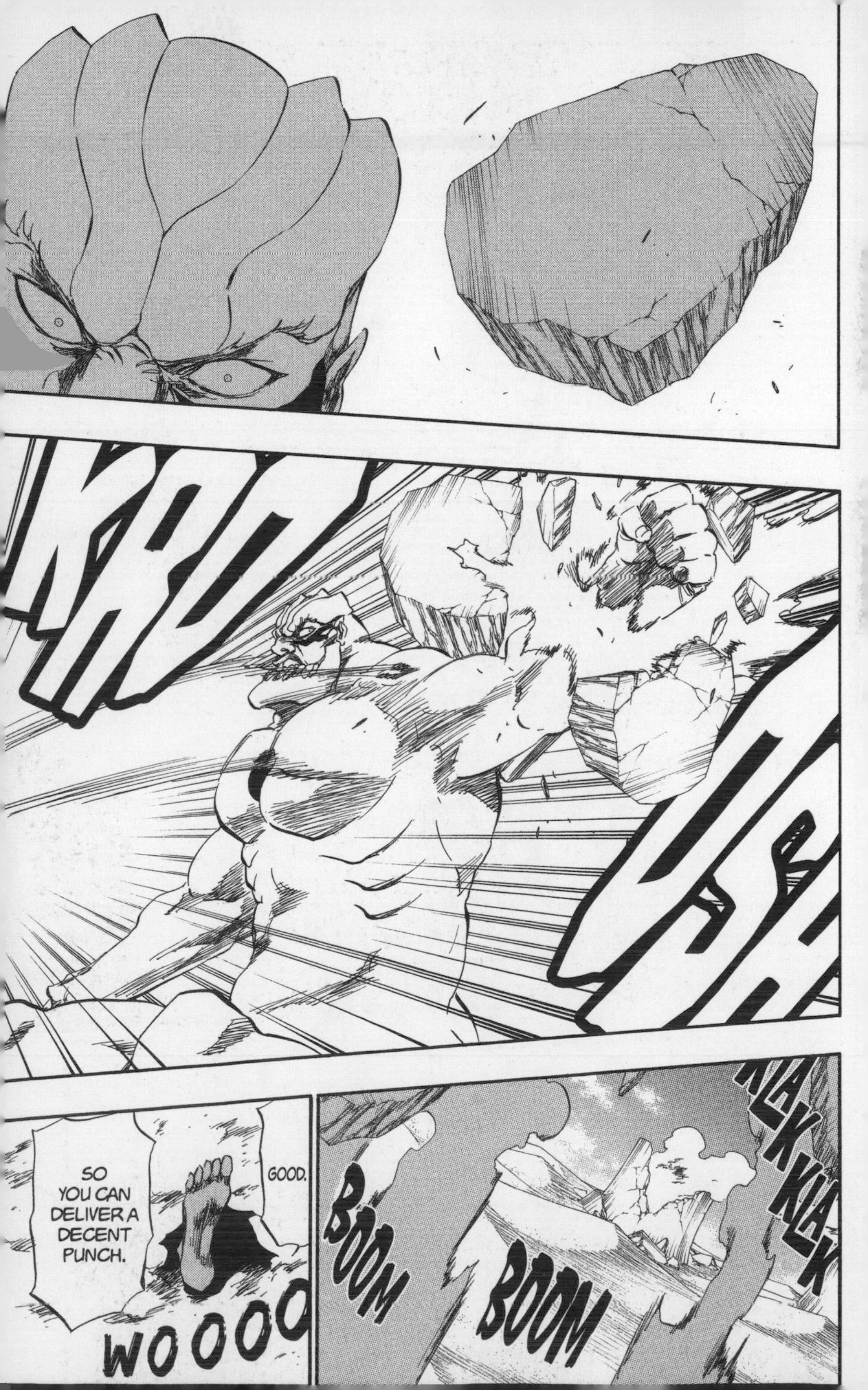
KLAK
KLAK
KLAK
BOOM
BOOM
GOOD.
SO YOU CAN DELIVER A DECENT PUNCH.
WOOOO

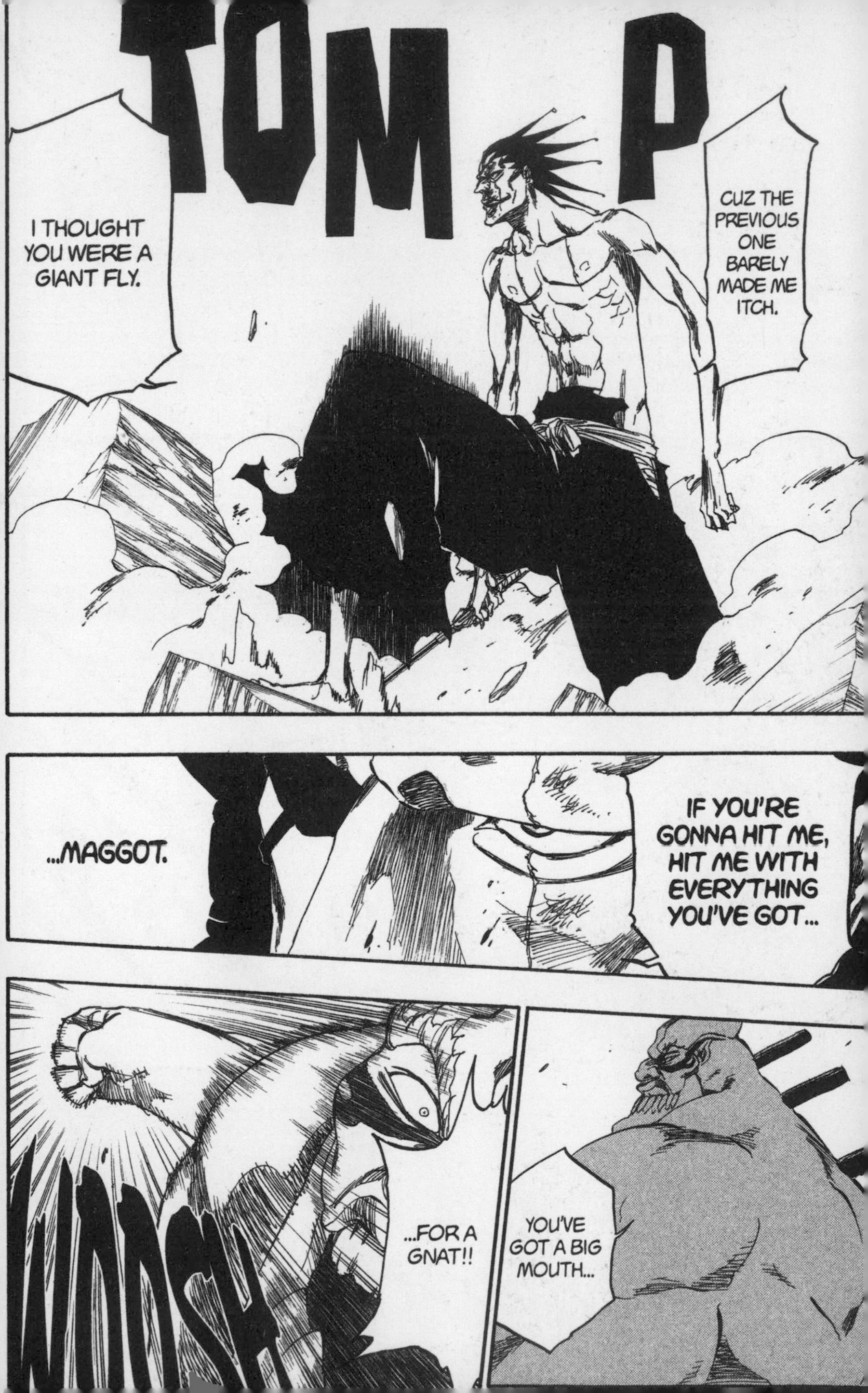
TOMP
CUZ THE PREVIOUS ONE BARELY MADE ME ITCH.
I THOUGHT YOU WERE A GIANT FLY.
IF YOU'RE GONNA HIT ME, HIT ME WITH EVERYTHING YOU'VE GOT...
...MAGGOT.
YOU'VE GOT A BIG MOUTH...
...FOR A GNAT!!

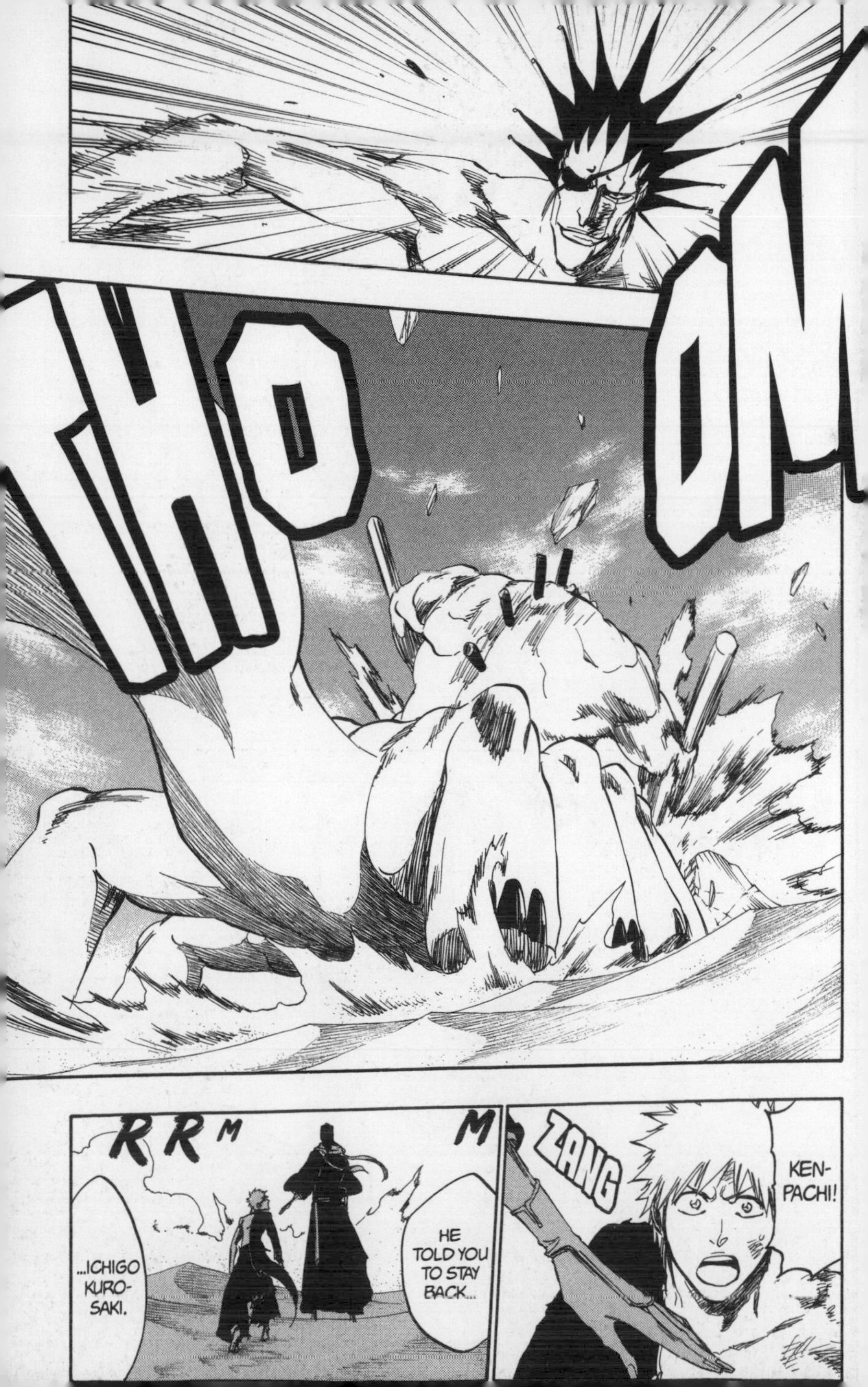
THOOM
ZANG
KEN-PACHI!
RRMM
HE TOLD YOU TO STAY BACK...
...ICHIGO KURO-SAKI.

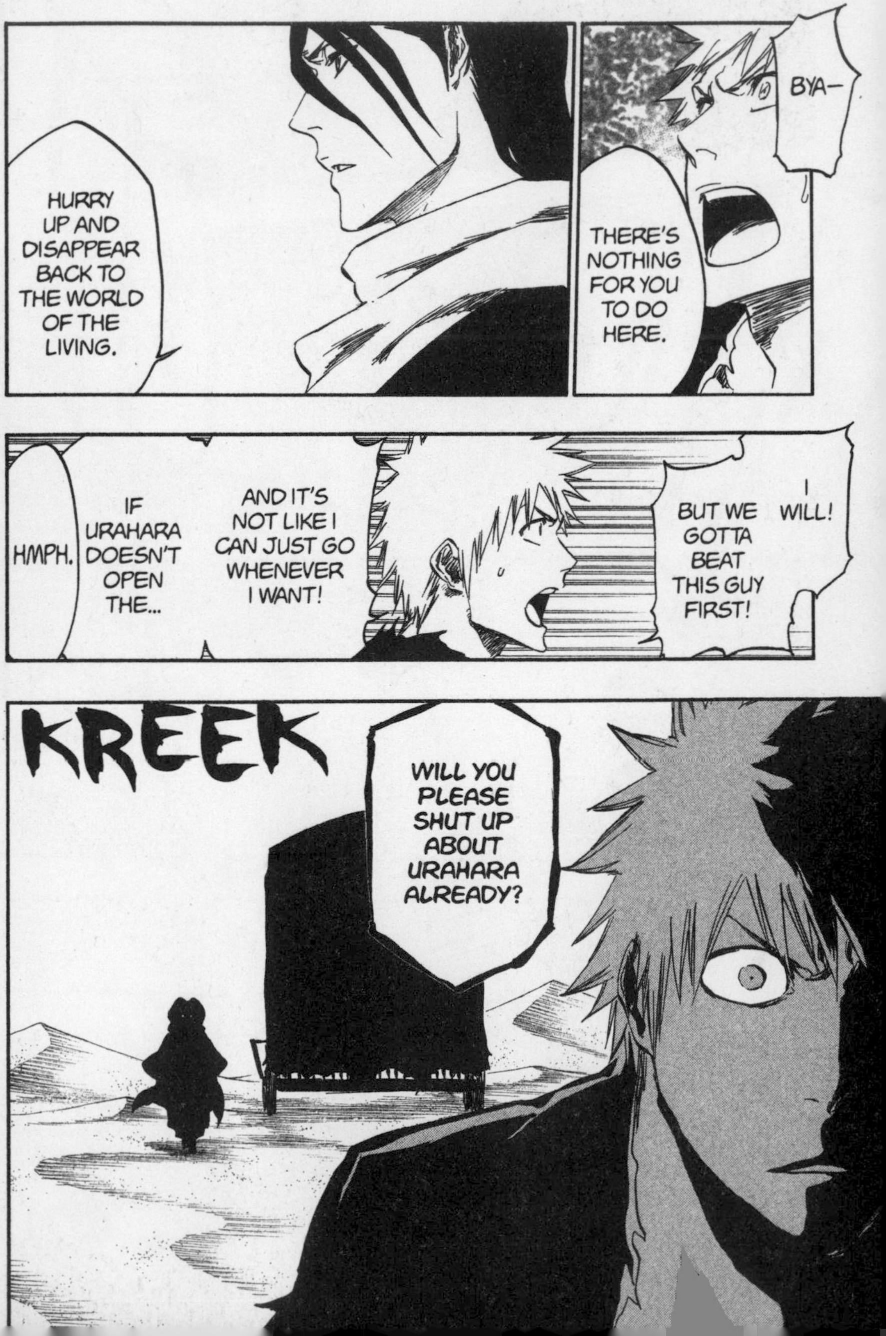
BYA—
THERE'S NOTHING FOR YOU TO DO HERE.
HURRY UP AND DISAPPEAR BACK TO THE WORLD OF THE LIVING.
I WILL!
BUT WE GOTTA BEAT THIS GUY FIRST!
AND IT'S NOT LIKE I CAN JUST GO WHENEVER I WANT!
IF URAHARA DOESN'T OPEN THE...
HMPH.
WILL YOU PLEASE SHUT UP ABOUT URAHARA ALREADY?
KREEK

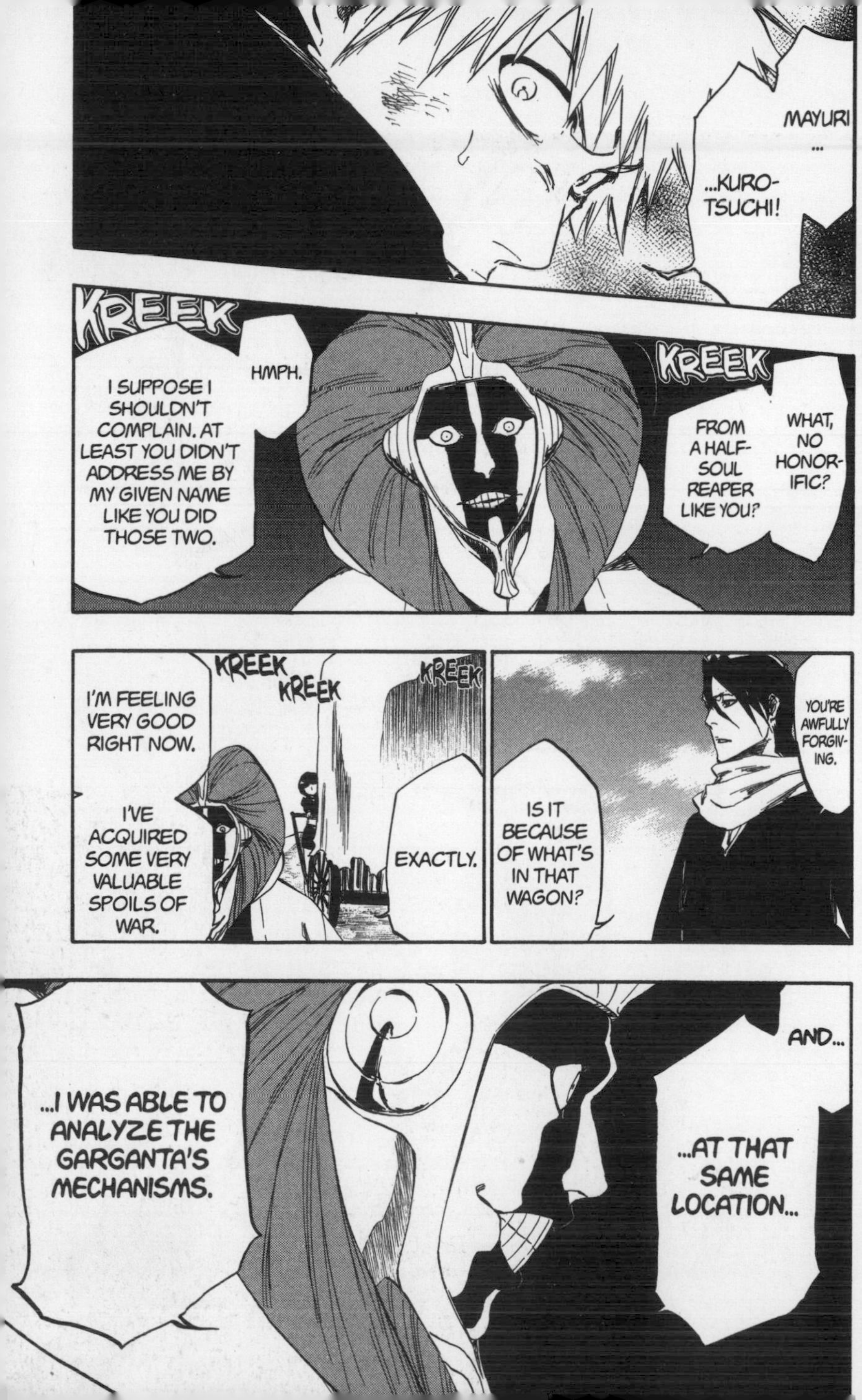
MAYURI ...
...KURO-TSUCHI!
KREEK
WHAT, NO HONOR-IFIC?
FROM A HALF-SOUL REAPER LIKE YOU?
KREEK
HMPH.
I SUPPOSE I SHOULDN'T COMPLAIN. AT LEAST YOU DIDN'T ADDRESS ME BY MY GIVEN NAME LIKE YOU DID THOSE TWO.
YOU'RE AWFULLY FORGIV-ING.
IS IT BECAUSE OF WHAT'S IN THAT WAGON?
KREEK
EXACTLY.
KREEK KREEK
I'M FEELING VERY GOOD RIGHT NOW.
I'VE ACQUIRED SOME VERY VALUABLE SPOILS OF WAR.
AND...
...AT THAT SAME LOCATION...
...I WAS ABLE TO ANALYZE THE GARGANTA'S MECHANISMS.

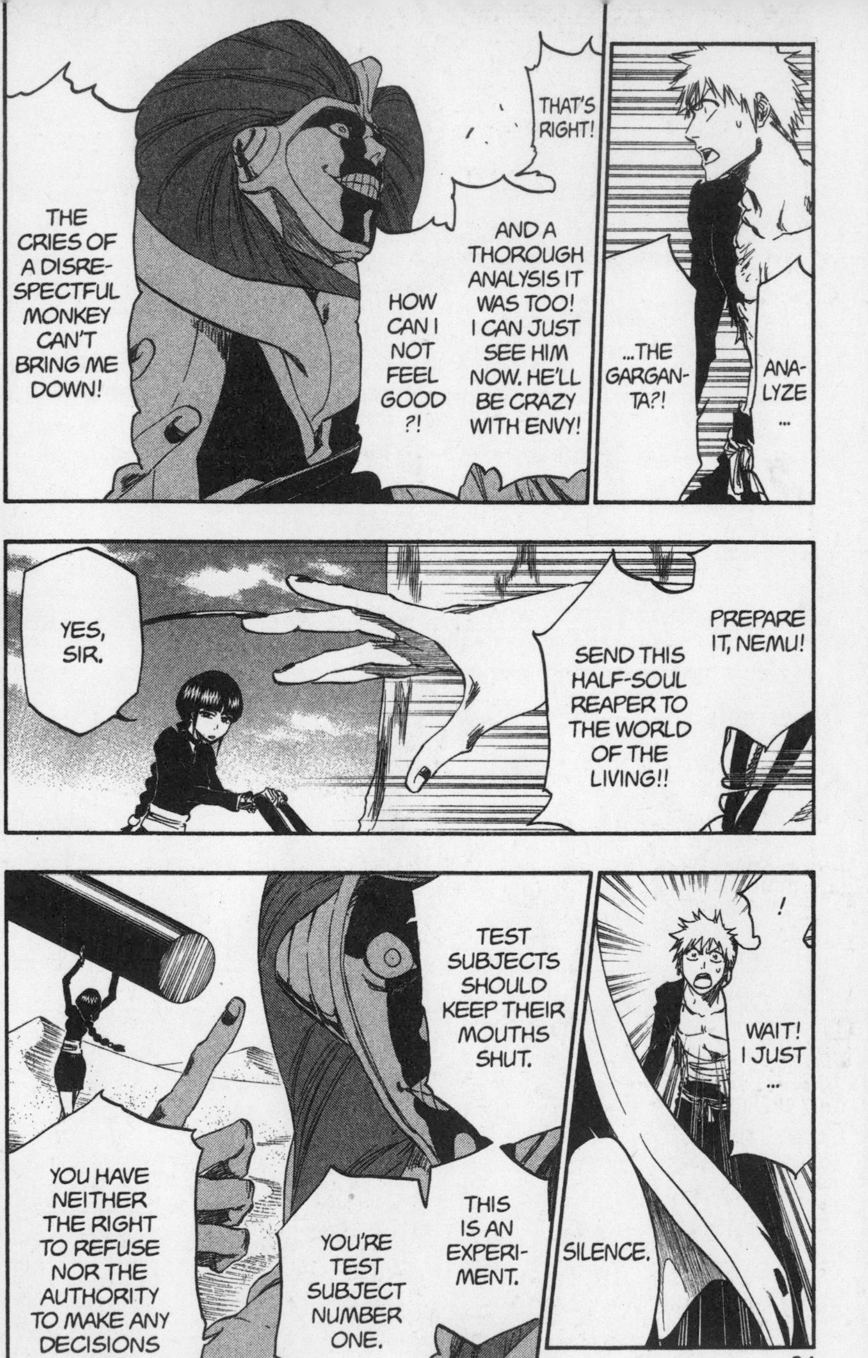

ANA-LYZE...
...THE GARGAN-TA?!
THAT'S RIGHT!
AND A THOROUGH ANALYSIS IT WAS TOO! I CAN JUST SEE HIM NOW. HE'LL BE CRAZY WITH ENVY!
HOW CAN I NOT FEEL GOOD ?!
THE CRIES OF A DISRE-SPECTFUL MONKEY CAN'T BRING ME DOWN!
PREPARE IT, NEMU!
SEND THIS HALF-SOUL REAPER TO THE WORLD OF THE LIVING!!
YES, SIR.
!
WAIT! I JUST ...
SILENCE.
TEST SUBJECTS SHOULD KEEP THEIR MOUTHS SHUT.
THIS IS AN EXPERI-MENT.
YOU'RE TEST SUBJECT NUMBER ONE.
YOU HAVE NEITHER THE RIGHT TO REFUSE NOR THE AUTHORITY TO MAKE ANY DECISIONS HERE!

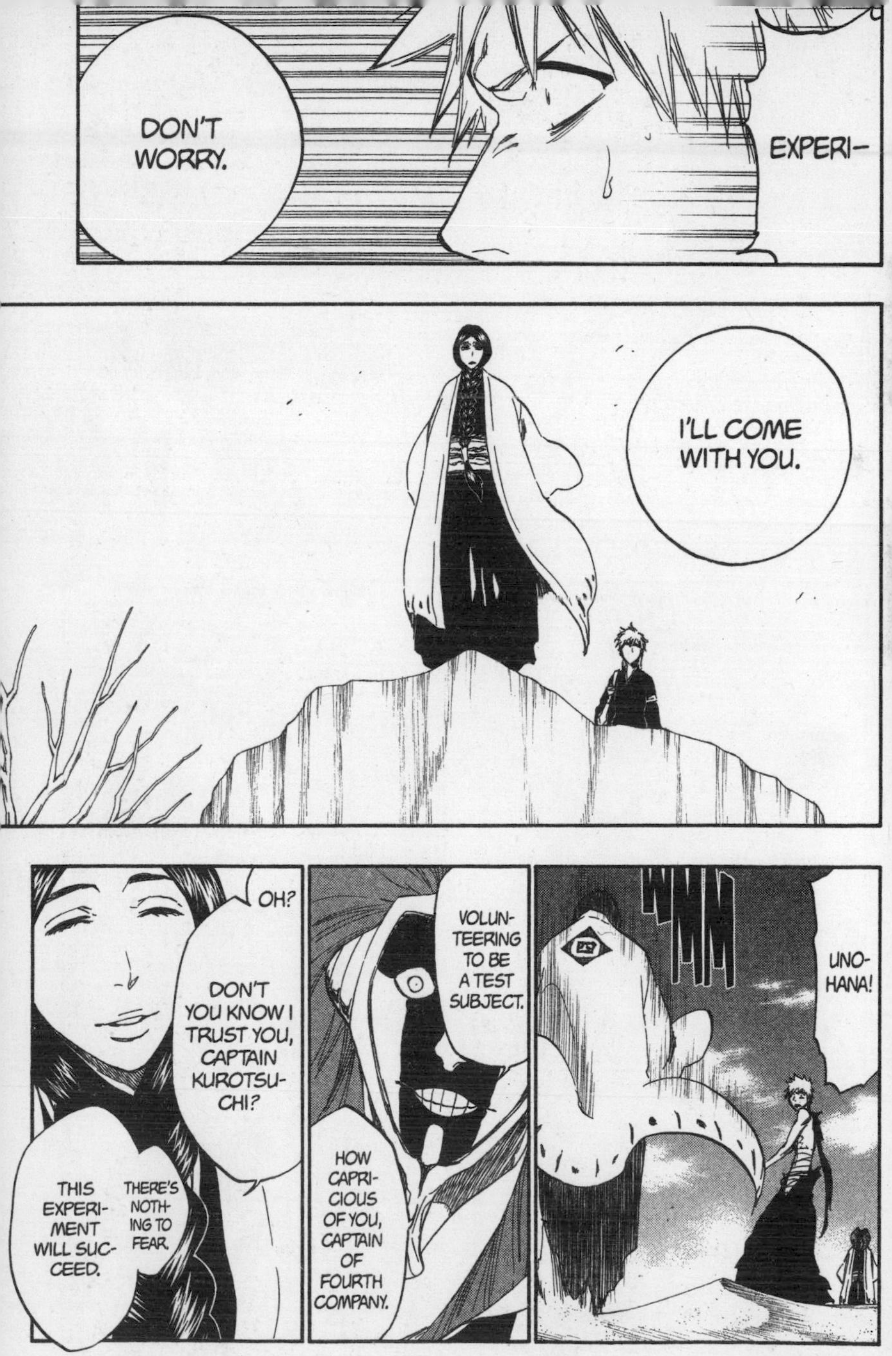
EXPERI-
DON'T WORRY.
I'LL COME WITH YOU.
UNO-HANA!
WMM
VOLUN-TEERING TO BE A TEST SUBJECT.
HOW CAPRI-CIOUS OF YOU, CAPTAIN OF FOURTH COMPANY.
OH?
DON'T YOU KNOW I TRUST YOU, CAPTAIN KUROTSU-CHI?
THERE'S NOTH-ING TO FEAR.
THIS EXPERI-MENT WILL SUC-CEED.

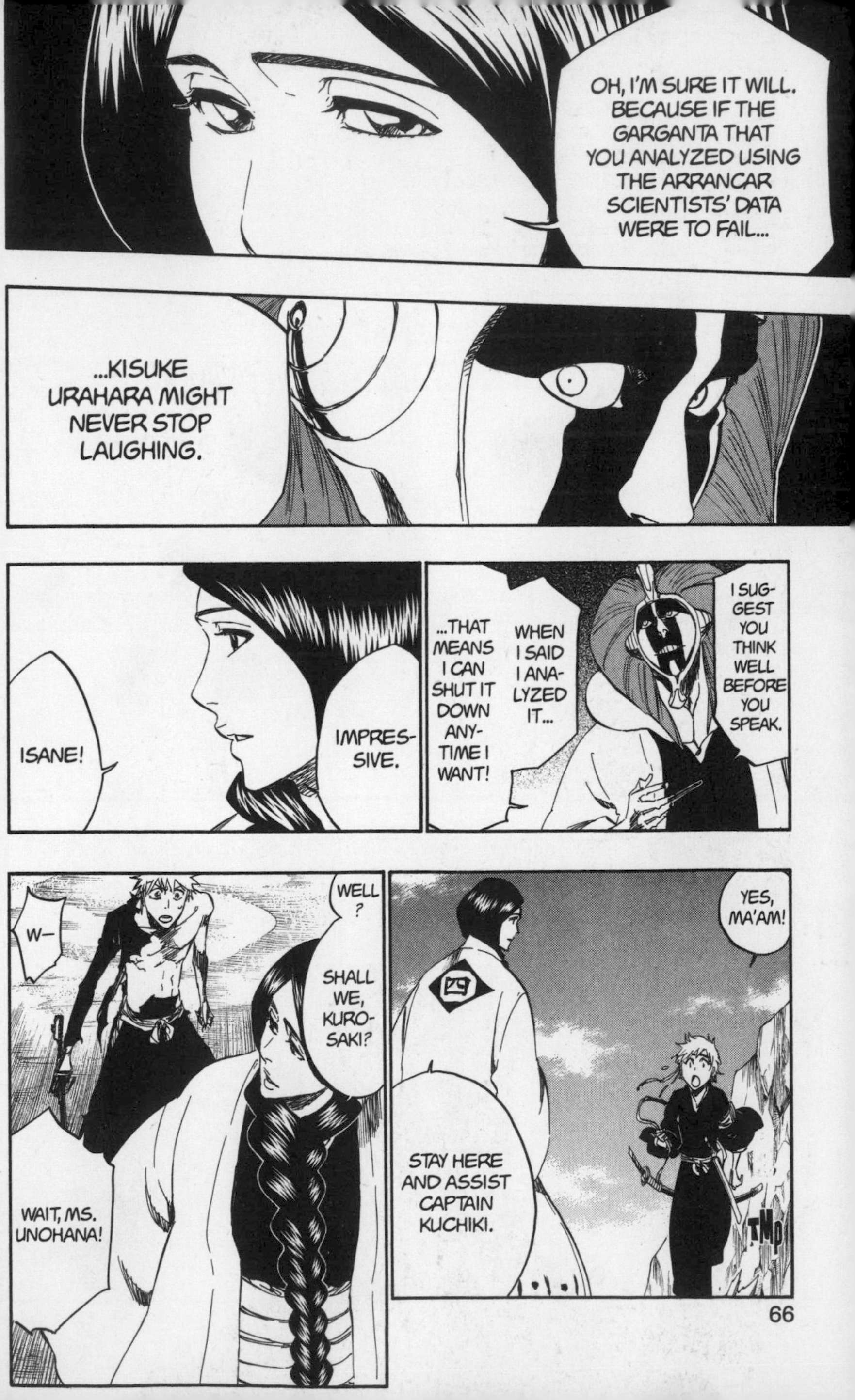
OH, I'M SURE IT WILL. BECAUSE IF THE GARGANTA THAT YOU ANALYZED USING THE ARRANCAR SCIENTISTS' DATA WERE TO FAIL...
...KISUKE URAHARA MIGHT NEVER STOP LAUGHING.
I SUG-GEST YOU THINK WELL BEFORE YOU SPEAK.
WHEN I SAID I ANA-LYZED IT...
...THAT MEANS I CAN SHUT IT DOWN ANY-TIME I WANT!
IMPRES-SIVE.
ISANE!
YES, MA'AM!
STAY HERE AND ASSIST CAPTAIN KUCHIKI.
TMP
WELL?
SHALL WE, KURO-SAKI?
W—
WAIT, MS. UNOHANA!

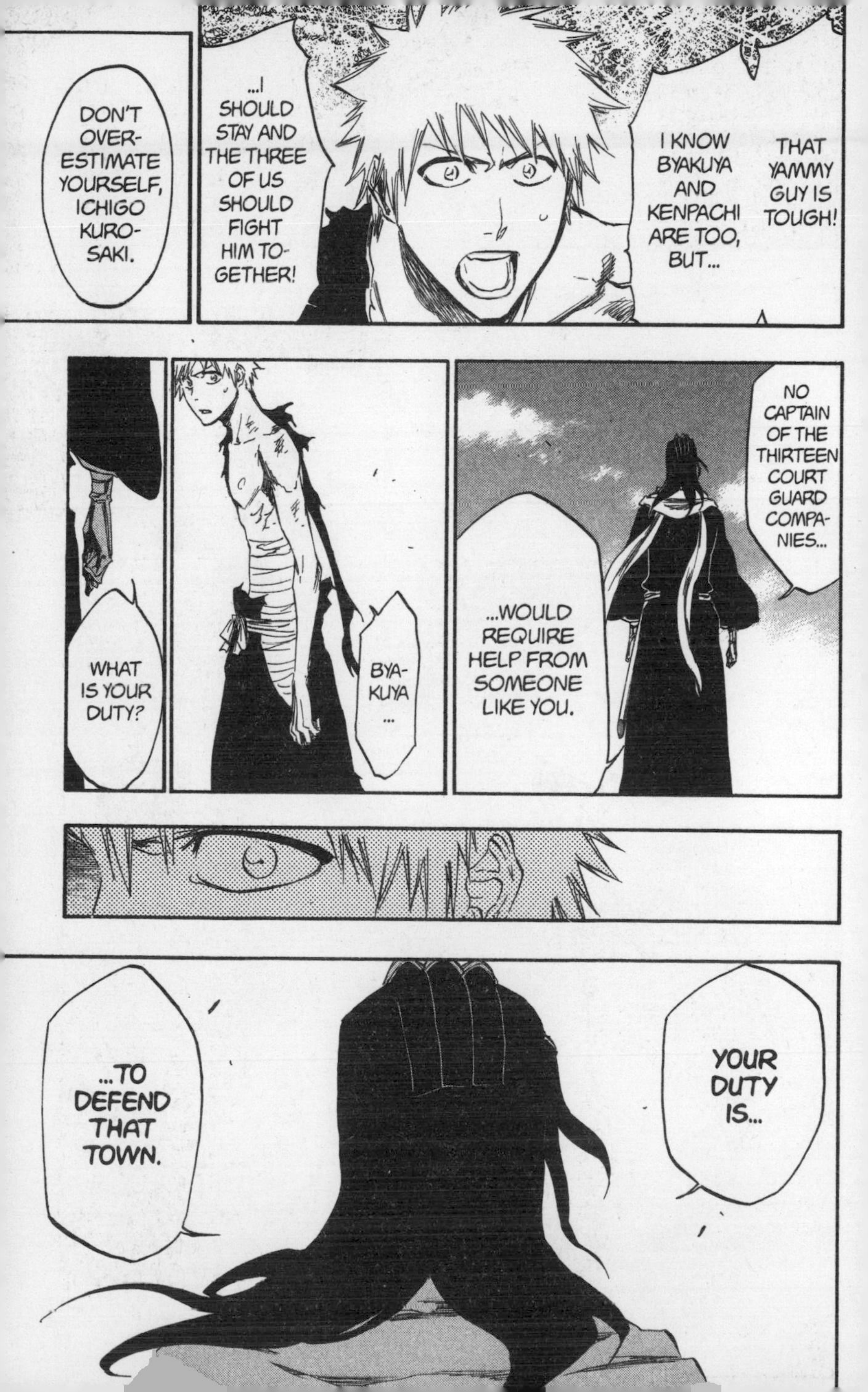
THAT YAMMY GUY IS TOUGH!
I KNOW BYAKUYA AND KENPACHI ARE TOO, BUT...
...I SHOULD STAY AND THE THREE OF US SHOULD FIGHT HIM TO-GETHER!
DON'T OVER-ESTIMATE YOURSELF, ICHIGO KURO-SAKI.
NO CAPTAIN OF THE THIRTEEN COURT GUARD COMPA-NIES...
...WOULD REQUIRE HELP FROM SOMEONE LIKE YOU.
BYA-KUYA...
WHAT IS YOUR DUTY?
YOUR DUTY IS...
...TO DEFEND THAT TOWN.

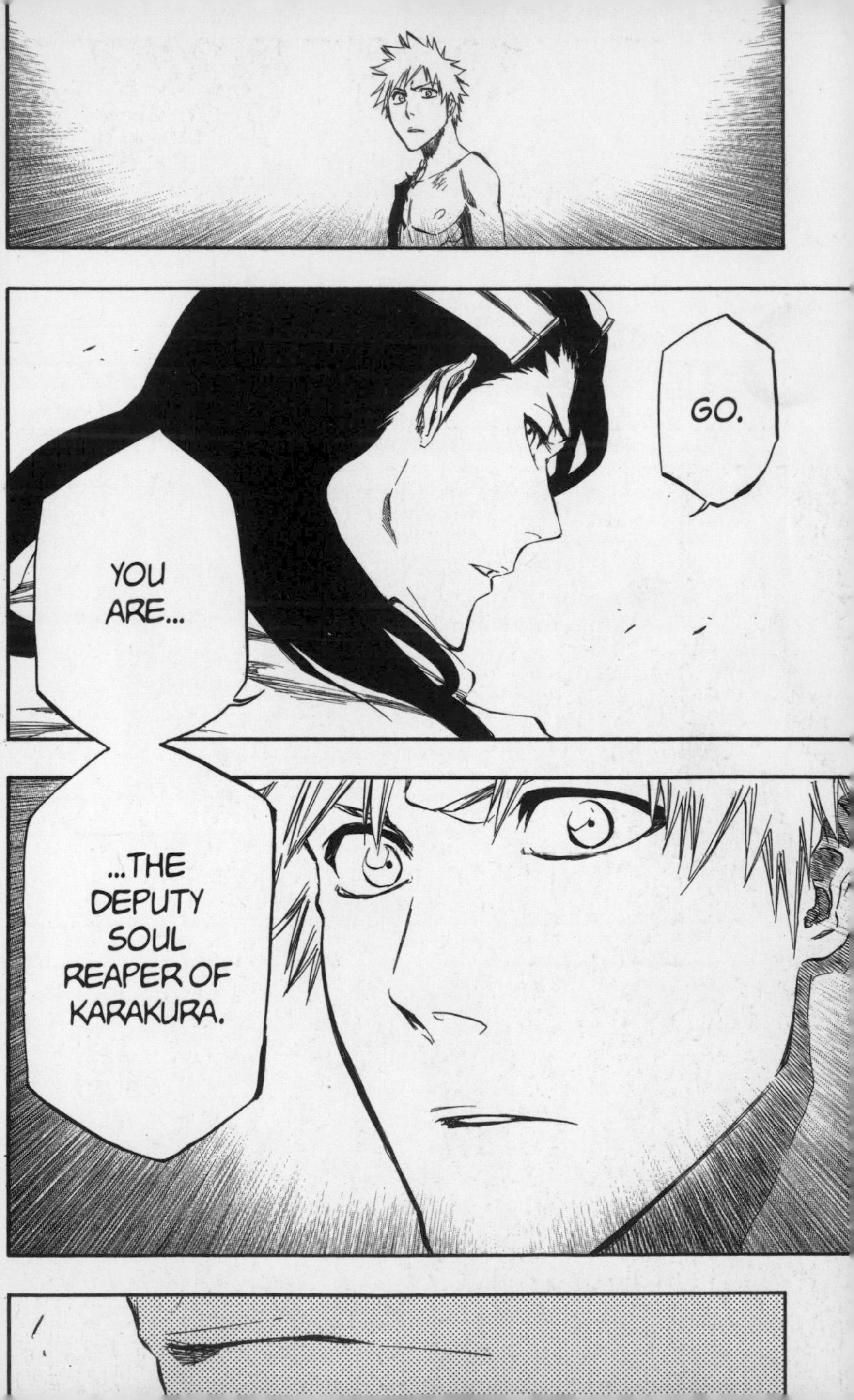
GO.
YOU ARE...
...THE DEPUTY SOUL REAPER OF KARAKURA.

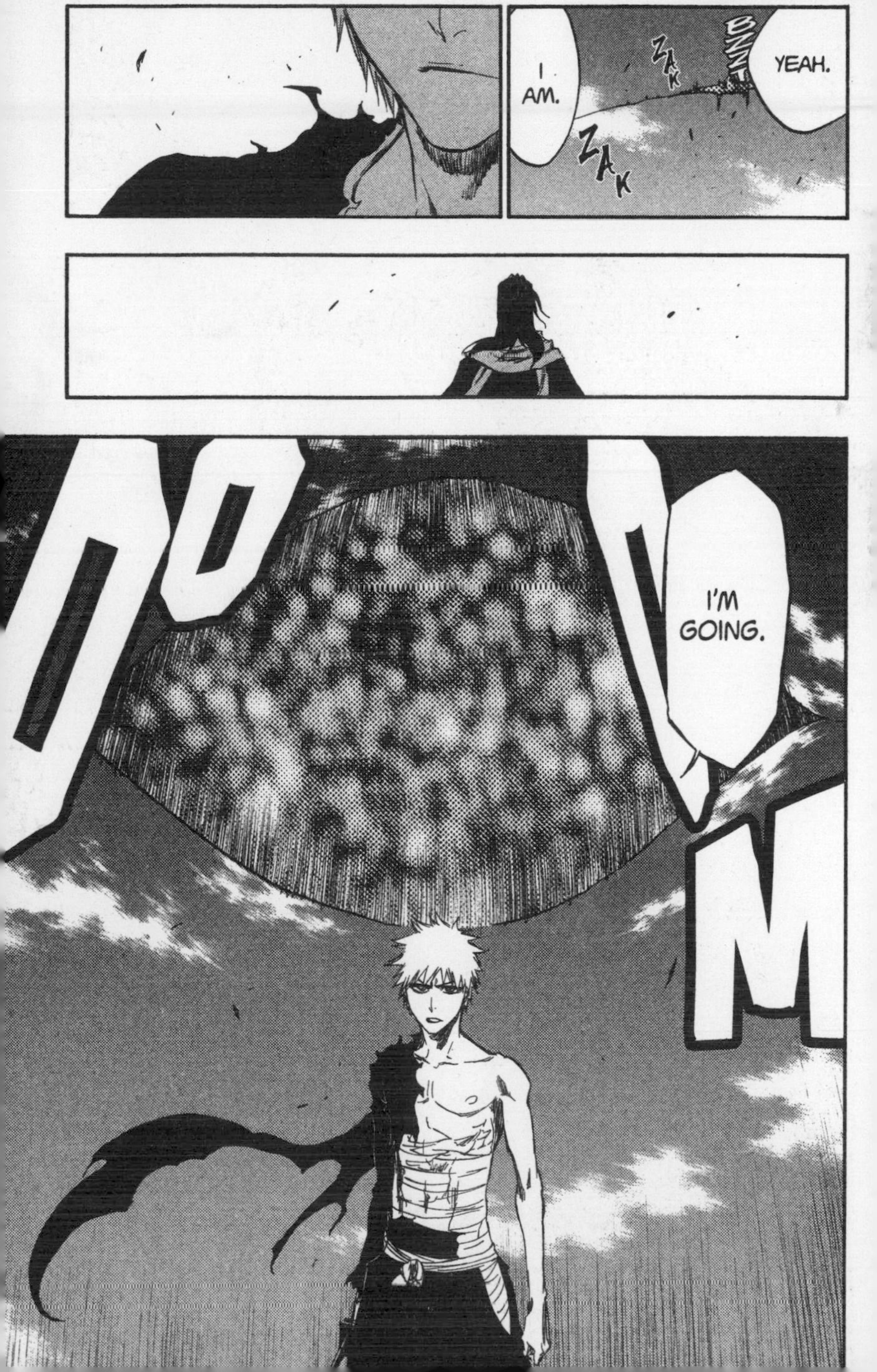
YEAH.
BZZT
ZAK
I AM.
ZAK
I'M GOING.

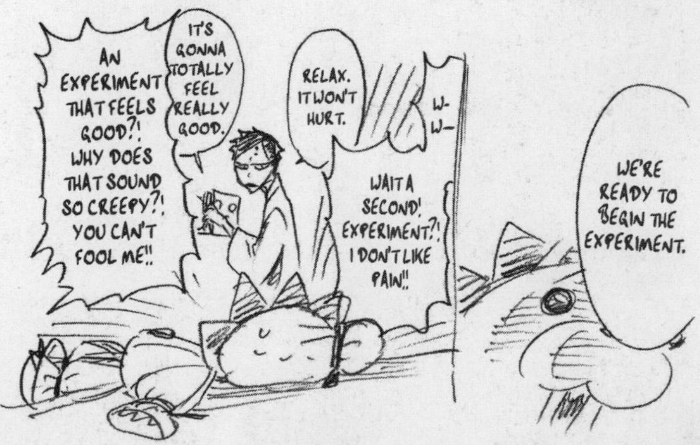
WE'RE READY TO BEGIN THE EXPERIMENT.
W-W—
WAIT A SECOND! EXPERIMENT?! I DON'T LIKE PAIN!!
RELAX. IT WON'T HURT.
IT'S GONNA TOTALLY FEEL REALLY GOOD.
AN EXPERIMENT THAT FEELS GOOD?! WHY DOES THAT SOUND SO CREEPY?! YOU CAN'T FOOL ME!!

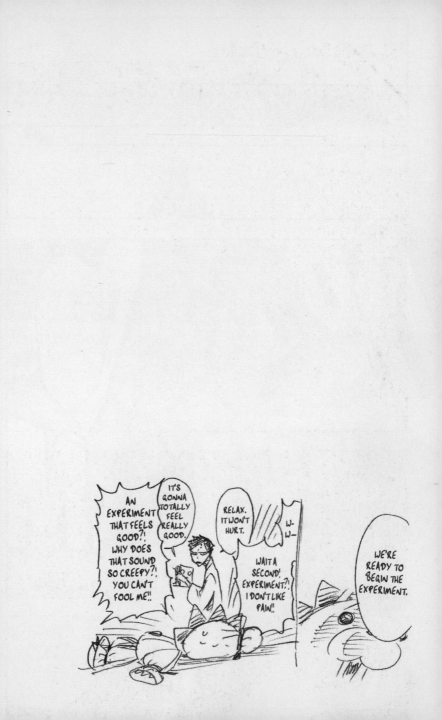

381. Words Just Don't Like You

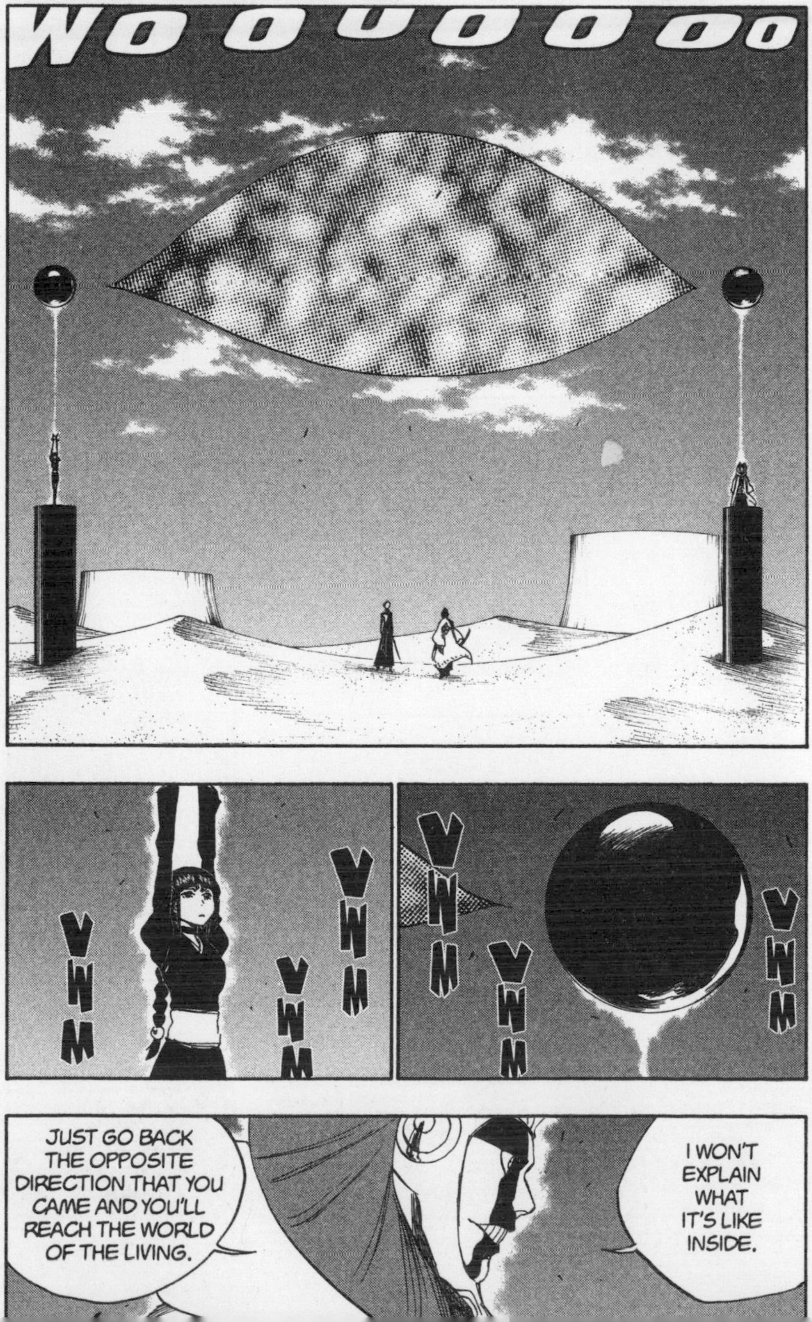
WOOOOOOOO
VWM
VWM
VWM
VWM
VWM
VWM
I WON'T EXPLAIN WHAT IT'S LIKE INSIDE.
JUST GO BACK THE OPPOSITE DIRECTION THAT YOU CAME AND YOU'LL REACH THE WORLD OF THE LIVING.

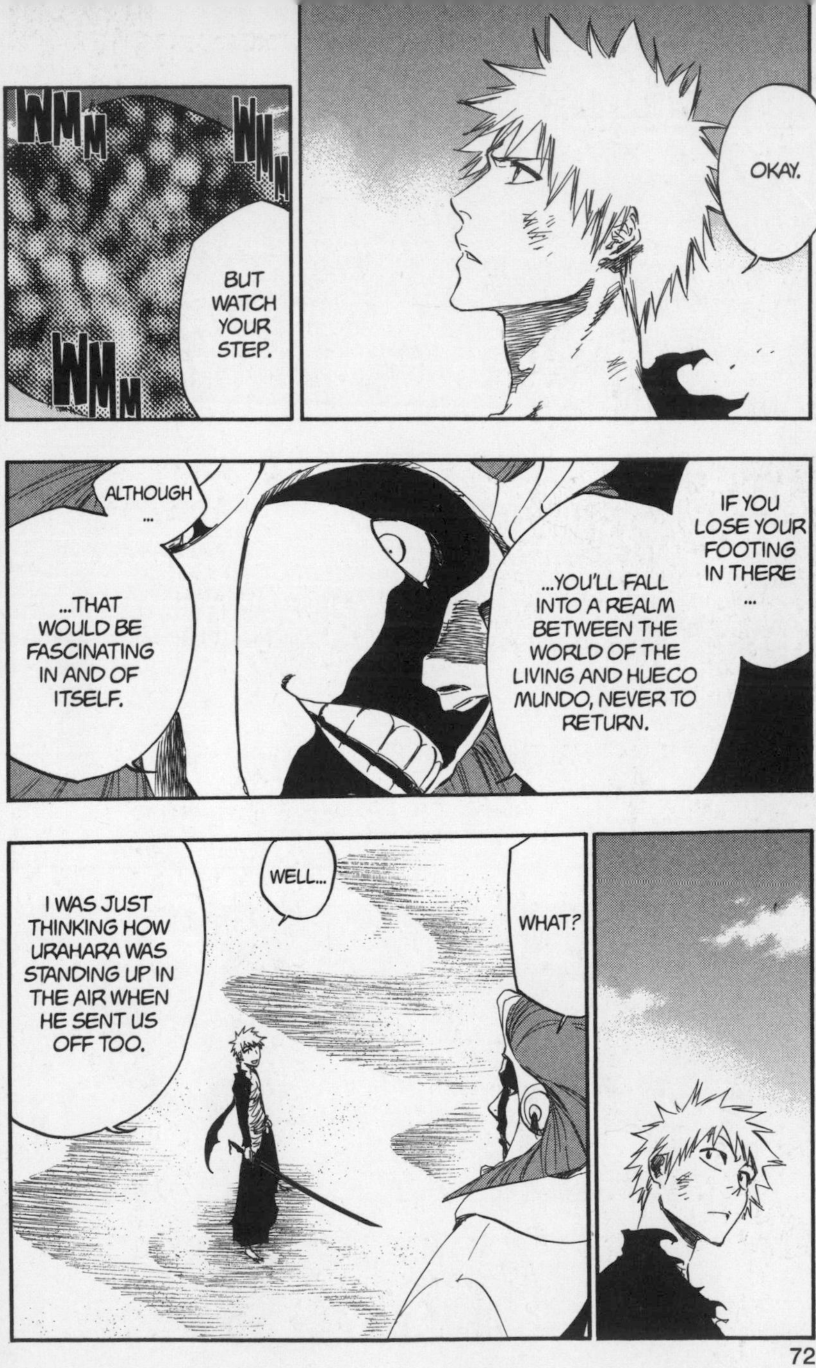
OKAY.
WMM
WMM
BUT WATCH YOUR STEP.
WMM
IF YOU LOSE YOUR FOOTING IN THERE ...
...YOU'LL FALL INTO A REALM BETWEEN THE WORLD OF THE LIVING AND HUECO MUNDO, NEVER TO RETURN.
ALTHOUGH ...
...THAT WOULD BE FASCINATING IN AND OF ITSELF.
WHAT?
WELL...
I WAS JUST THINKING HOW URAHARA WAS STANDING UP IN THE AIR WHEN HE SENT US OFF TOO.

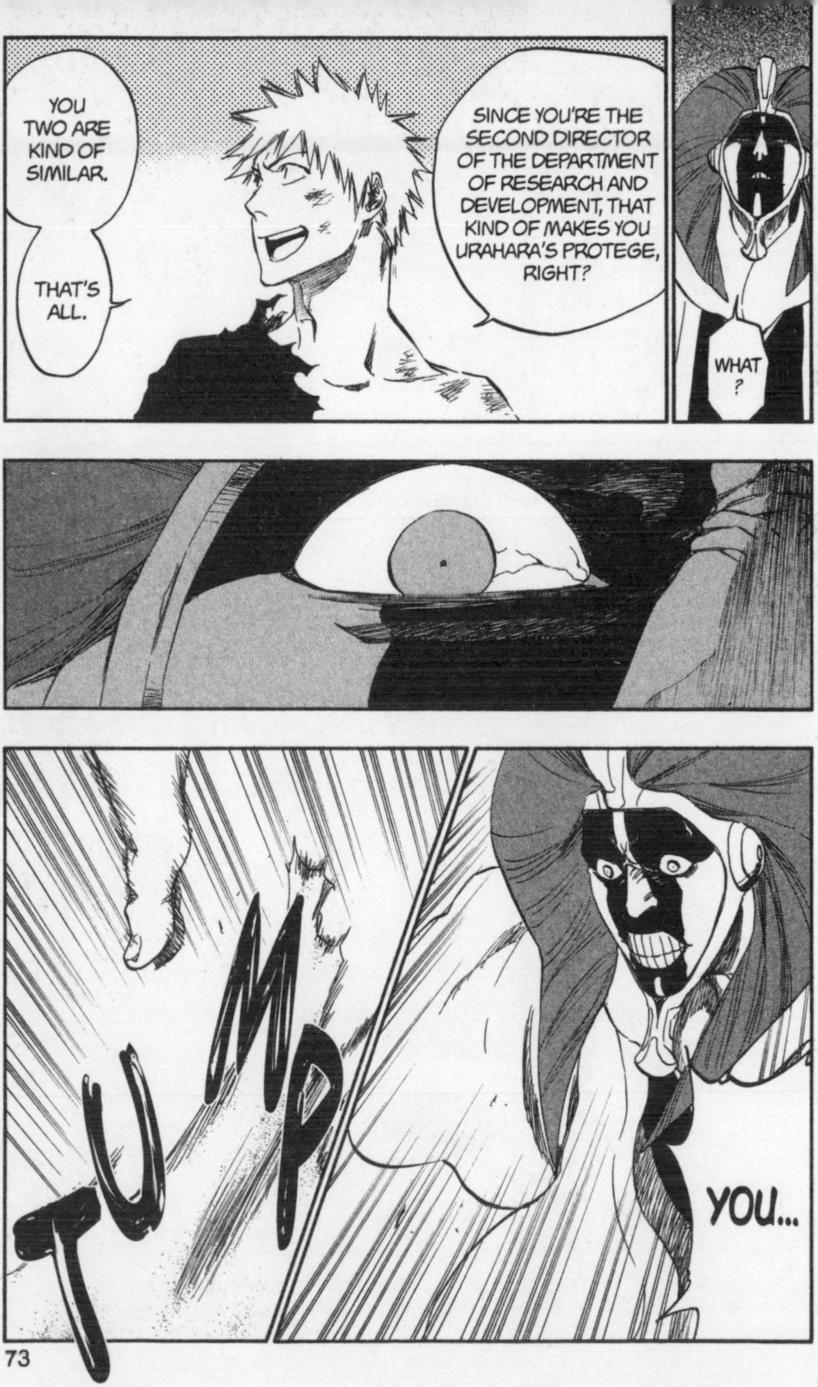
WHAT?
SINCE YOU'RE THE SECOND DIRECTOR OF THE DEPARTMENT OF RESEARCH AND DEVELOPMENT, THAT KIND OF MAKES YOU URAHARA'S PROTEGE, RIGHT?
YOU TWO ARE KIND OF SIMILAR.
THAT'S ALL.
YOU...
TUMP

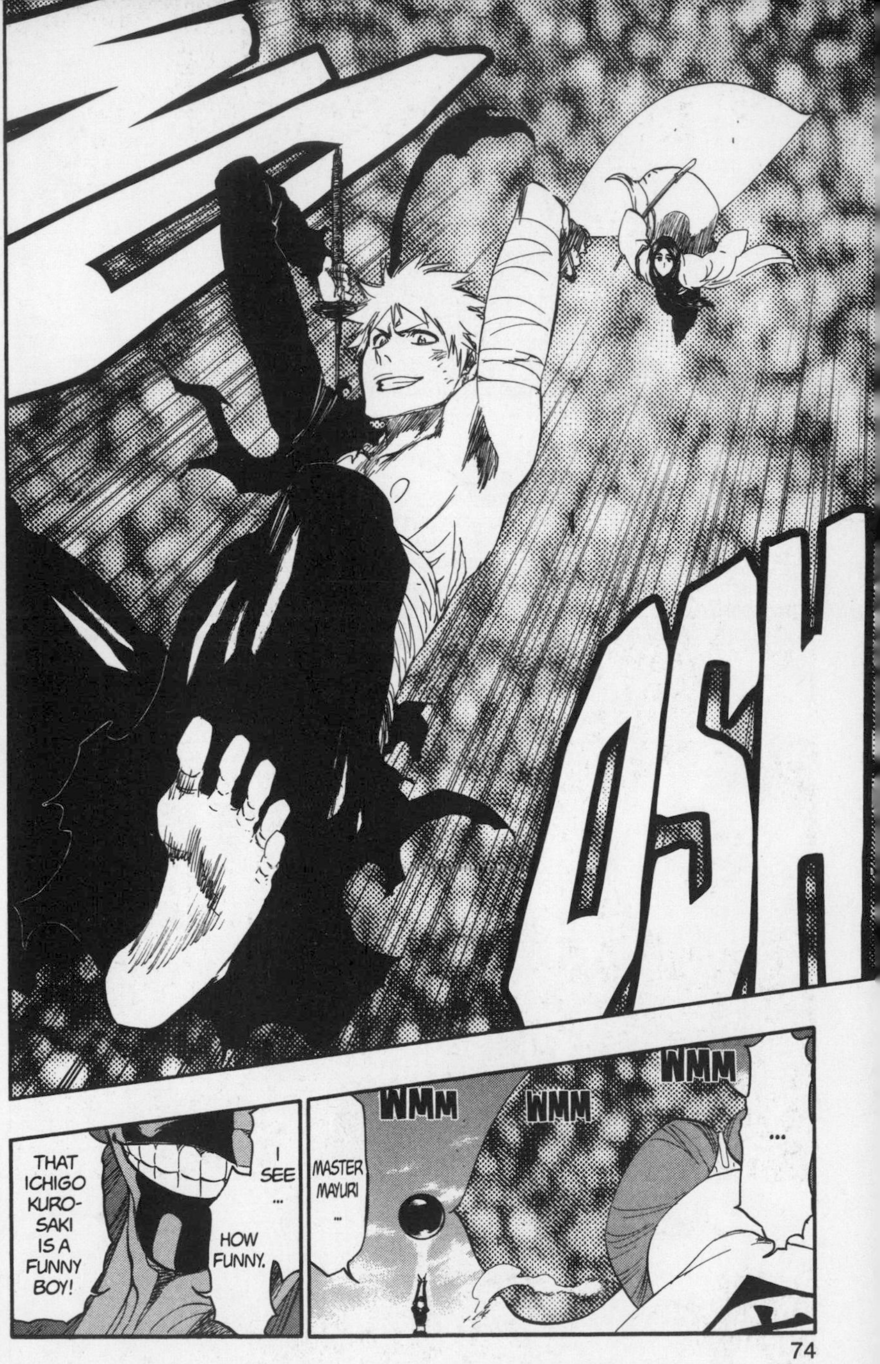
OSH
WMM
...
WMM
WMM
MASTER MAYURI ...
I SEE ...
HOW FUNNY.
THAT ICHIGO KURO-SAKI IS A FUNNY BOY!

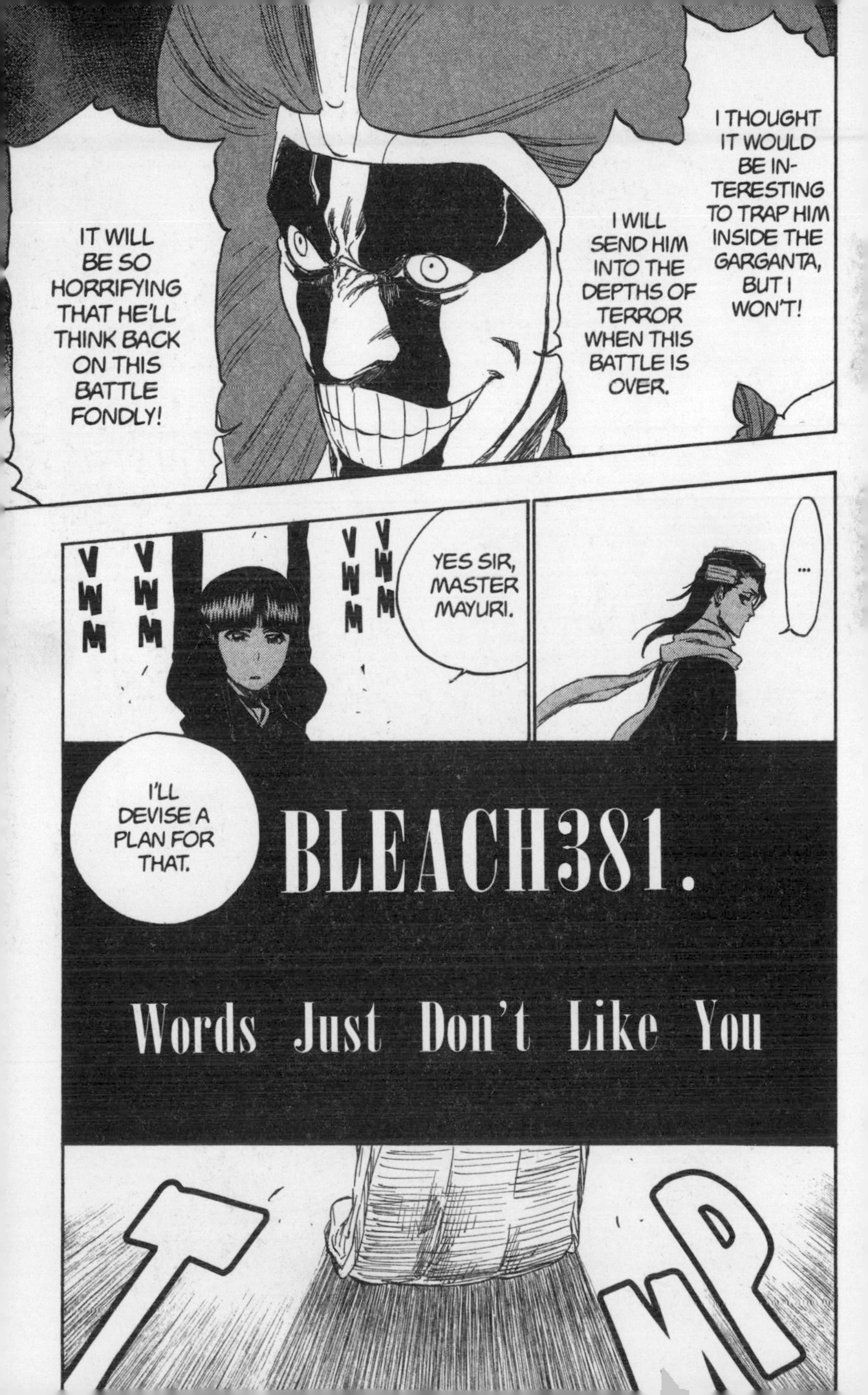
I THOUGHT IT WOULD BE IN-TERESTING TO TRAP HIM INSIDE THE GARGANTA, BUT I WON'T!
I WILL SEND HIM INTO THE DEPTHS OF TERROR WHEN THIS BATTLE IS OVER.
IT WILL BE SO HORRIFYING THAT HE'LL THINK BACK ON THIS BATTLE FONDLY!
...
VWM VWM
YES SIR, MASTER MAYURI.
VWM VWM
BLEACH381.
Words Just Don't Like You
I'LL DEVISE A PLAN FOR THAT.
T MP

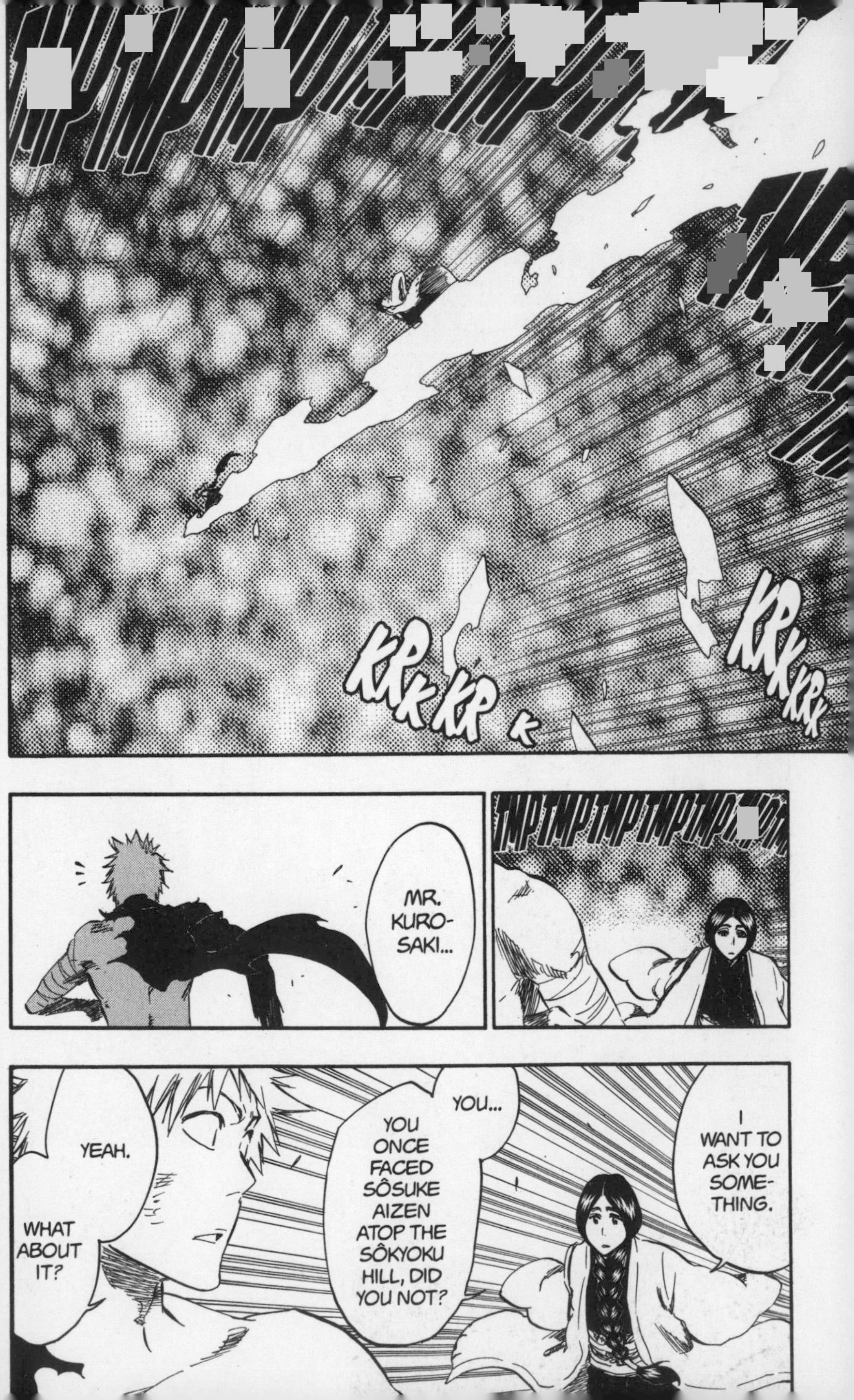
KRKKRK
KRK KRK K
TMP TMP TMP TMP TMP
MR. KURO-SAKI...
I WANT TO ASK YOU SOME-THING.
YOU...
YOU ONCE FACED SÔSUKE AIZEN ATOP THE SÔKYOKU HILL, DID YOU NOT?
YEAH.
WHAT ABOUT IT?

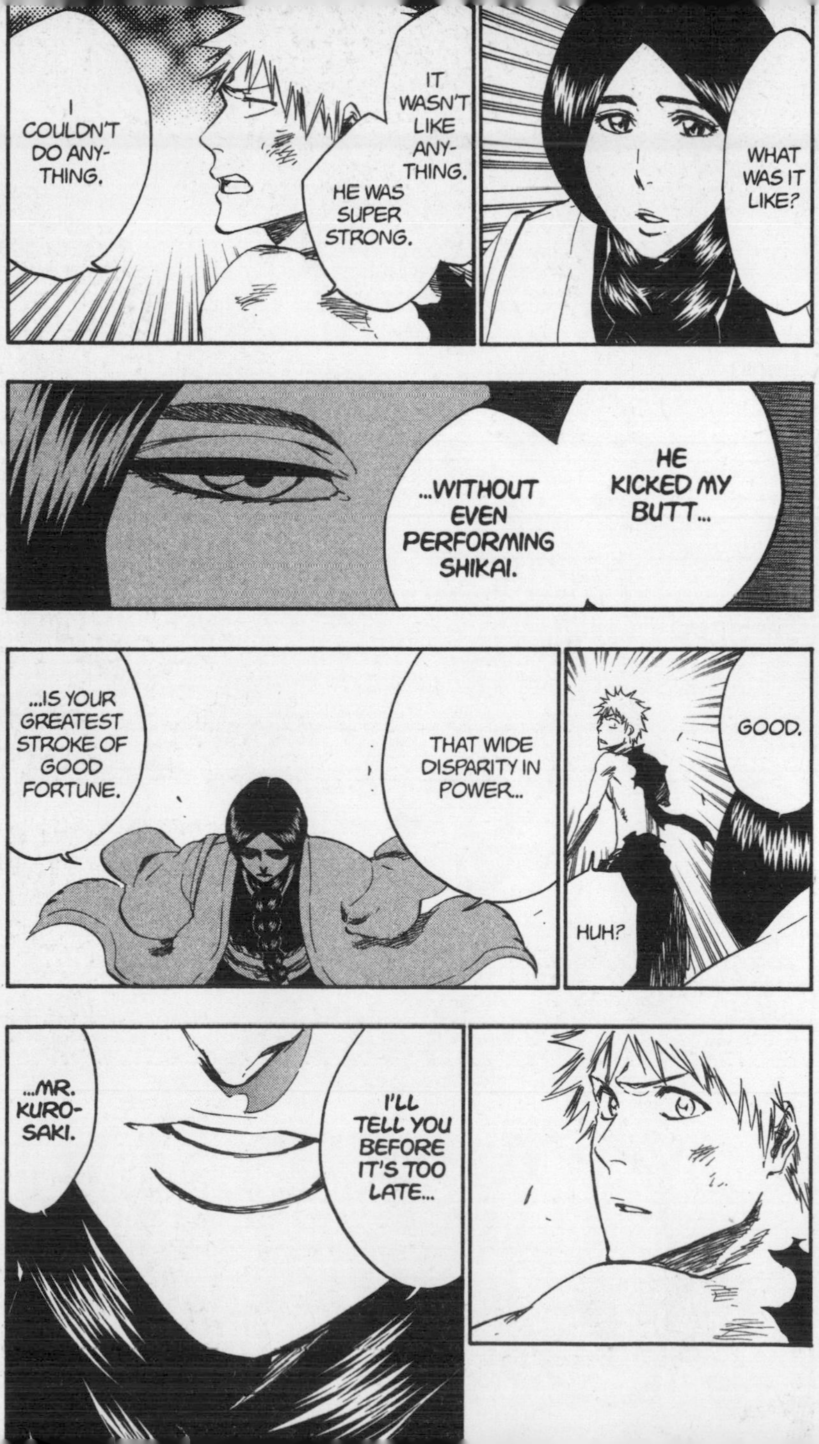
WHAT WAS IT LIKE?
IT WASN'T LIKE ANYTHING.
HE WAS SUPER STRONG.
I COULDN'T DO ANYTHING.
HE KICKED MY BUTT...
...WITHOUT EVEN PERFORMING SHIKAI.
GOOD.
HUH?
THAT WIDE DISPARITY IN POWER...
...IS YOUR GREATEST STROKE OF GOOD FORTUNE.
I'LL TELL YOU BEFORE IT'S TOO LATE...
...MR. KUROSAKI.

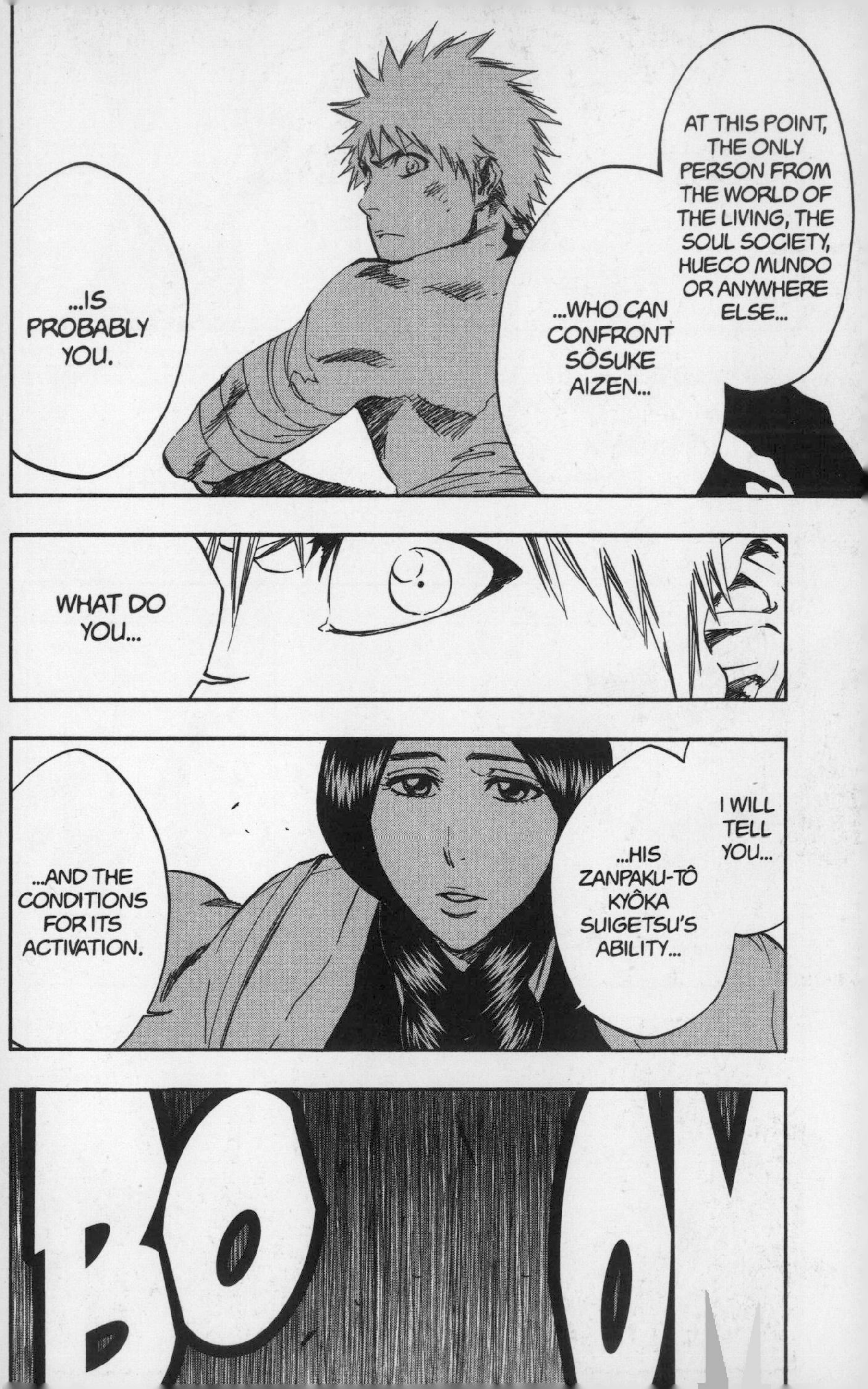
AT THIS POINT, THE ONLY PERSON FROM THE WORLD OF THE LIVING, THE SOUL SOCIETY, HUECO MUNDO OR ANYWHERE ELSE...
...WHO CAN CONFRONT SÔSUKE AIZEN...
...IS PROBABLY YOU.
WHAT DO YOU...
I WILL TELL YOU...
...HIS ZANPAKU-TÔ KYÔKA SUIGETSU'S ABILITY...
...AND THE CONDITIONS FOR ITS ACTIVATION.
BOOM

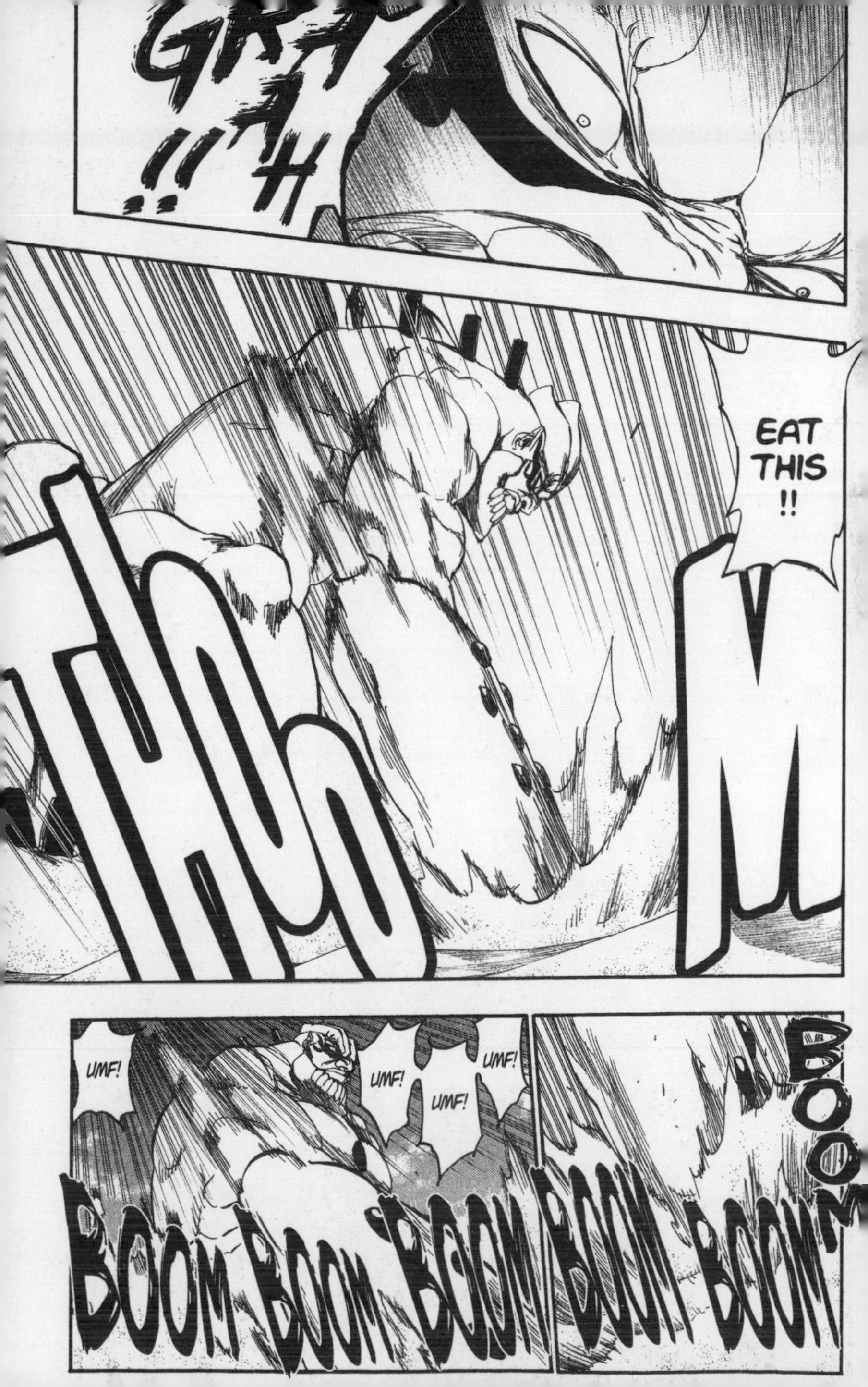
GRAAH!!
EAT THIS!!
HOOM
BOOOM
UMF!
UMF!
UMF!
UMF!
BOOM BOOM BOOM BOOM BOOM

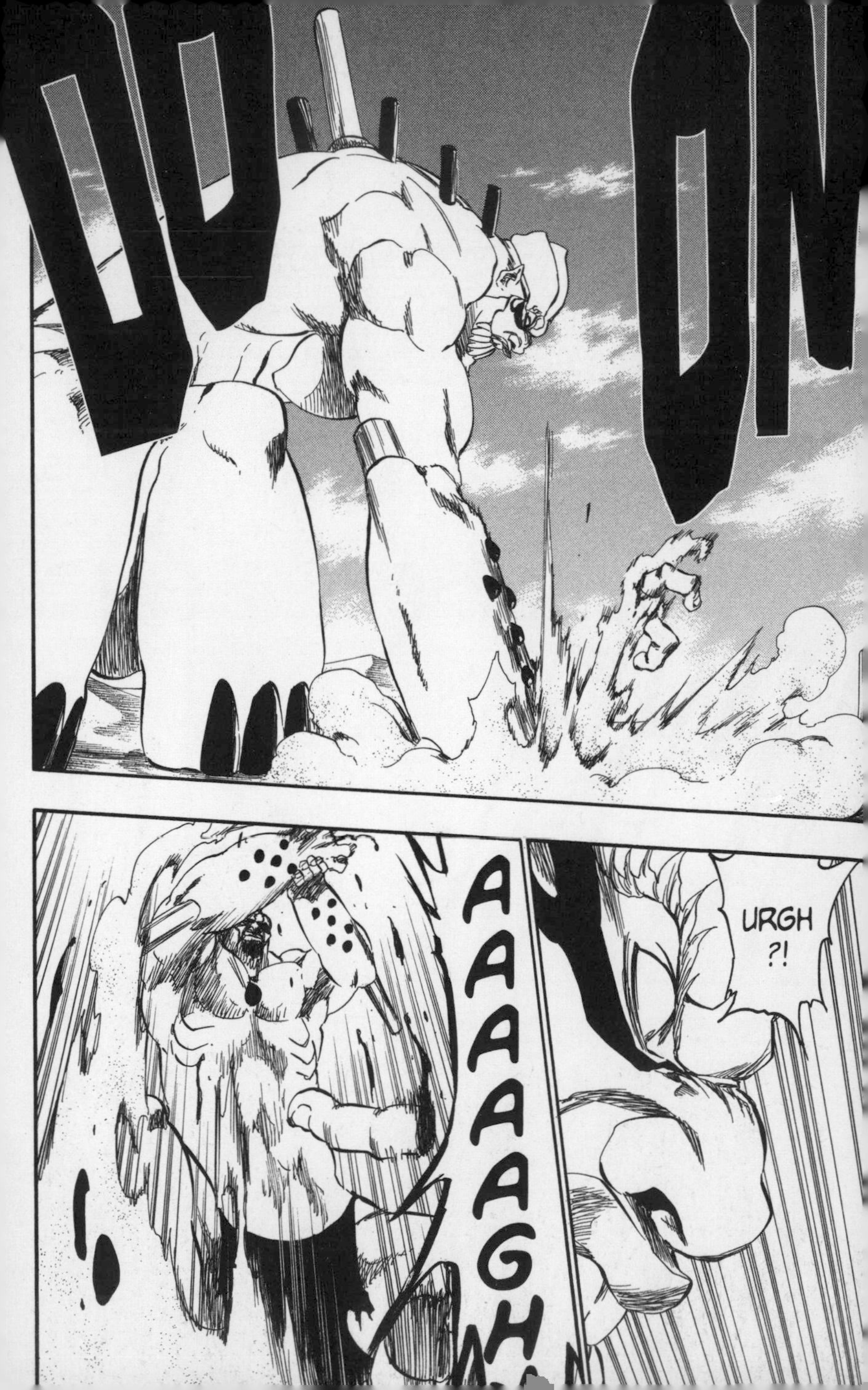
URGH ?!
AAAAAGH

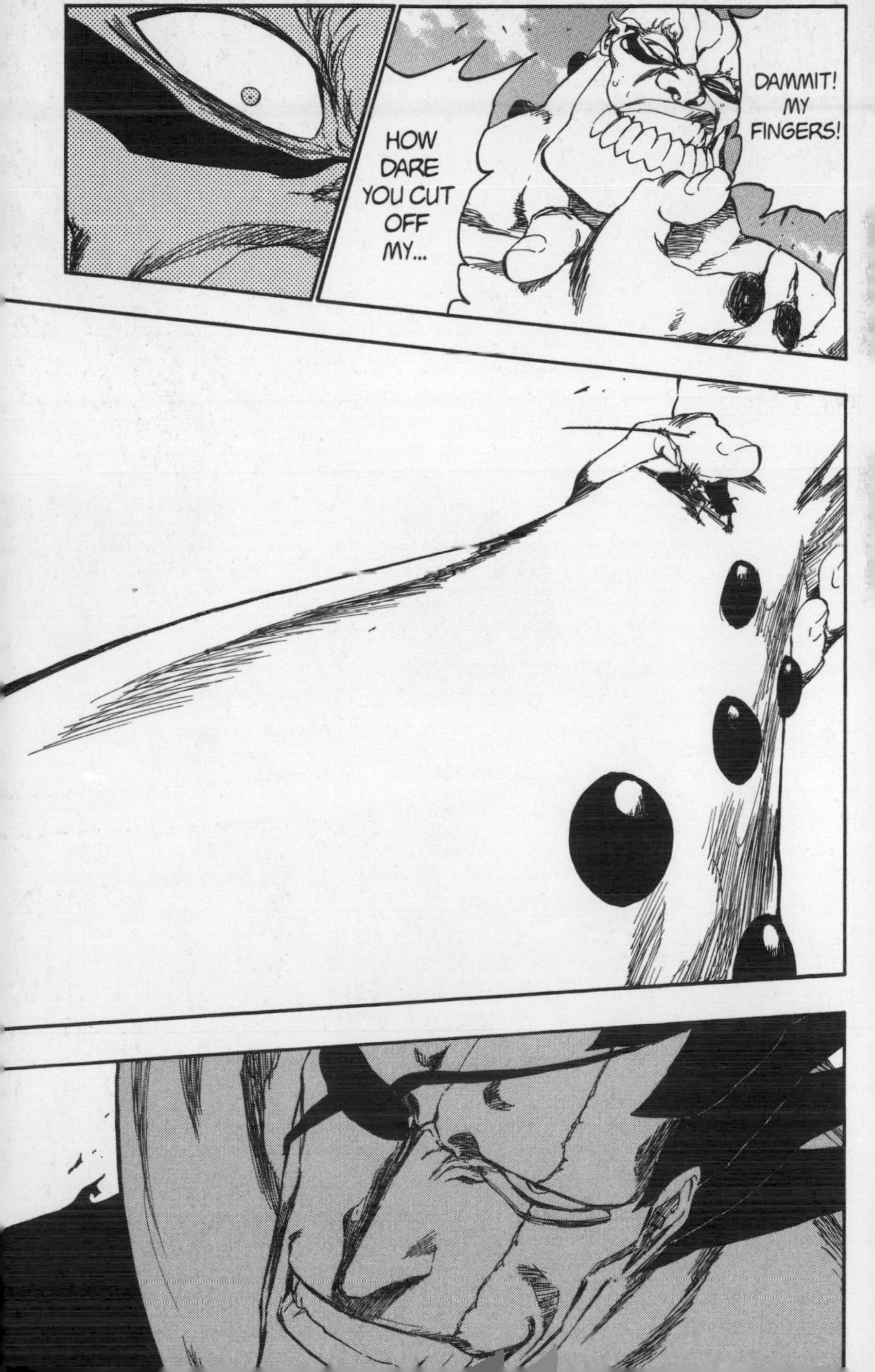
DAMMIT! MY FINGERS!
HOW DARE YOU CUT OFF MY...

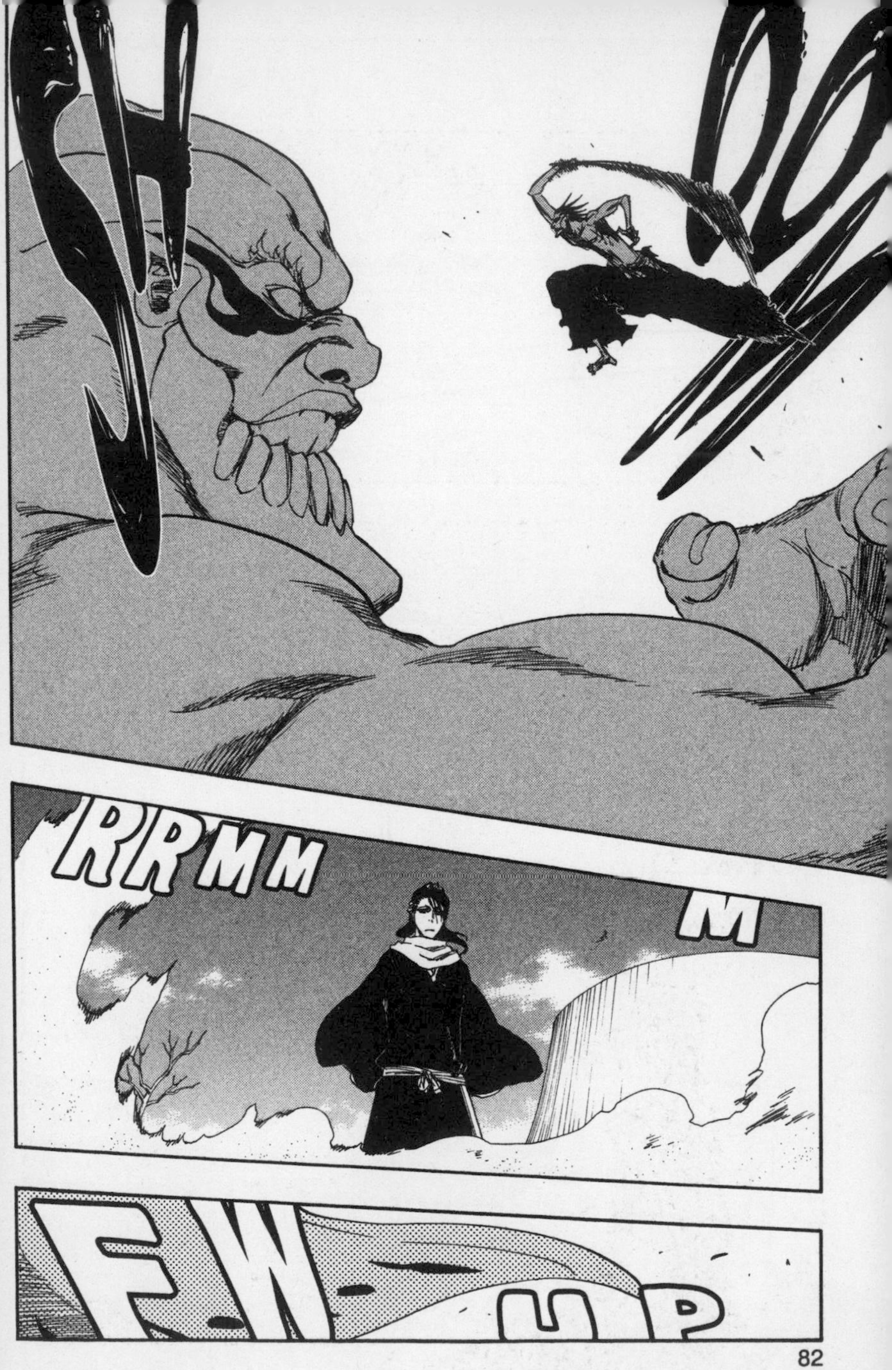
RRMMM

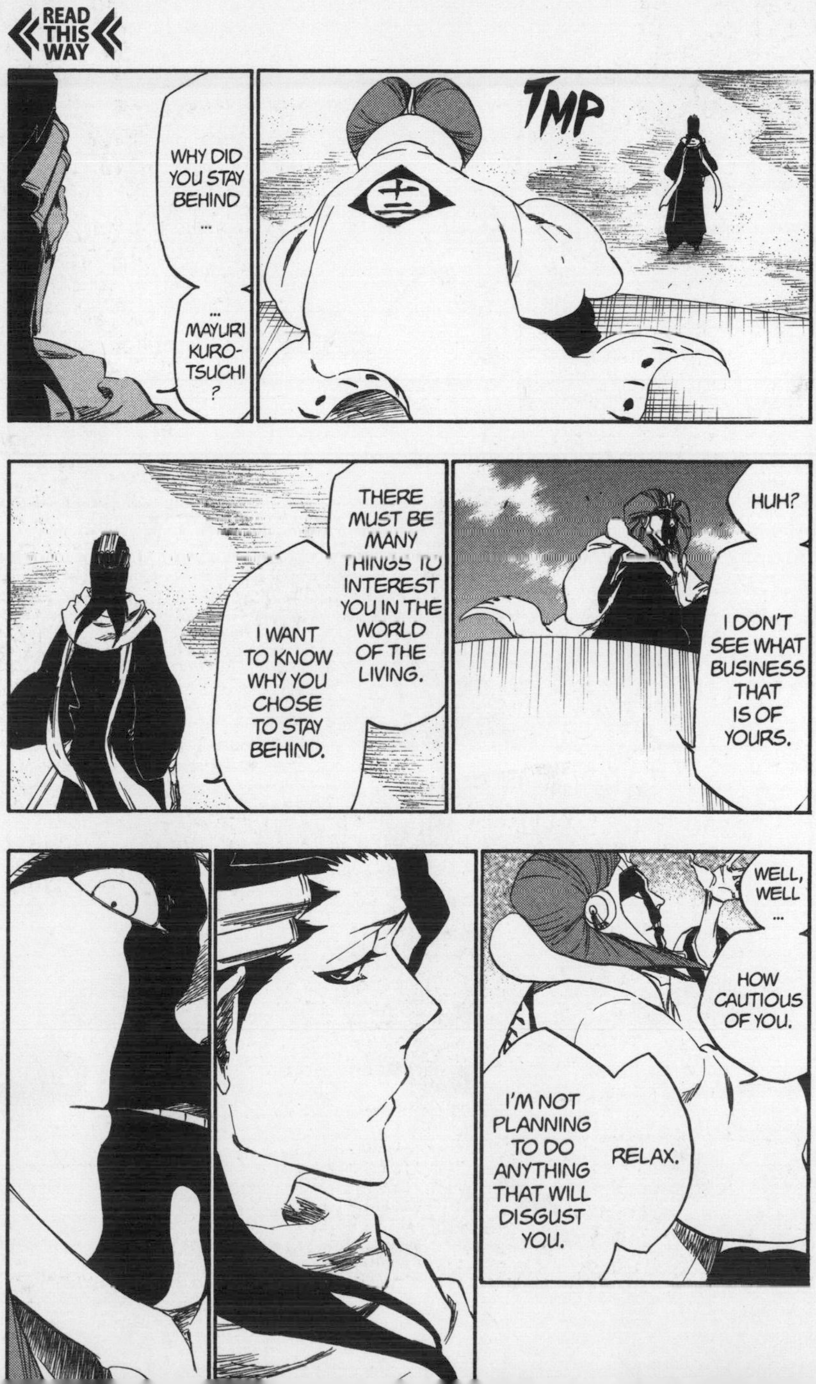
READ THIS WAY
TMP
WHY DID YOU STAY BEHIND ...
... MAYURI KURO-TSUCHI ?
HUH?
I DON'T SEE WHAT BUSINESS THAT IS OF YOURS.
THERE MUST BE MANY THINGS TO INTEREST YOU IN THE WORLD OF THE LIVING.
I WANT TO KNOW WHY YOU CHOSE TO STAY BEHIND.
WELL, WELL ...
HOW CAUTIOUS OF YOU.
RELAX.
I'M NOT PLANNING TO DO ANYTHING THAT WILL DISGUST YOU.

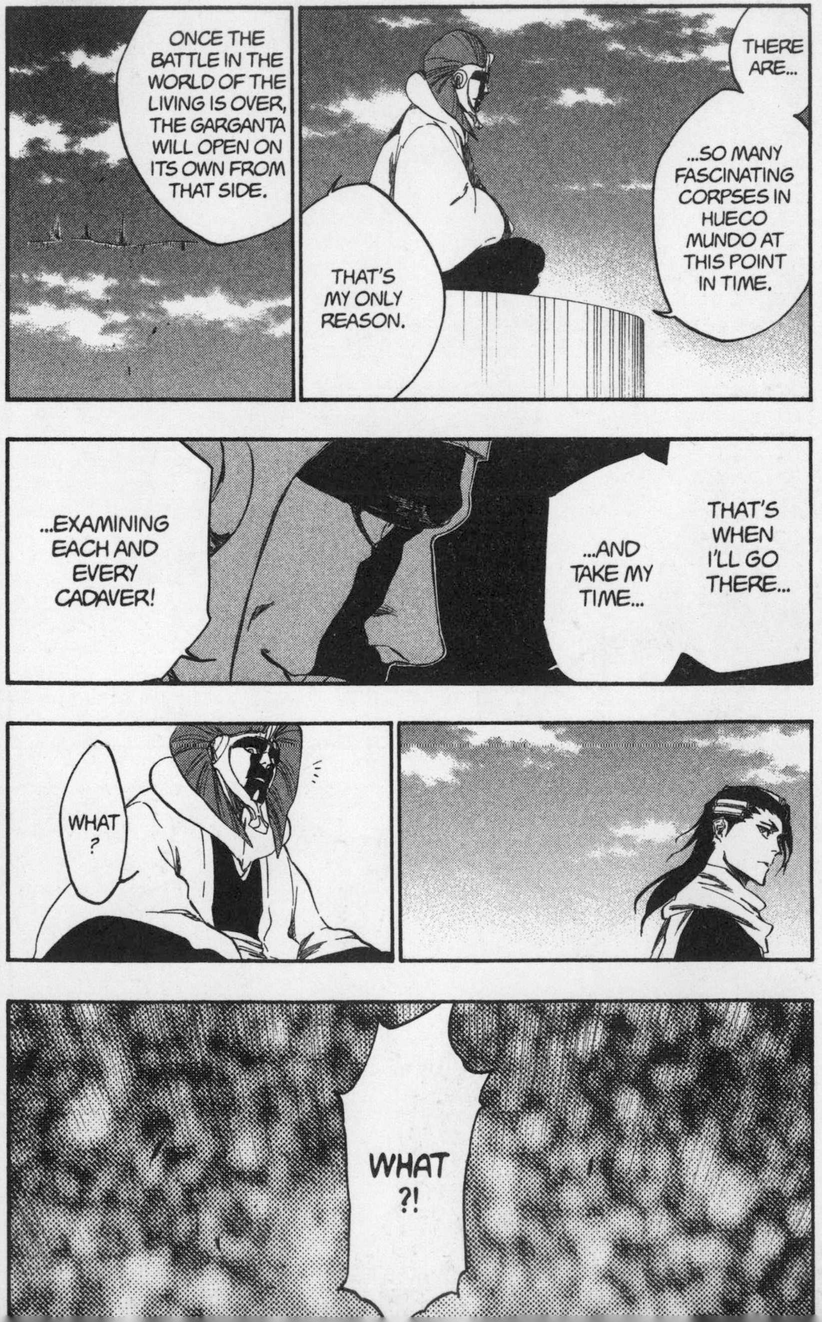
THERE ARE...
...SO MANY FASCINATING CORPSES IN HUECO MUNDO AT THIS POINT IN TIME.
THAT'S MY ONLY REASON.
ONCE THE BATTLE IN THE WORLD OF THE LIVING IS OVER, THE GARGANTA WILL OPEN ON ITS OWN FROM THAT SIDE.
THAT'S WHEN I'LL GO THERE...
...AND TAKE MY TIME...
...EXAMINING EACH AND EVERY CADAVER!
WHAT ?
WHAT ?!

READ THIS WAY

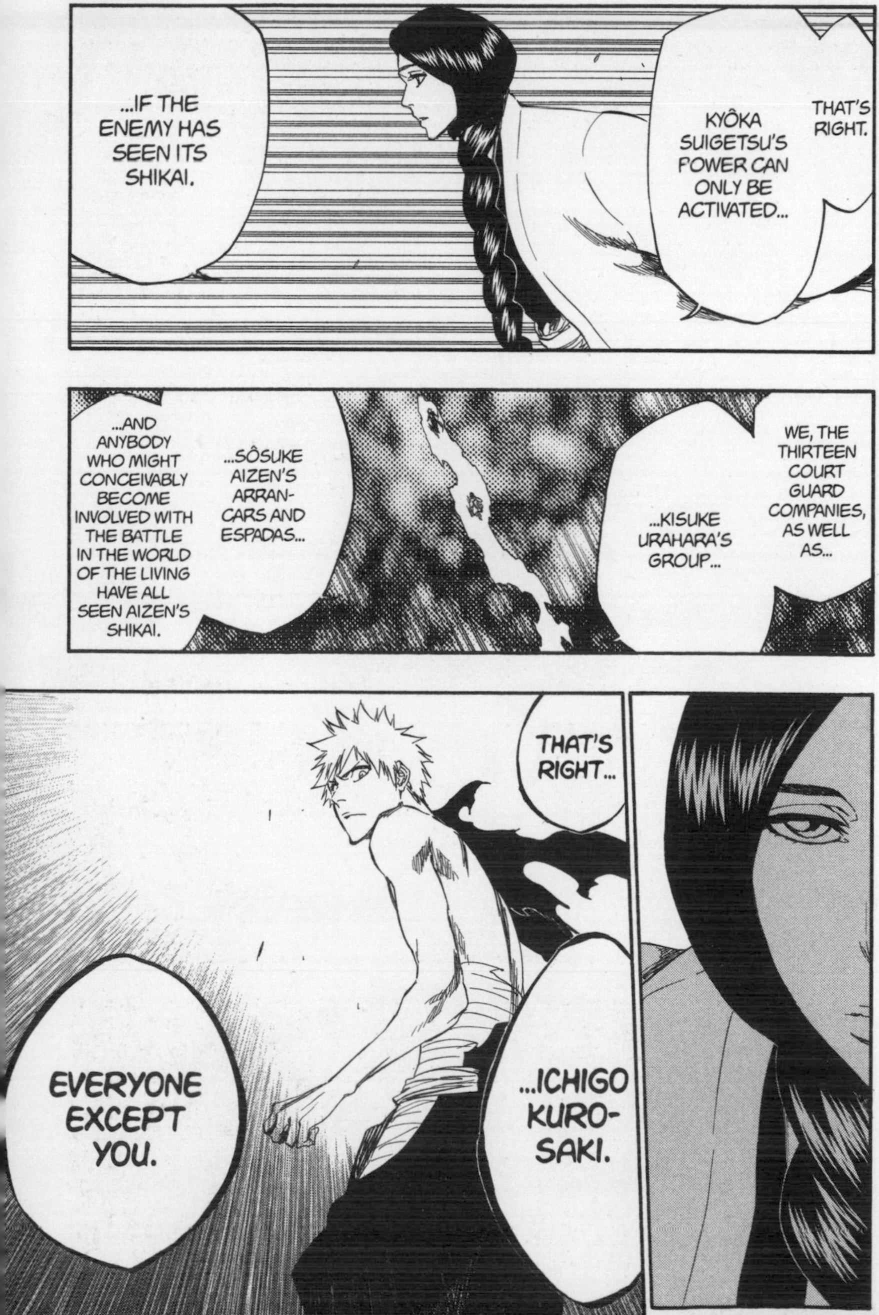
THAT'S RIGHT.
KYÔKA SUIGETSU'S POWER CAN ONLY BE ACTIVATED...
...IF THE ENEMY HAS SEEN ITS SHIKAI.
WE, THE THIRTEEN COURT GUARD COMPANIES, AS WELL AS...
...KISUKE URAHARA'S GROUP...
...SÔSUKE AIZEN'S ARRANCARS AND ESPADAS...
...AND ANYBODY WHO MIGHT CONCEIVABLY BECOME INVOLVED WITH THE BATTLE IN THE WORLD OF THE LIVING HAVE ALL SEEN AIZEN'S SHIKAI.
THAT'S RIGHT...
...ICHIGO KUROSAKI.
EVERYONE EXCEPT YOU.

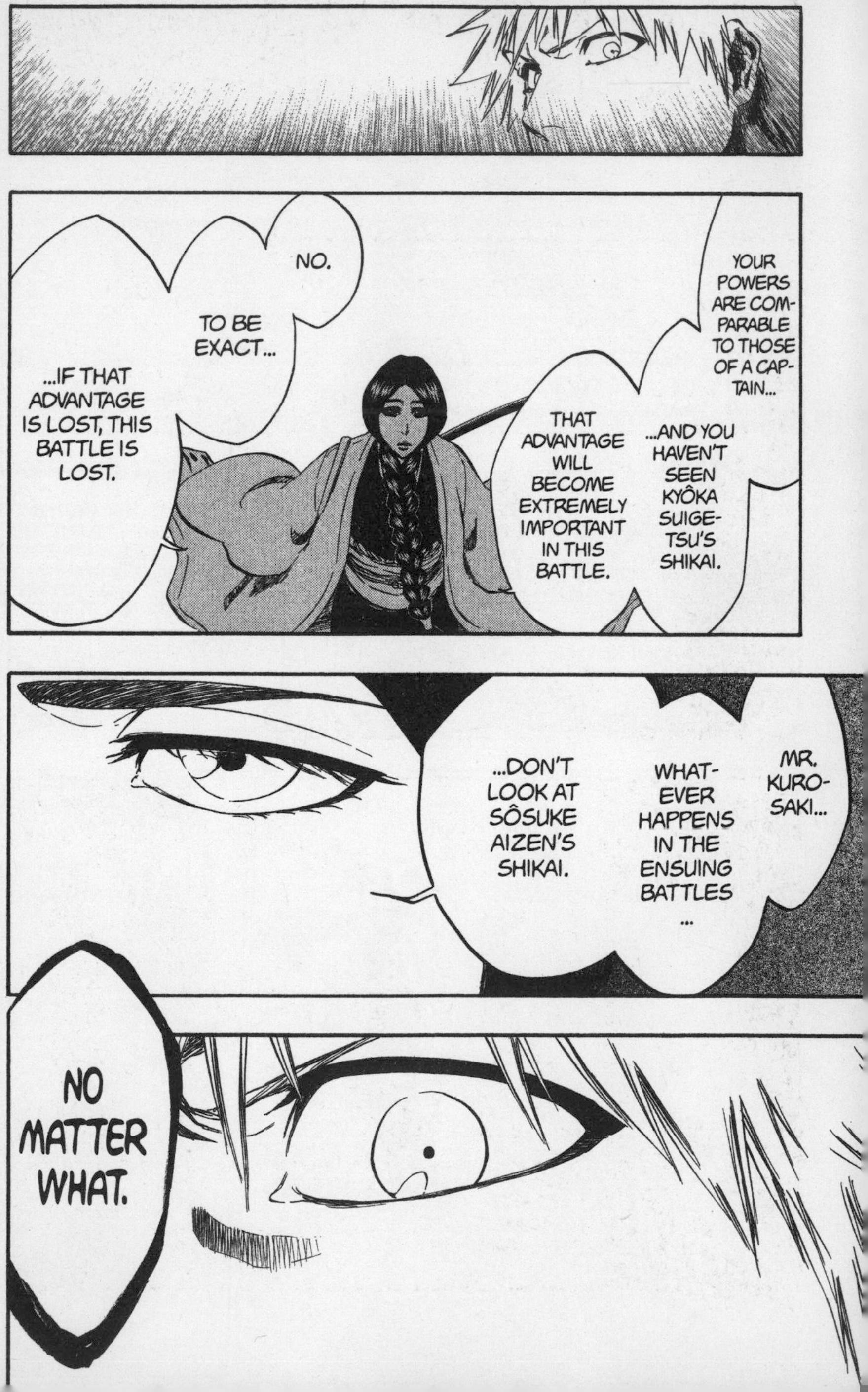
YOUR POWERS ARE COMPARABLE TO THOSE OF A CAPTAIN...
...AND YOU HAVEN'T SEEN KYÔKA SUIGETSU'S SHIKAI.
THAT ADVANTAGE WILL BECOME EXTREMELY IMPORTANT IN THIS BATTLE.
NO.
TO BE EXACT...
...IF THAT ADVANTAGE IS LOST, THIS BATTLE IS LOST.
MR. KUROSAKI...
WHATEVER HAPPENS IN THE ENSUING BATTLES...
...DON'T LOOK AT SÔSUKE AIZEN'S SHIKAI.
NO MATTER WHAT.

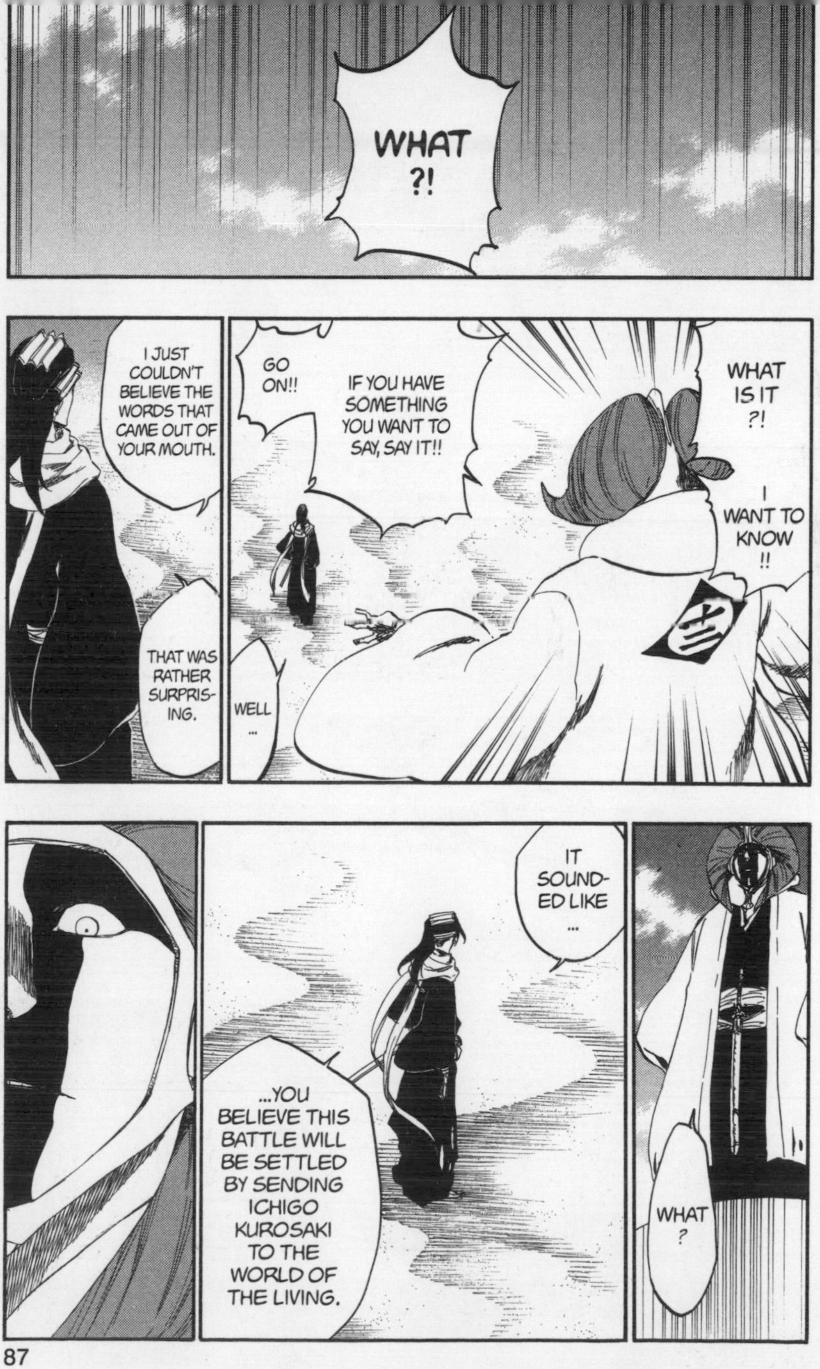
WHAT ?!
WHAT IS IT ?!
I WANT TO KNOW !!
IF YOU HAVE SOMETHING YOU WANT TO SAY, SAY IT!!
GO ON!!
WELL ...
I JUST COULDN'T BELIEVE THE WORDS THAT CAME OUT OF YOUR MOUTH.
THAT WAS RATHER SURPRIS-ING.
WHAT ?
IT SOUND-ED LIKE ...
...YOU BELIEVE THIS BATTLE WILL BE SETTLED BY SENDING ICHIGO KUROSAKI TO THE WORLD OF THE LIVING.

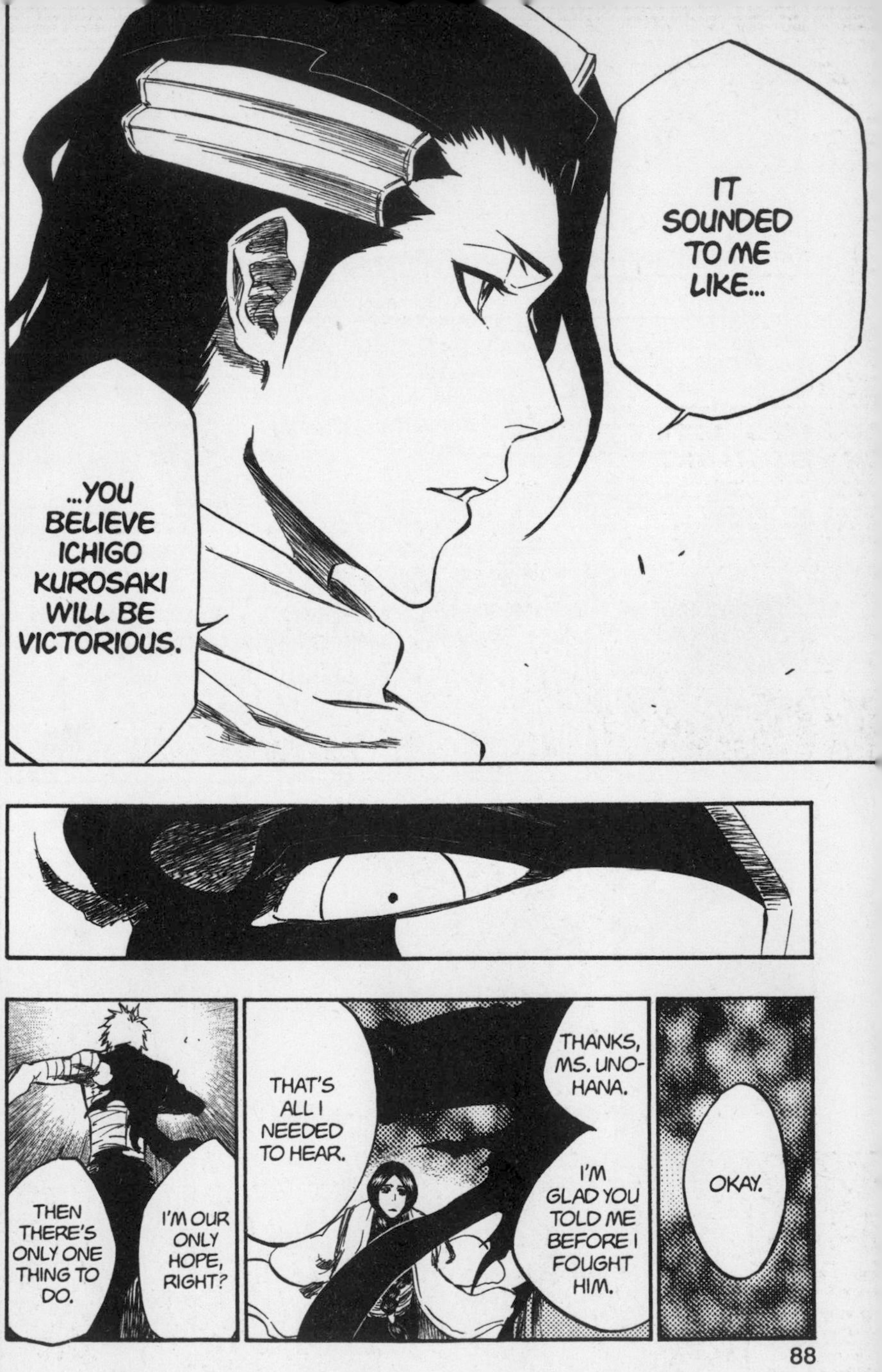
IT SOUNDED TO ME LIKE...
...YOU BELIEVE ICHIGO KUROSAKI WILL BE VICTORIOUS.
OKAY.
THANKS, MS. UNO-HANA.
I'M GLAD YOU TOLD ME BEFORE I FOUGHT HIM.
THAT'S ALL I NEEDED TO HEAR.
I'M OUR ONLY HOPE, RIGHT?
THEN THERE'S ONLY ONE THING TO DO.

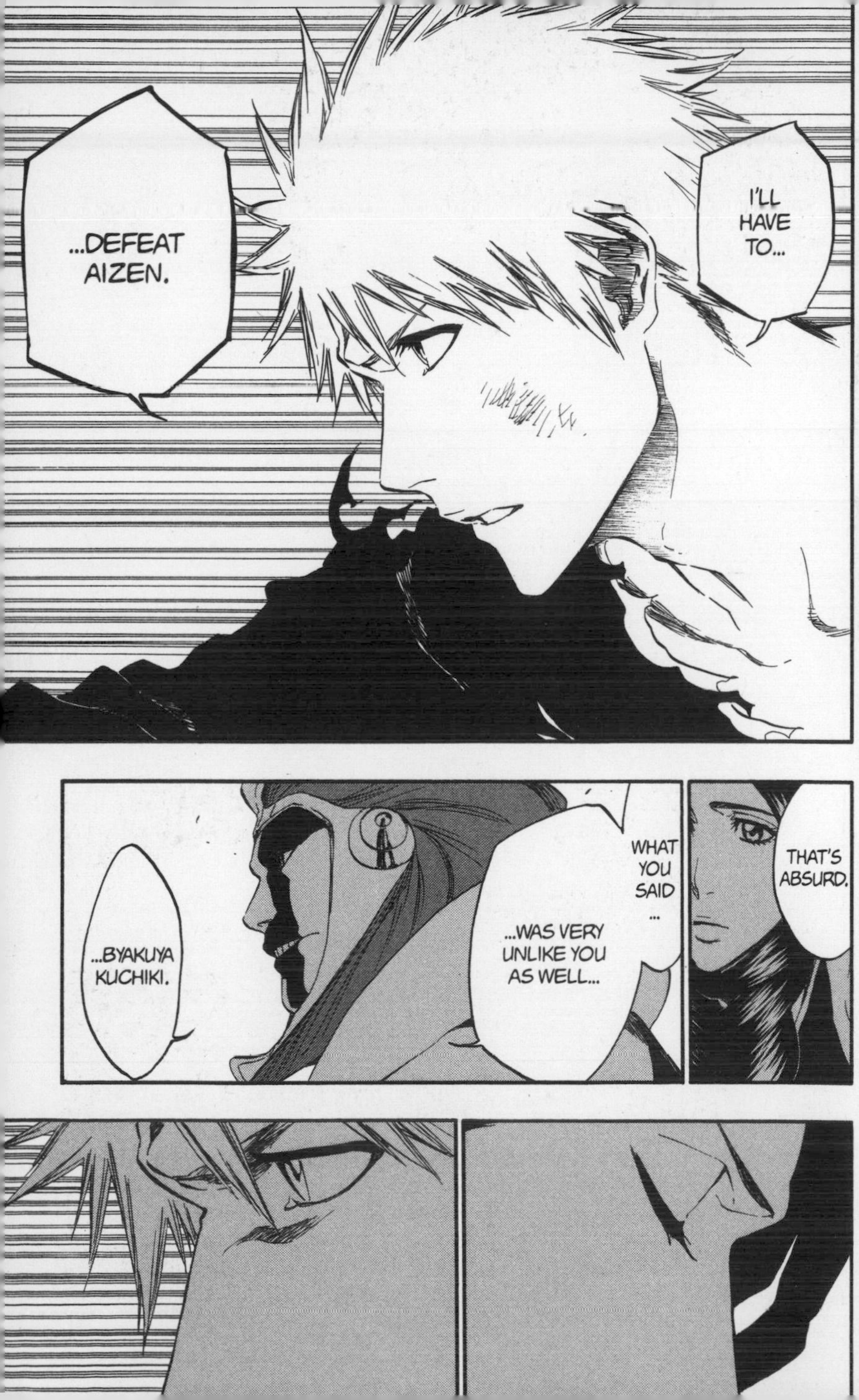
I'LL HAVE TO...
...DEFEAT AIZEN.
THAT'S ABSURD.
WHAT YOU SAID ...
...WAS VERY UNLIKE YOU AS WELL...
...BYAKUYA KUCHIKI.

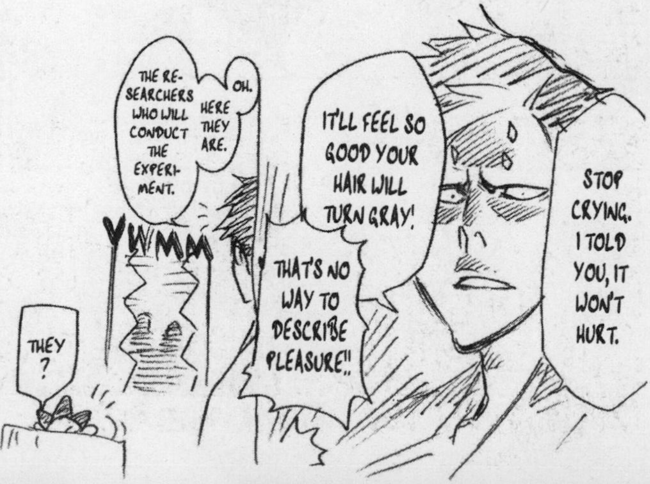
STOP CRYING. I TOLD YOU, IT WON'T HURT.
IT'LL FEEL SO GOOD YOUR HAIR WILL TURN GRAY!
THAT'S NO WAY TO DESCRIBE PLEASURE!!
OH. HERE THEY ARE.
THE RESEARCHERS WHO WILL CONDUCT THE EXPERIMENT.
VWMM
THEY ?

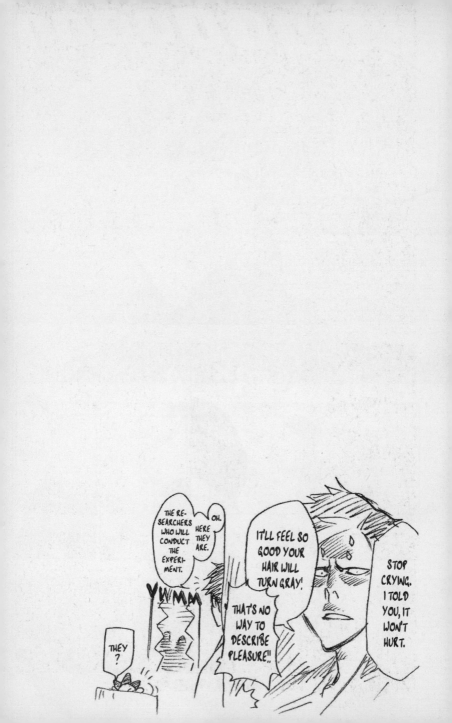

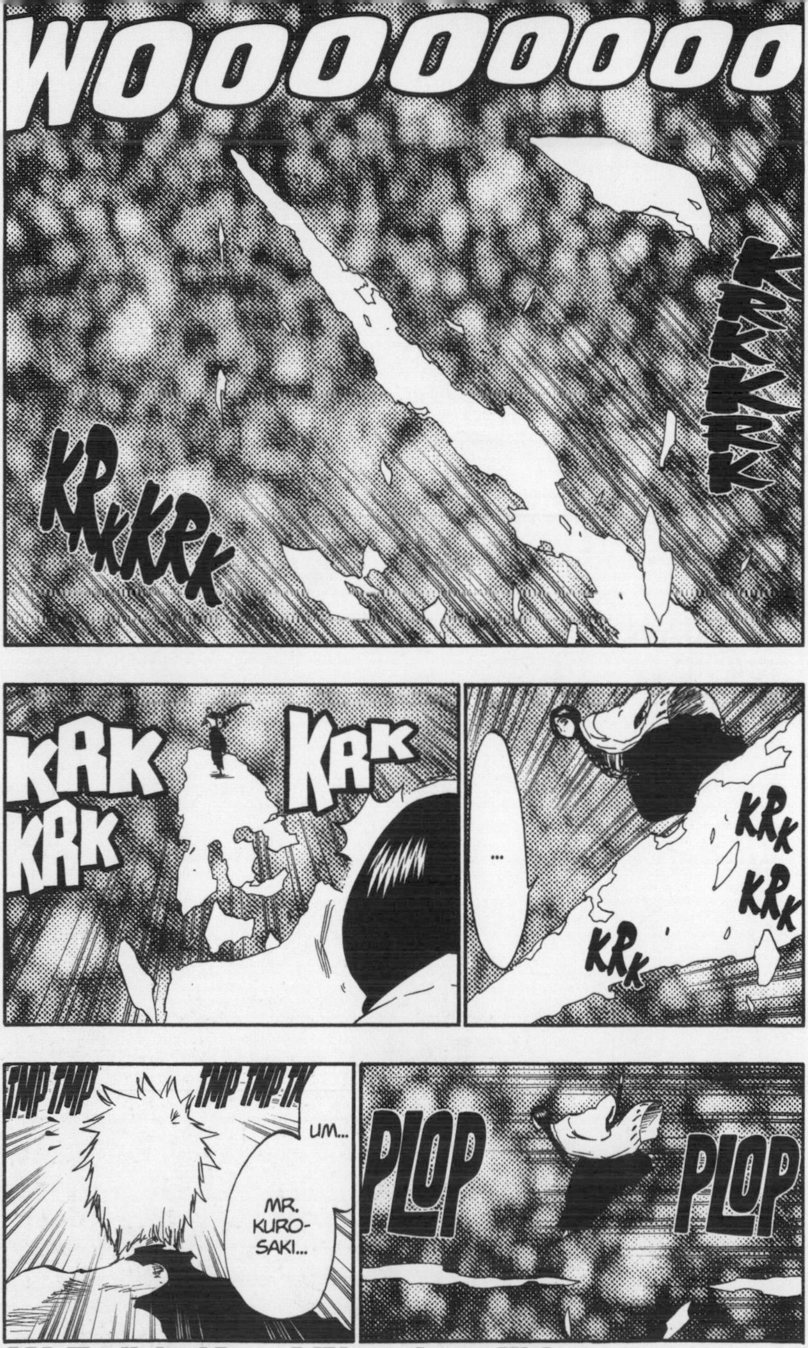
WOOOOOOOOO
KRKKRKRK
KRKKRKRK
...
KRK
KRK
KRK
KRK
KRK KRK
TMP TMP TK
UM...
MR. KURO-SAKI...
TMP TMP
PLOP
PLOP

382. The United Front 2 (Discordeque Mix)

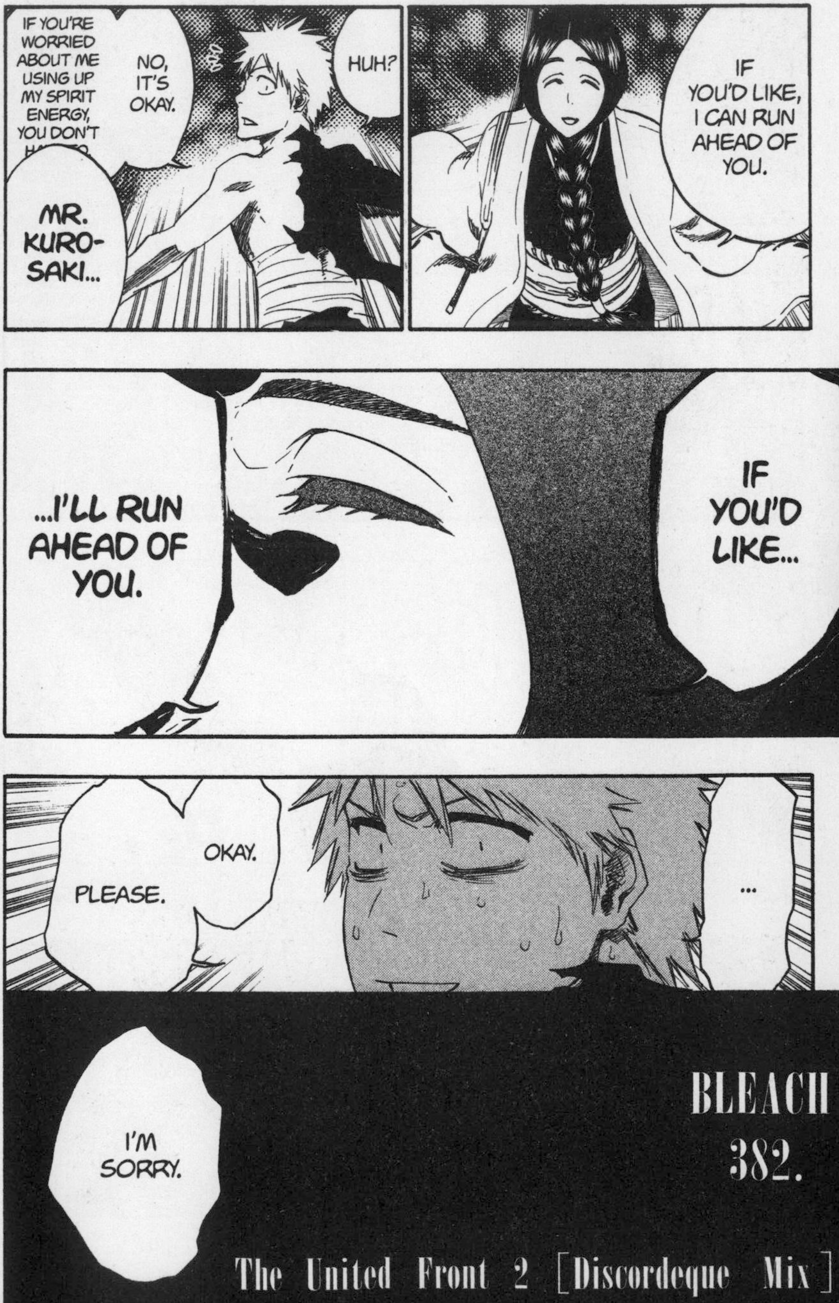
IF YOU'D LIKE, I CAN RUN AHEAD OF YOU.
HUH?
NO, IT'S OKAY.
IF YOU'RE WORRIED ABOUT ME USING UP MY SPIRIT ENERGY, YOU DON'T
MR. KURO-SAKI...
IF YOU'D LIKE...
...I'LL RUN AHEAD OF YOU.
...
OKAY.
PLEASE.
I'M SORRY.
BLEACH 382.
The United Front 2 [Discordeque Mix]

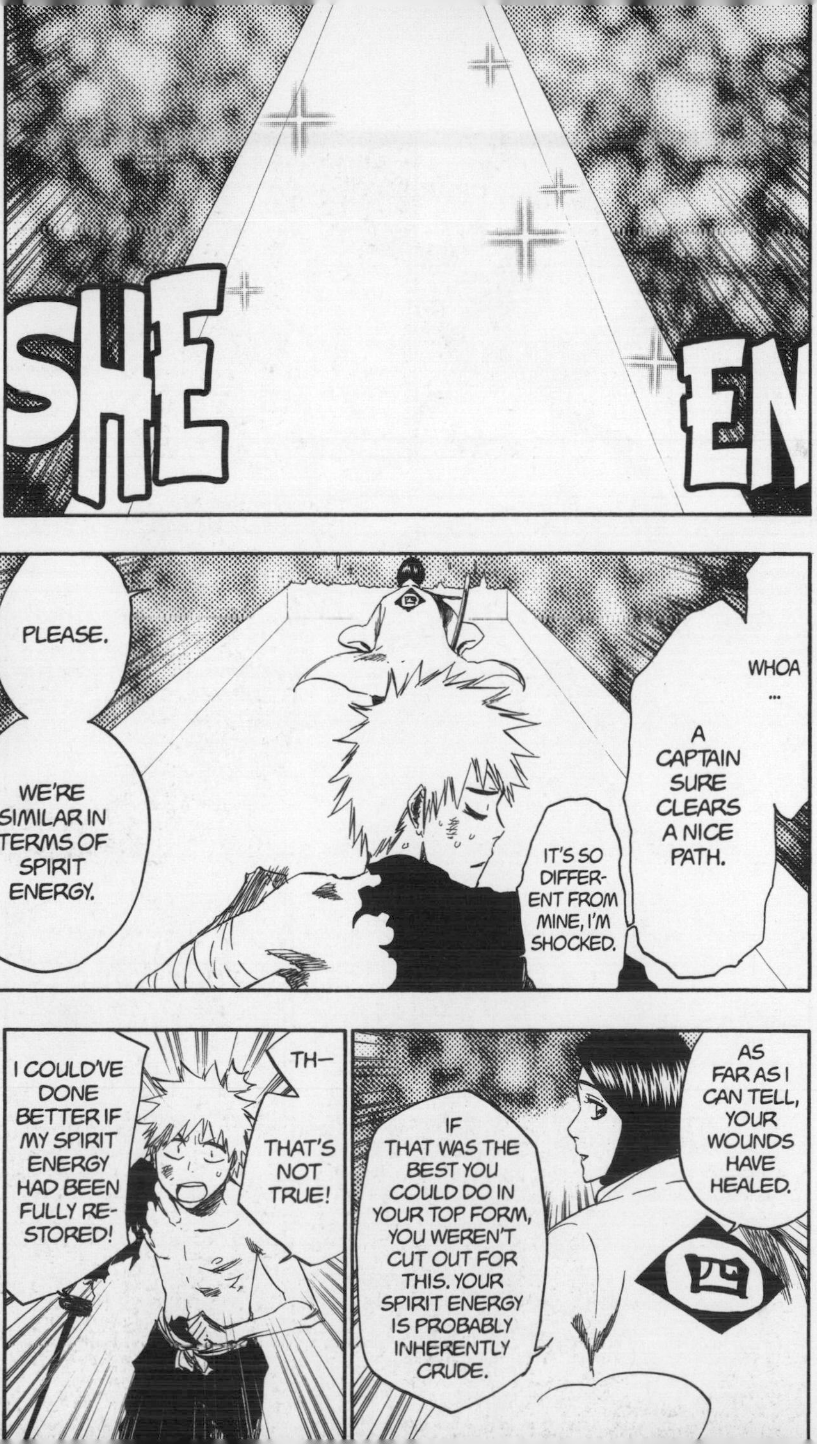

SHE
EN
WHOA...
A CAPTAIN SURE CLEARS A NICE PATH.
IT'S SO DIFFER-ENT FROM MINE, I'M SHOCKED.
PLEASE.
WE'RE SIMILAR IN TERMS OF SPIRIT ENERGY.
AS FAR AS I CAN TELL, YOUR WOUNDS HAVE HEALED.
IF THAT WAS THE BEST YOU COULD DO IN YOUR TOP FORM, YOU WEREN'T CUT OUT FOR THIS. YOUR SPIRIT ENERGY IS PROBABLY INHERENTLY CRUDE.
TH—
THAT'S NOT TRUE!
I COULD'VE DONE BETTER IF MY SPIRIT ENERGY HAD BEEN FULLY RE-STORED!

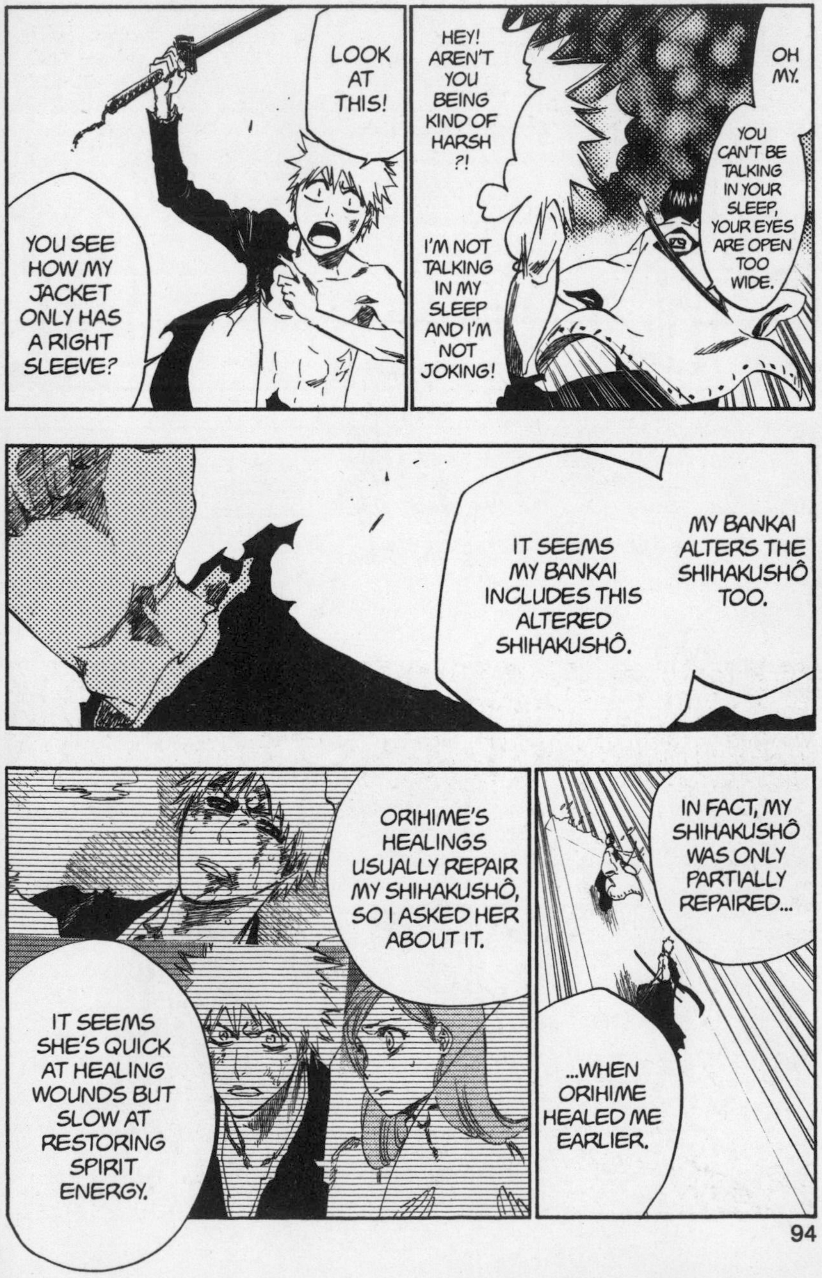
OH MY.
YOU CAN'T BE TALKING IN YOUR SLEEP, YOUR EYES ARE OPEN TOO WIDE.
HEY! AREN'T YOU BEING KIND OF HARSH ?!
I'M NOT TALKING IN MY SLEEP AND I'M NOT JOKING!
LOOK AT THIS!
YOU SEE HOW MY JACKET ONLY HAS A RIGHT SLEEVE?
MY BANKAI ALTERS THE SHIHAKUSHÔ TOO.
IT SEEMS MY BANKAI INCLUDES THIS ALTERED SHIHAKUSHÔ.
IN FACT, MY SHIHAKUSHÔ WAS ONLY PARTIALLY REPAIRED...
...WHEN ORIHIME HEALED ME EARLIER.
ORIHIME'S HEALINGS USUALLY REPAIR MY SHIHAKUSHÔ, SO I ASKED HER ABOUT IT.
IT SEEMS SHE'S QUICK AT HEALING WOUNDS BUT SLOW AT RESTORING SPIRIT ENERGY.

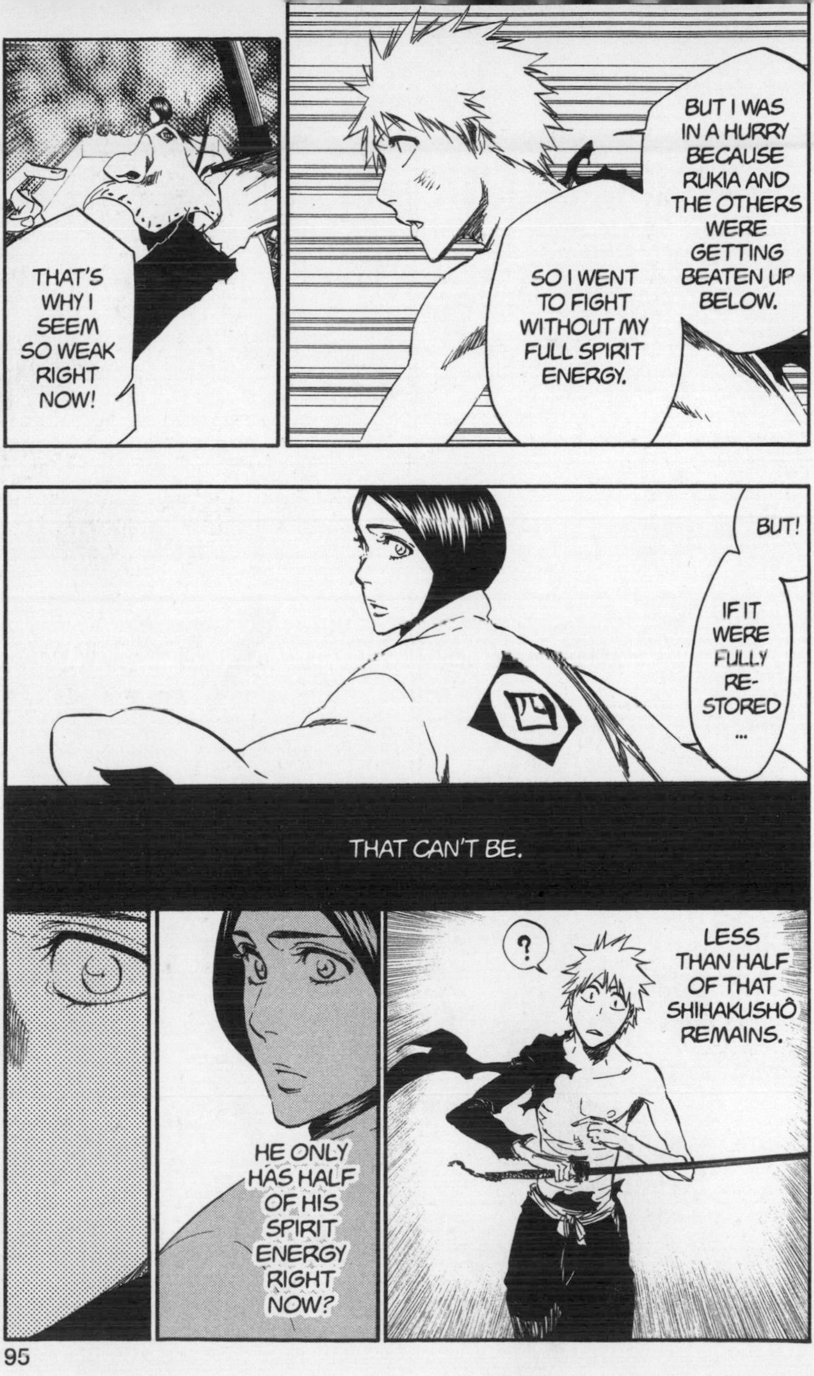
BUT I WAS IN A HURRY BECAUSE RUKIA AND THE OTHERS WERE GETTING BEATEN UP BELOW.
SO I WENT TO FIGHT WITHOUT MY FULL SPIRIT ENERGY.
THAT'S WHY I SEEM SO WEAK RIGHT NOW!
BUT!
IF IT WERE FULLY RE-STORED...
THAT CAN'T BE.
?
LESS THAN HALF OF THAT SHIHAKUSHÔ REMAINS.
HE ONLY HAS HALF OF HIS SPIRIT ENERGY RIGHT NOW?

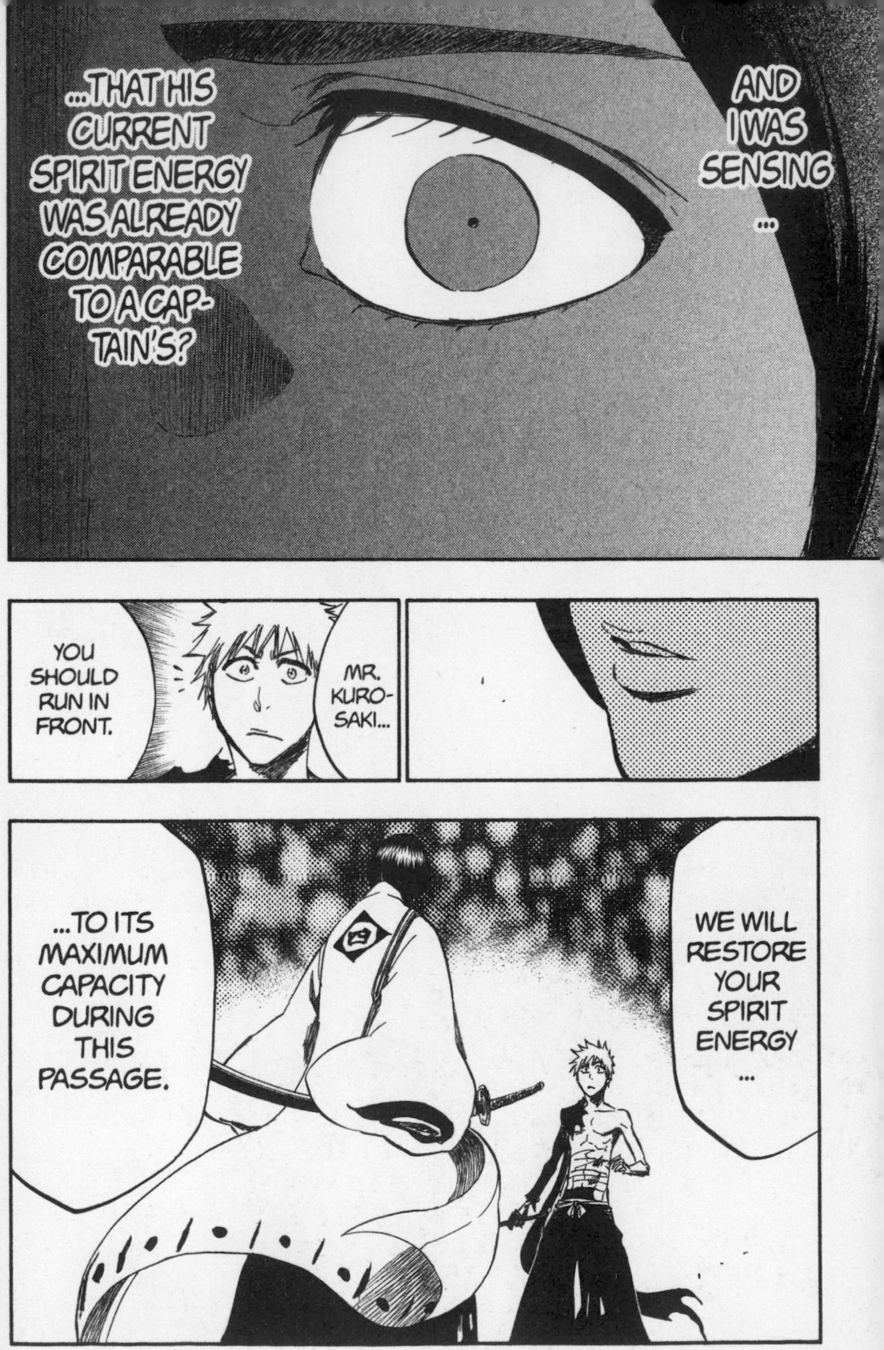
AND I WAS SENSING...
...THAT HIS CURRENT SPIRIT ENERGY WAS ALREADY COMPARABLE TO A CAPTAIN'S?
MR. KURO-SAKI...
YOU SHOULD RUN IN FRONT.
WE WILL RESTORE YOUR SPIRIT ENERGY...
...TO ITS MAXIMUM CAPACITY DURING THIS PASSAGE.

READ THIS WAY

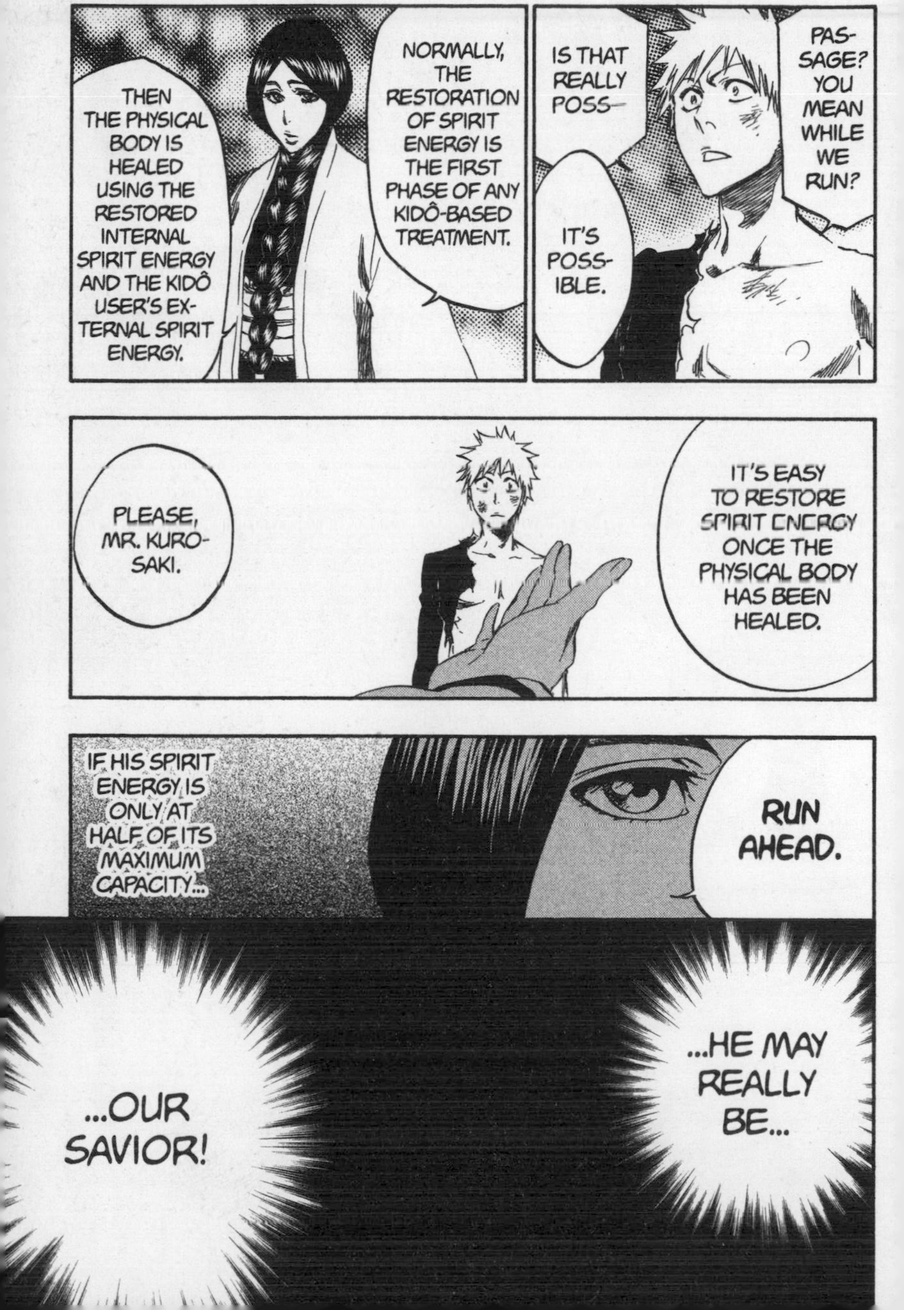
PAS-SAGE? YOU MEAN WHILE WE RUN?
IS THAT REALLY POSS—
IT'S POSS-IBLE.
NORMALLY, THE RESTORATION OF SPIRIT ENERGY IS THE FIRST PHASE OF ANY KIDÔ-BASED TREATMENT.
THEN THE PHYSICAL BODY IS HEALED USING THE RESTORED INTERNAL SPIRIT ENERGY AND THE KIDÔ USER'S EX-TERNAL SPIRIT ENERGY.
IT'S EASY TO RESTORE SPIRIT ENERGY ONCE THE PHYSICAL BODY HAS BEEN HEALED.
PLEASE, MR. KURO-SAKI.
RUN AHEAD.
IF HIS SPIRIT ENERGY IS ONLY AT HALF OF ITS MAXIMUM CAPACITY...
...HE MAY REALLY BE...
...OUR SAVIOR!

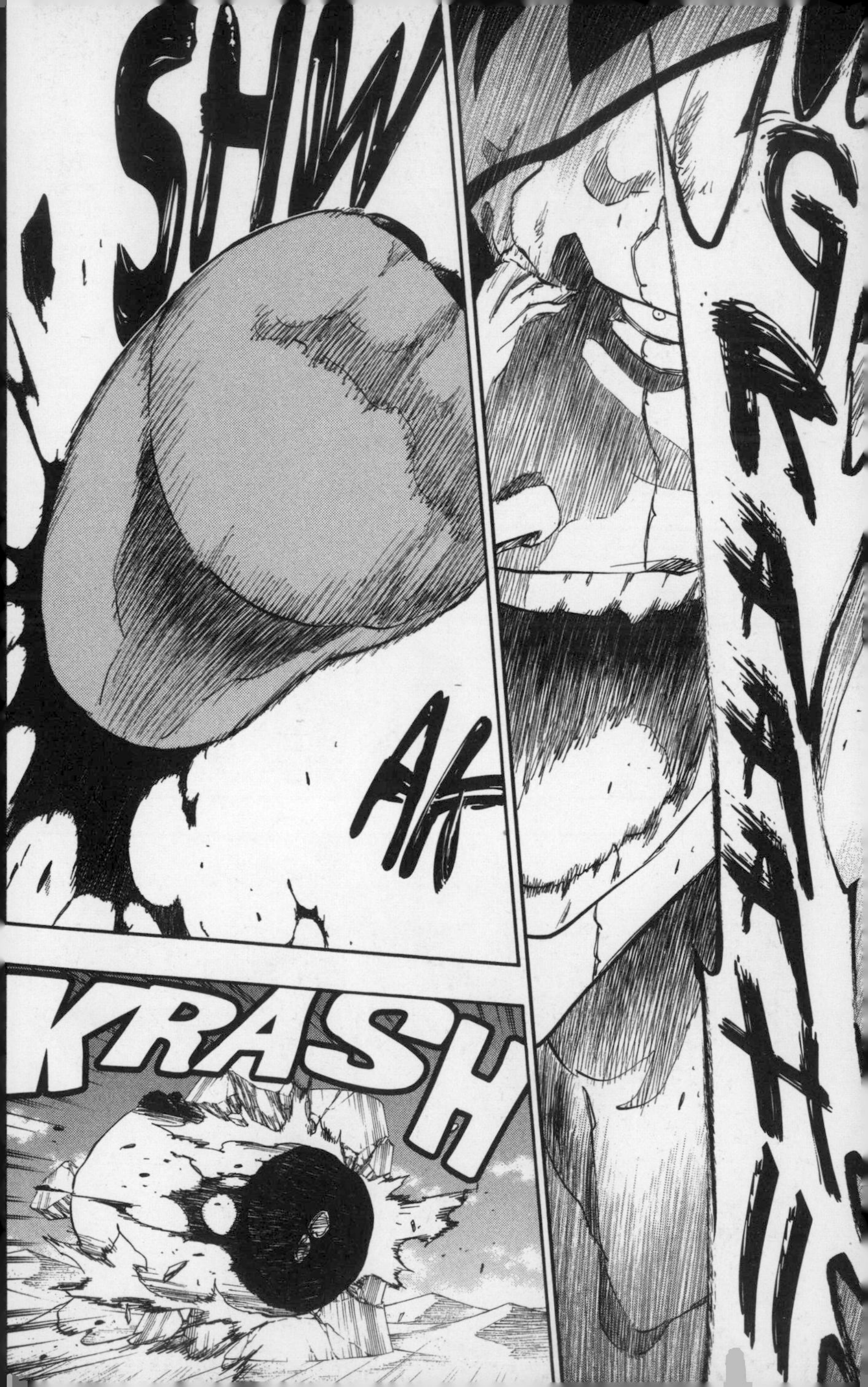
SHW
AH
KRASH

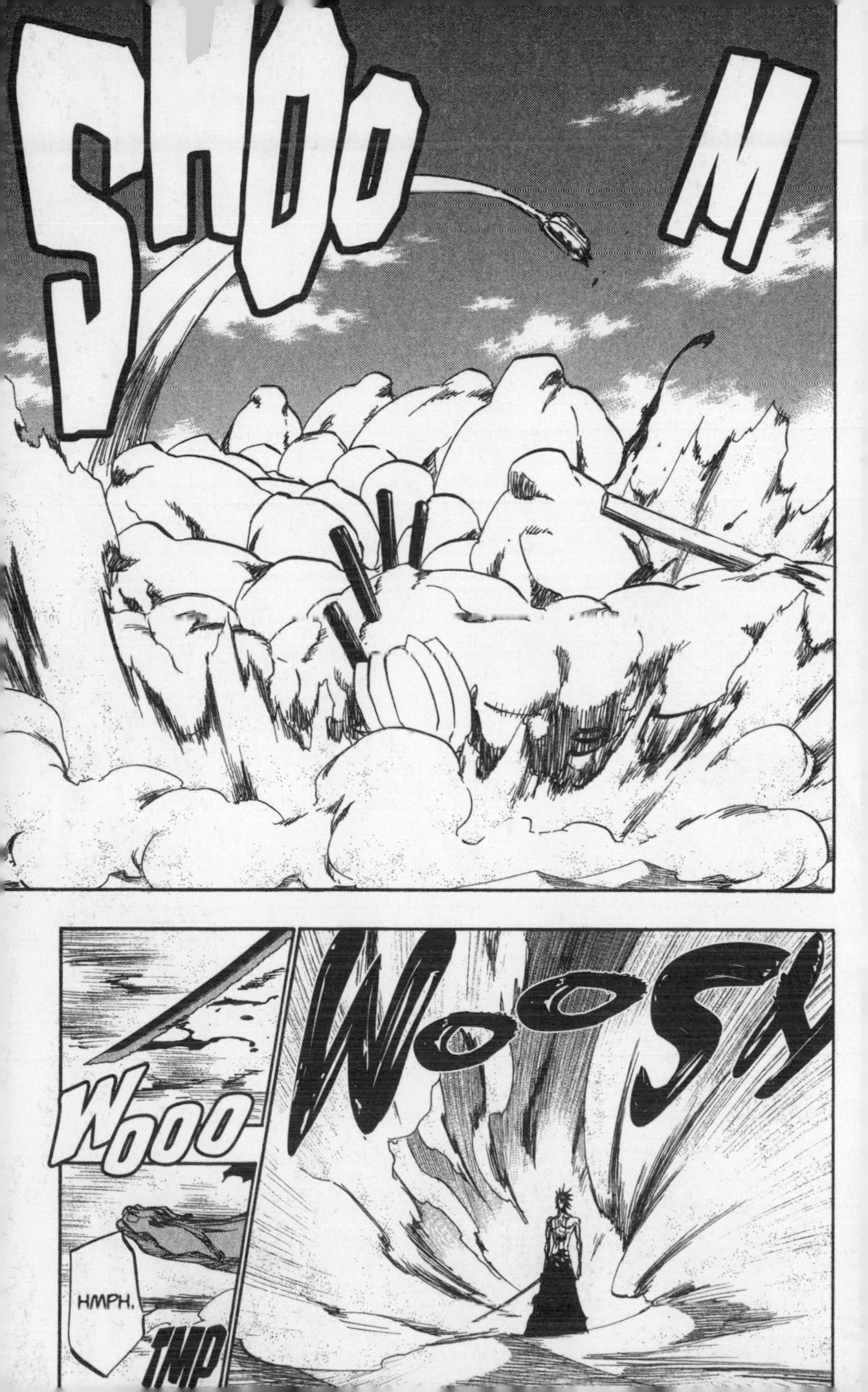
SHOOM
WOOSH
WOOO
HMPH.
TMP

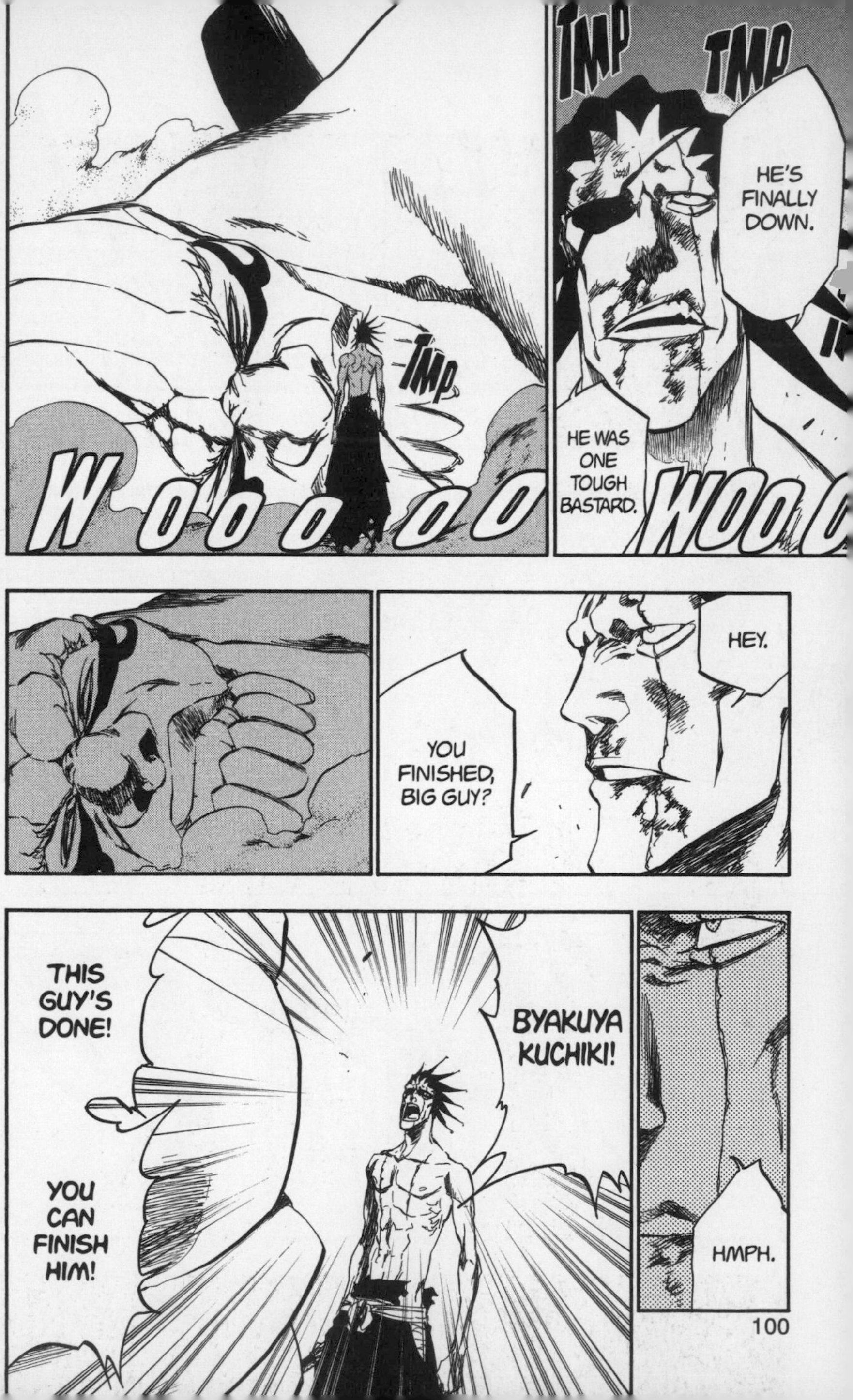
TMP
TMP
HE'S FINALLY DOWN.
HE WAS ONE TOUGH BASTARD.
WOOO
TMP
WOOOOOO
HEY.
YOU FINISHED, BIG GUY?
HMPH.
BYAKUYA KUCHIKI!
THIS GUY'S DONE!
YOU CAN FINISH HIM!

READ THIS WAY

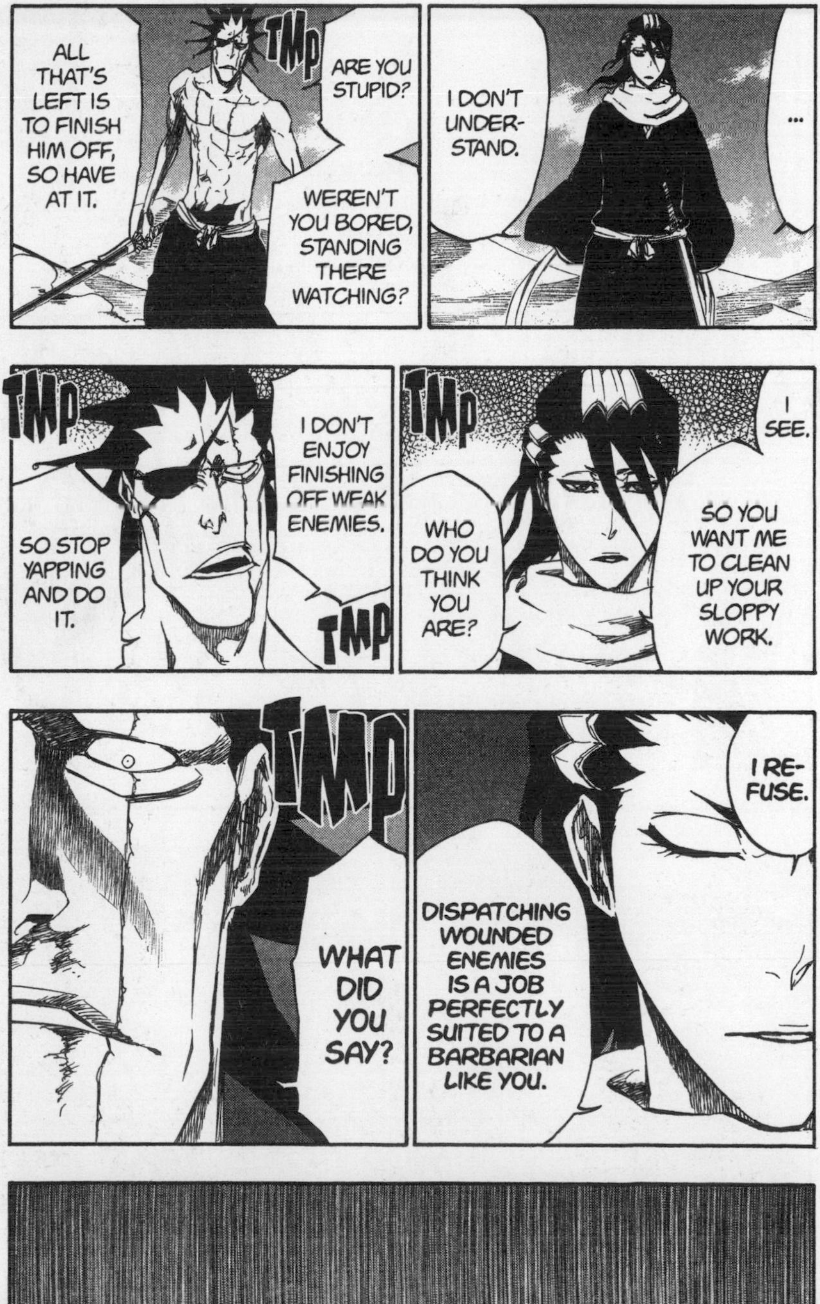
...
I DON'T UNDERSTAND.
ARE YOU STUPID?
WEREN'T YOU BORED, STANDING THERE WATCHING?
TMP
ALL THAT'S LEFT IS TO FINISH HIM OFF, SO HAVE AT IT.
I SEE.
SO YOU WANT ME TO CLEAN UP YOUR SLOPPY WORK.
TMP
WHO DO YOU THINK YOU ARE?
I DON'T ENJOY FINISHING OFF WEAK ENEMIES.
TMP
TMP
SO STOP YAPPING AND DO IT.
I REFUSE.
DISPATCHING WOUNDED ENEMIES IS A JOB PERFECTLY SUITED TO A BARBARIAN LIKE YOU.
TMP
WHAT DID YOU SAY?

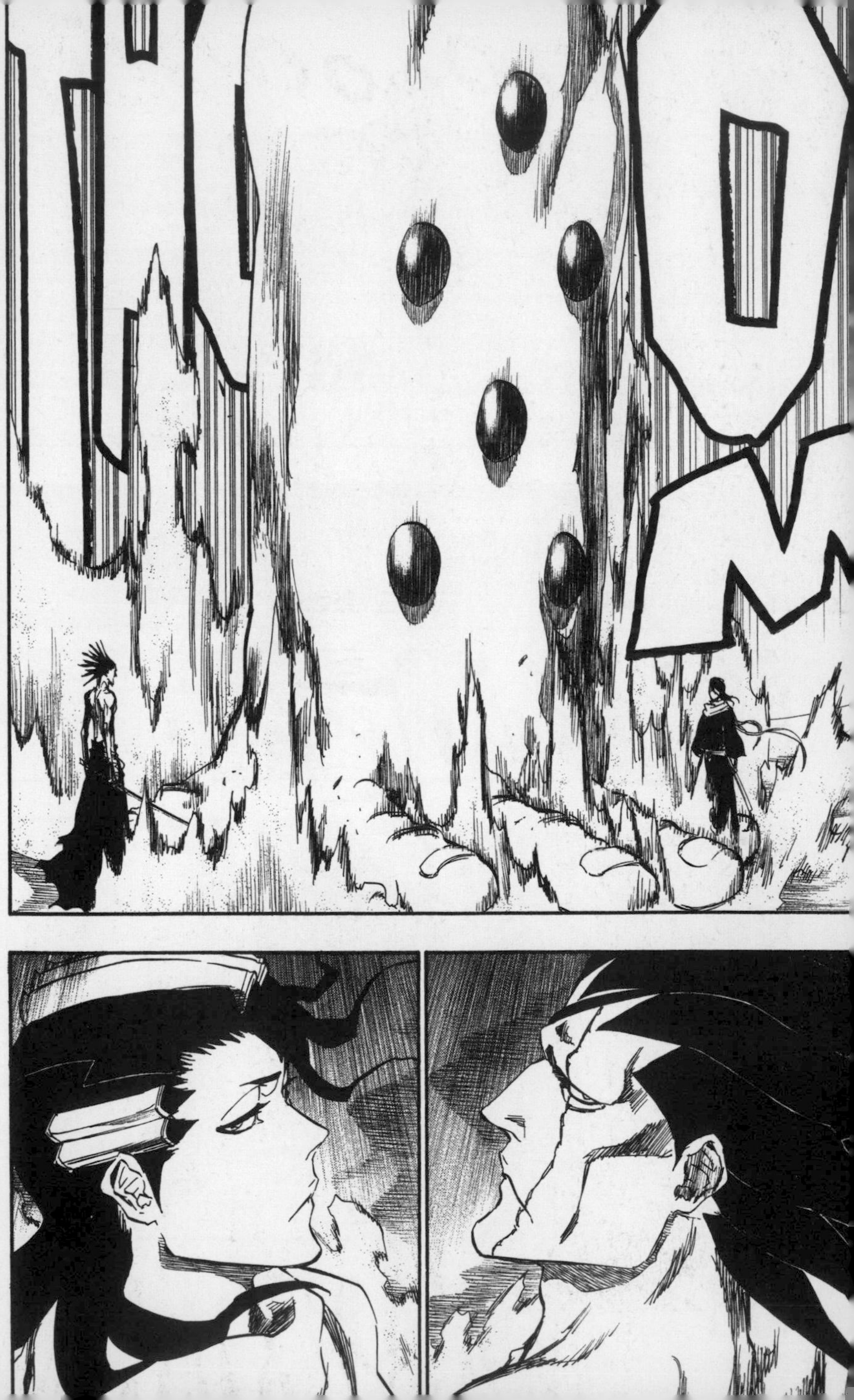

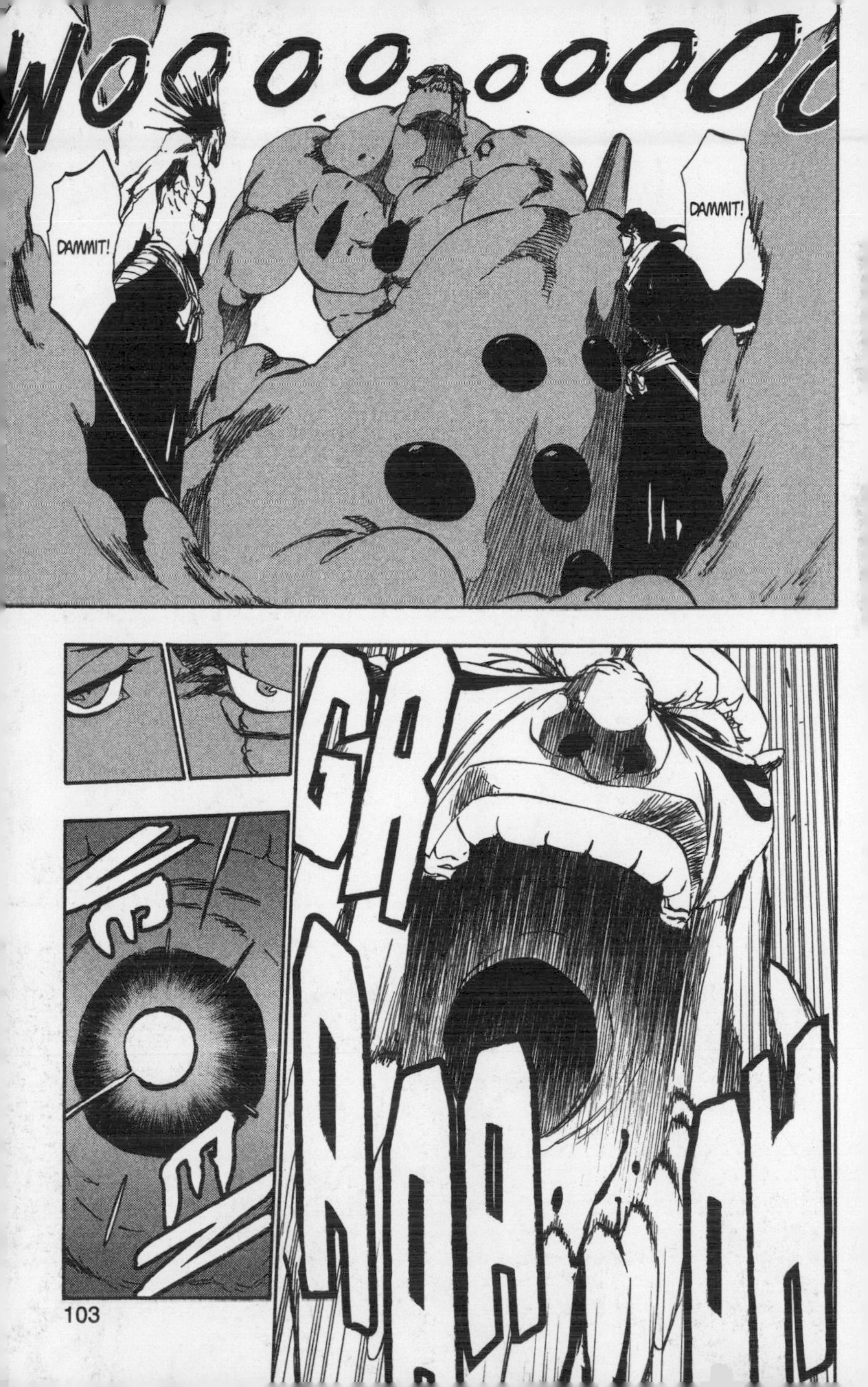
DAMMIT!
DAMMIT!

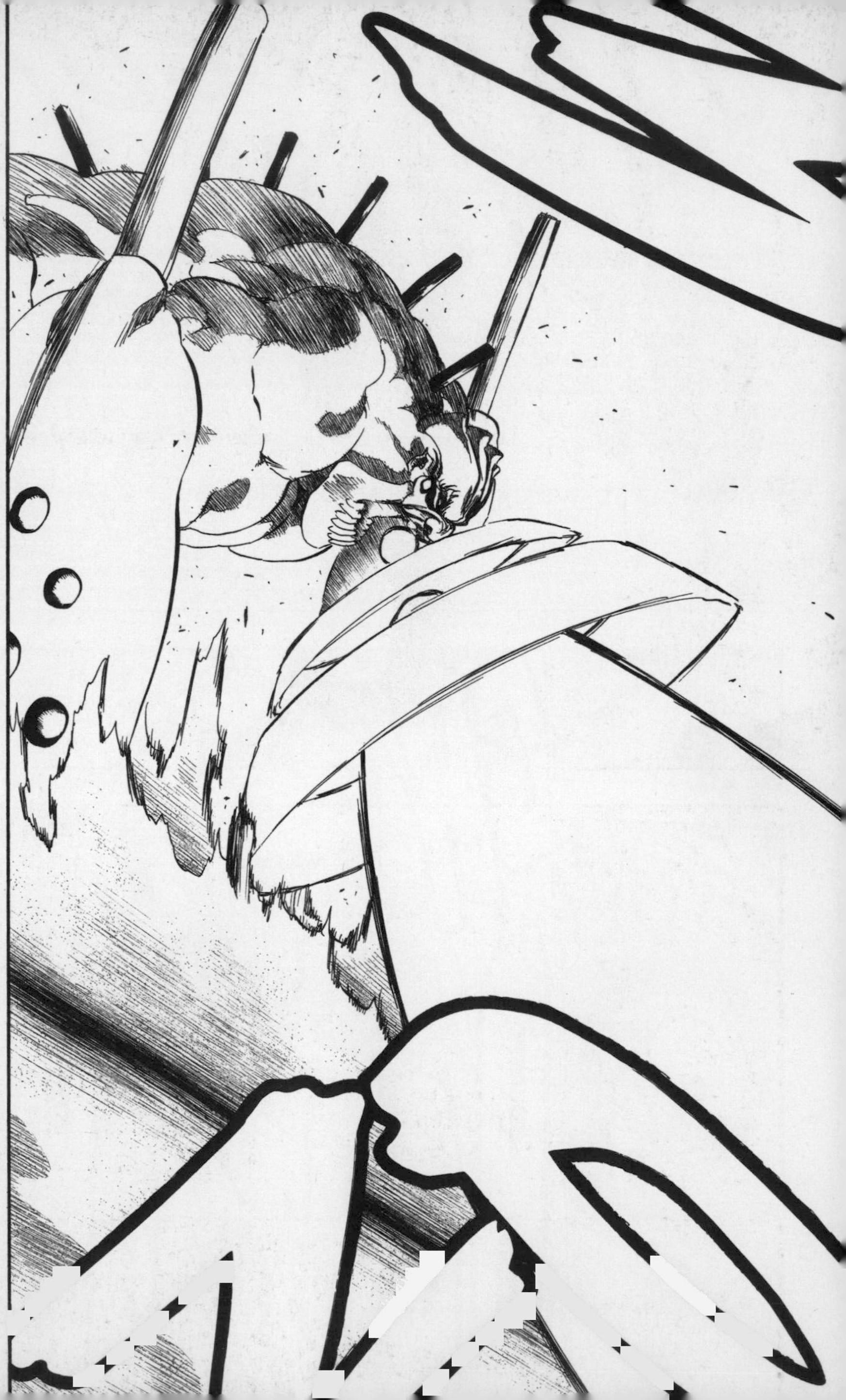

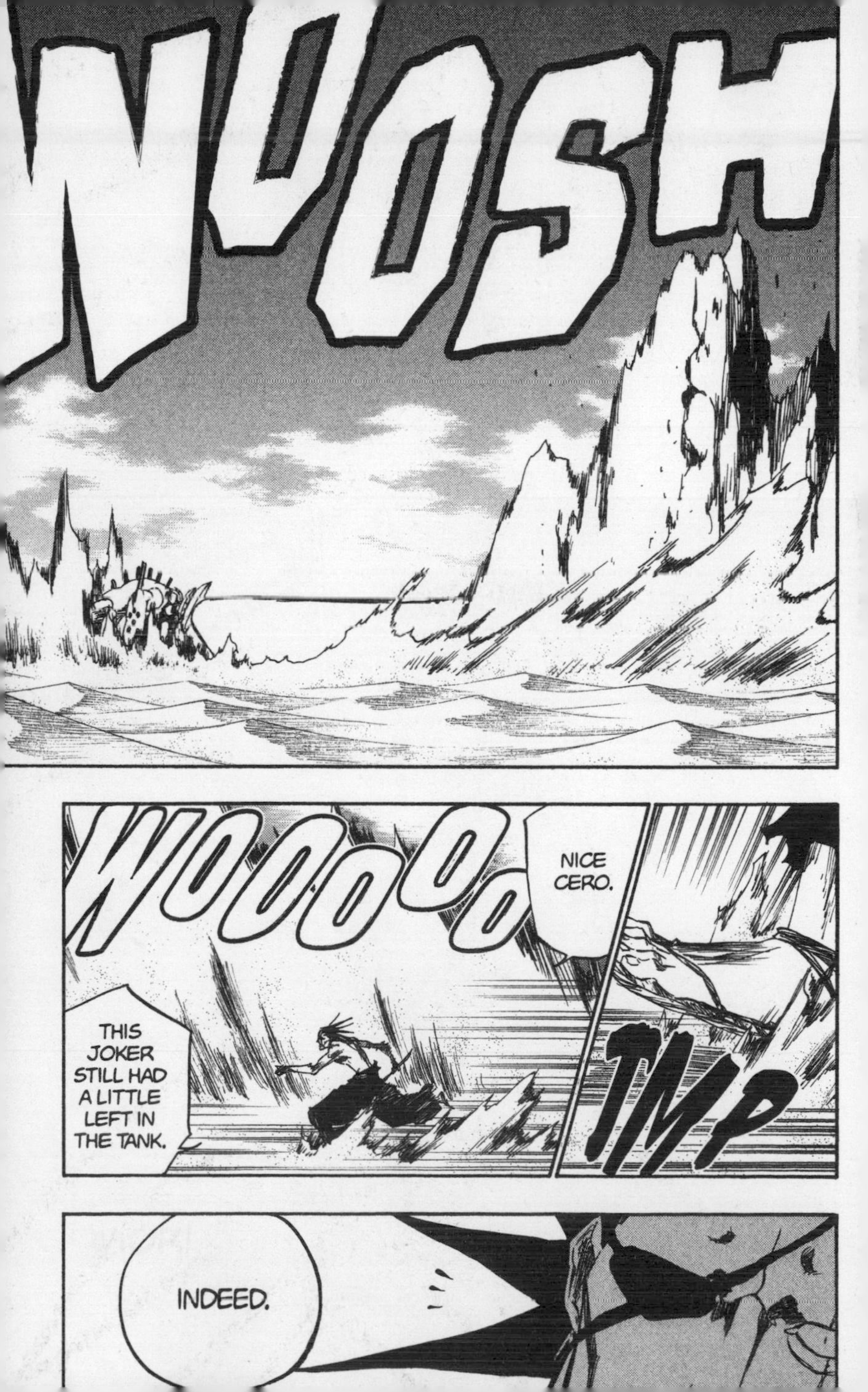
WHOSH
TMP
WOOOOO
NICE CERO.
THIS JOKER STILL HAD A LITTLE LEFT IN THE TANK.
INDEED.

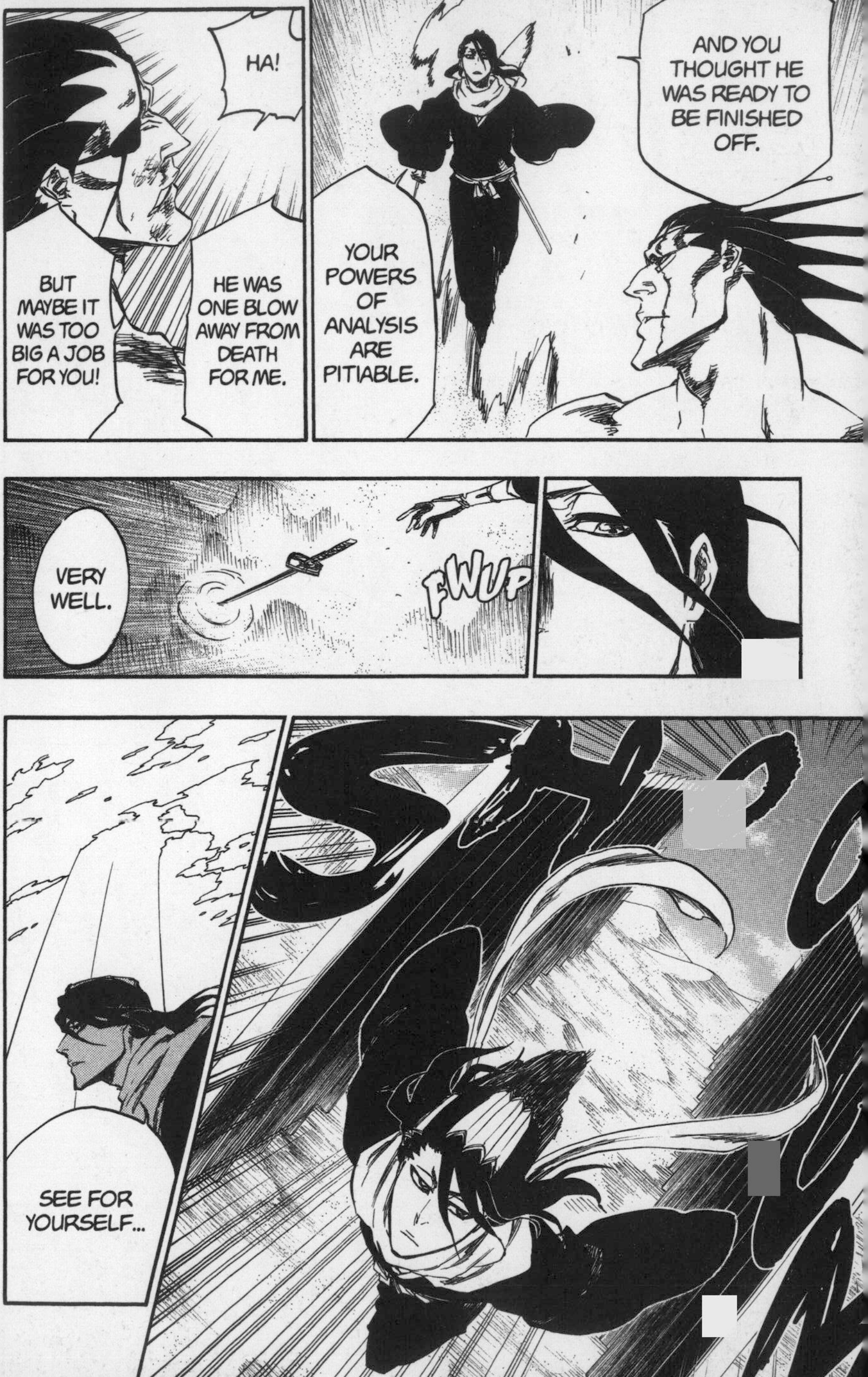
AND YOU THOUGHT HE WAS READY TO BE FINISHED OFF.
YOUR POWERS OF ANALYSIS ARE PITIABLE.
HA!
HE WAS ONE BLOW AWAY FROM DEATH FOR ME.
BUT MAYBE IT WAS TOO BIG A JOB FOR YOU!
FWUP
VERY WELL.
SEE FOR YOURSELF...

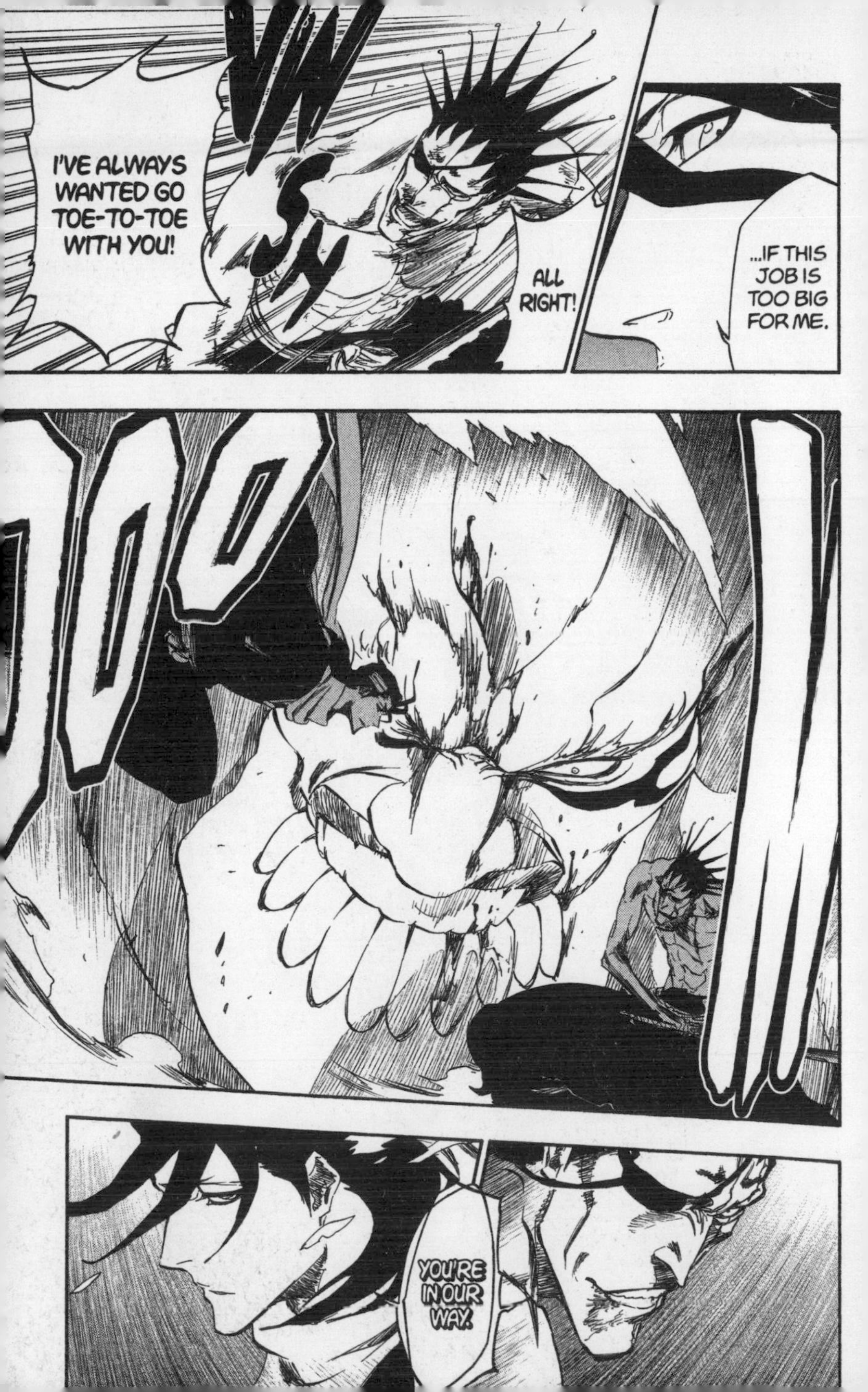
...IF THIS JOB IS TOO BIG FOR ME.
ALL RIGHT!
I'VE ALWAYS WANTED GO TOE-TO-TOE WITH YOU!
YOU'RE IN OUR WAY.

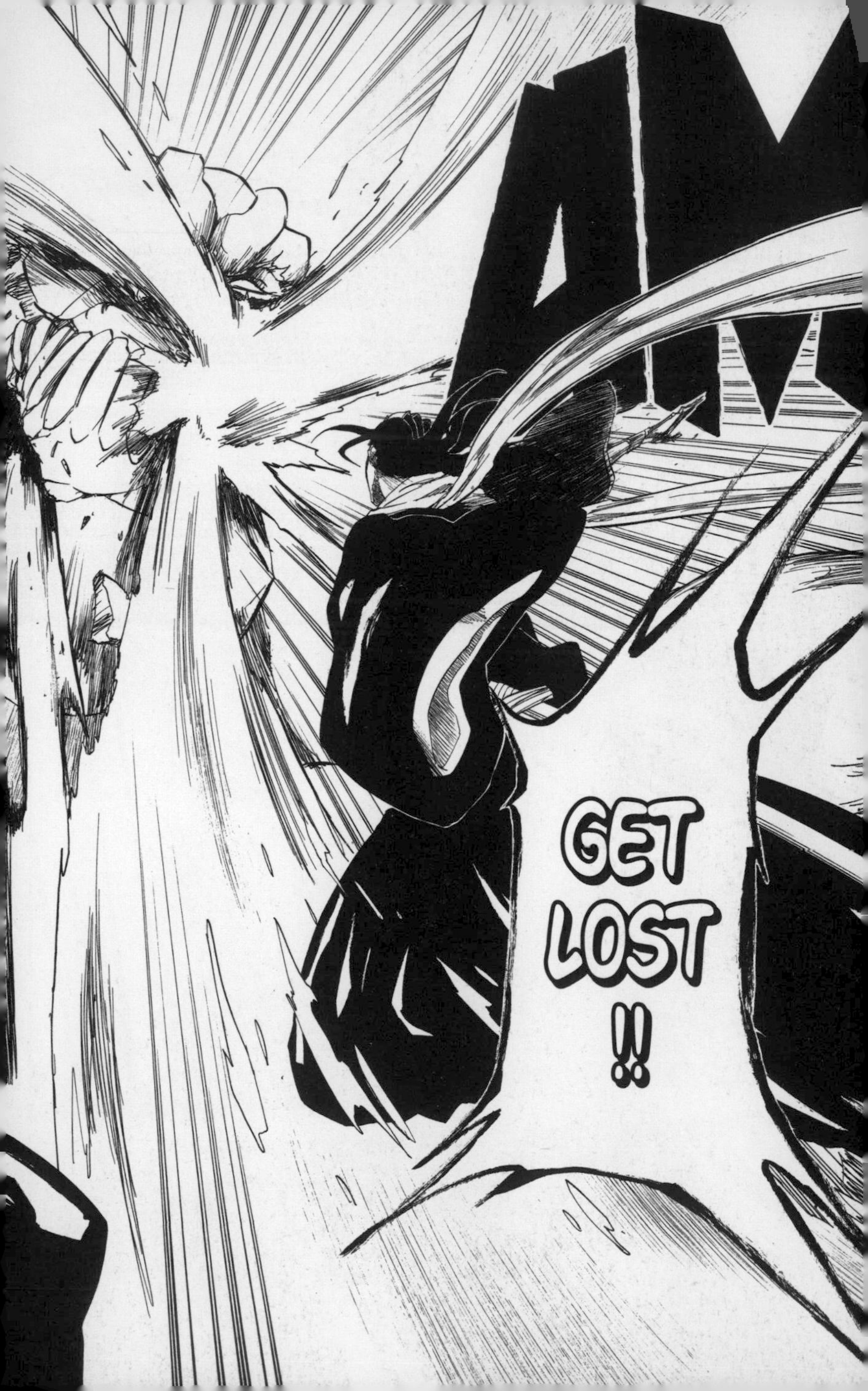
GET LOST !!

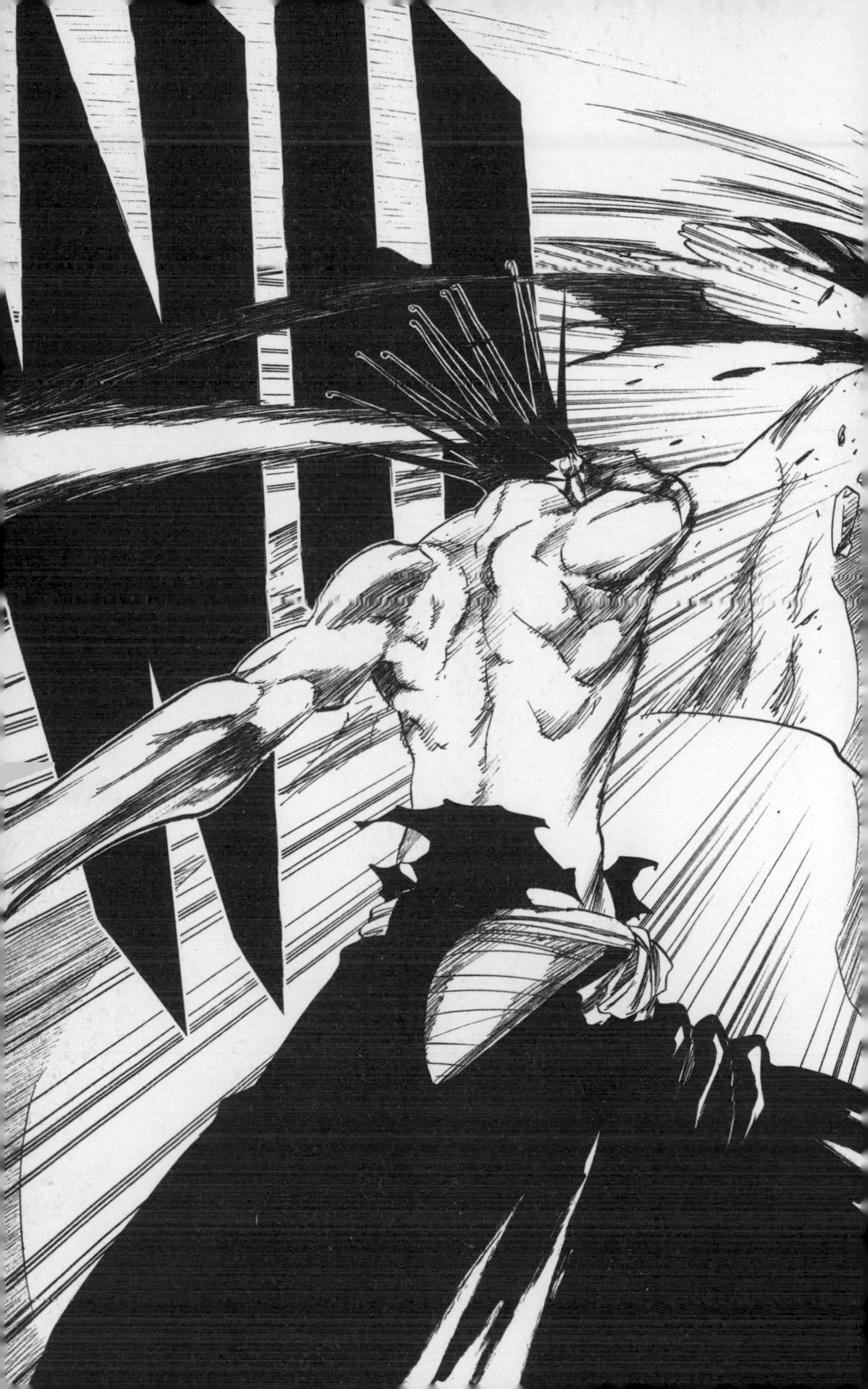

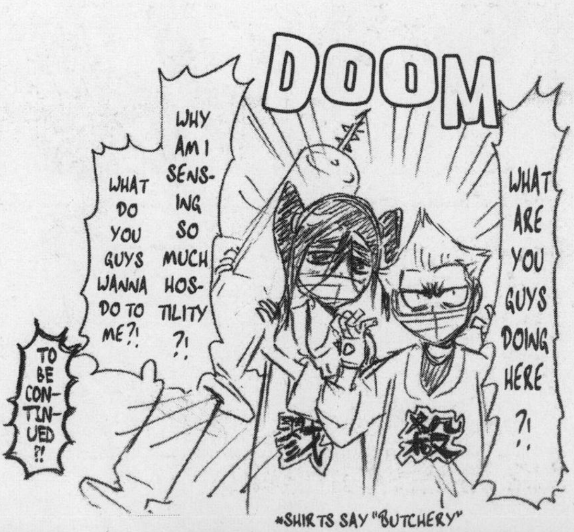
DOOM
WHAT ARE YOU GUYS DOING HERE ?!
WHY AM I SENSING SO MUCH HOSTILITY ?!
WHAT DO YOU GUYS WANNA DO TO ME?!
TO BE CONTINUED ?!
*SHIRTS SAY "BUTCHERY"

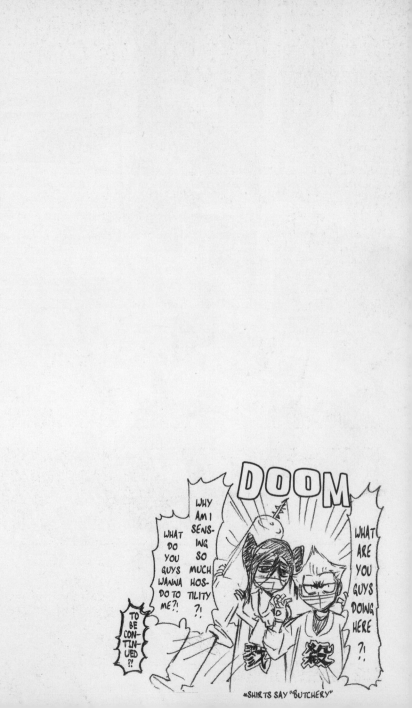

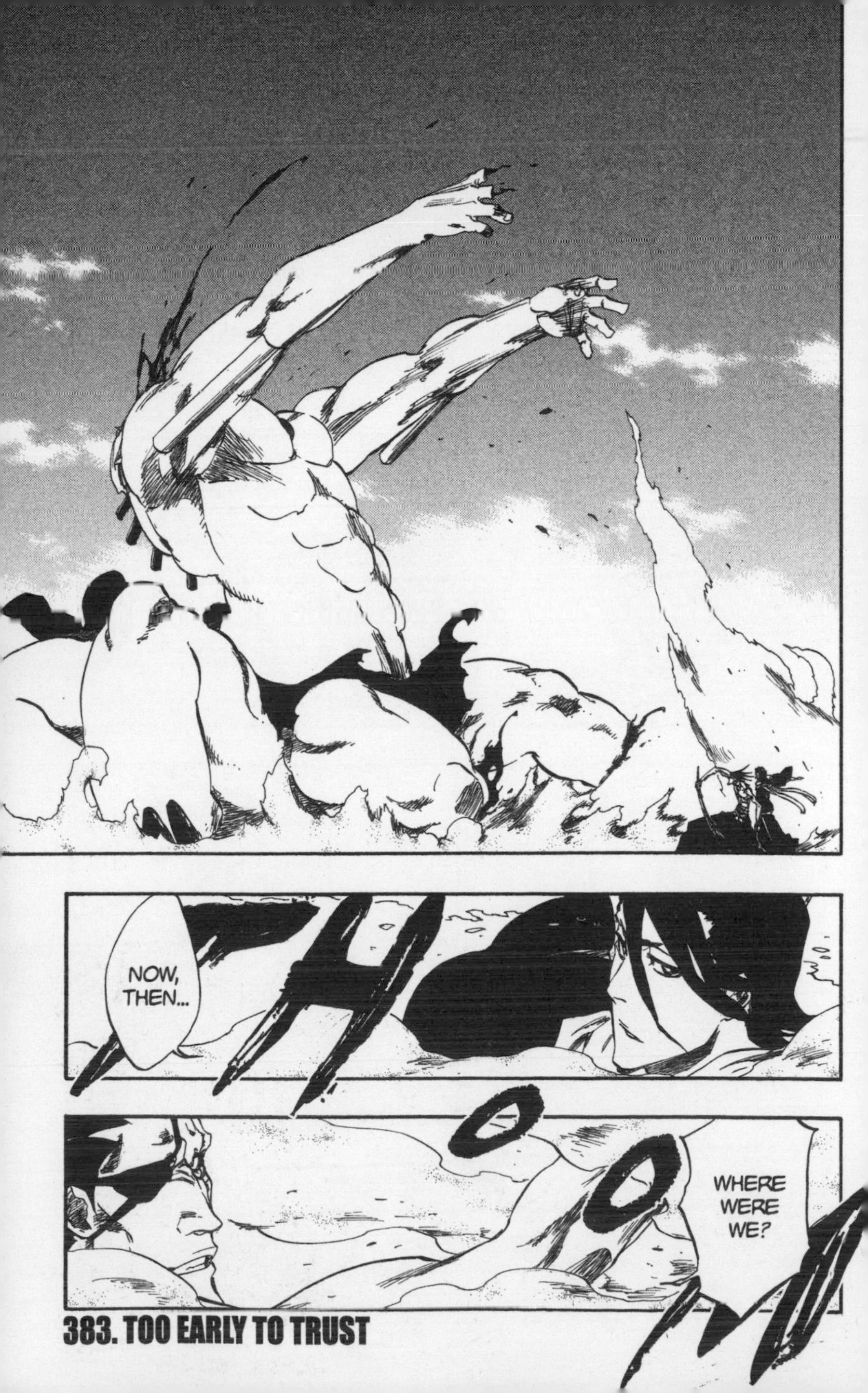
NOW, THEN...
WHERE WERE WE?

383. TOO EARLY TO TRUST

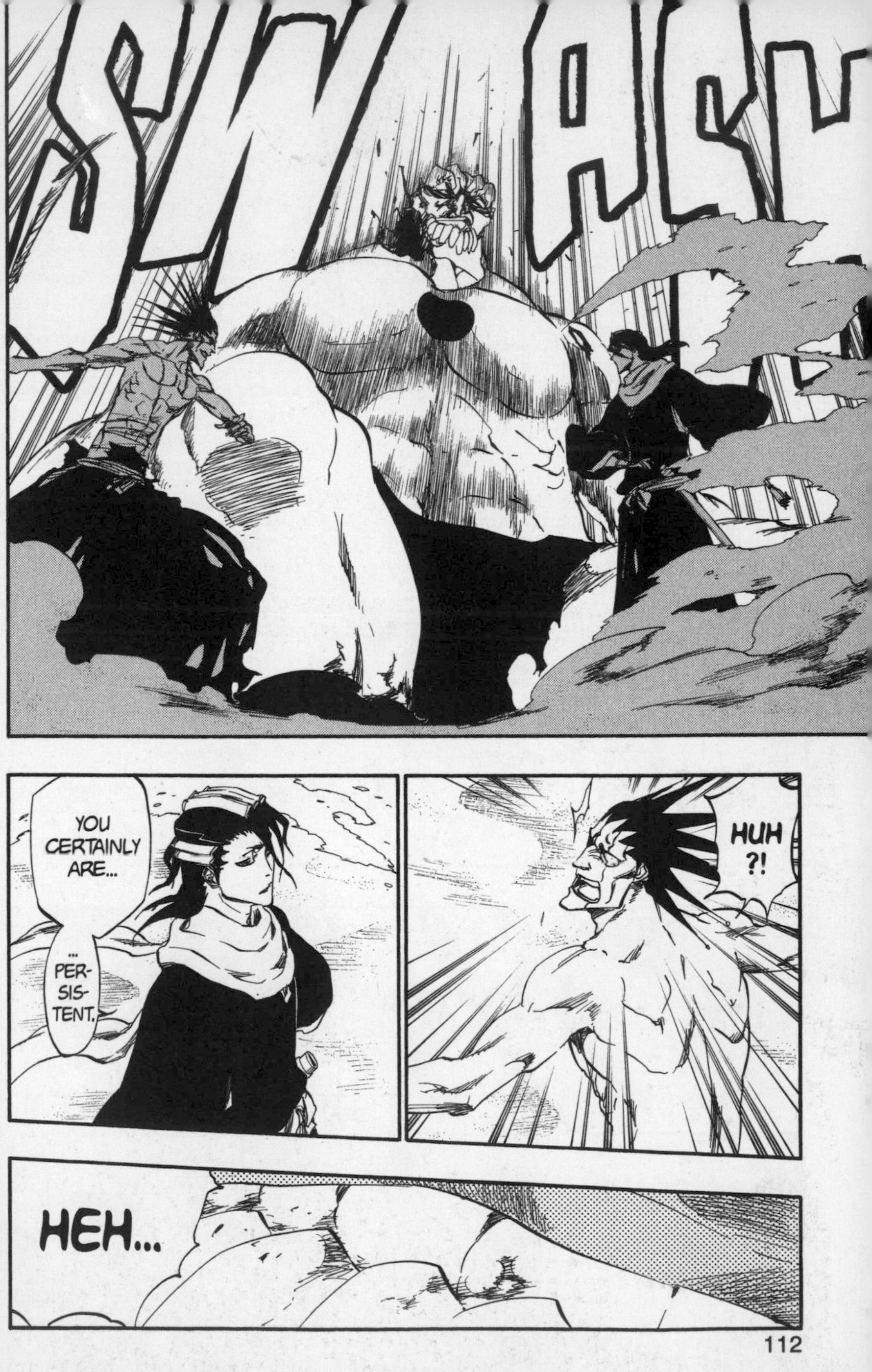
HUH ?!
YOU CERTAINLY ARE...
... PER-SIS-TENT.
HEH...

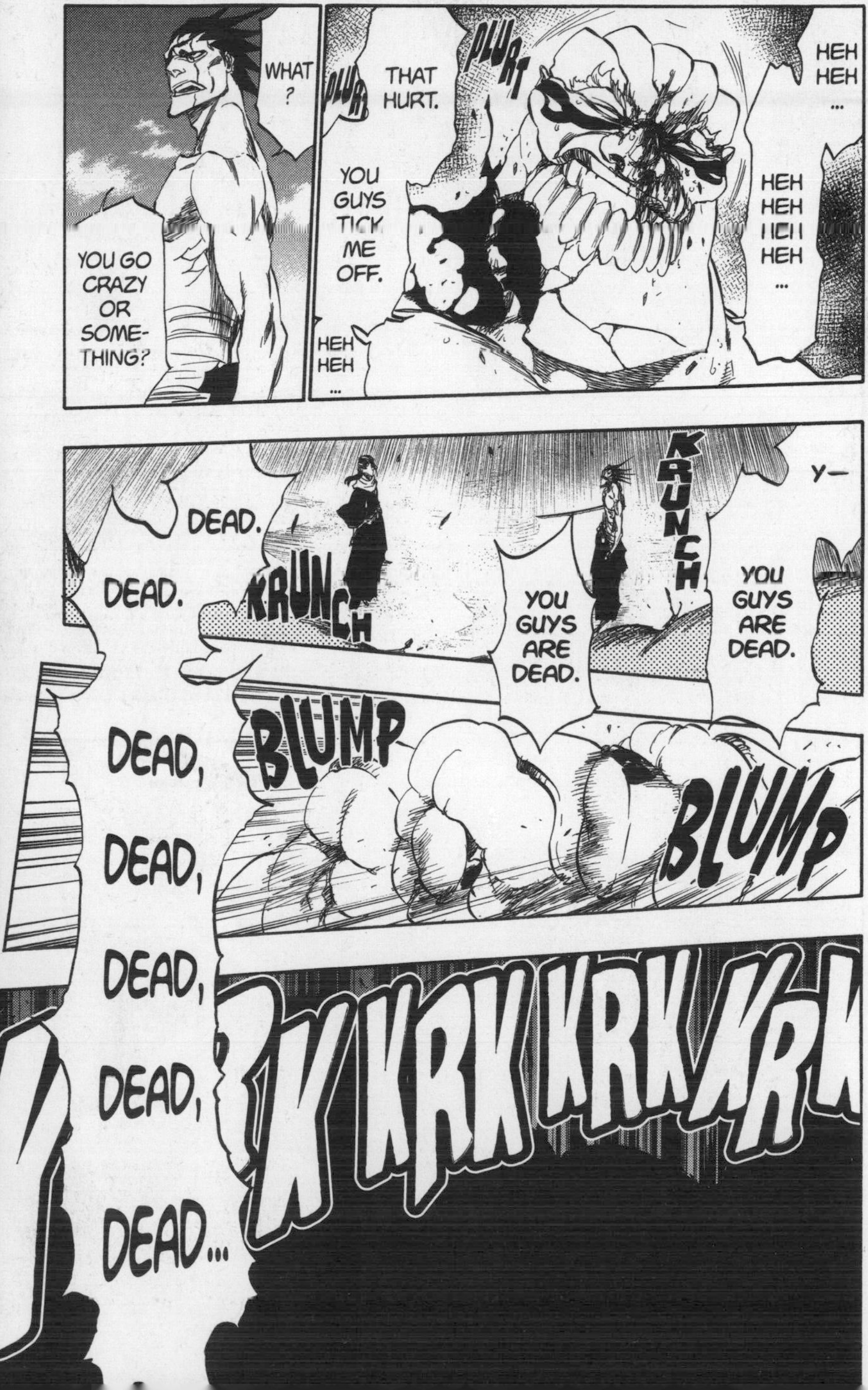
HEH HEH ...
HEH HEH HEH HEH ...
PLURT
THAT HURT.
PLURT
YOU GUYS TICK ME OFF.
HEH HEH ...
WHAT?
YOU GO CRAZY OR SOMETHING?
Y—
YOU GUYS ARE DEAD.
KRUNCH
YOU GUYS ARE DEAD.
KRUNCH
DEAD.
DEAD.
BLUMP
BLUMP
DEAD, DEAD, DEAD, DEAD, DEAD...
KRK KRK KRK KRK

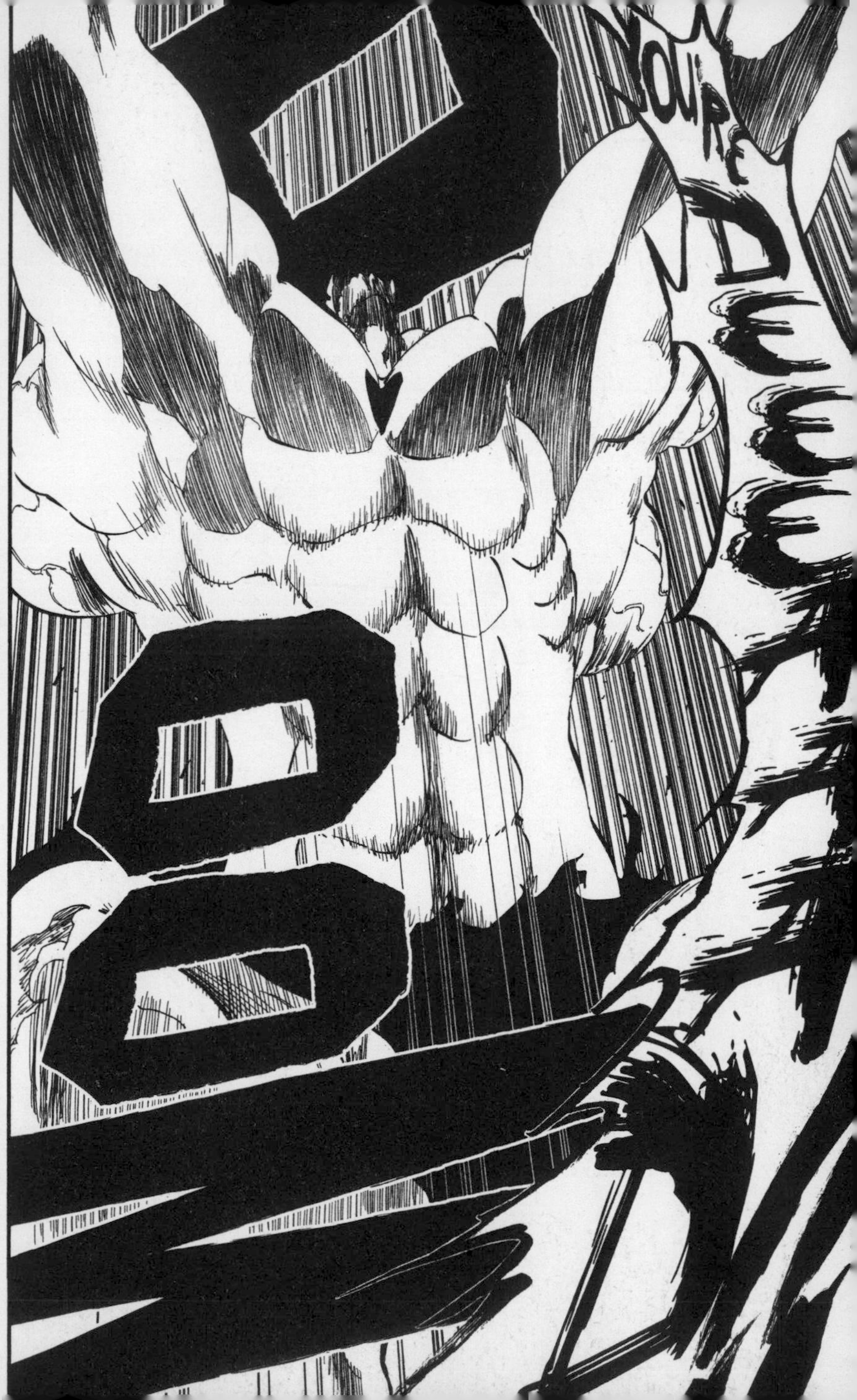
YOU'RE DEEEE

READ THIS WAY

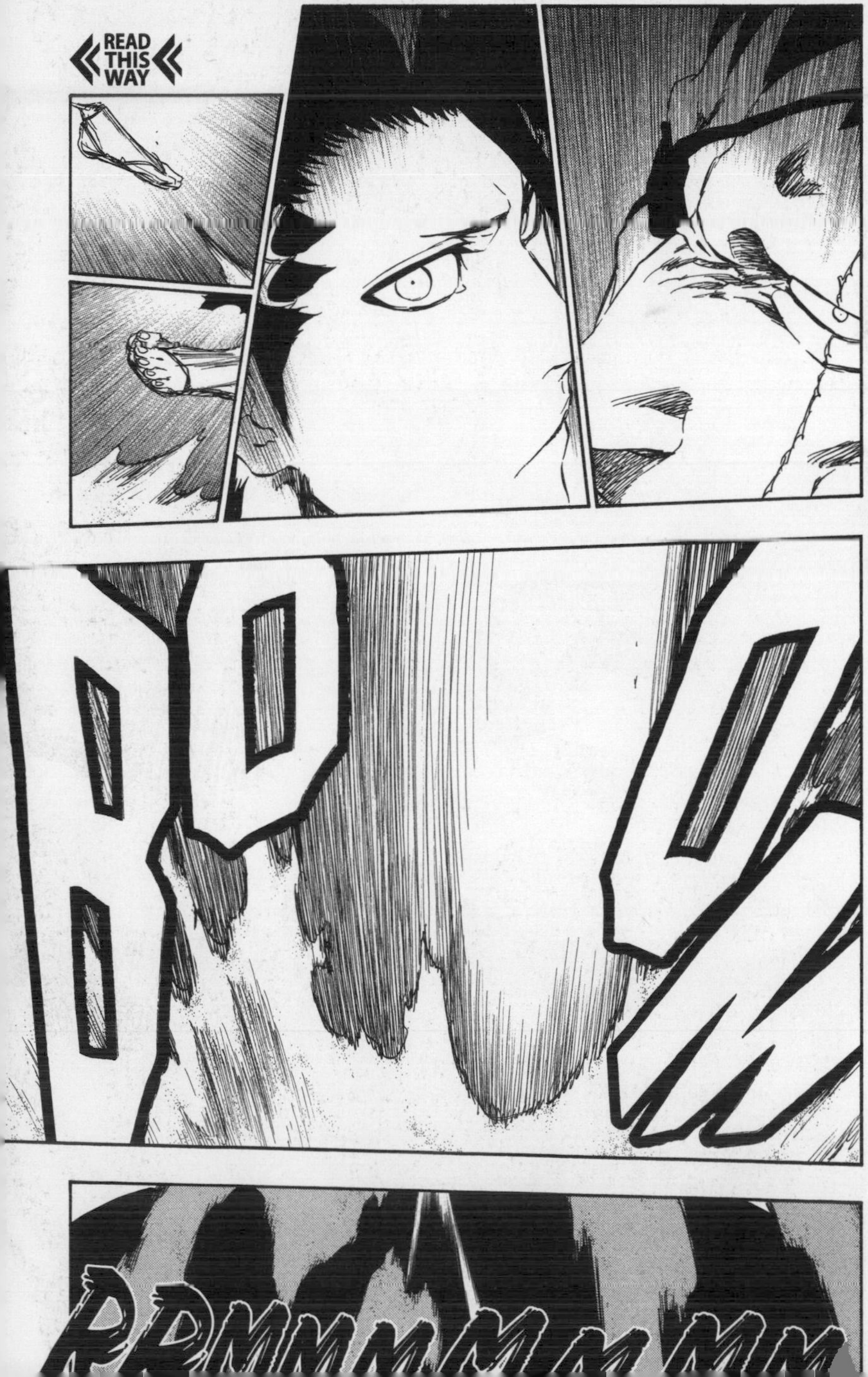

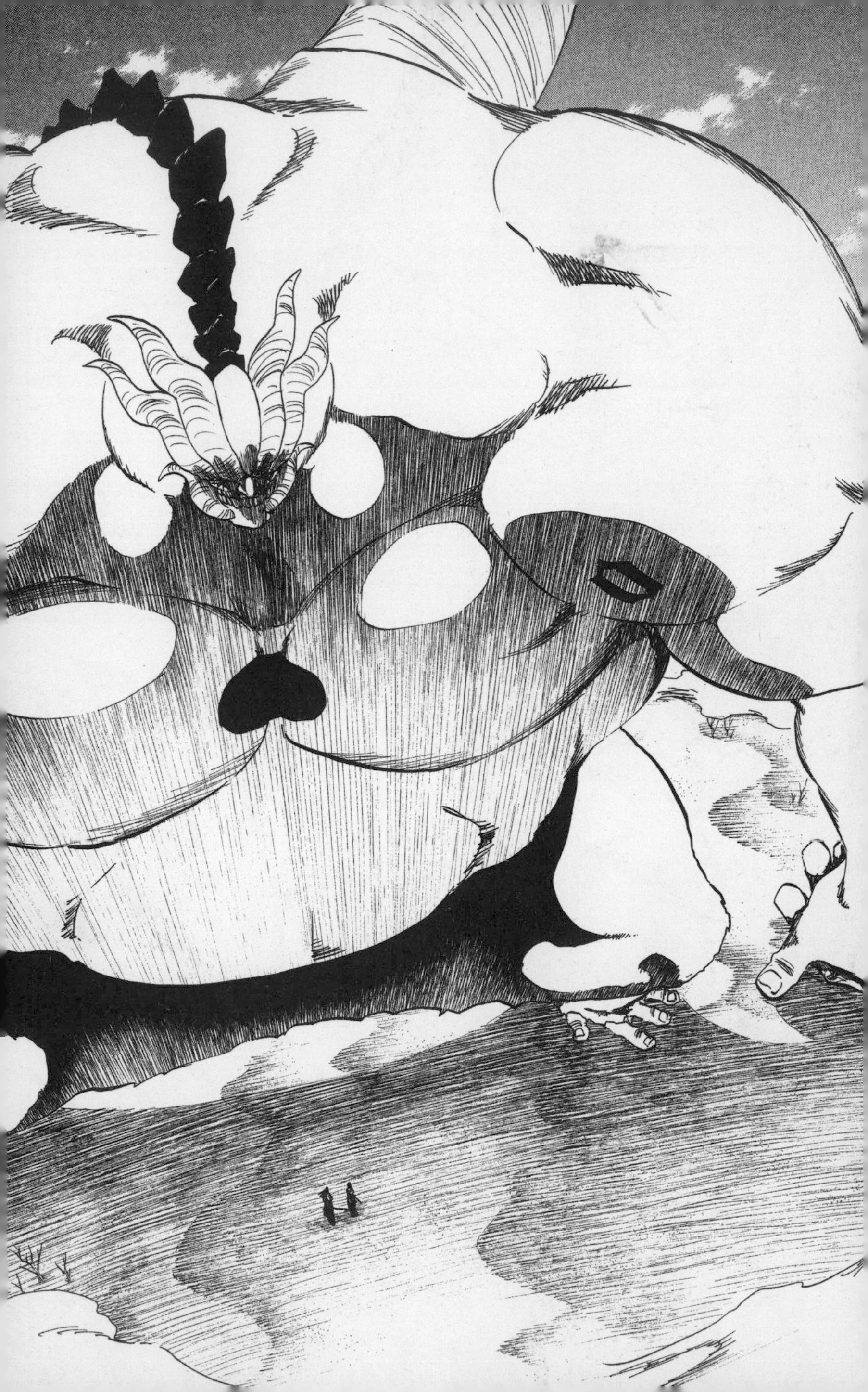

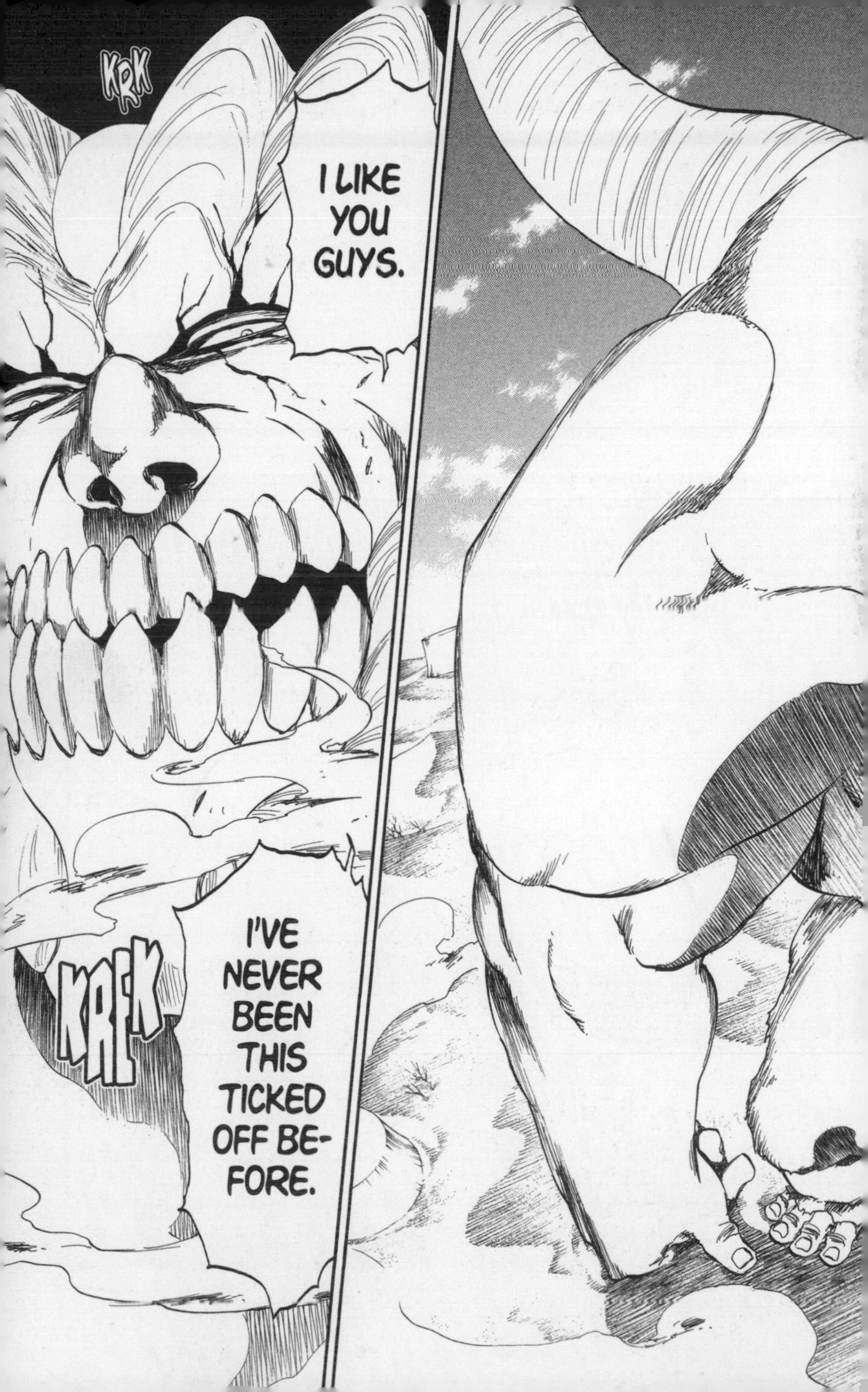
KRK
I LIKE YOU GUYS.
I'VE NEVER BEEN THIS TICKED OFF BE-FORE.

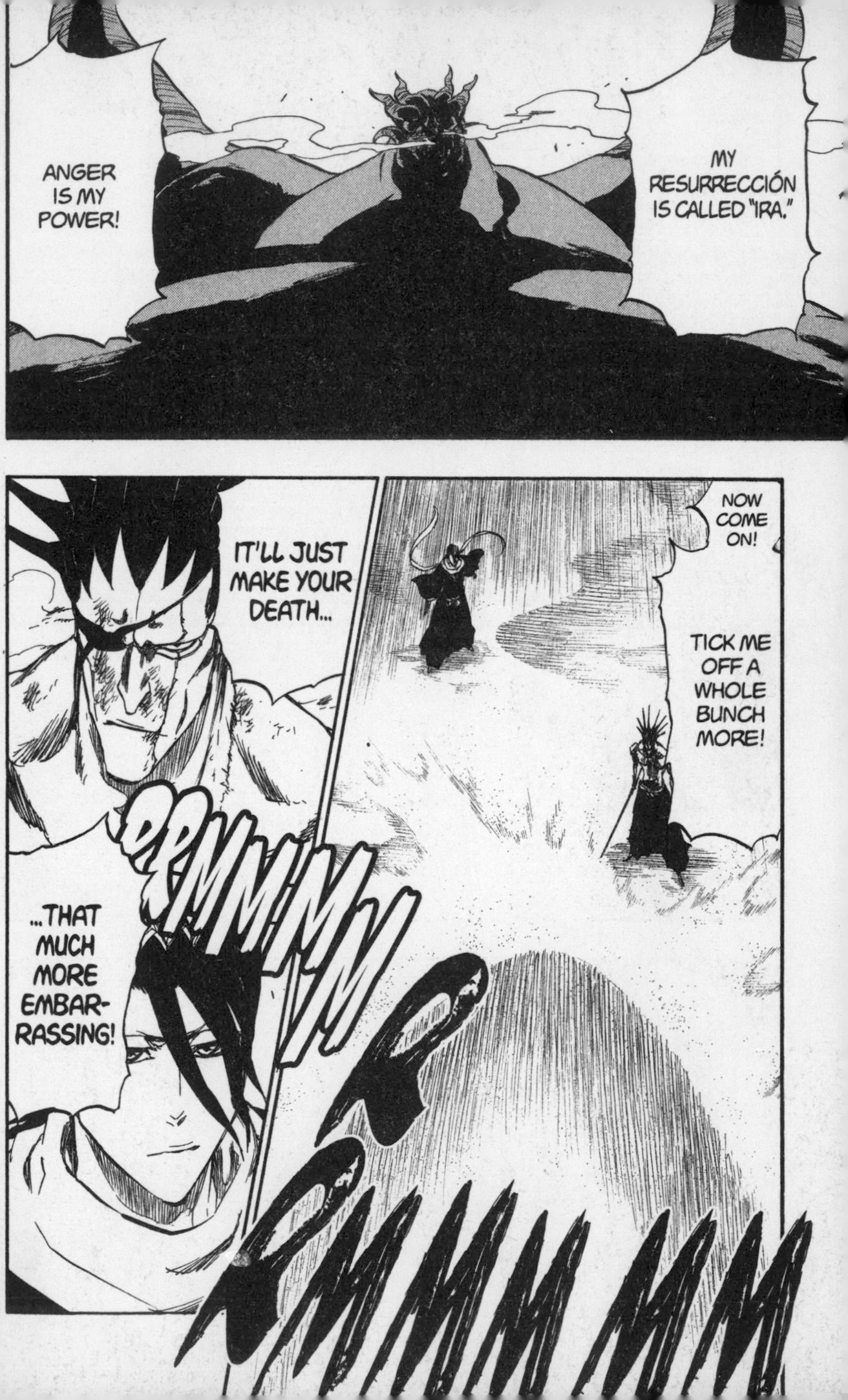
MY RESURRECCIÓN IS CALLED "IRA."
ANGER IS MY POWER!
NOW COME ON!
TICK ME OFF A WHOLE BUNCH MORE!
IT'LL JUST MAKE YOUR DEATH...
...THAT MUCH MORE EMBARRASSING!

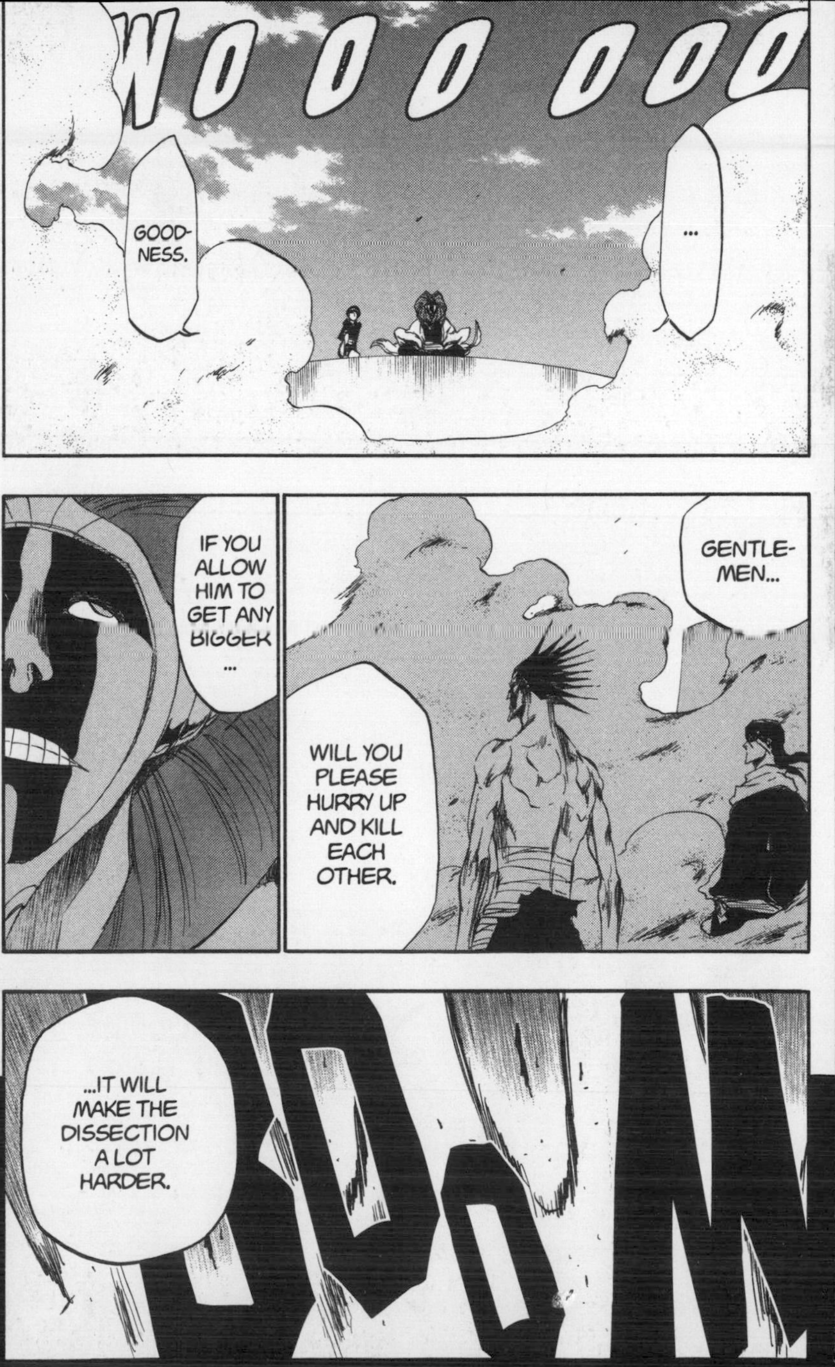
WOOO OOO
...
GOOD-NESS.
GENTLE-MEN...
WILL YOU PLEASE HURRY UP AND KILL EACH OTHER.
IF YOU ALLOW HIM TO GET ANY BIGGER ...
...IT WILL MAKE THE DISSECTION A LOT HARDER.

383. TOO EARLY TO TRUST

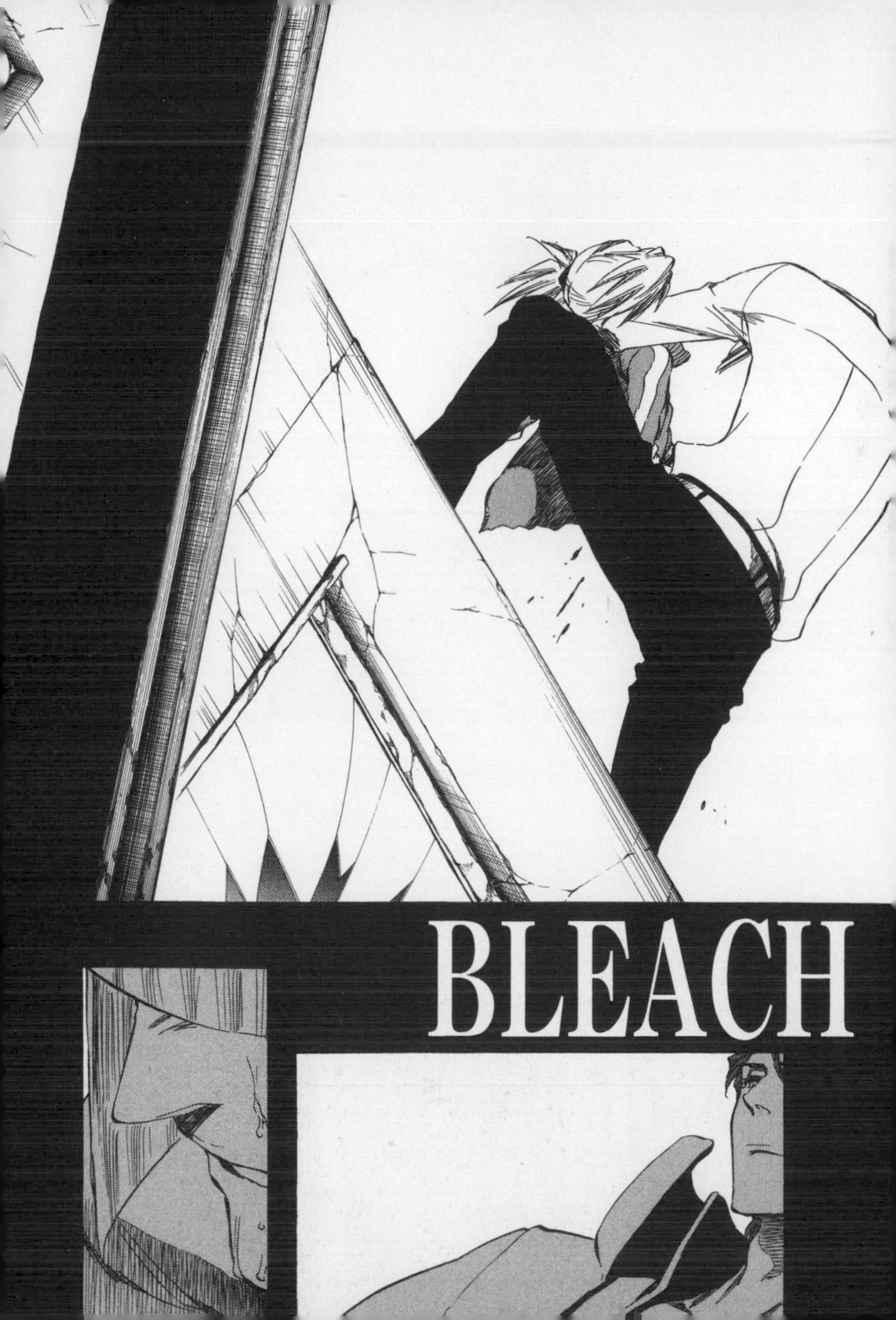
BLEACH

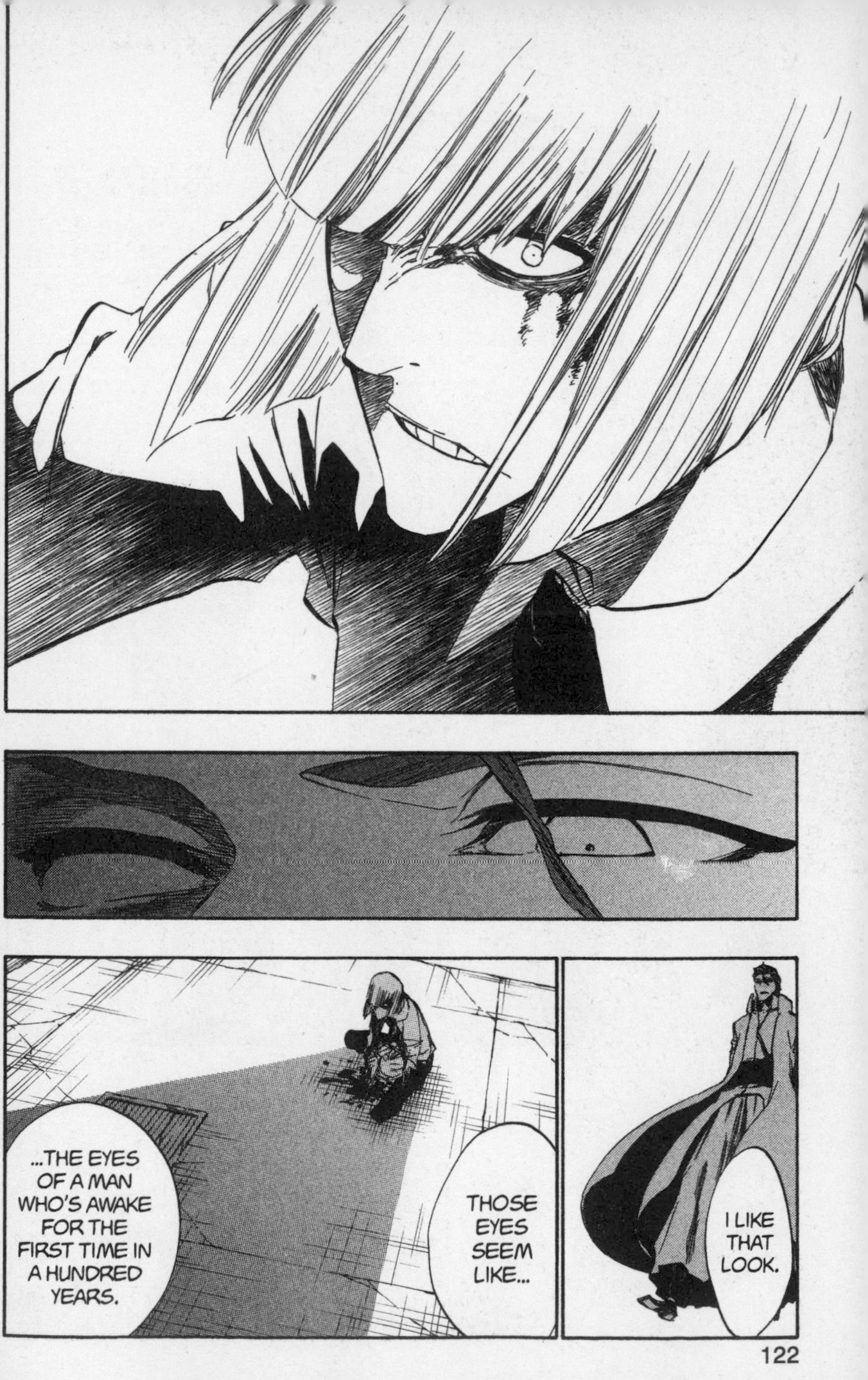
I LIKE THAT LOOK.
THOSE EYES SEEM LIKE...
...THE EYES OF A MAN WHO'S AWAKE FOR THE FIRST TIME IN A HUNDRED YEARS.

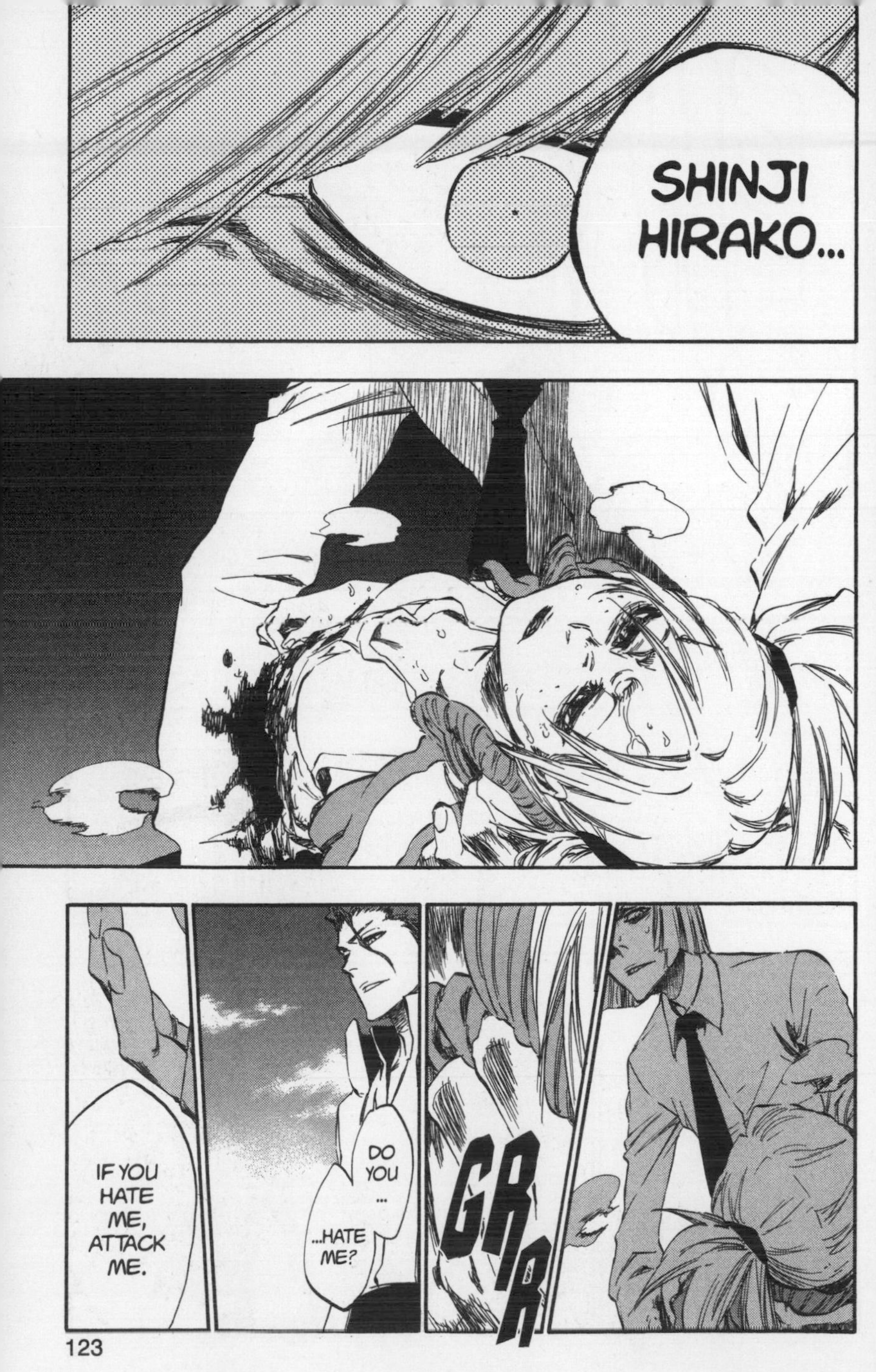
SHINJI HIRAKO...
GRR
DO YOU ...
...HATE ME?
IF YOU HATE ME, ATTACK ME.

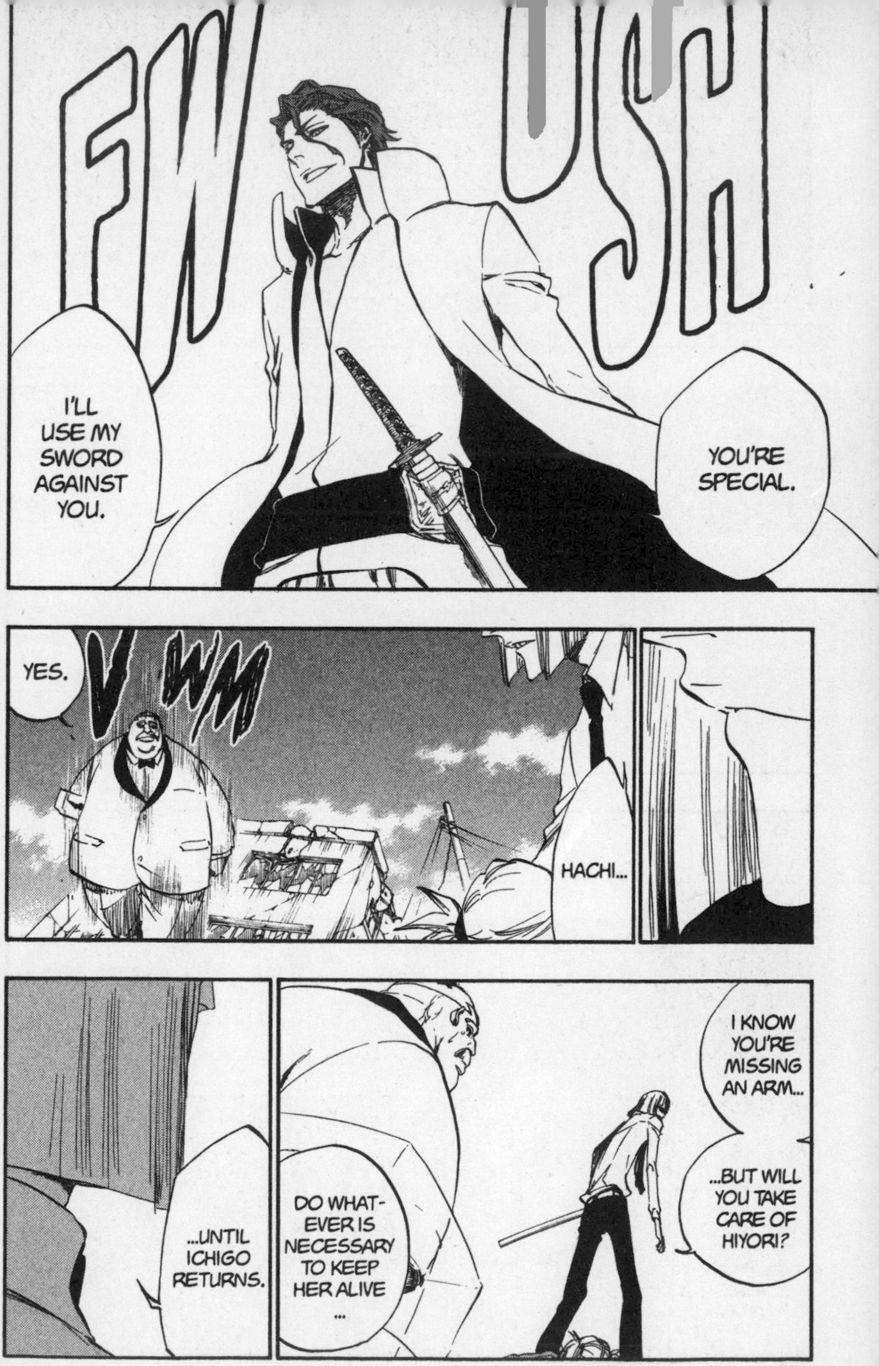
FWUSH
YOU'RE SPECIAL.
I'LL USE MY SWORD AGAINST YOU.
HACHI...
VWM
YES.
I KNOW YOU'RE MISSING AN ARM...
...BUT WILL YOU TAKE CARE OF HIYORI?
DO WHATEVER IS NECESSARY TO KEEP HER ALIVE...
...UNTIL ICHIGO RETURNS.

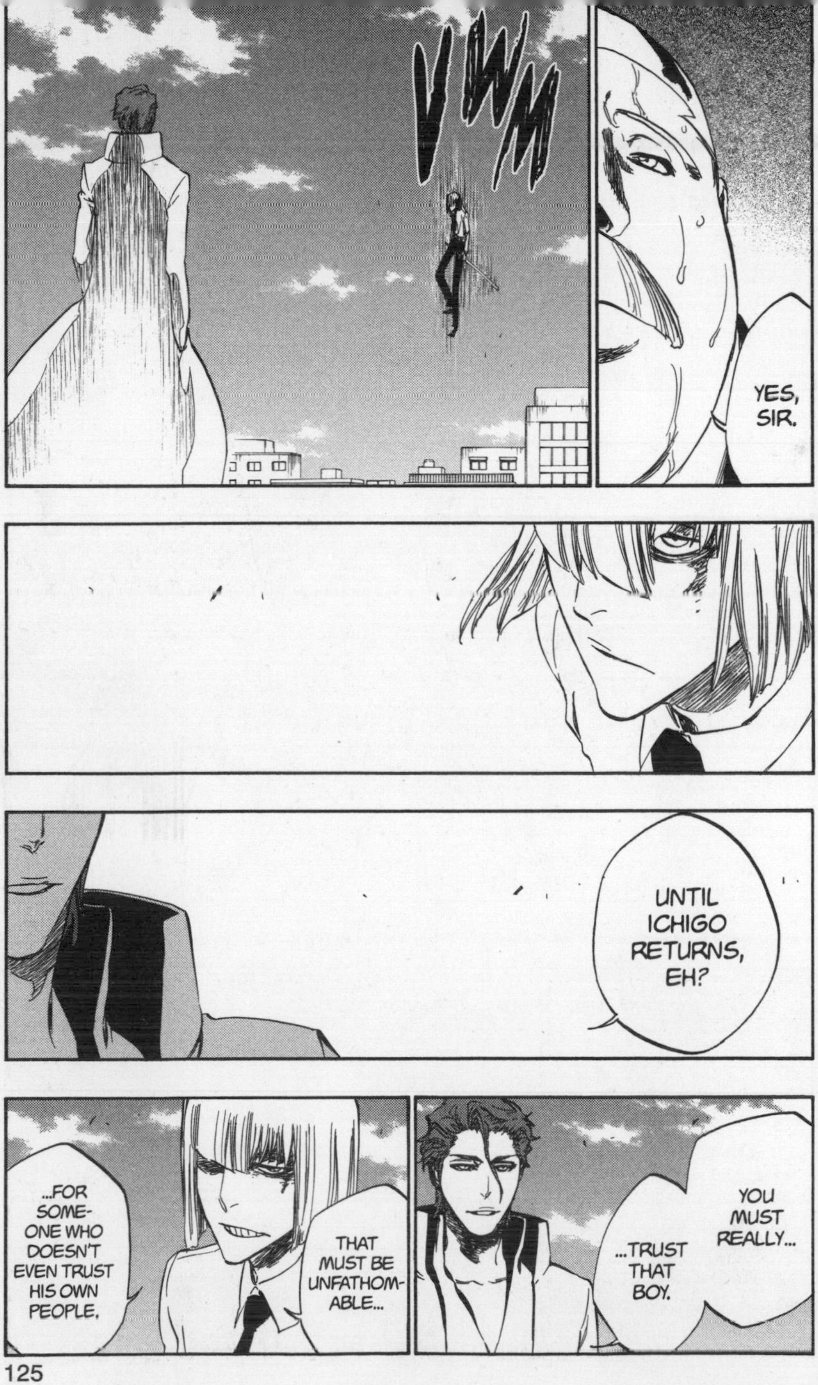
YES, SIR.
VWM
UNTIL ICHIGO RETURNS, EH?
YOU MUST REALLY...
...TRUST THAT BOY.
THAT MUST BE UNFATHOMABLE...
...FOR SOMEONE WHO DOESN'T EVEN TRUST HIS OWN PEOPLE.

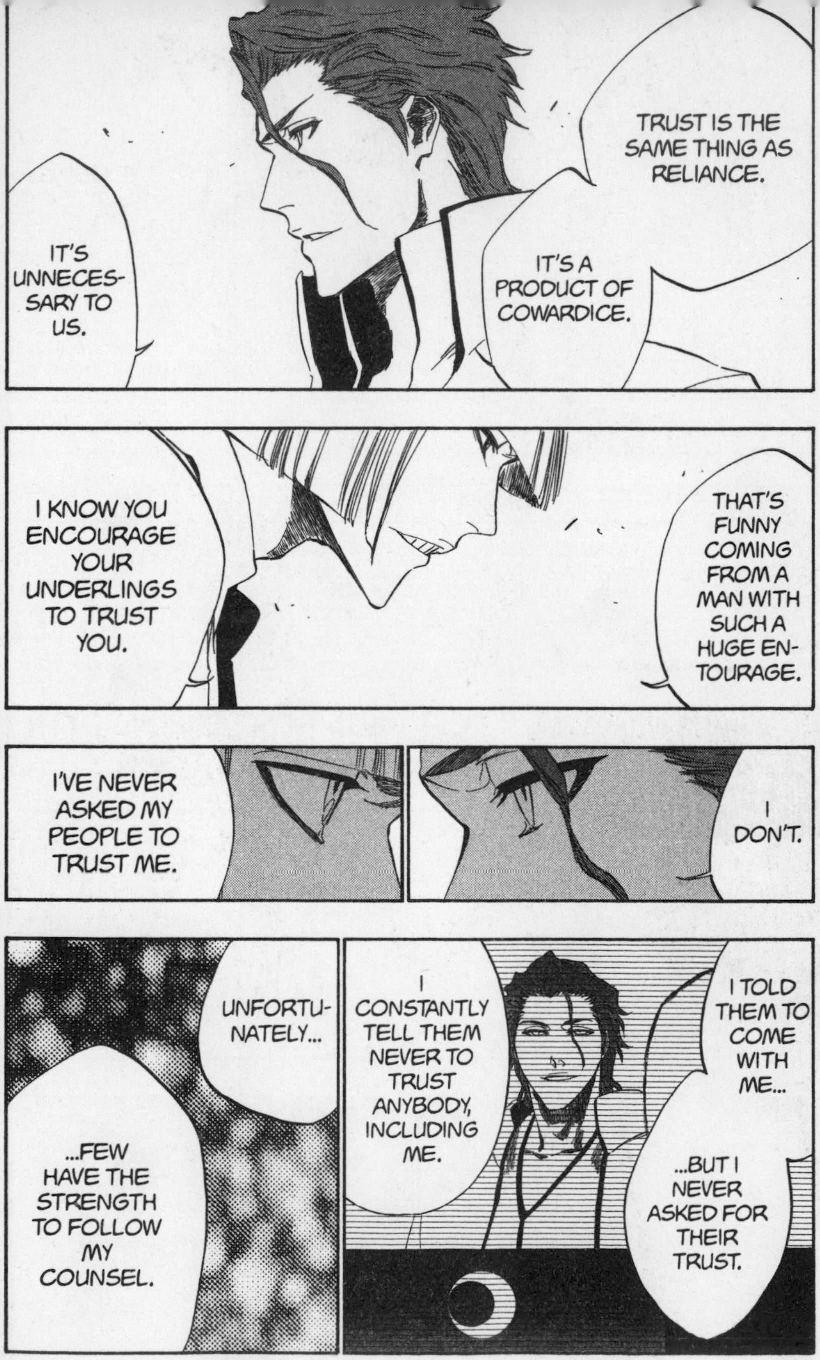
TRUST IS THE SAME THING AS RELIANCE.
IT'S A PRODUCT OF COWARDICE.
IT'S UNNECESSARY TO US.
THAT'S FUNNY COMING FROM A MAN WITH SUCH A HUGE ENTOURAGE.
I KNOW YOU ENCOURAGE YOUR UNDERLINGS TO TRUST YOU.
I DON'T.
I'VE NEVER ASKED MY PEOPLE TO TRUST ME.
I TOLD THEM TO COME WITH ME...
...BUT I NEVER ASKED FOR THEIR TRUST.
I CONSTANTLY TELL THEM NEVER TO TRUST ANYBODY, INCLUDING ME.
UNFORTUNATELY...
...FEW HAVE THE STRENGTH TO FOLLOW MY COUNSEL.

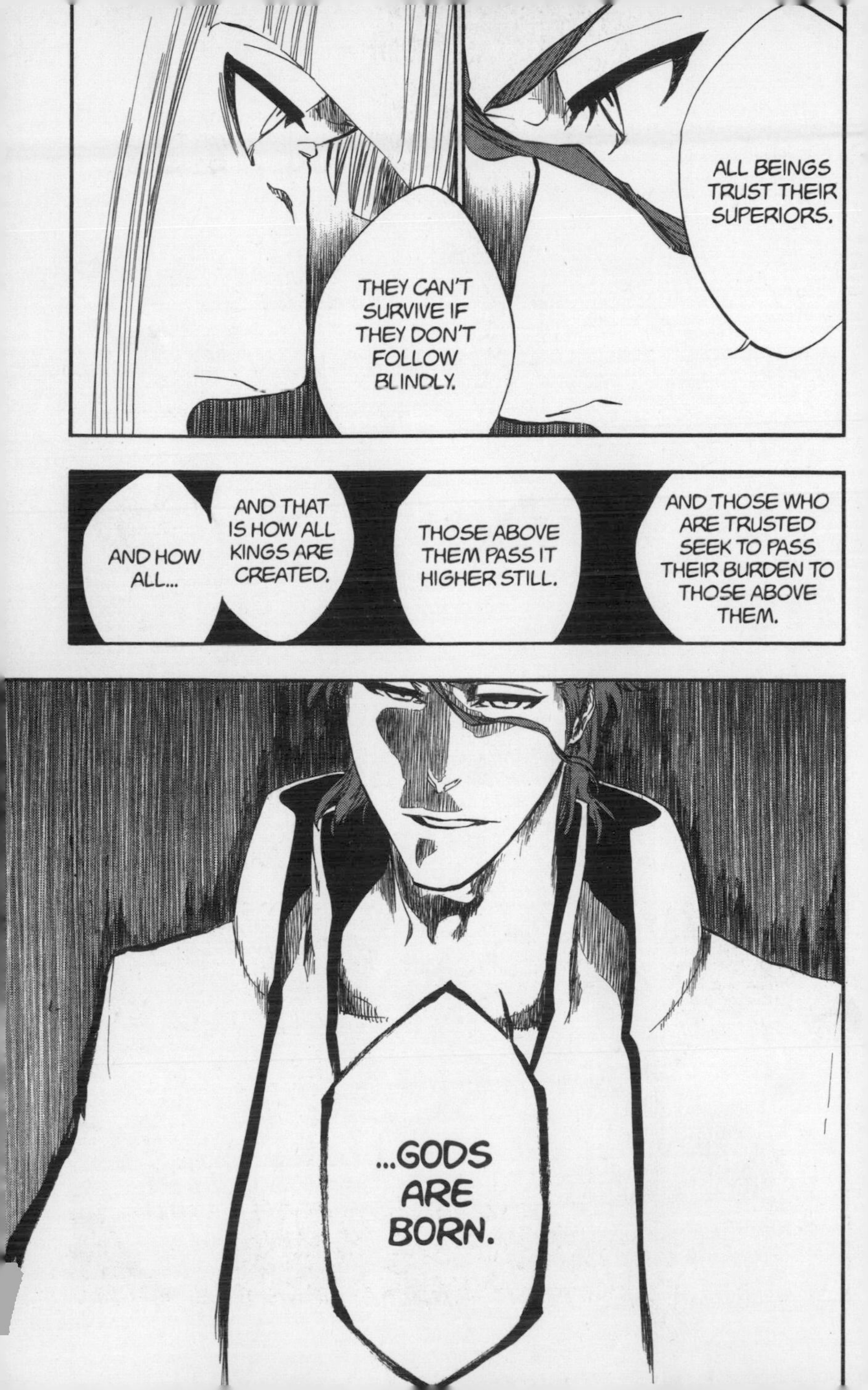
ALL BEINGS TRUST THEIR SUPERIORS.
THEY CAN'T SURVIVE IF THEY DON'T FOLLOW BLINDLY.
AND THOSE WHO ARE TRUSTED SEEK TO PASS THEIR BURDEN TO THOSE ABOVE THEM.
THOSE ABOVE THEM PASS IT HIGHER STILL.
AND THAT IS HOW ALL KINGS ARE CREATED.
AND HOW ALL...
...GODS ARE BORN.

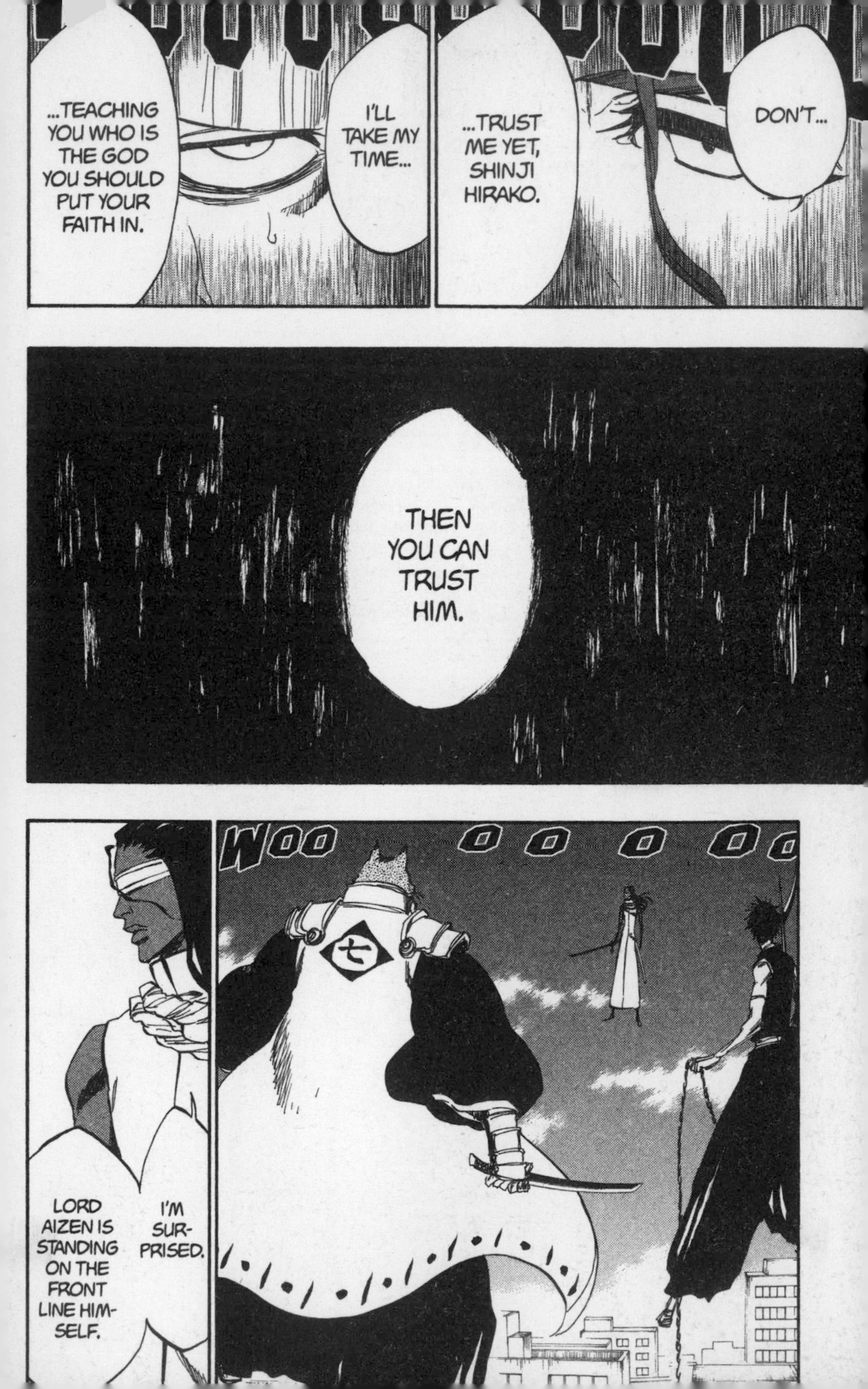
DON'T...
...TRUST ME YET, SHINJI HIRAKO.
I'LL TAKE MY TIME...
...TEACHING YOU WHO IS THE GOD YOU SHOULD PUT YOUR FAITH IN.
THEN YOU CAN TRUST HIM.
WOOOOOOO
I'M SUR-PRISED.
LORD AIZEN IS STANDING ON THE FRONT LINE HIM-SELF.

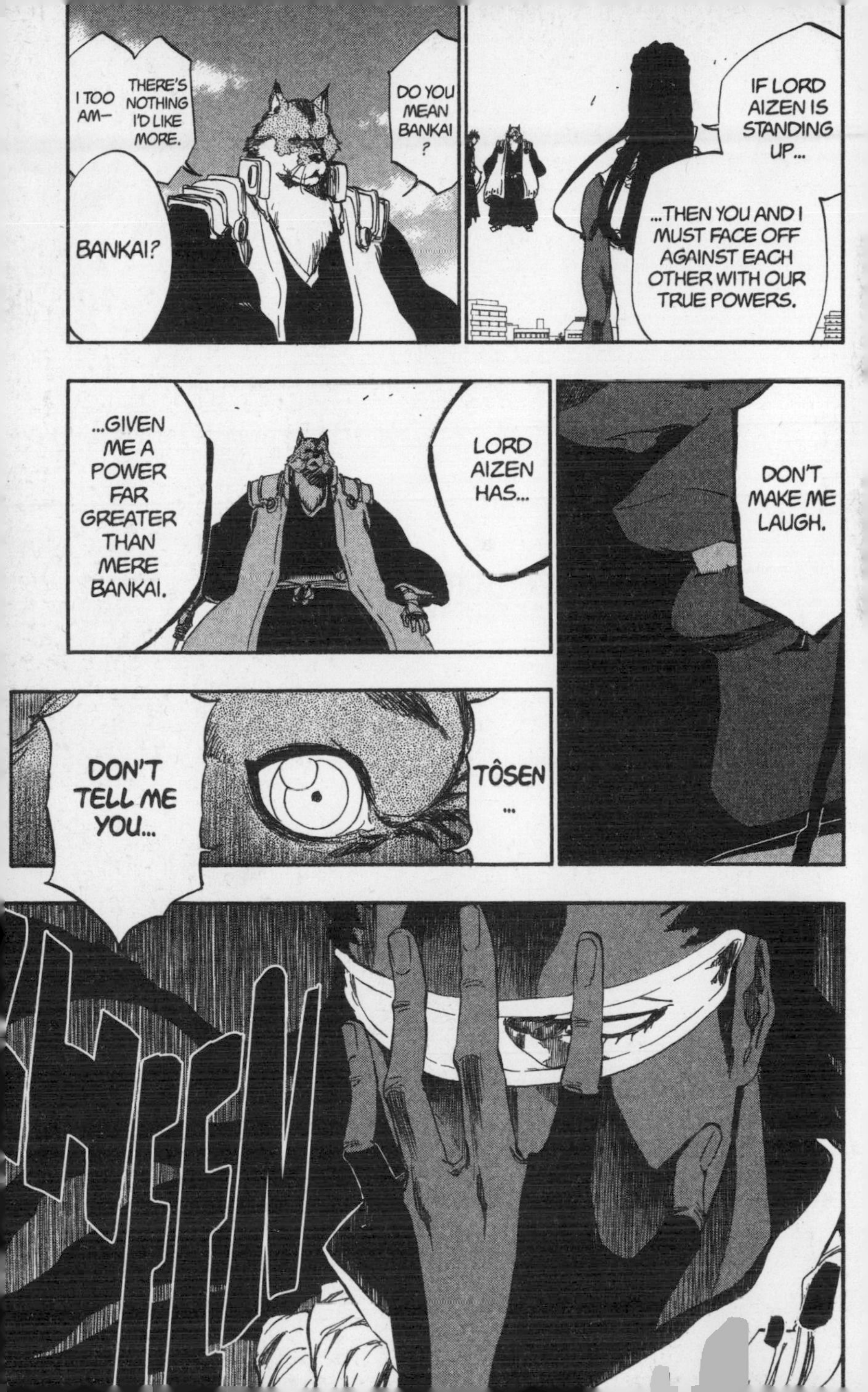
IF LORD AIZEN IS STANDING UP...
...THEN YOU AND I MUST FACE OFF AGAINST EACH OTHER WITH OUR TRUE POWERS.
DO YOU MEAN BANKAI?
THERE'S NOTHING I'D LIKE MORE.
I TOO AM—
BANKAI?
DON'T MAKE ME LAUGH.
LORD AIZEN HAS...
...GIVEN ME A POWER FAR GREATER THAN MERE BANKAI.
TÔSEN...
DON'T TELL ME YOU...

384. Can't Fear Your Own Sword

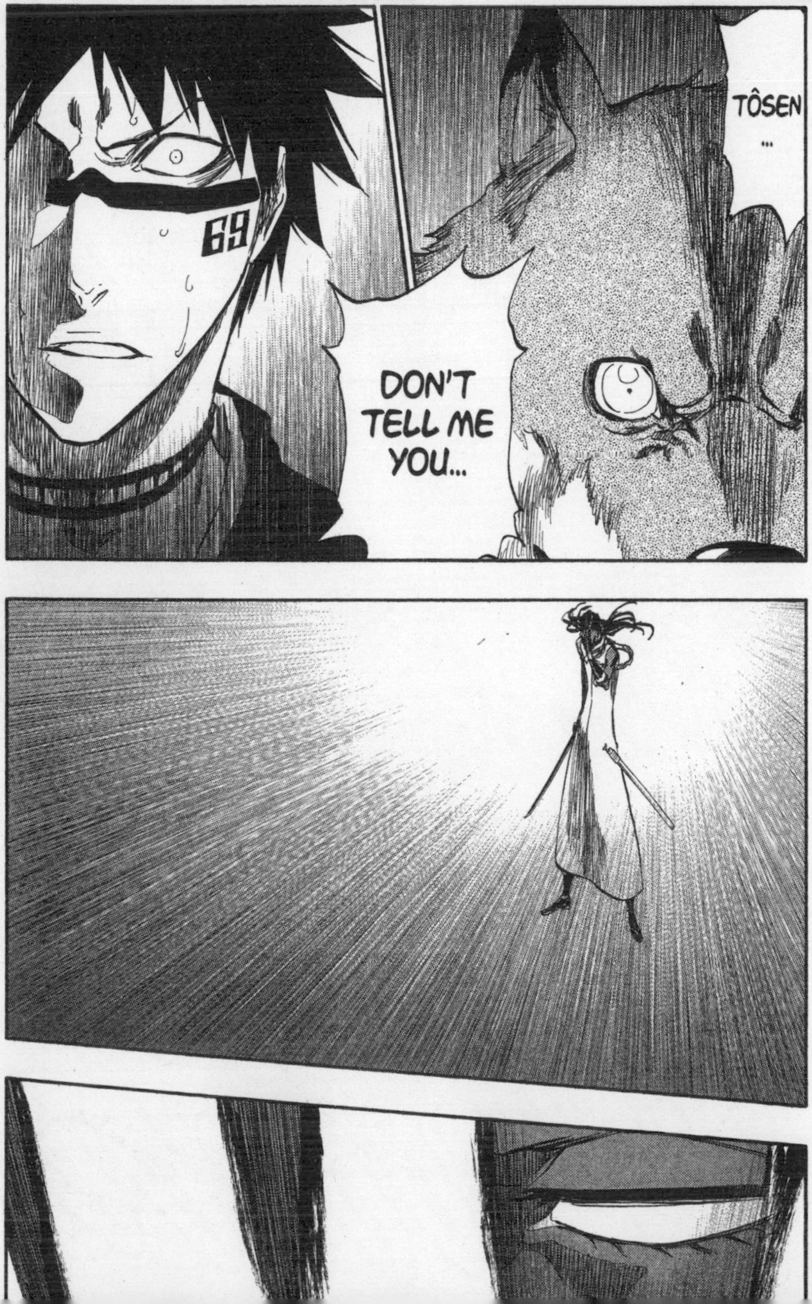
TÔSEN
...
DON'T TELL ME YOU...

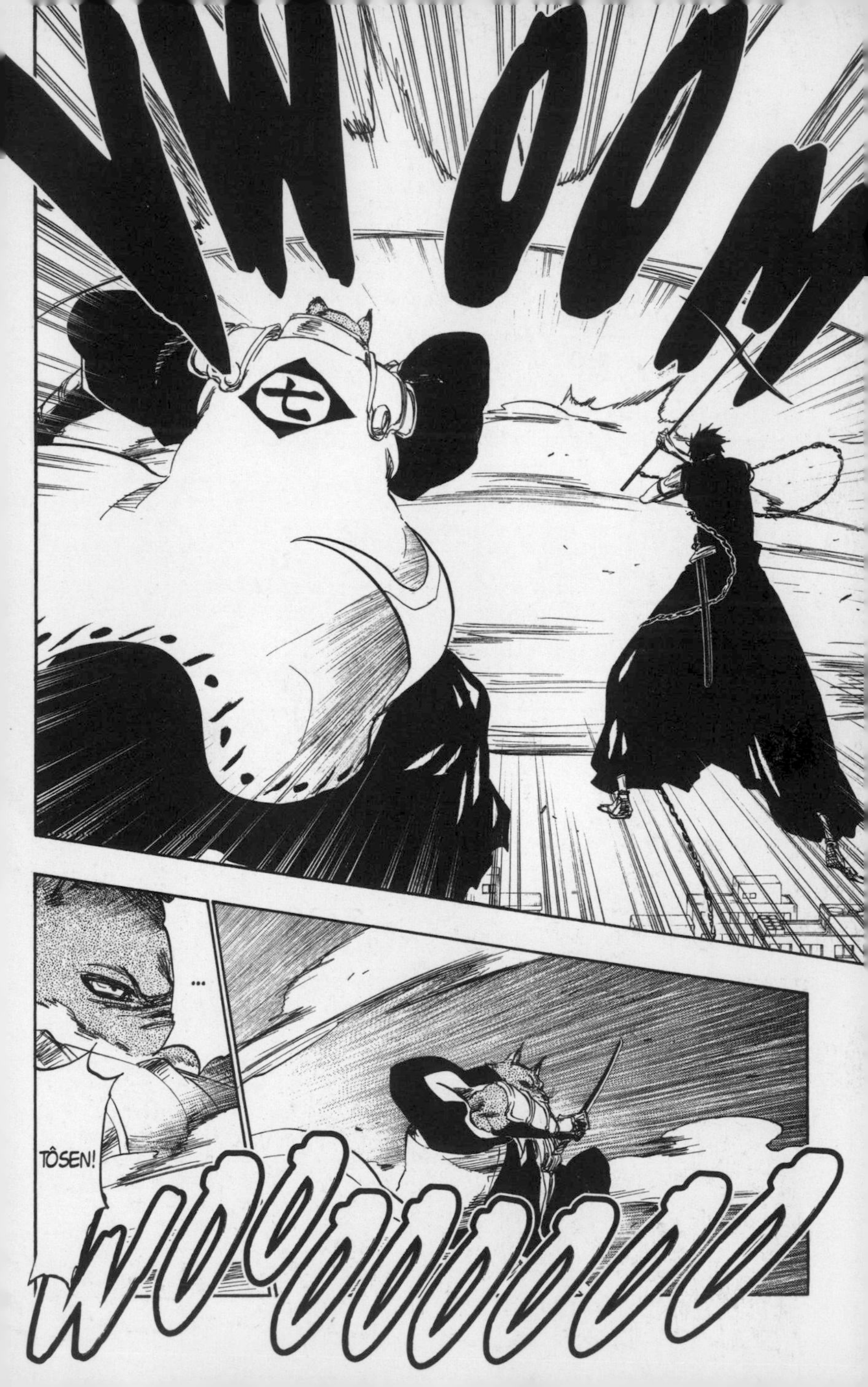
VWOOM
...
TÔSEN!
WOOMMMMMM

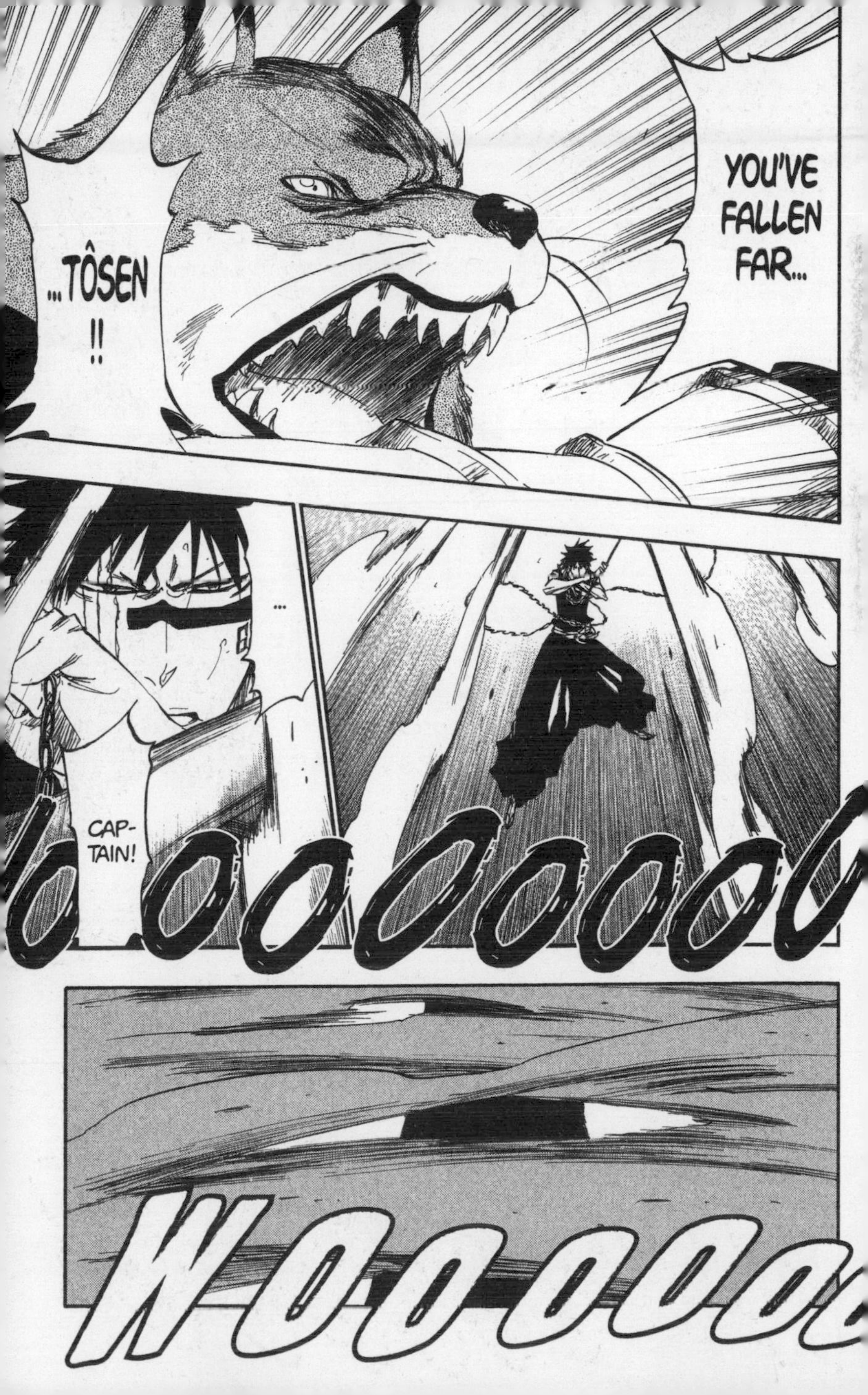
YOU'VE FALLEN FAR...
...TÔSEN!!
...
CAP-TAIN!
OOOOOOO
WOOOO

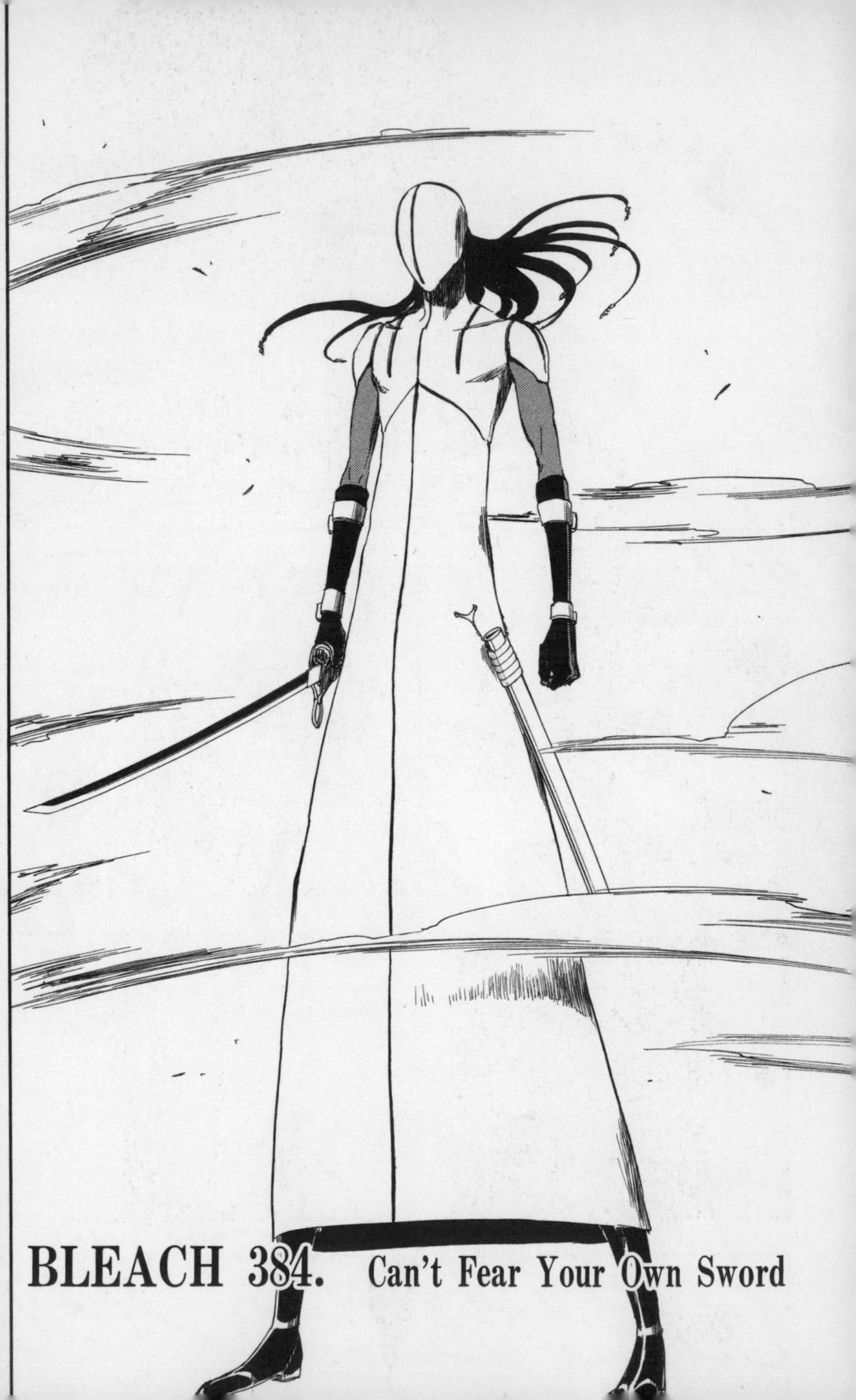
BLEACH 384. Can't Fear Your Own Sword

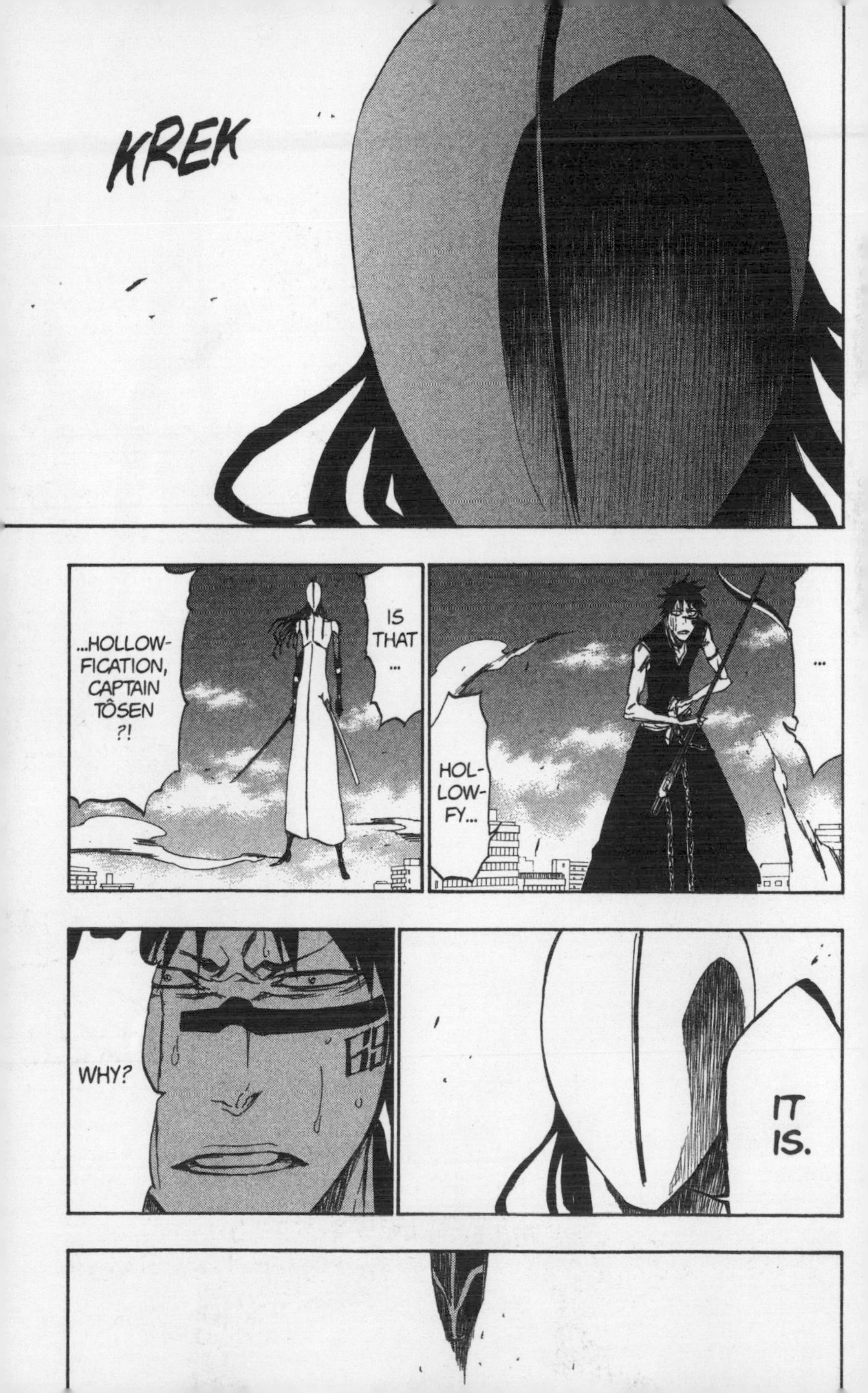
KREK
...
HOL-LOW-FY...
IS THAT ...
...HOLLOW-FICATION, CAPTAIN TÔSEN ?!
IT IS.
WHY?

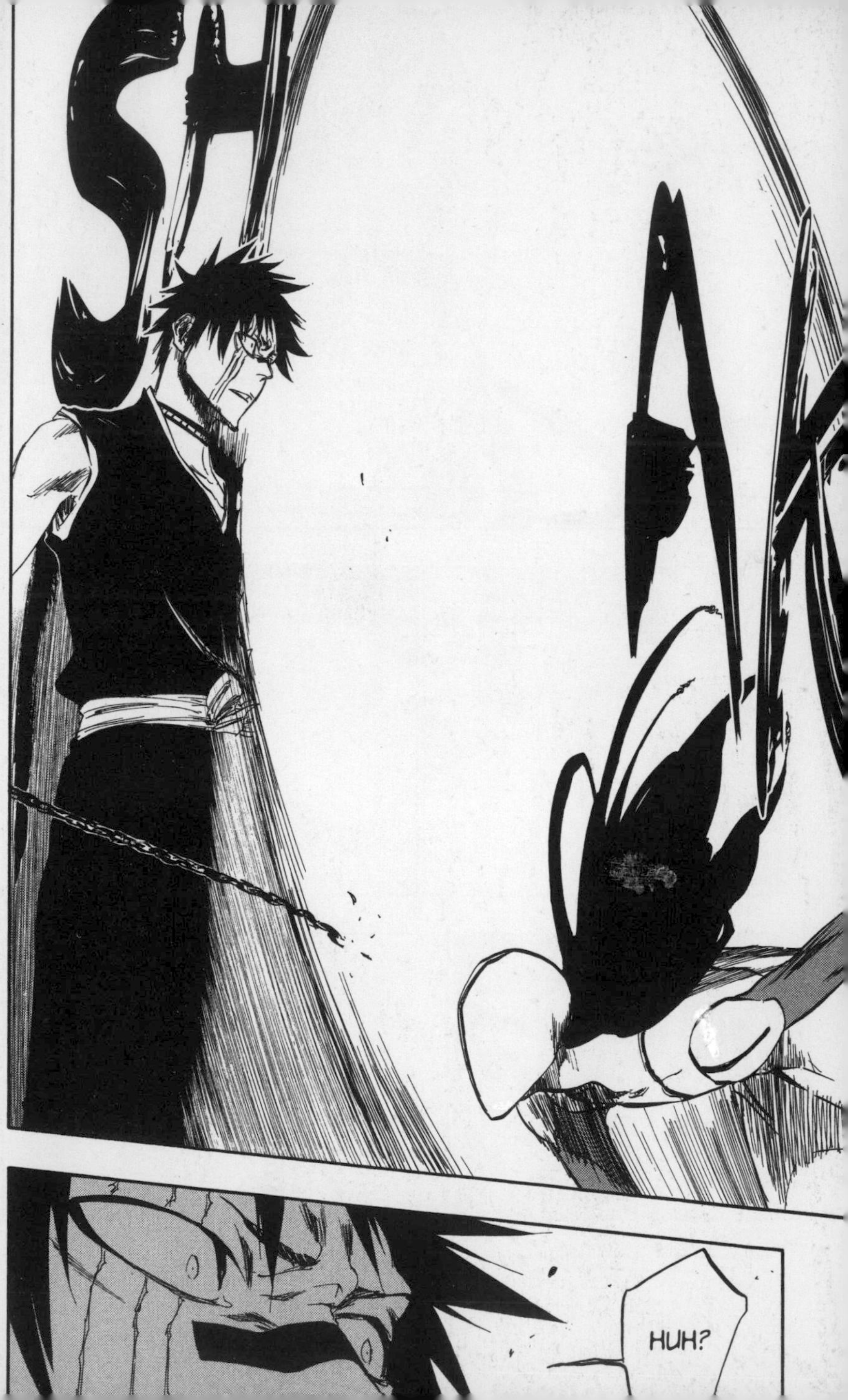
HUH?

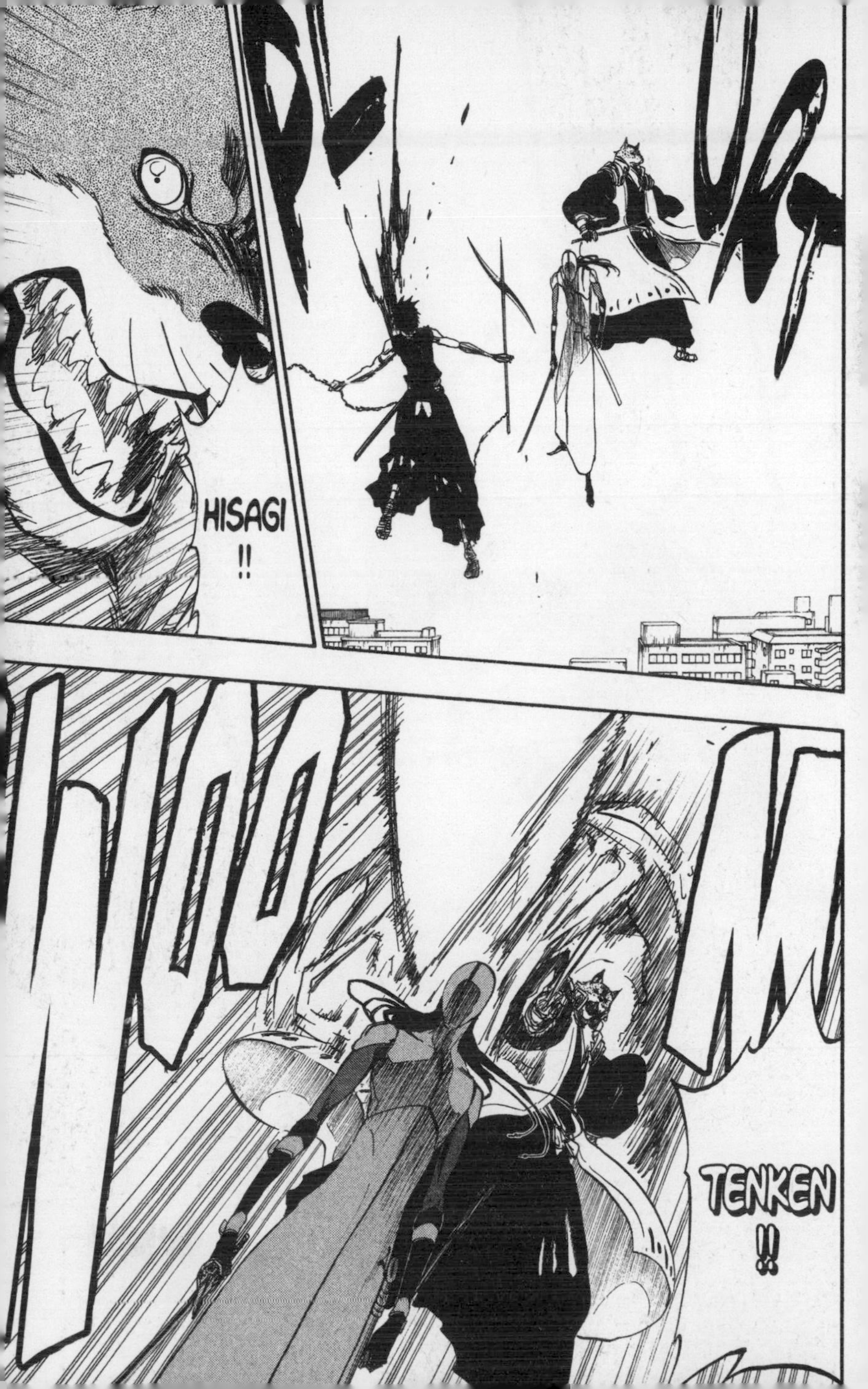
HISAGI !!
TENKEN !!

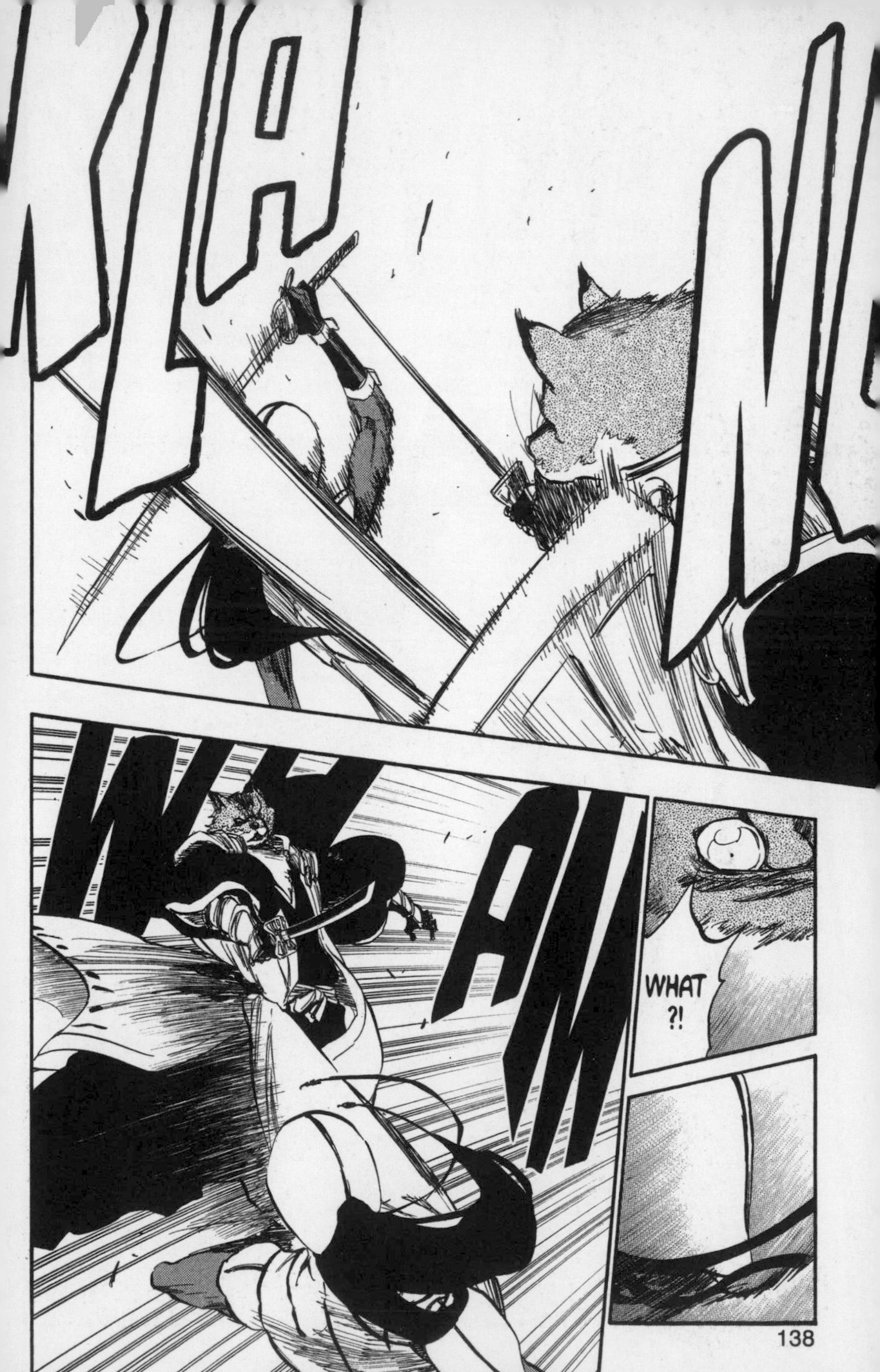
WHAT ?!

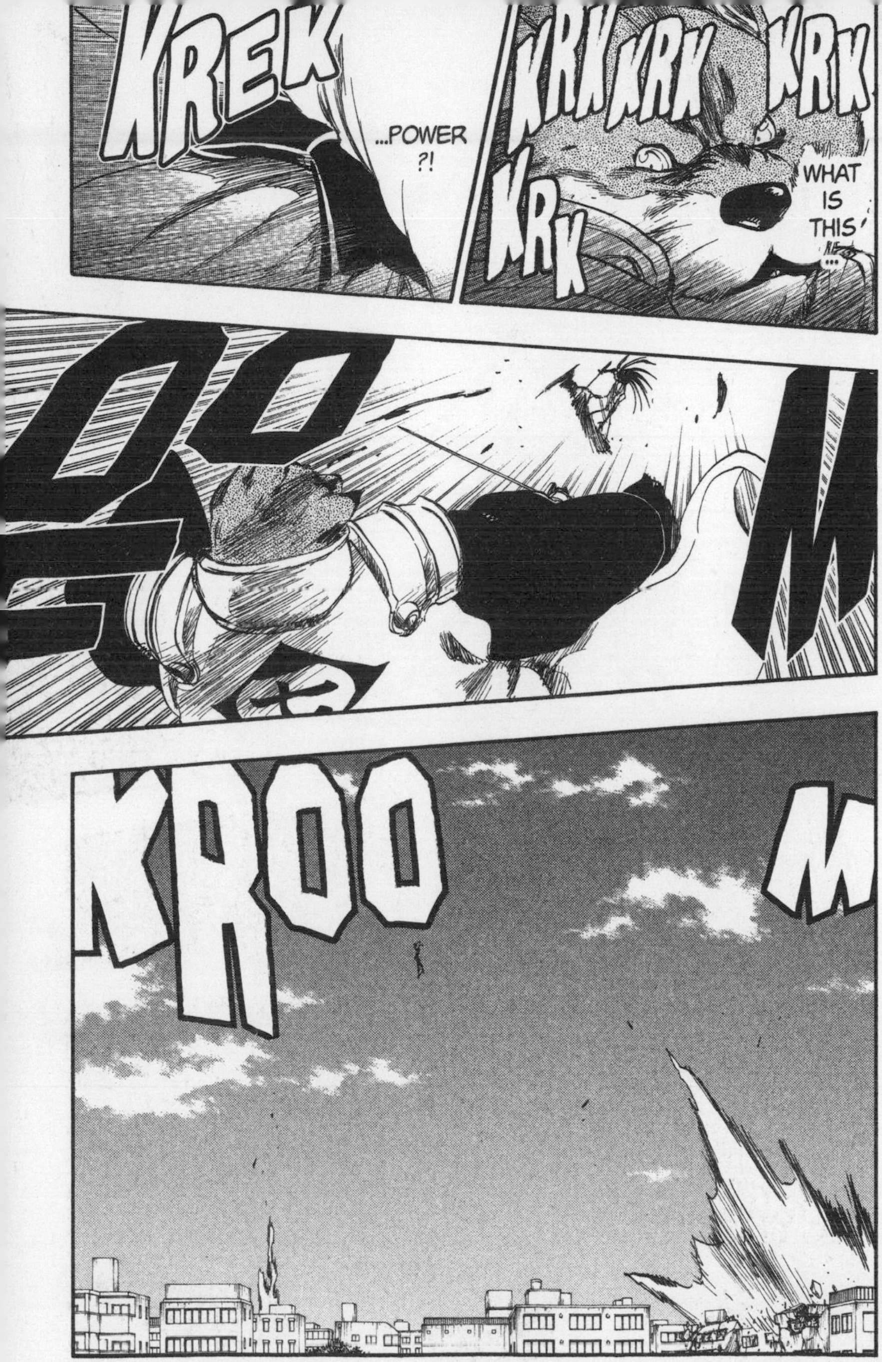
KRK KRK KRK
WHAT IS THIS...
KRK
KREK
...POWER ?!
KROOM

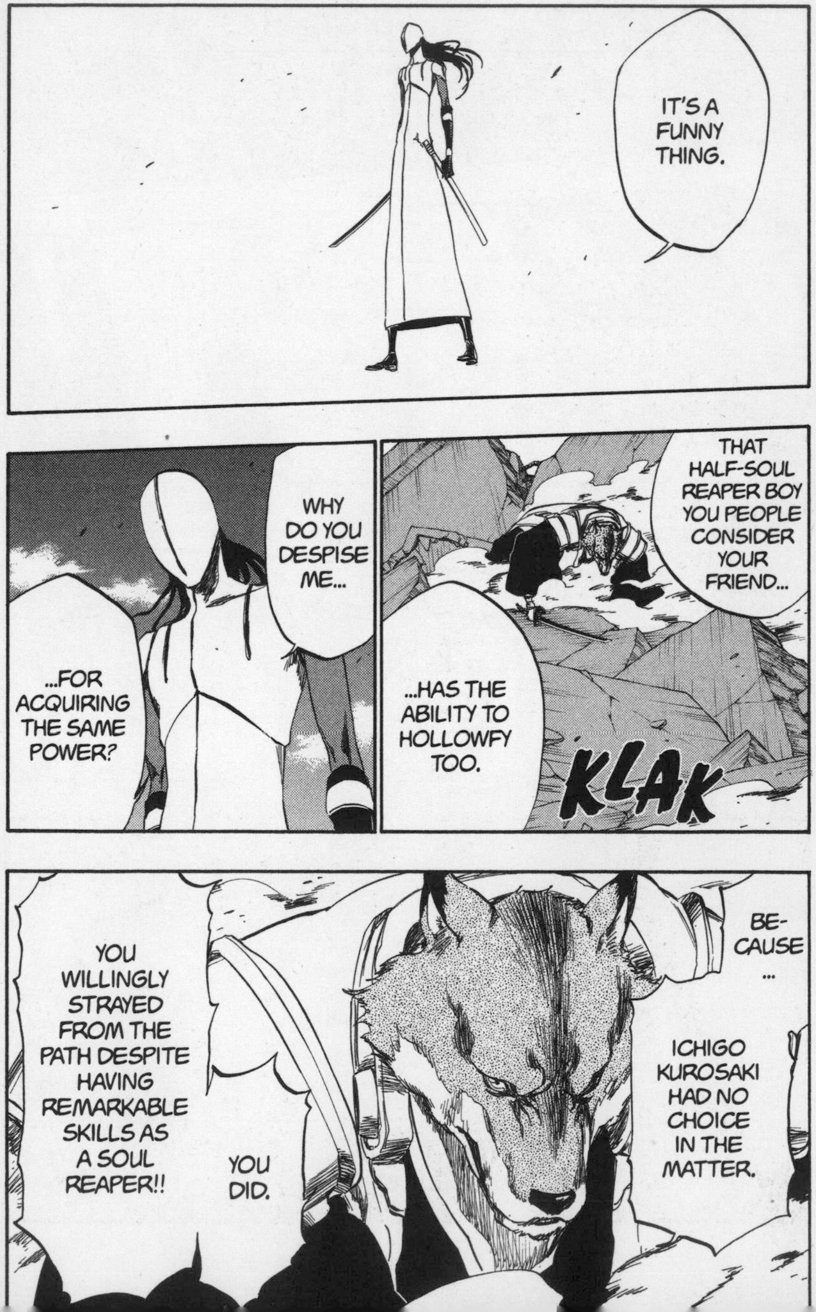
IT'S A FUNNY THING.
THAT HALF-SOUL REAPER BOY YOU PEOPLE CONSIDER YOUR FRIEND...
...HAS THE ABILITY TO HOLLOWFY TOO.
KLAK
WHY DO YOU DESPISE ME...
...FOR ACQUIRING THE SAME POWER?
BE-CAUSE...
ICHIGO KUROSAKI HAD NO CHOICE IN THE MATTER.
YOU DID.
YOU WILLINGLY STRAYED FROM THE PATH DESPITE HAVING REMARKABLE SKILLS AS A SOUL REAPER!!

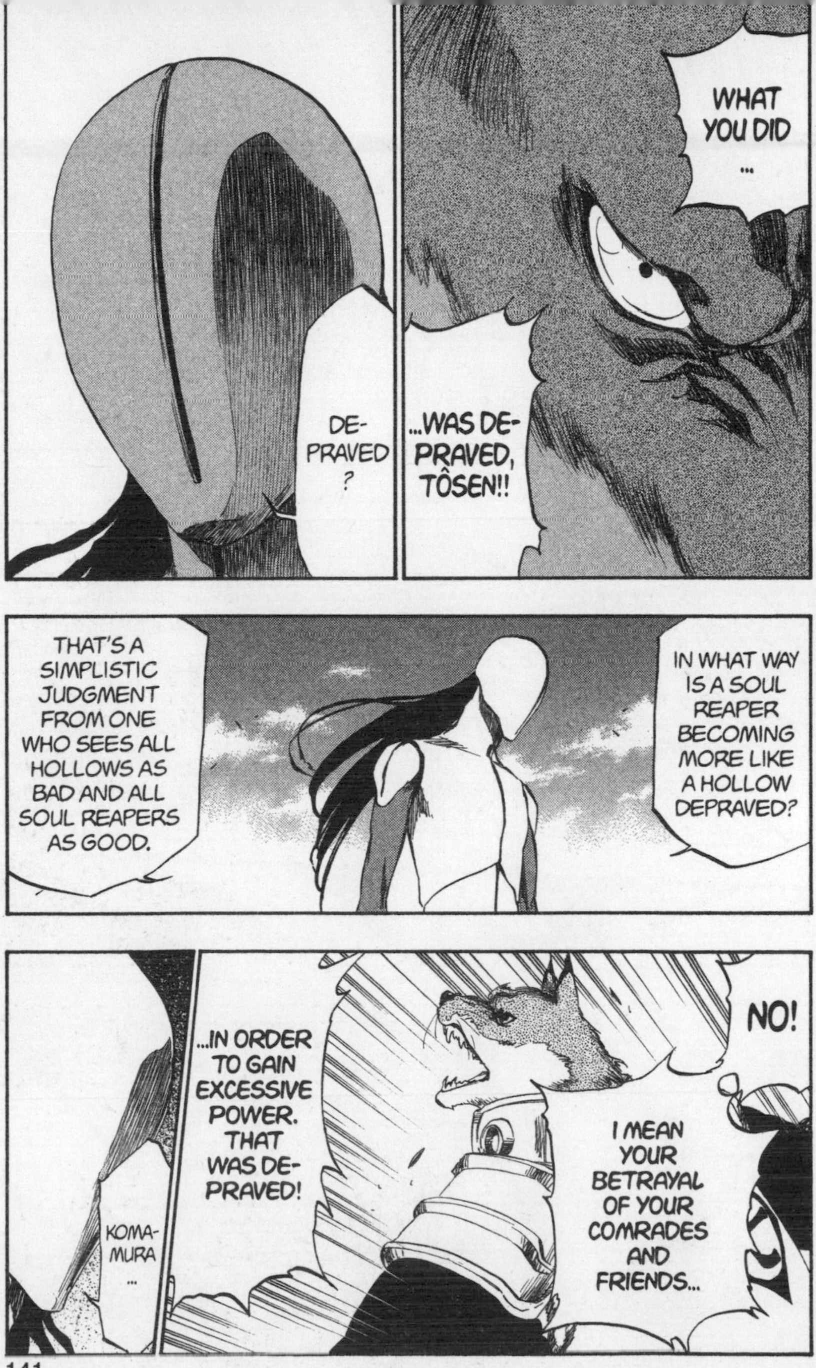
WHAT YOU DID ...
...WAS DEPRAVED, TÔSEN!!
DEPRAVED?
IN WHAT WAY IS A SOUL REAPER BECOMING MORE LIKE A HOLLOW DEPRAVED?
THAT'S A SIMPLISTIC JUDGMENT FROM ONE WHO SEES ALL HOLLOWS AS BAD AND ALL SOUL REAPERS AS GOOD.
NO!
I MEAN YOUR BETRAYAL OF YOUR COMRADES AND FRIENDS...
...IN ORDER TO GAIN EXCESSIVE POWER. THAT WAS DEPRAVED!
KOMAMURA ...

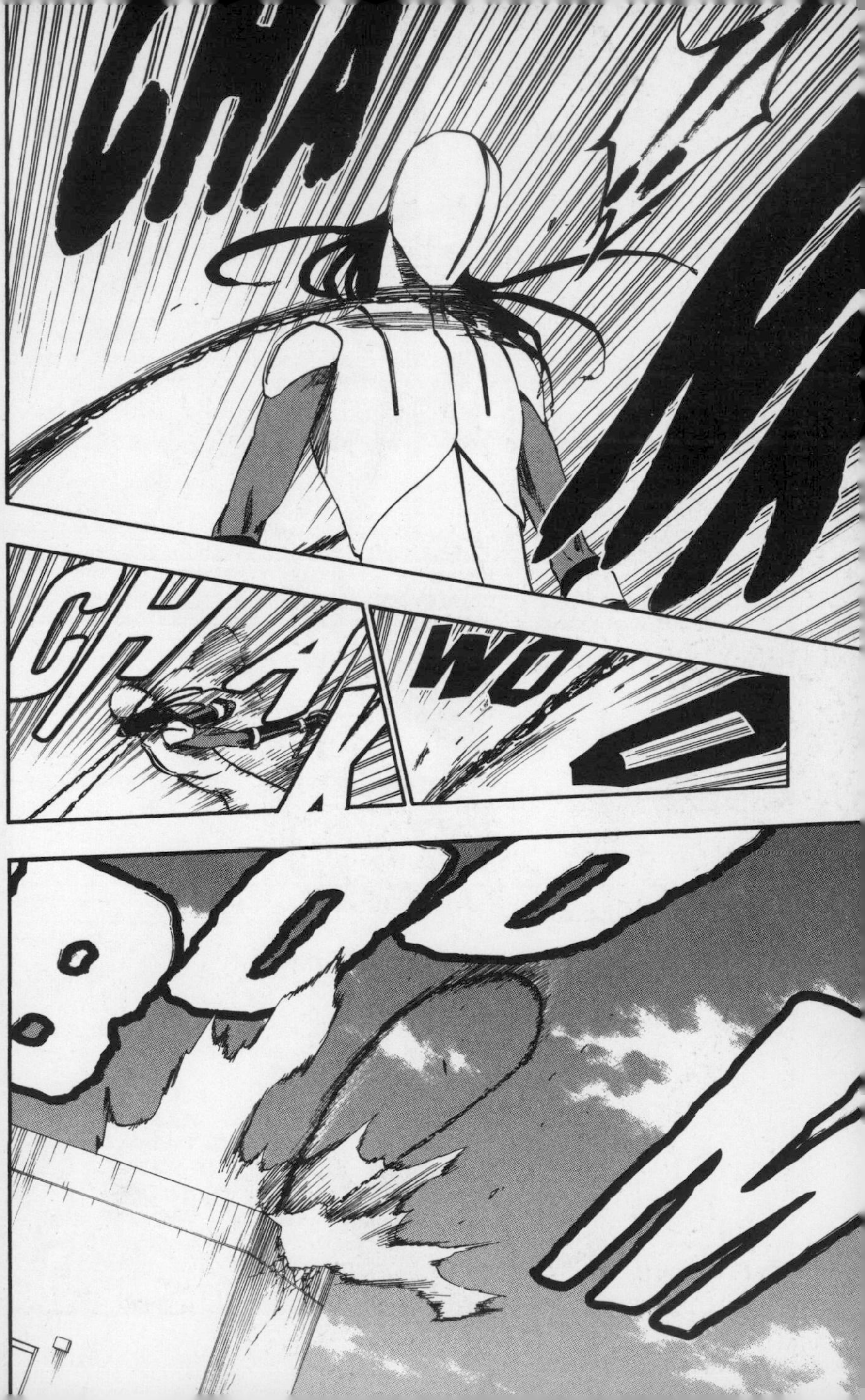
CHA
WO
CHA

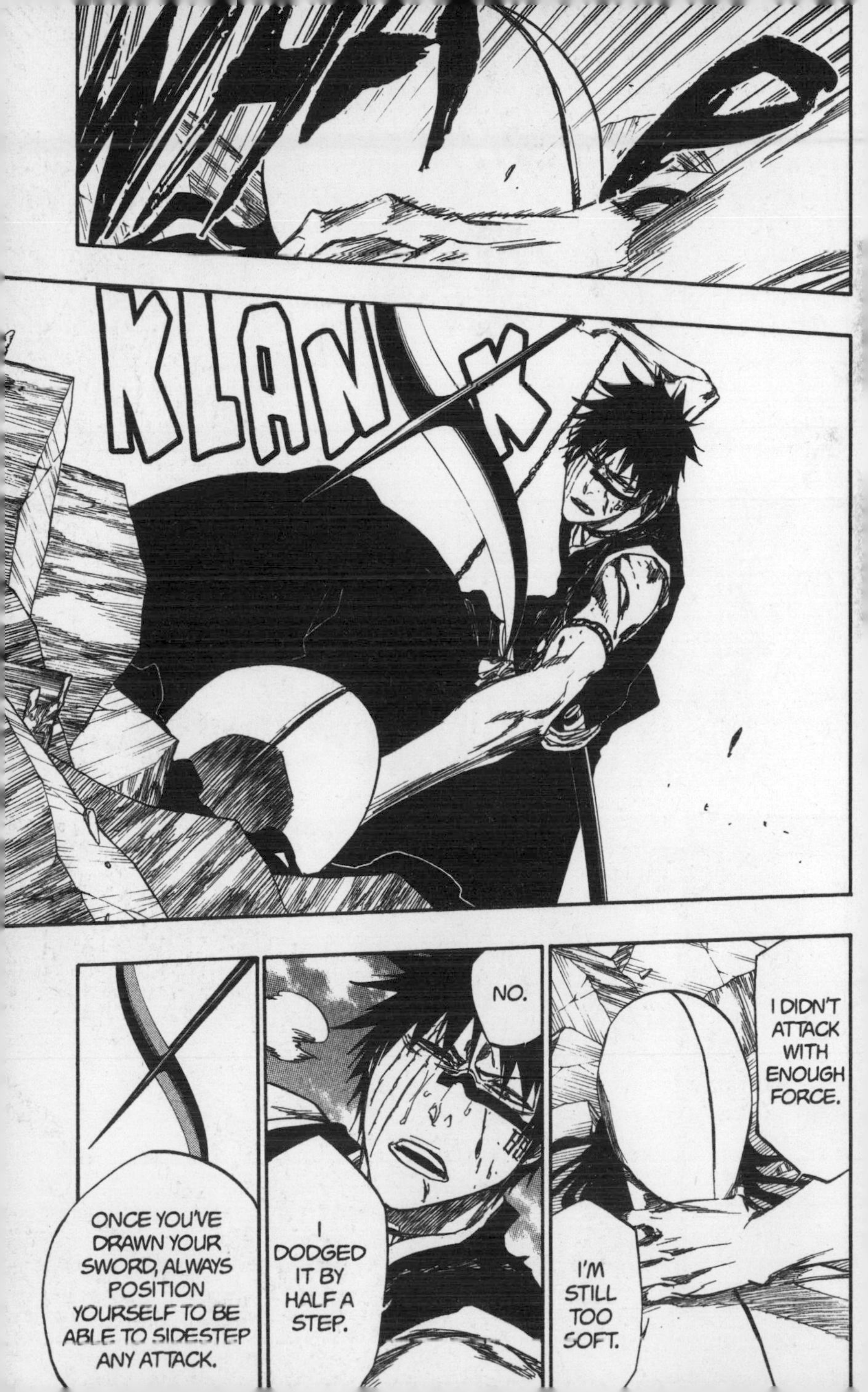
KLANK
I DIDN'T ATTACK WITH ENOUGH FORCE.
I'M STILL TOO SOFT.
NO.
I DODGED IT BY HALF A STEP.
ONCE YOU'VE DRAWN YOUR SWORD, ALWAYS POSITION YOURSELF TO BE ABLE TO SIDESTEP ANY ATTACK.

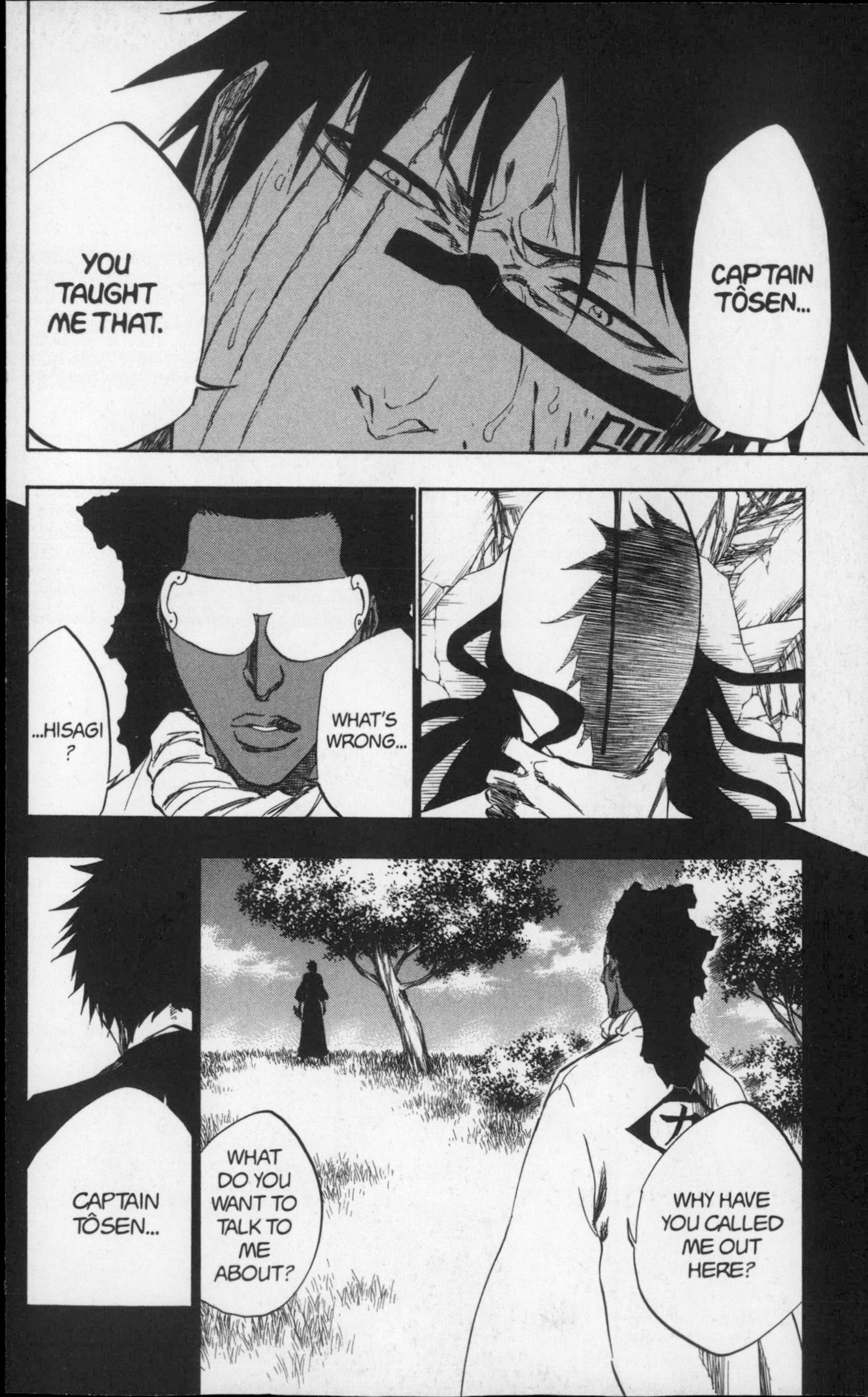
CAPTAIN TÔSEN...
YOU TAUGHT ME THAT.
WHAT'S WRONG...
...HISAGI ?
WHY HAVE YOU CALLED ME OUT HERE?
WHAT DO YOU WANT TO TALK TO ME ABOUT?
CAPTAIN TÔSEN...

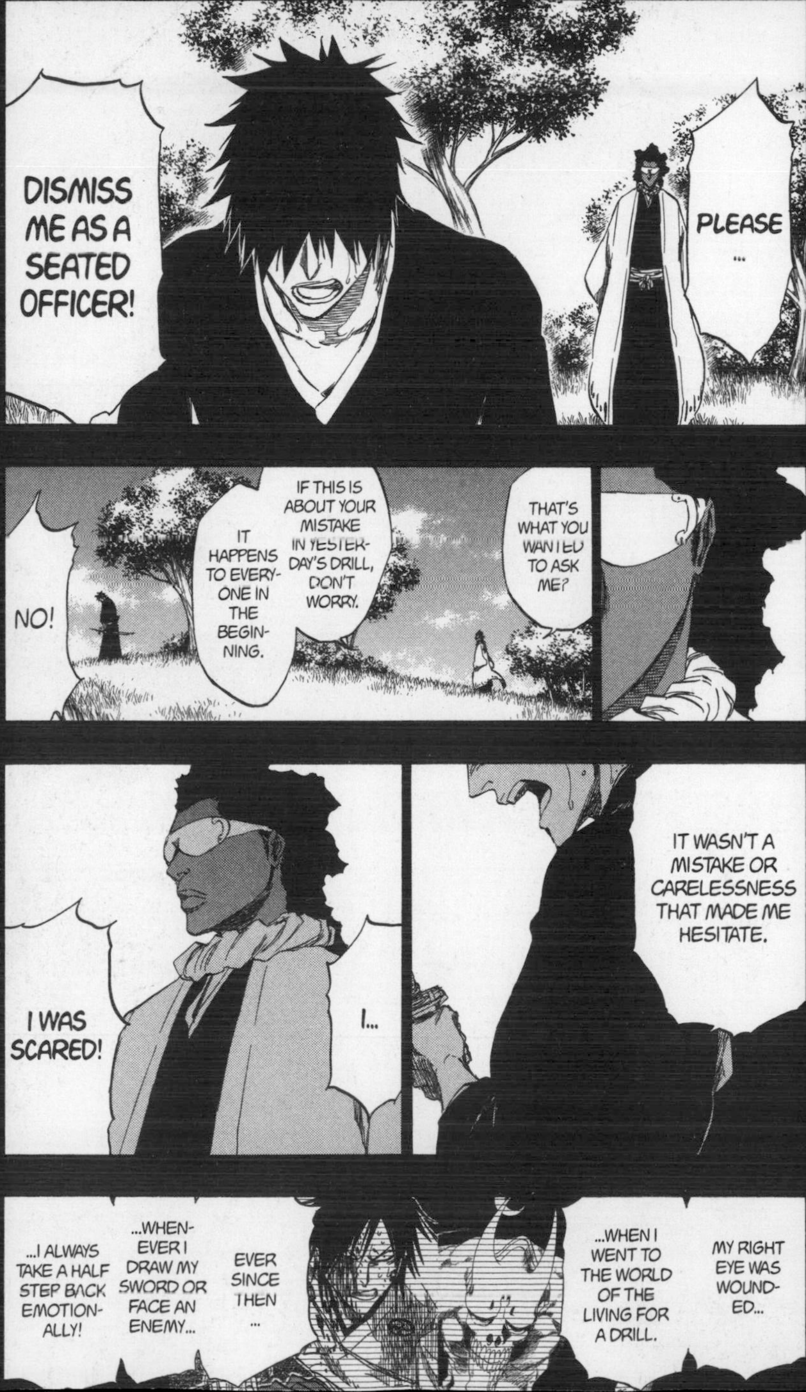
PLEASE ...
DISMISS ME AS A SEATED OFFICER!
THAT'S WHAT YOU WANTED TO ASK ME?
IF THIS IS ABOUT YOUR MISTAKE IN YESTERDAY'S DRILL, DON'T WORRY.
IT HAPPENS TO EVERYONE IN THE BEGINNING.
NO!
IT WASN'T A MISTAKE OR CARELESSNESS THAT MADE ME HESITATE.
I...
I WAS SCARED!
MY RIGHT EYE WAS WOUNDED...
...WHEN I WENT TO THE WORLD OF THE LIVING FOR A DRILL.
EVER SINCE THEN ...
...WHENEVER I DRAW MY SWORD OR FACE AN ENEMY...
...I ALWAYS TAKE A HALF STEP BACK EMOTIONALLY!

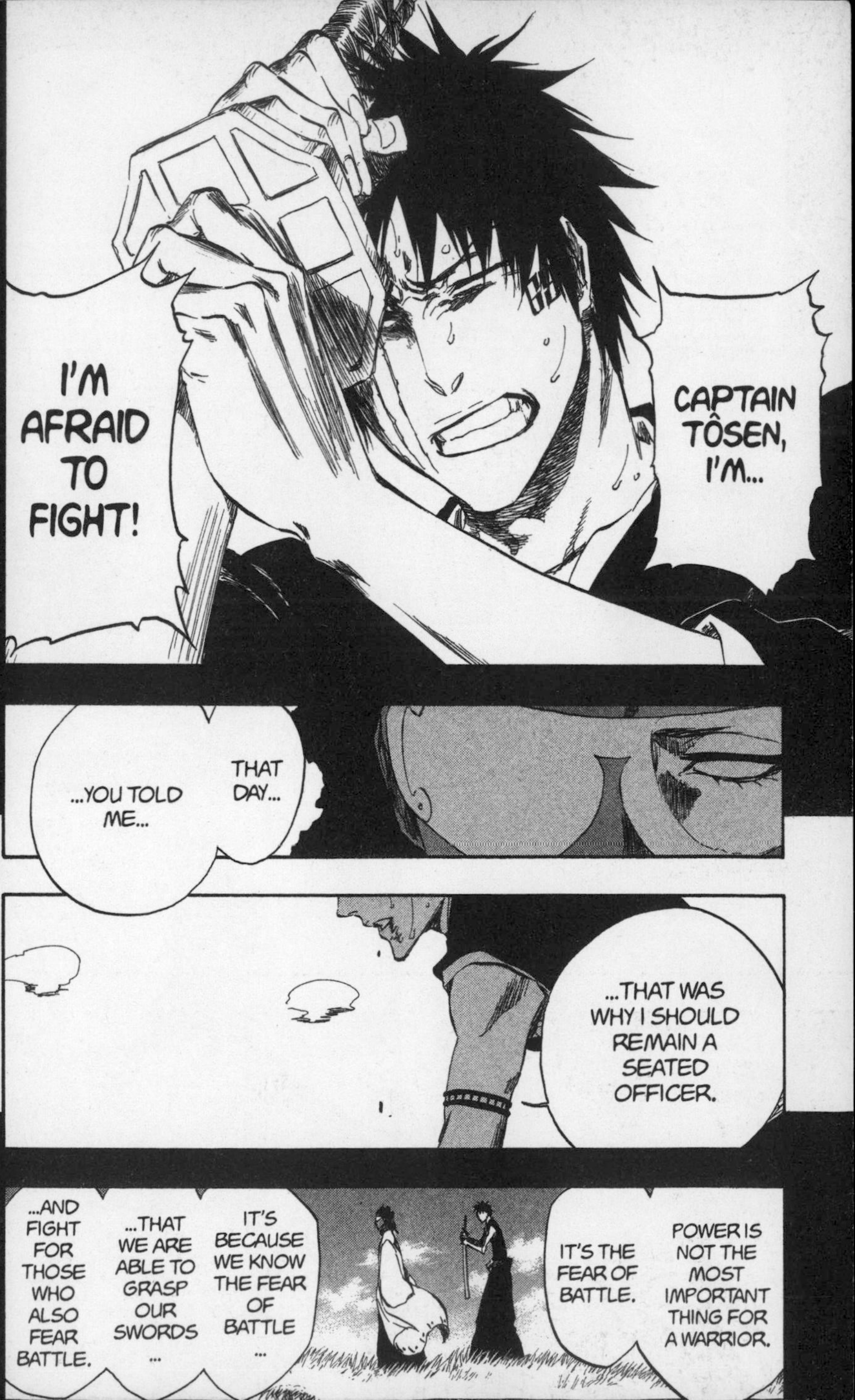
CAPTAIN TÔSEN, I'M...
I'M AFRAID TO FIGHT!
THAT DAY...
...YOU TOLD ME...
...THAT WAS WHY I SHOULD REMAIN A SEATED OFFICER.
POWER IS NOT THE MOST IMPORTANT THING FOR A WARRIOR.
IT'S THE FEAR OF BATTLE.
IT'S BECAUSE WE KNOW THE FEAR OF BATTLE...
...THAT WE ARE ABLE TO GRASP OUR SWORDS...
...AND FIGHT FOR THOSE WHO ALSO FEAR BATTLE.

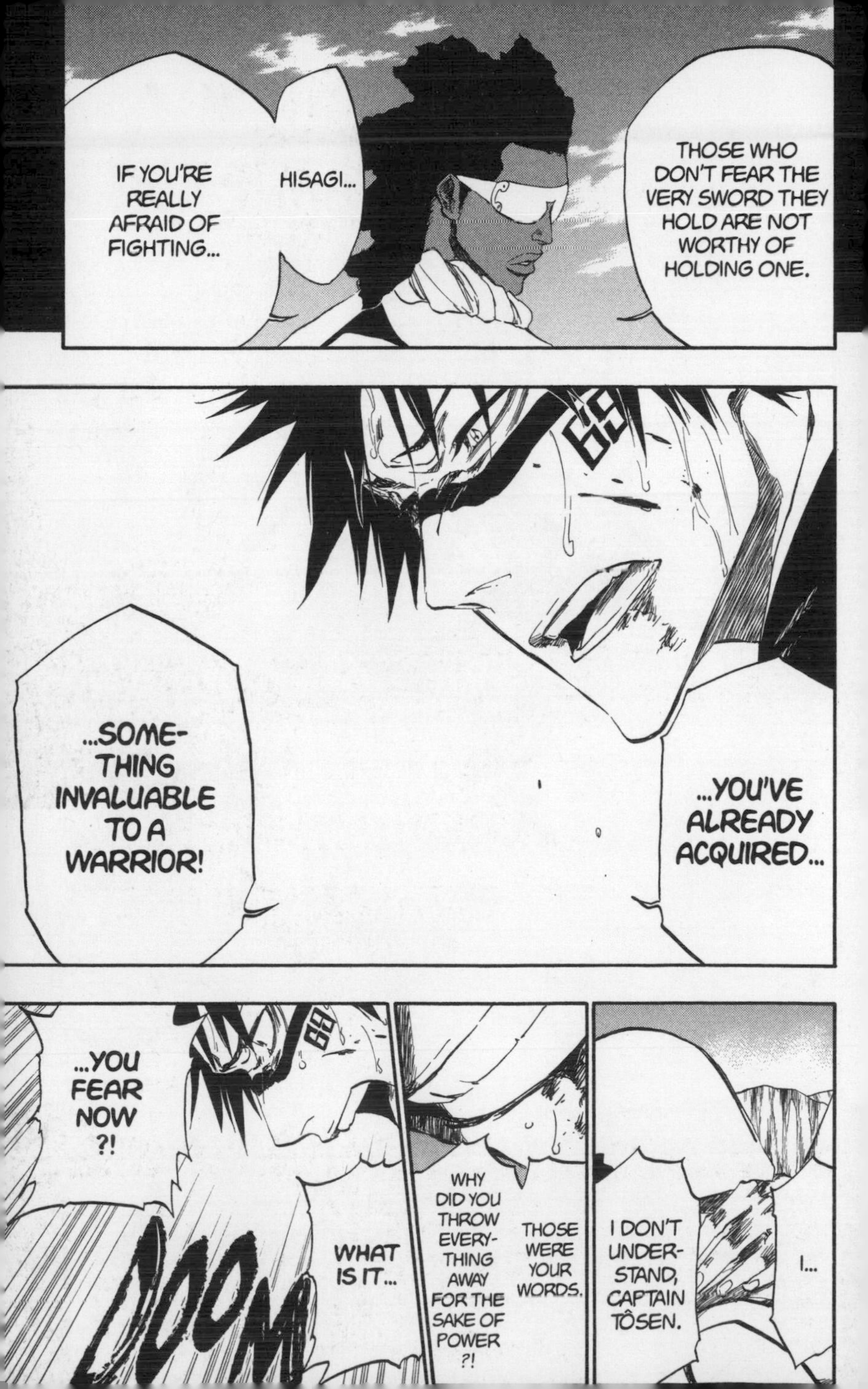
THOSE WHO DON'T FEAR THE VERY SWORD THEY HOLD ARE NOT WORTHY OF HOLDING ONE.
HISAGI...
IF YOU'RE REALLY AFRAID OF FIGHTING...
...YOU'VE ALREADY ACQUIRED...
...SOME-THING INVALUABLE TO A WARRIOR!
I...
I DON'T UNDER-STAND, CAPTAIN TÔSEN.
THOSE WERE YOUR WORDS.
WHY DID YOU THROW EVERY-THING AWAY FOR THE SAKE OF POWER ?!
WHAT IS IT...
...YOU FEAR NOW ?!
DOOM

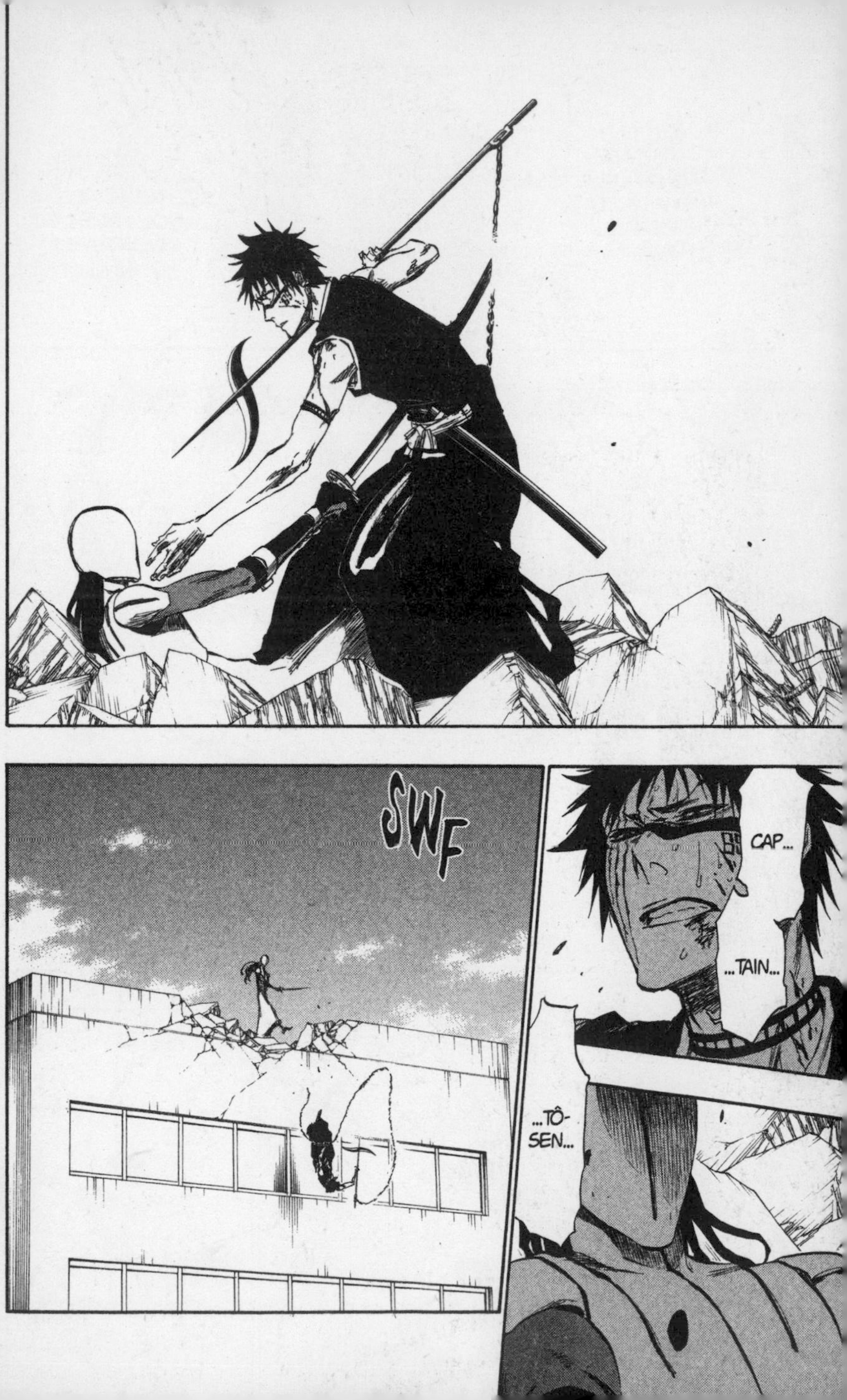
CAP...
...TAIN...
...TÔ-SEN...
SWF

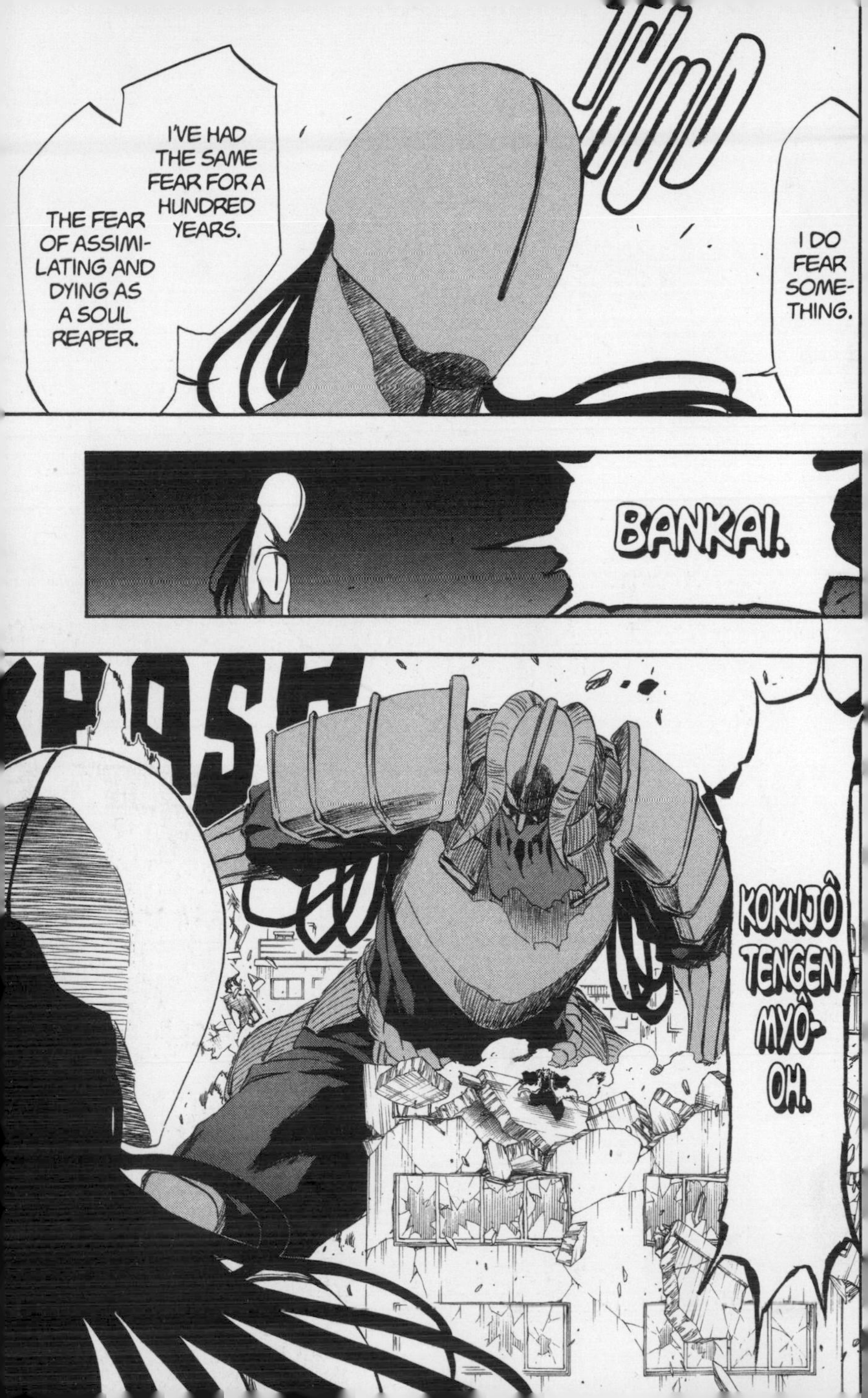
I DO FEAR SOME-THING.
I'VE HAD THE SAME FEAR FOR A HUNDRED YEARS.
THE FEAR OF ASSIMI-LATING AND DYING AS A SOUL REAPER.
BANKAI.
KOKUJÔ TENGEN MYÔ-OH.

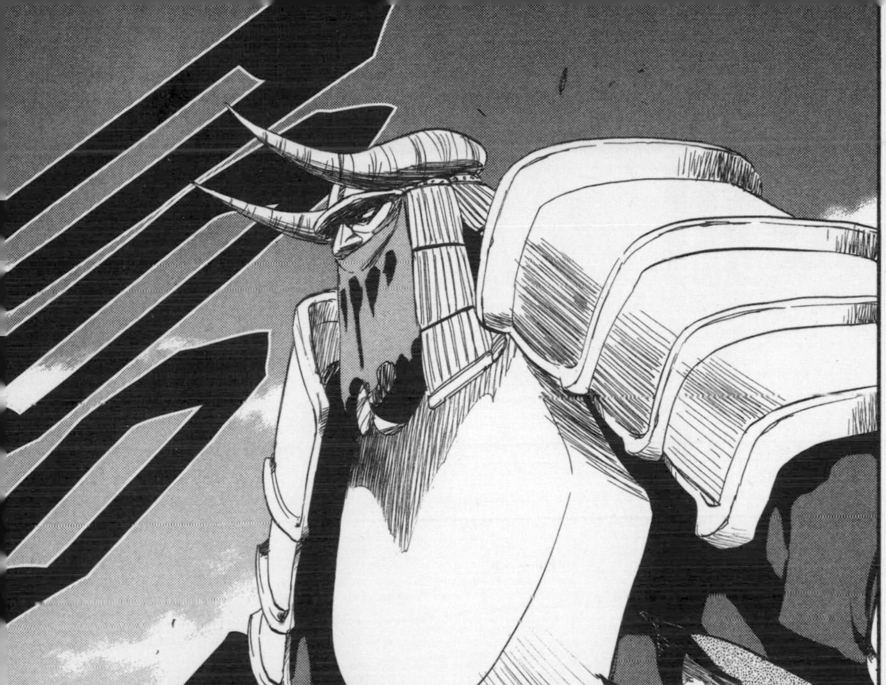

385. Vice It

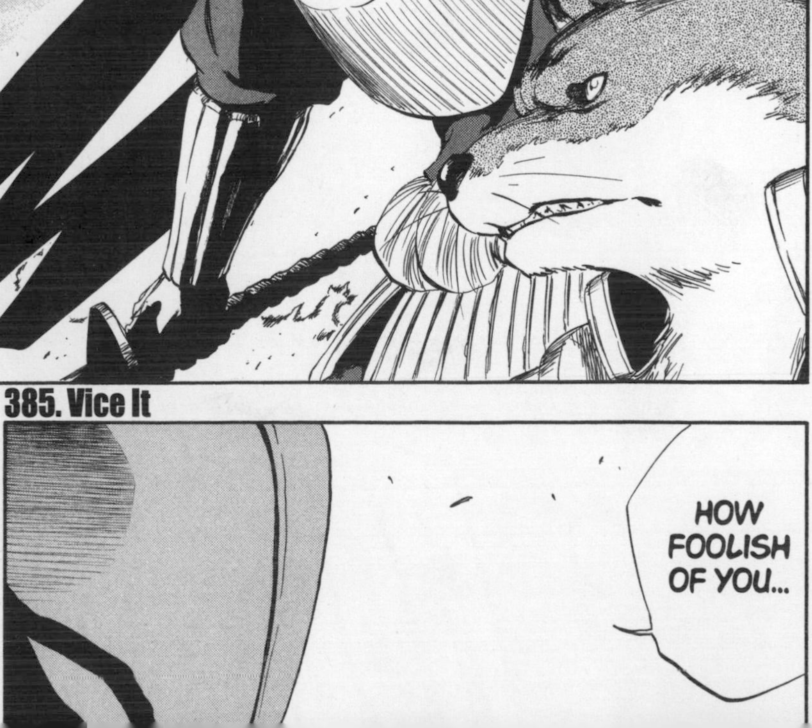
HOW FOOLISH OF YOU...

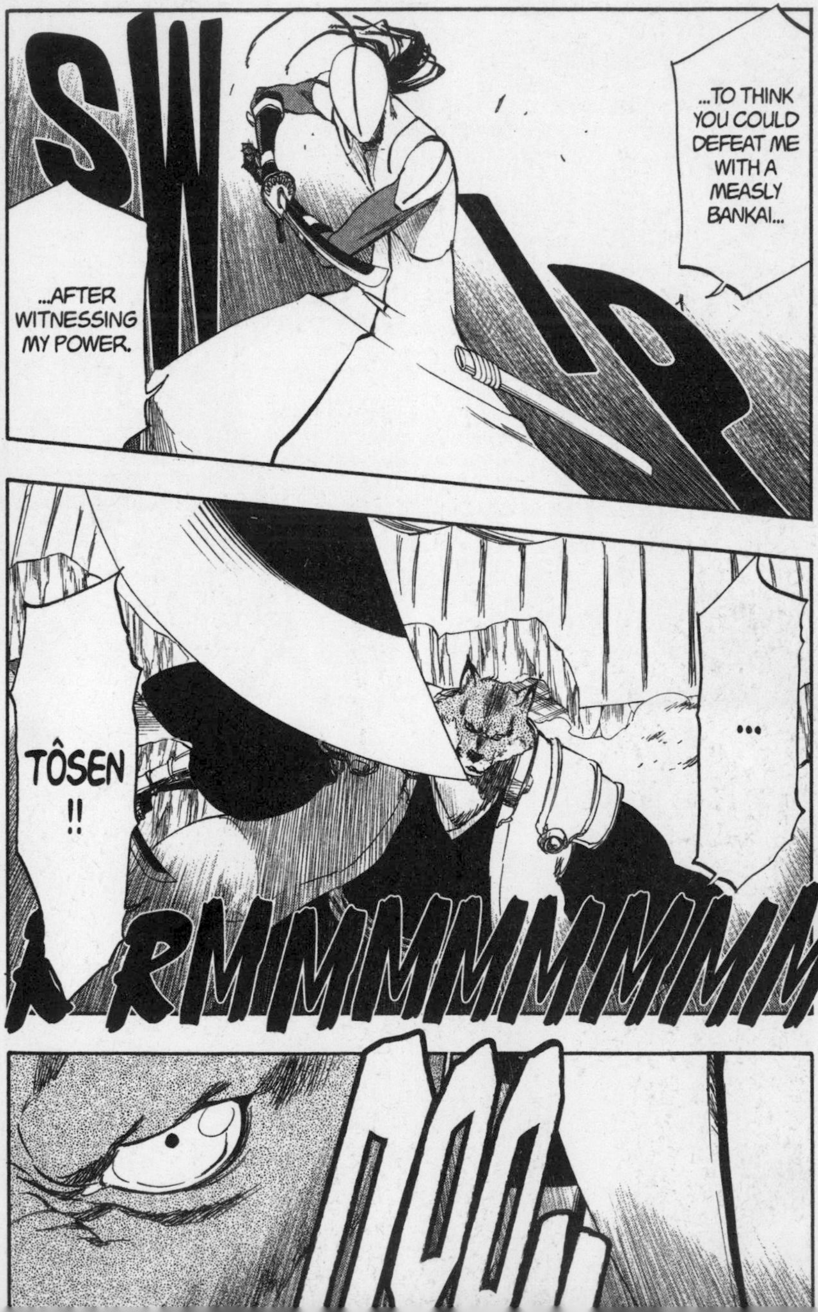
...TO THINK YOU COULD DEFEAT ME WITH A MEASLY BANKAI...
...AFTER WITNESSING MY POWER.
SW
...
TÔSEN !!
RMMMMMMMMMM

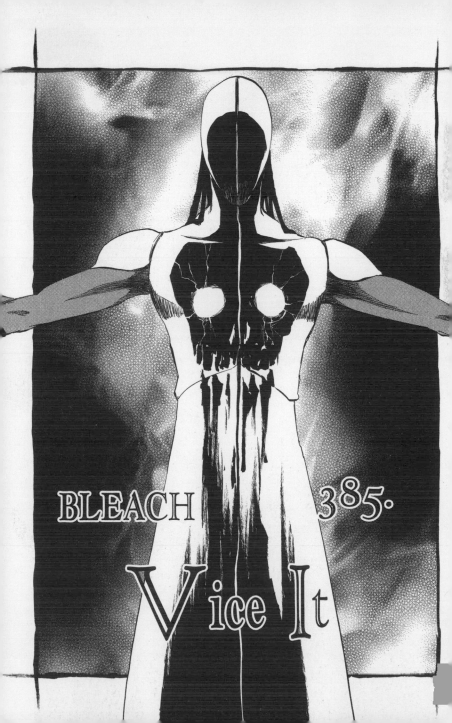

BLEACH 385.

Vice It

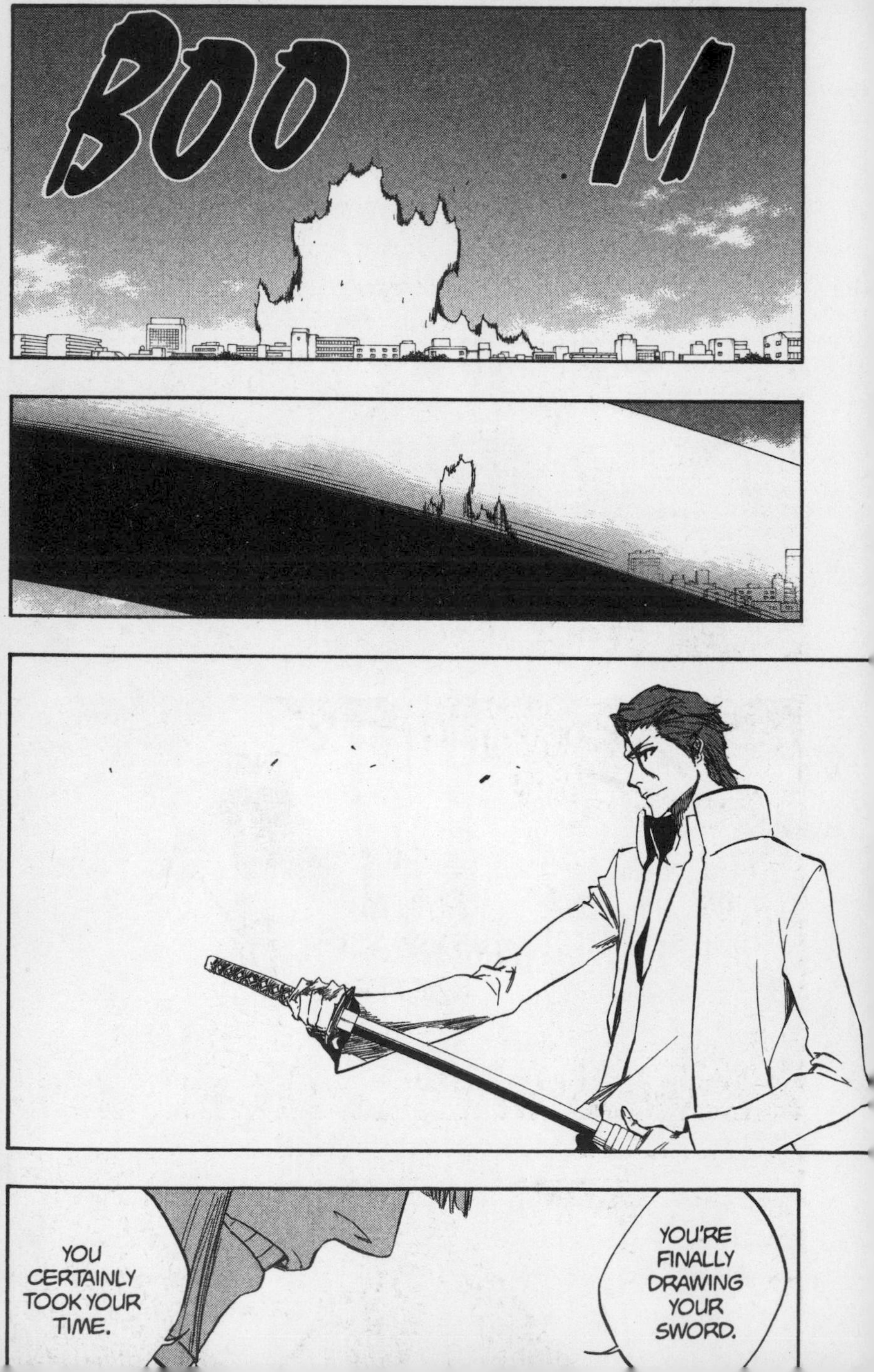
BOOOM
YOU'RE FINALLY DRAWING YOUR SWORD.
YOU CERTAINLY TOOK YOUR TIME.

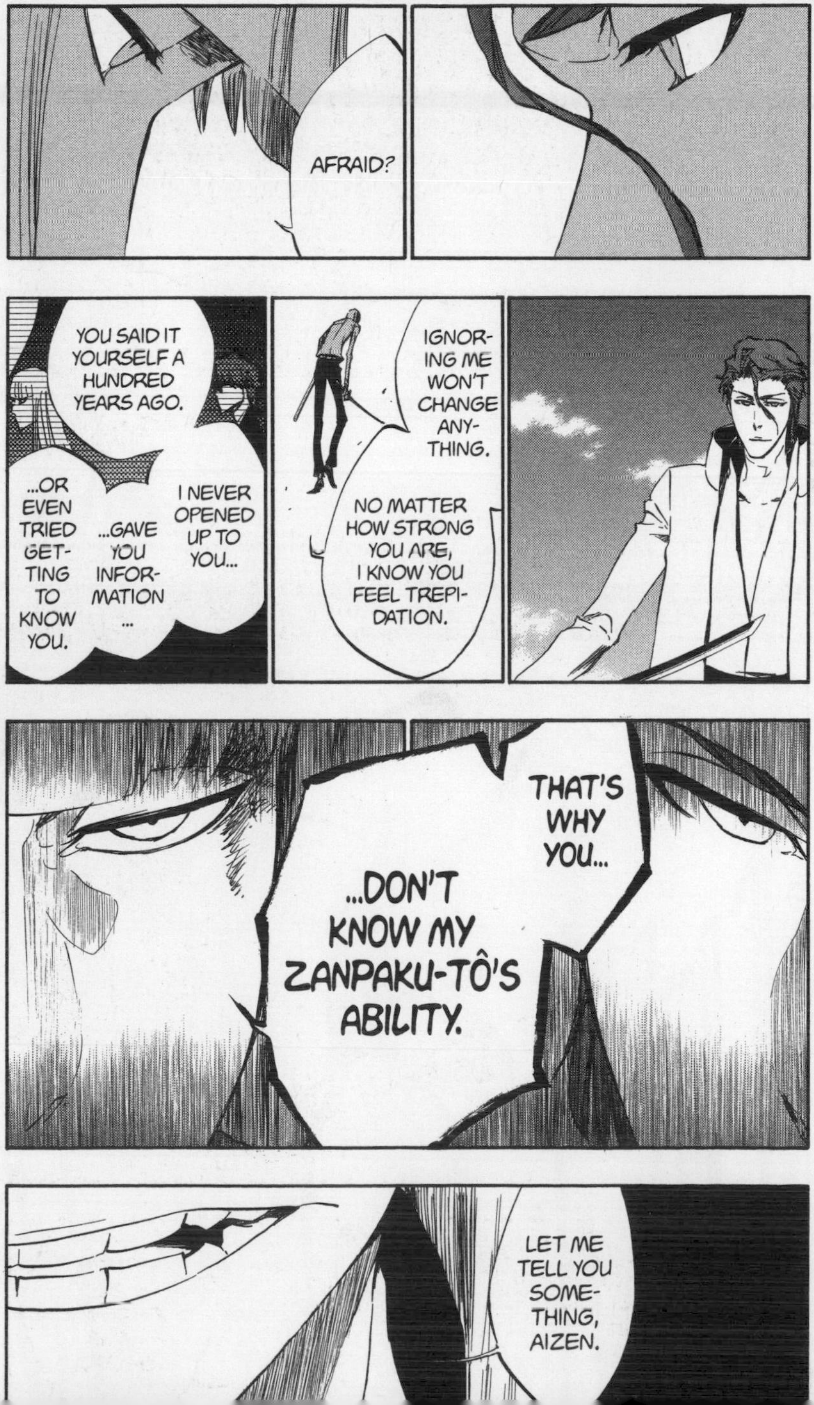
AFRAID?
IGNORING ME WON'T CHANGE ANYTHING.
NO MATTER HOW STRONG YOU ARE, I KNOW YOU FEEL TREPIDATION.
YOU SAID IT YOURSELF A HUNDRED YEARS AGO.
I NEVER OPENED UP TO YOU...
...GAVE YOU INFORMATION...
...OR EVEN TRIED GETTING TO KNOW YOU.
THAT'S WHY YOU...
...DON'T KNOW MY ZANPAKU-TÔ'S ABILITY.
LET ME TELL YOU SOMETHING, AIZEN.

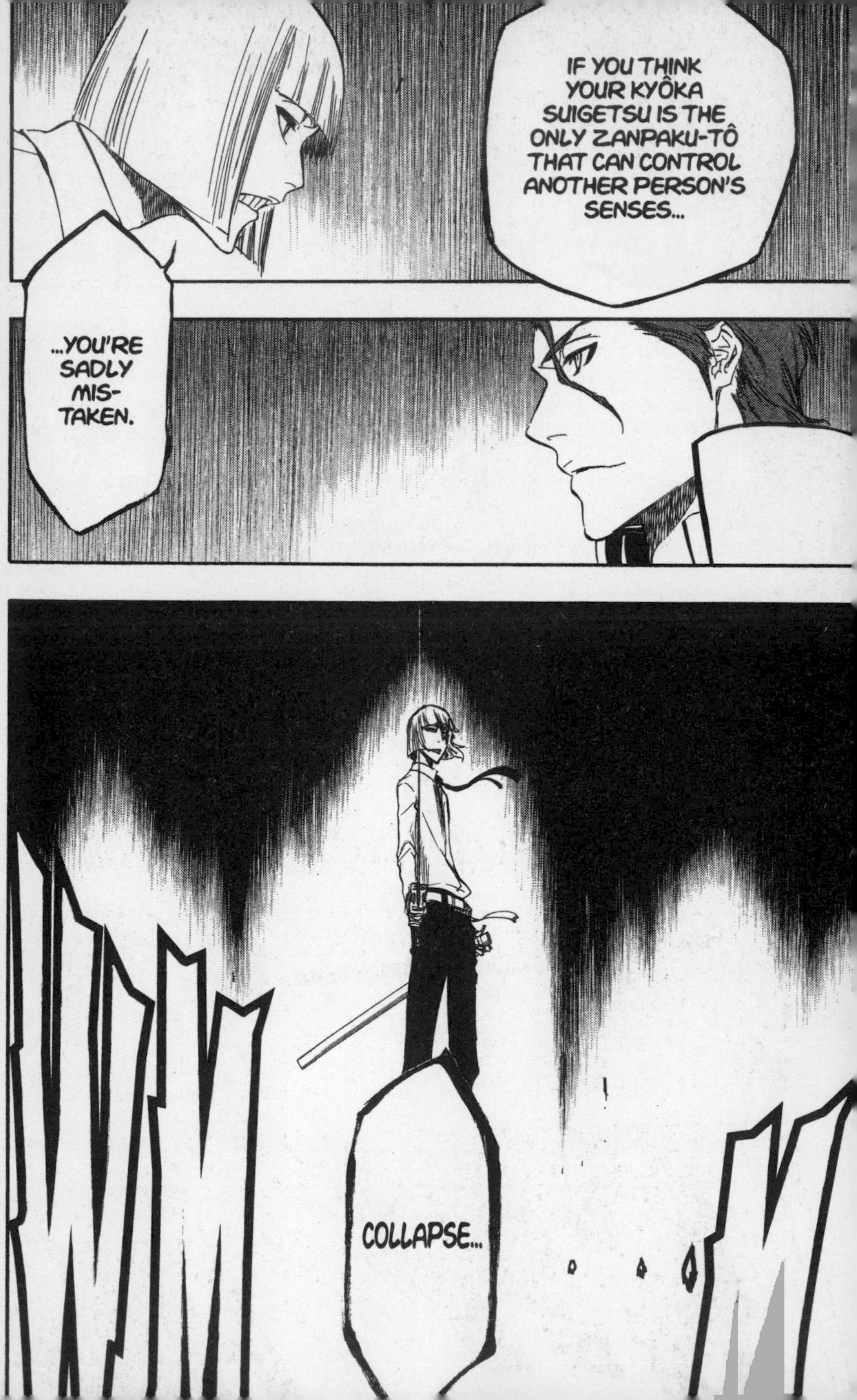
IF YOU THINK YOUR KYÔKA SUIGETSU IS THE ONLY ZANPAKU-TÔ THAT CAN CONTROL ANOTHER PERSON'S SENSES...
...YOU'RE SADLY MIS-TAKEN.
COLLAPSE...

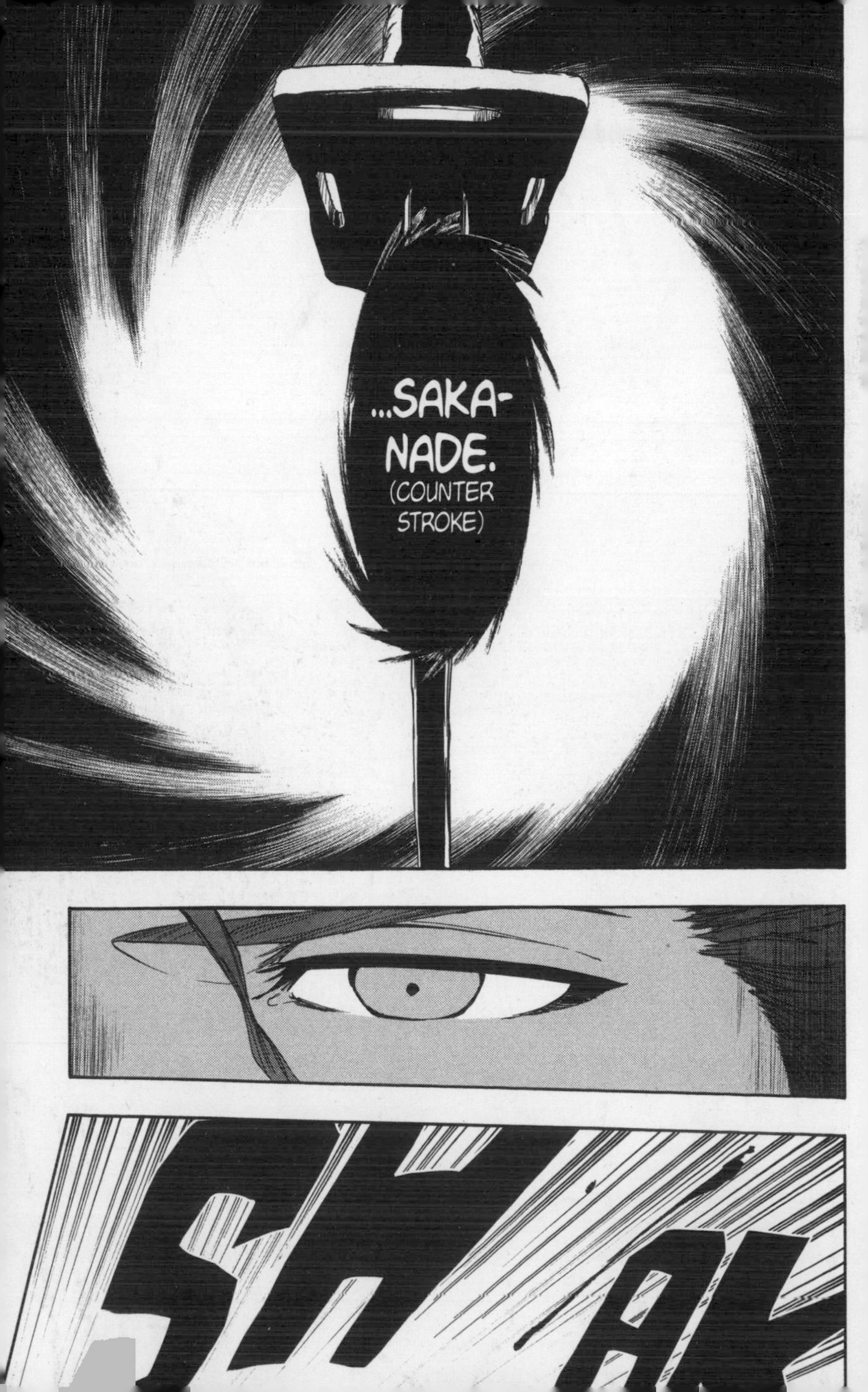
...SAKA-NADE. (COUNTER STROKE)

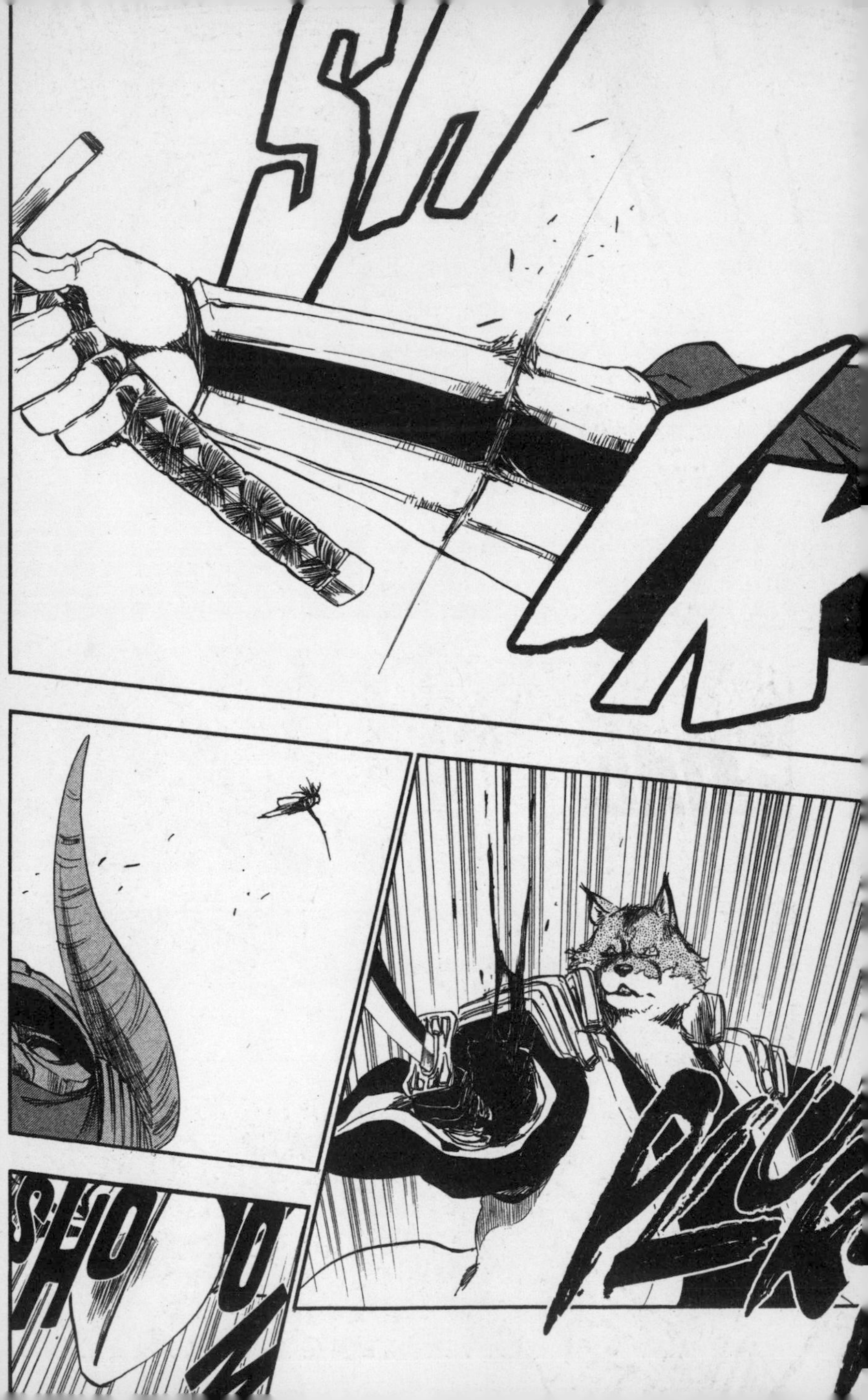
SHOOM

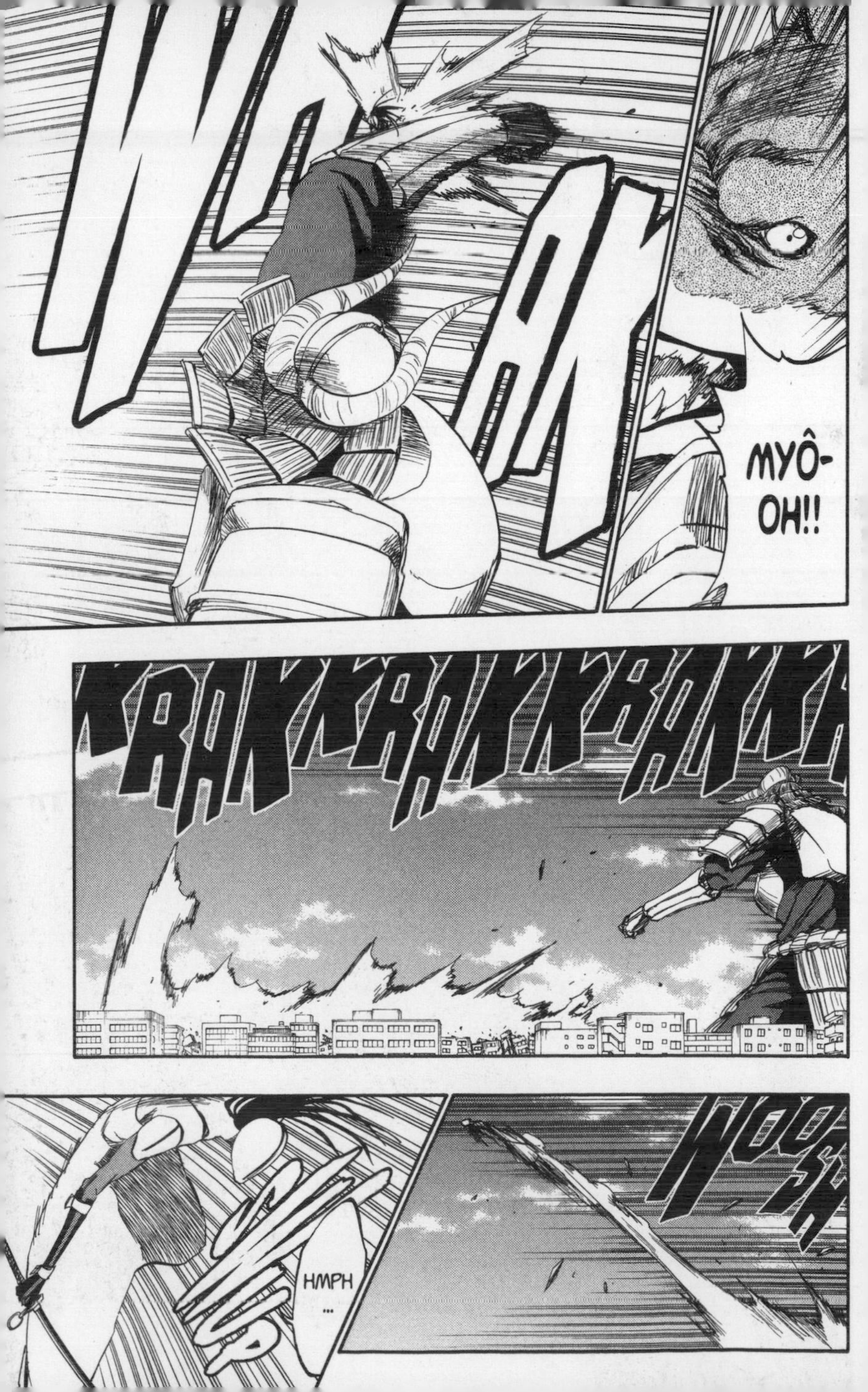

MYÔ-OH!!
HMPH
...

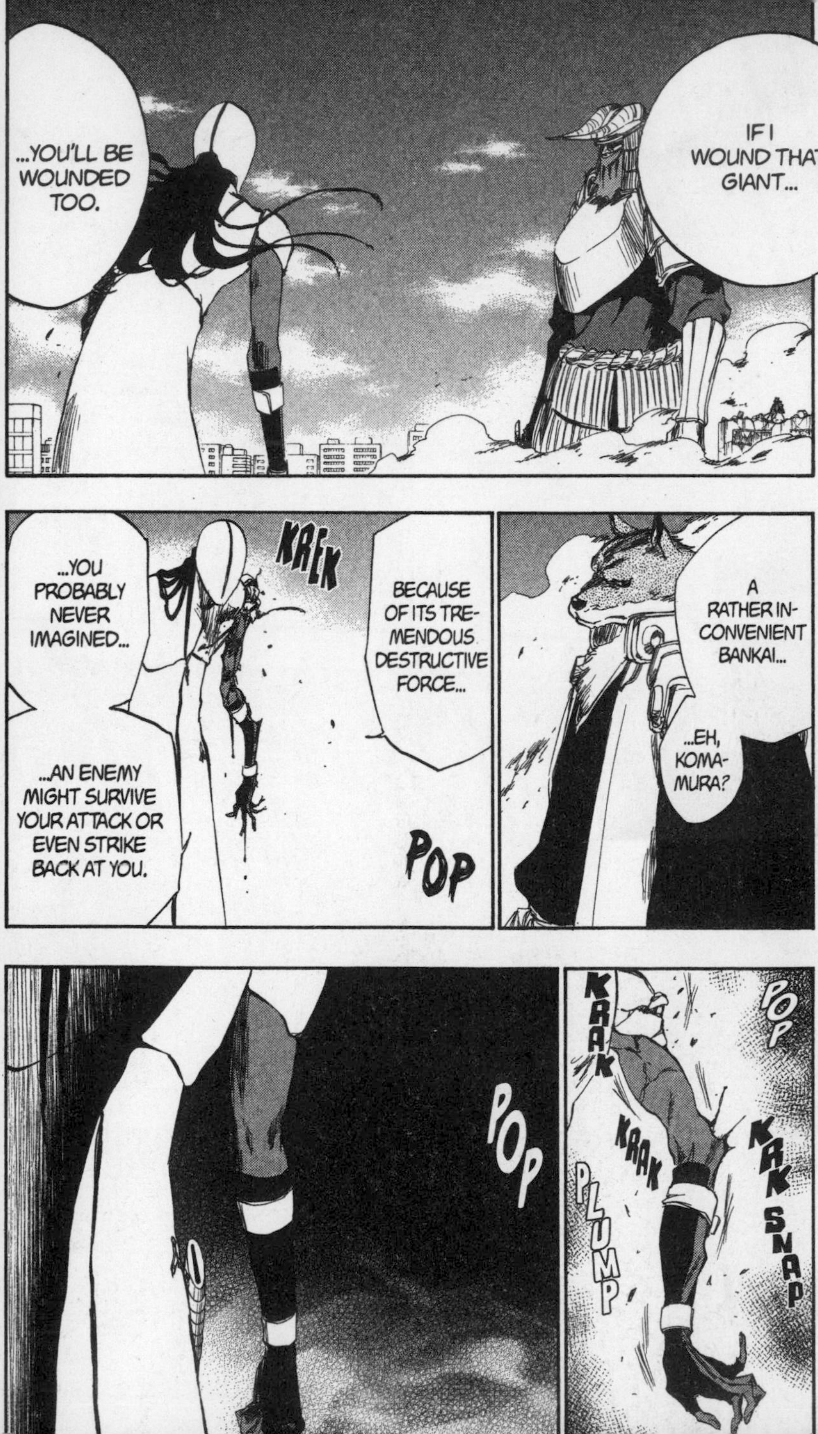
IF I WOUND THAT GIANT...
...YOU'LL BE WOUNDED TOO.
A RATHER INCONVENIENT BANKAI...
...EH, KOMAMURA?
BECAUSE OF ITS TREMENDOUS DESTRUCTIVE FORCE...
KREK
...YOU PROBABLY NEVER IMAGINED...
...AN ENEMY MIGHT SURVIVE YOUR ATTACK OR EVEN STRIKE BACK AT YOU.
POP
POP
KRAK
KRAK
KRK
SNAP
PLUMP
POP

READ THIS WAY

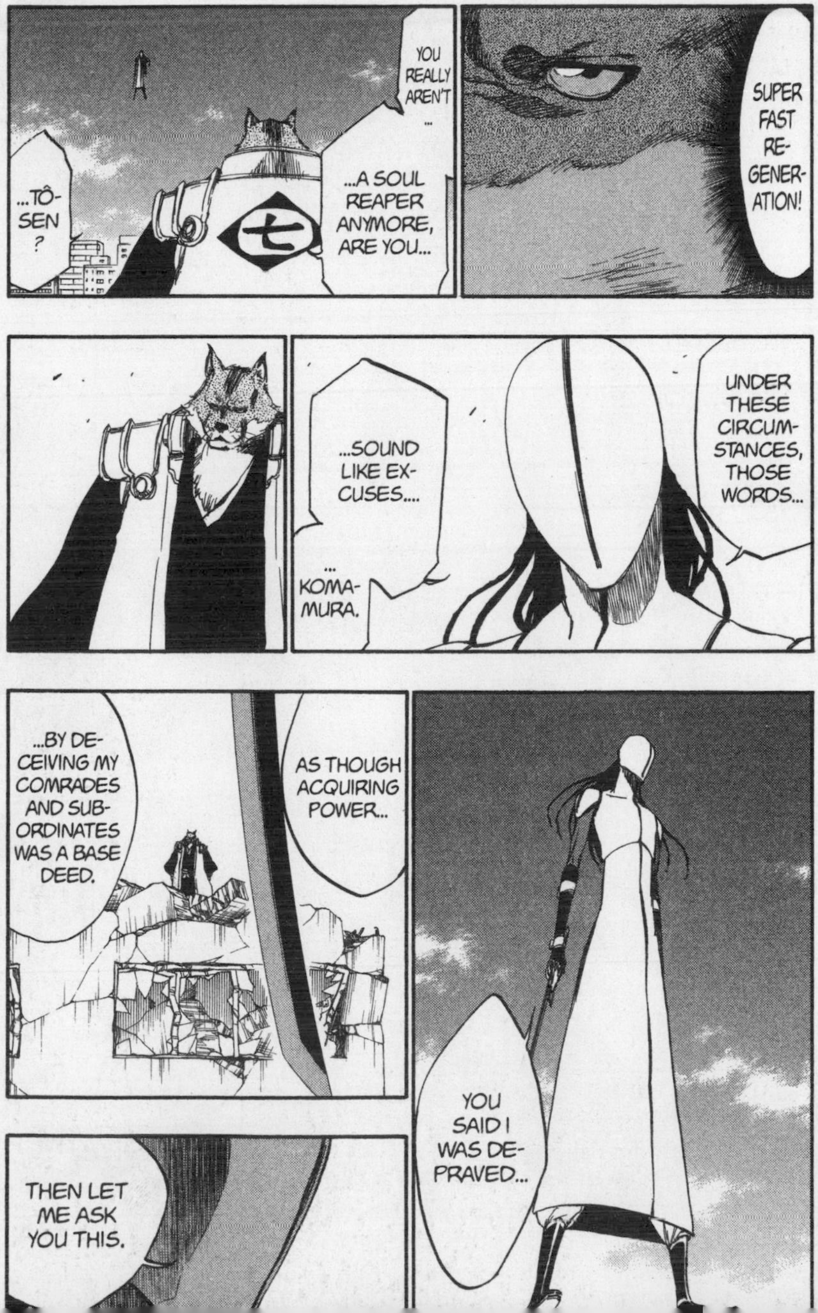
SUPER FAST REGENERATION!
YOU REALLY AREN'T ...
...A SOUL REAPER ANYMORE, ARE YOU...
...TÔSEN?
UNDER THESE CIRCUMSTANCES, THOSE WORDS...
...SOUND LIKE EXCUSES....
...KOMAMURA.
YOU SAID I WAS DEPRAVED...
AS THOUGH ACQUIRING POWER...
...BY DECEIVING MY COMRADES AND SUBORDINATES WAS A BASE DEED.
THEN LET ME ASK YOU THIS.

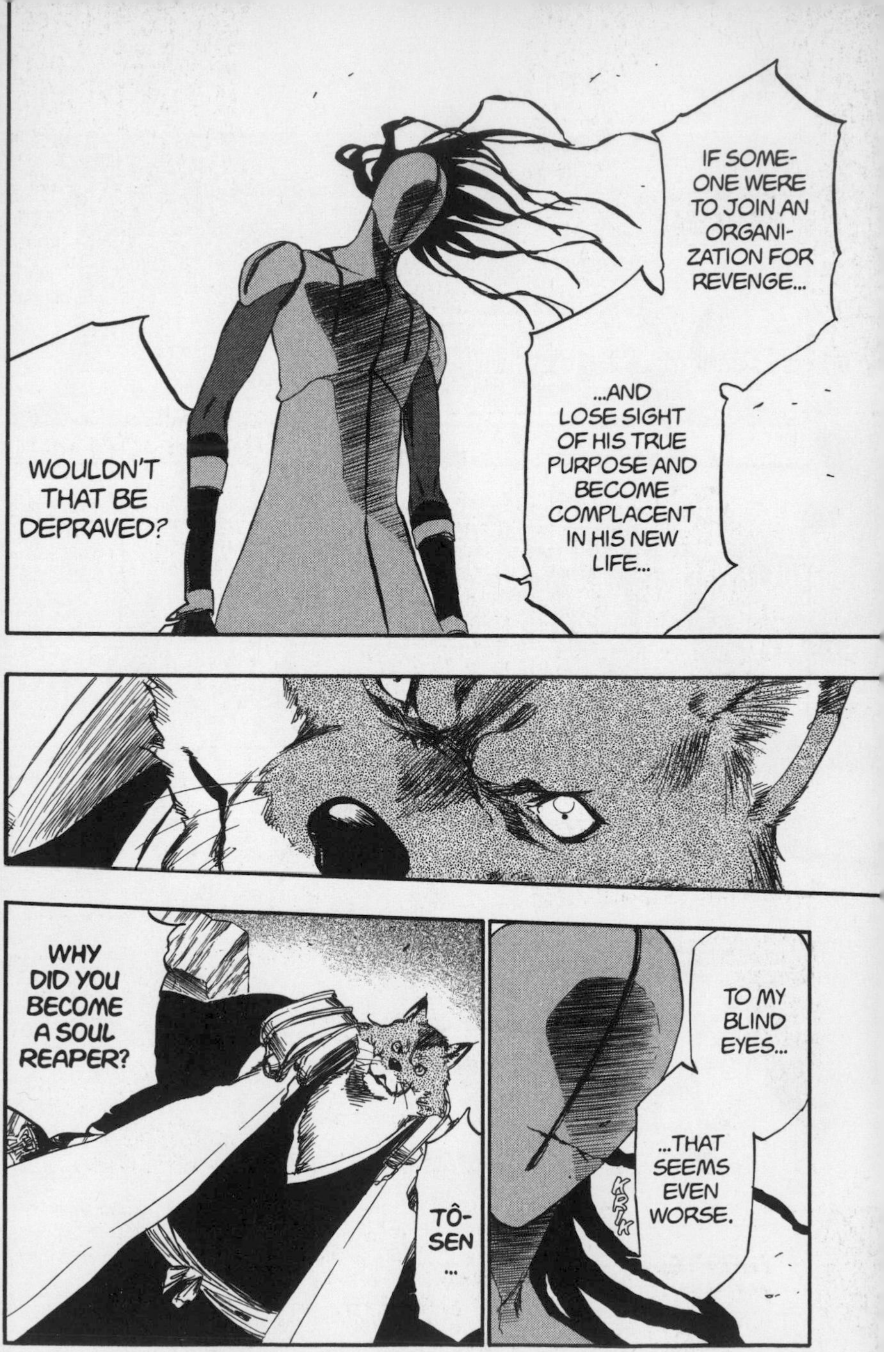
IF SOME-ONE WERE TO JOIN AN ORGANI-ZATION FOR REVENGE...
...AND LOSE SIGHT OF HIS TRUE PURPOSE AND BECOME COMPLACENT IN HIS NEW LIFE...
WOULDN'T THAT BE DEPRAVED?
TO MY BLIND EYES...
...THAT SEEMS EVEN WORSE.
KRIK
WHY DID YOU BECOME A SOUL REAPER?
TÔ-SEN
...

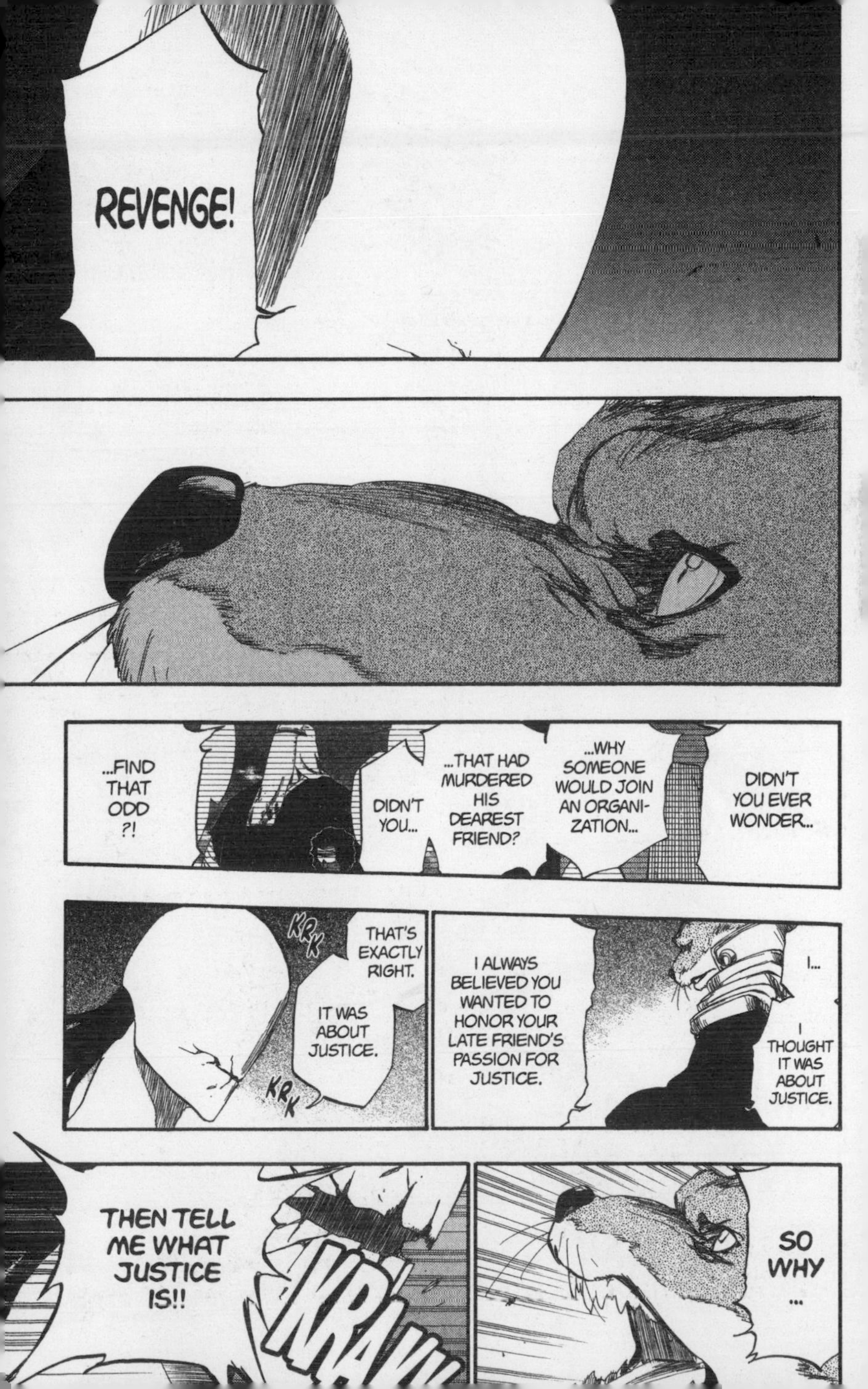
REVENGE!
DIDN'T YOU EVER WONDER...
...WHY SOMEONE WOULD JOIN AN ORGANIZATION...
...THAT HAD MURDERED HIS DEAREST FRIEND?
DIDN'T YOU...
...FIND THAT ODD?!
I...
I THOUGHT IT WAS ABOUT JUSTICE.
I ALWAYS BELIEVED YOU WANTED TO HONOR YOUR LATE FRIEND'S PASSION FOR JUSTICE.
KRK
THAT'S EXACTLY RIGHT.
IT WAS ABOUT JUSTICE.
KRK
SO WHY...
THEN TELL ME WHAT JUSTICE IS!!

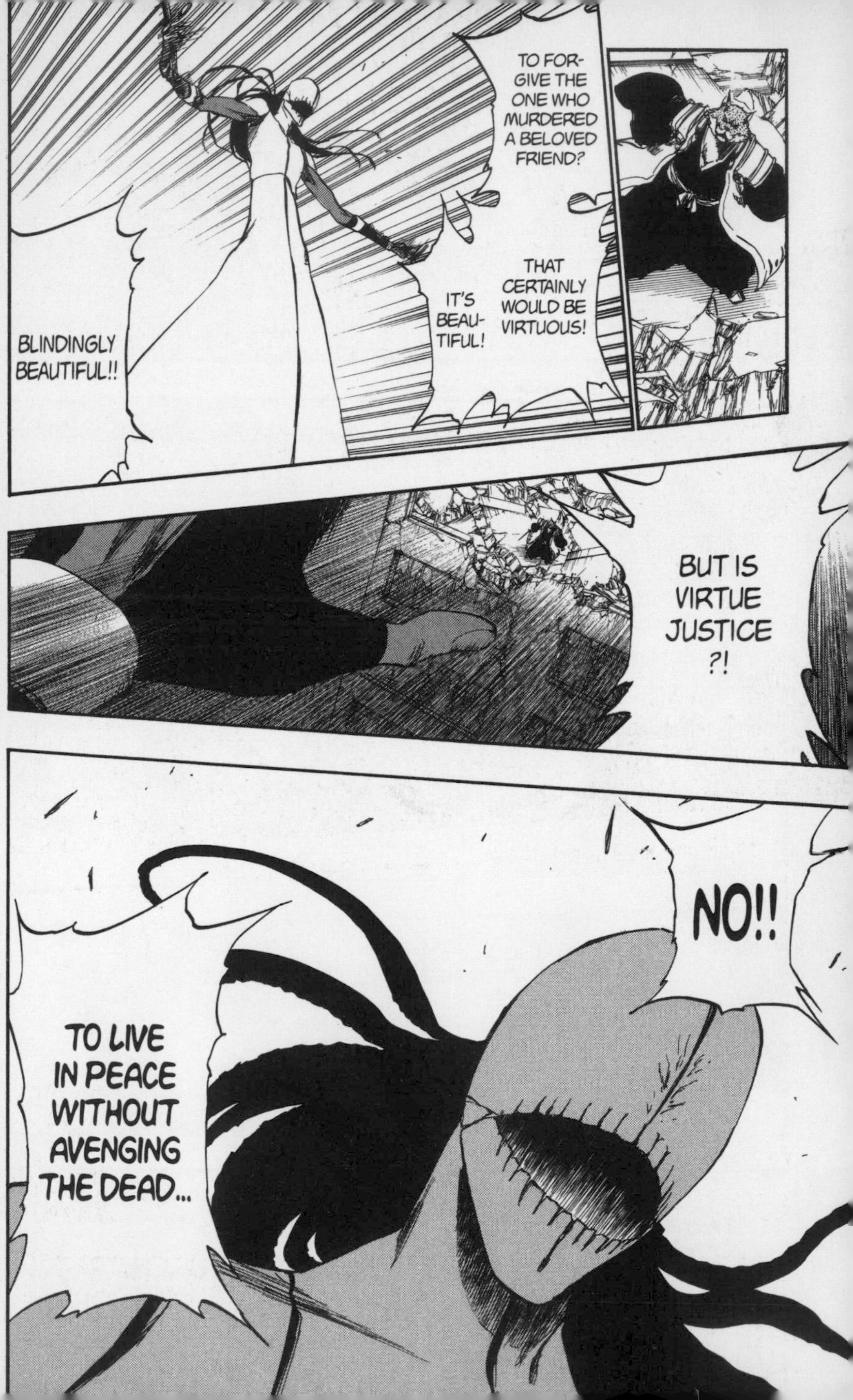
TO FOR-GIVE THE ONE WHO MURDERED A BELOVED FRIEND?
THAT CERTAINLY WOULD BE VIRTUOUS!
IT'S BEAU-TIFUL!
BLINDINGLY BEAUTIFUL!!
BUT IS VIRTUE JUSTICE ?!
NO!!
TO LIVE IN PEACE WITHOUT AVENGING THE DEAD...

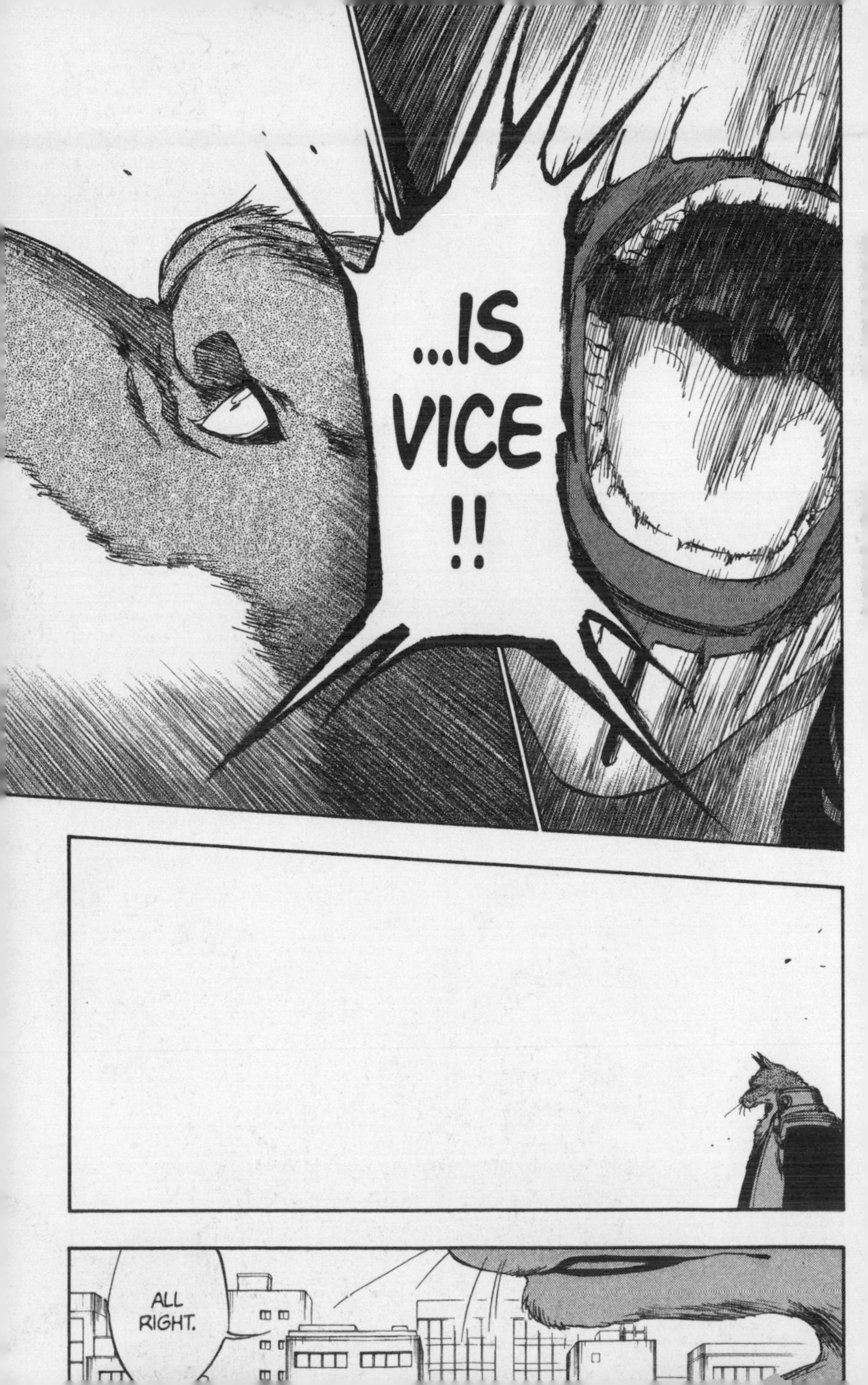
...IS VICE!!
ALL RIGHT.

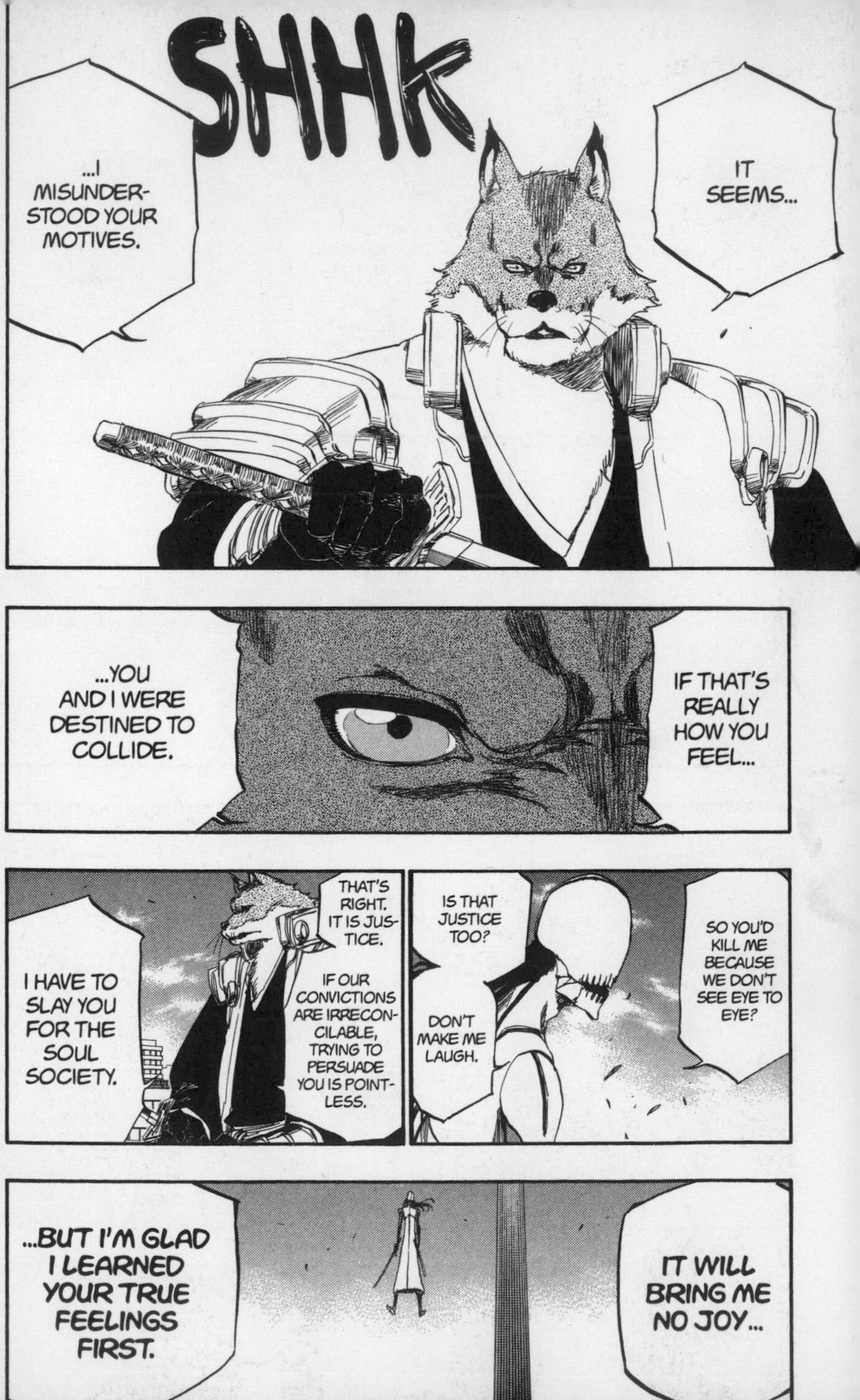
SHHK
IT SEEMS...
...I MISUNDERSTOOD YOUR MOTIVES.
IF THAT'S REALLY HOW YOU FEEL...
...YOU AND I WERE DESTINED TO COLLIDE.
SO YOU'D KILL ME BECAUSE WE DON'T SEE EYE TO EYE?
IS THAT JUSTICE TOO?
DON'T MAKE ME LAUGH.
THAT'S RIGHT. IT IS JUSTICE.
IF OUR CONVICTIONS ARE IRRECONCILABLE, TRYING TO PERSUADE YOU IS POINTLESS.
I HAVE TO SLAY YOU FOR THE SOUL SOCIETY.
IT WILL BRING ME NO JOY...
...BUT I'M GLAD I LEARNED YOUR TRUE FEELINGS FIRST.

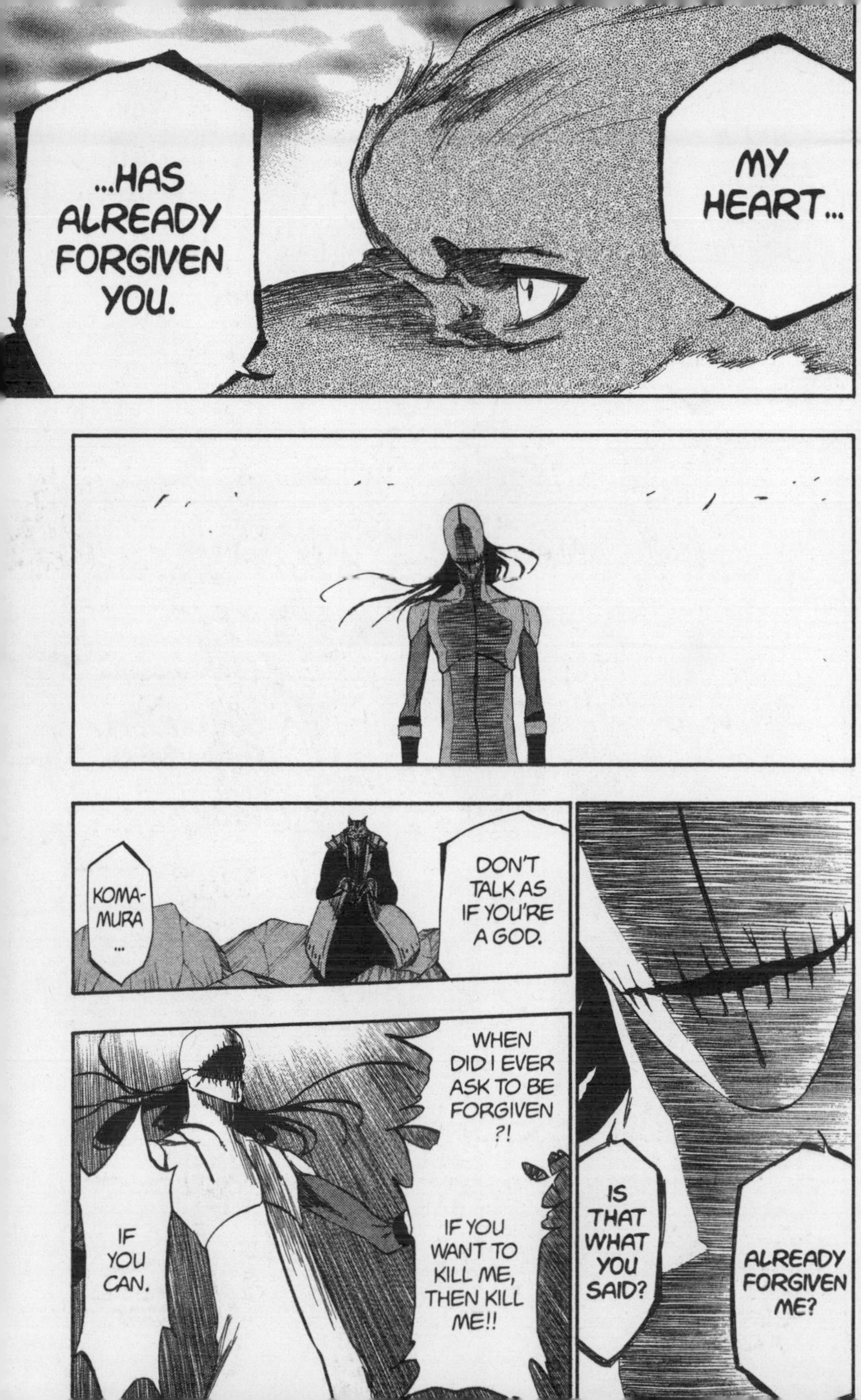
MY HEART...
...HAS ALREADY FORGIVEN YOU.
ALREADY FORGIVEN ME?
IS THAT WHAT YOU SAID?
DON'T TALK AS IF YOU'RE A GOD.
KOMA-MURA...
WHEN DID I EVER ASK TO BE FORGIVEN?!
IF YOU WANT TO KILL ME, THEN KILL ME!!
IF YOU CAN.

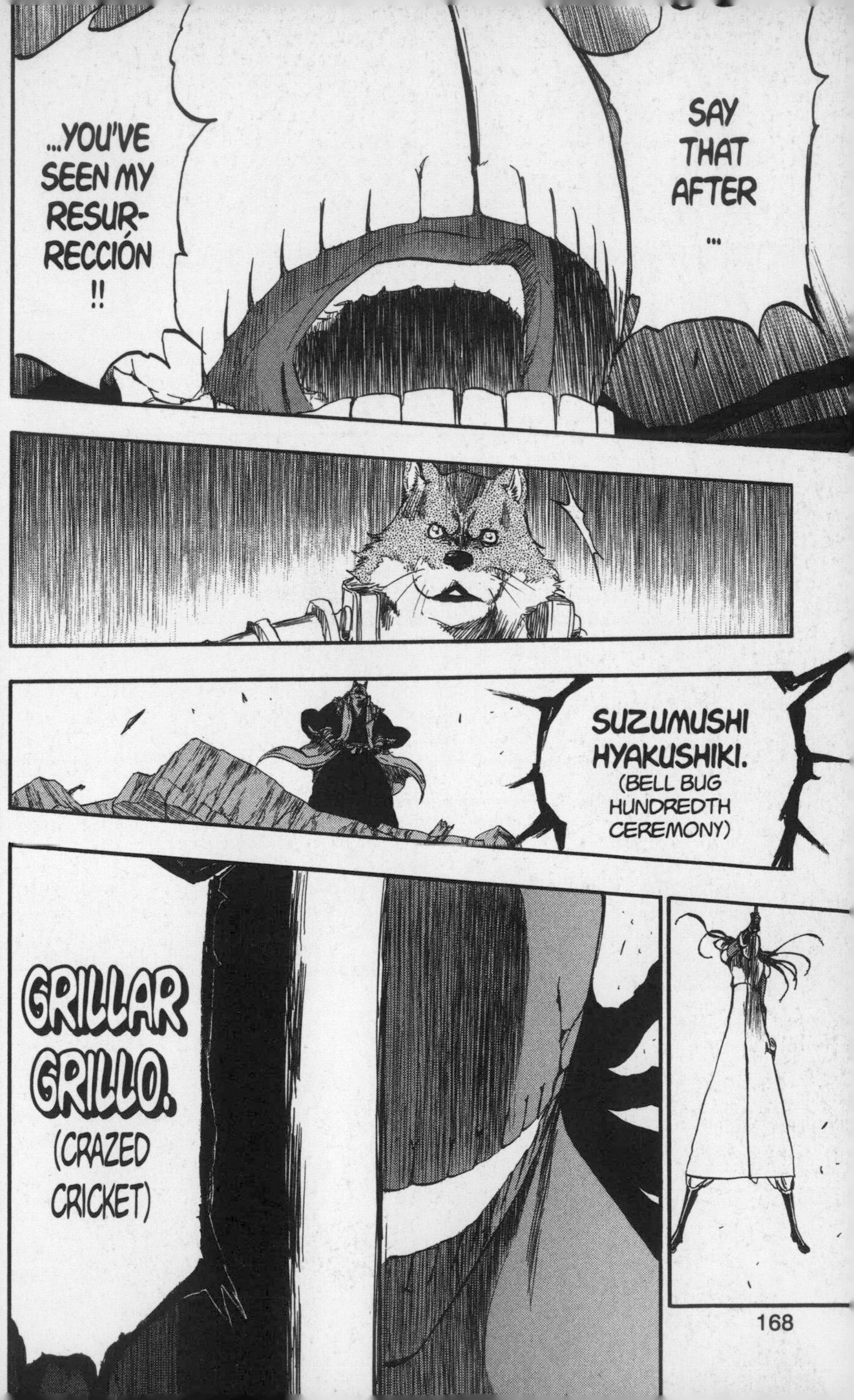
SAY THAT AFTER ...
...YOU'VE SEEN MY RESUR-RECCIÓN !!
SUZUMUSHI HYAKUSHIKI.
(BELL BUG HUNDREDTH CEREMONY)
GRILLAR GRILLO.
(CRAZED CRICKET)

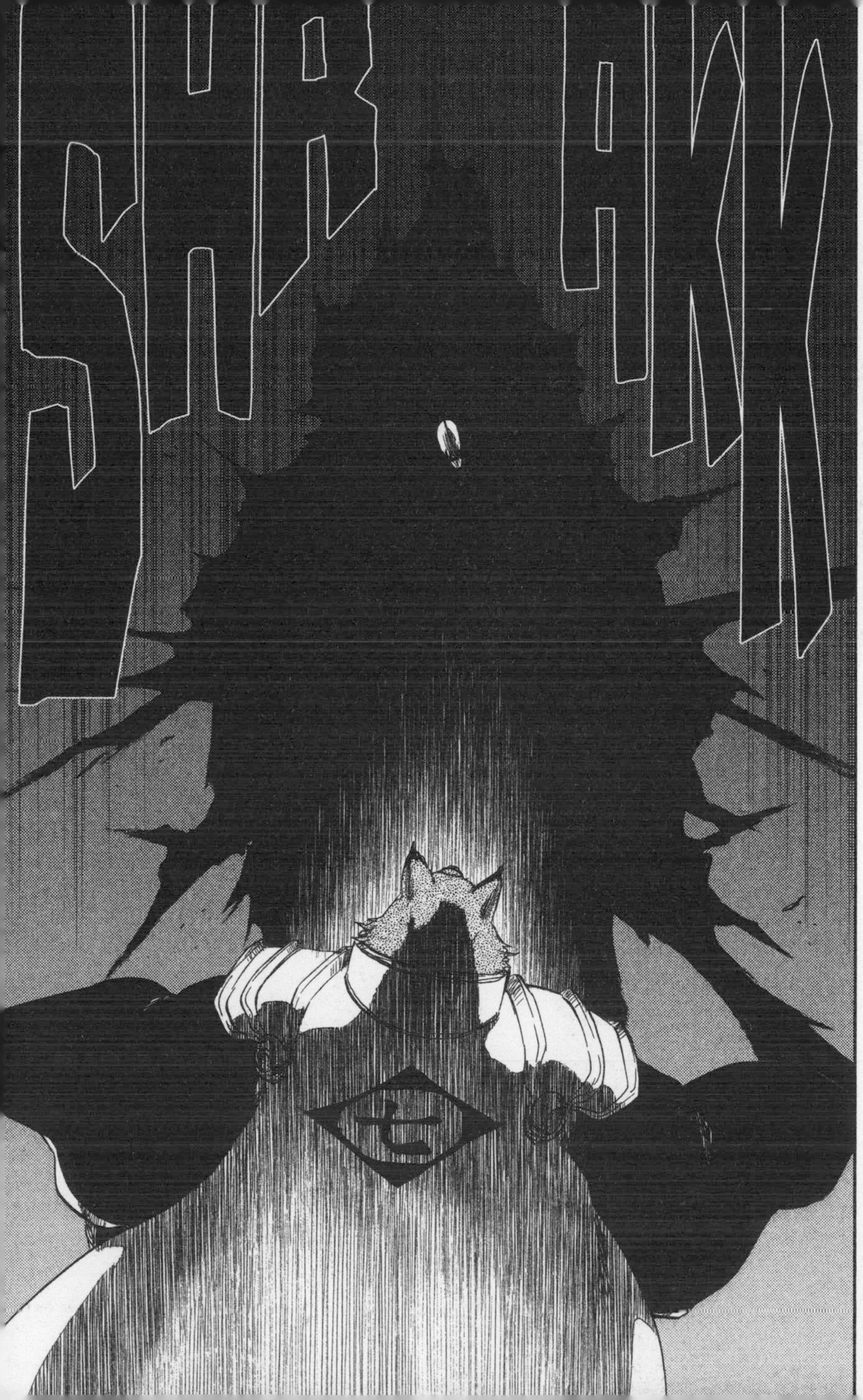
SHBCHKK
七

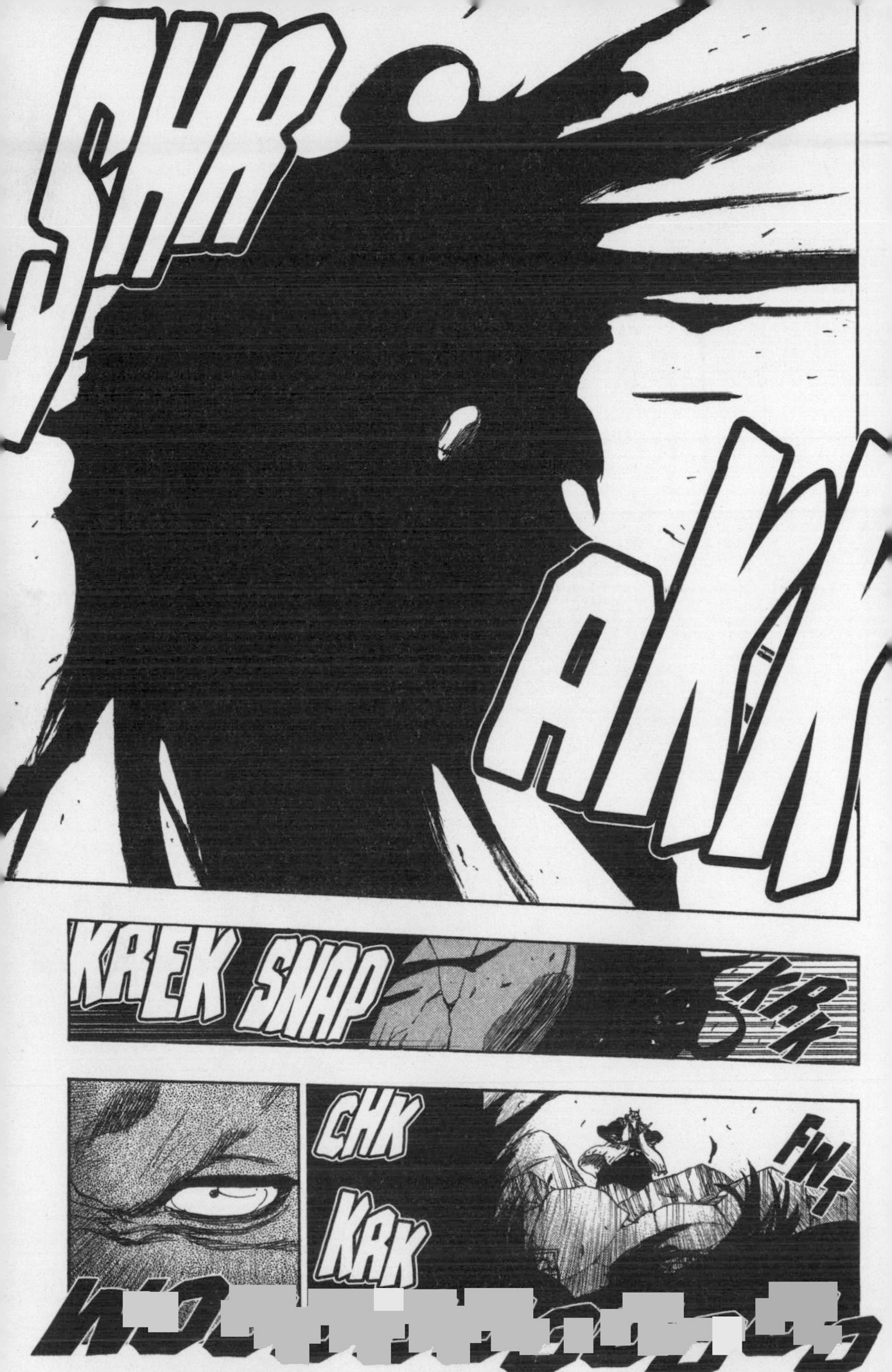
SHR
AKK
KRK
KREK
SNAP
FWT
CHK
KRK

386. Bells Are Blue

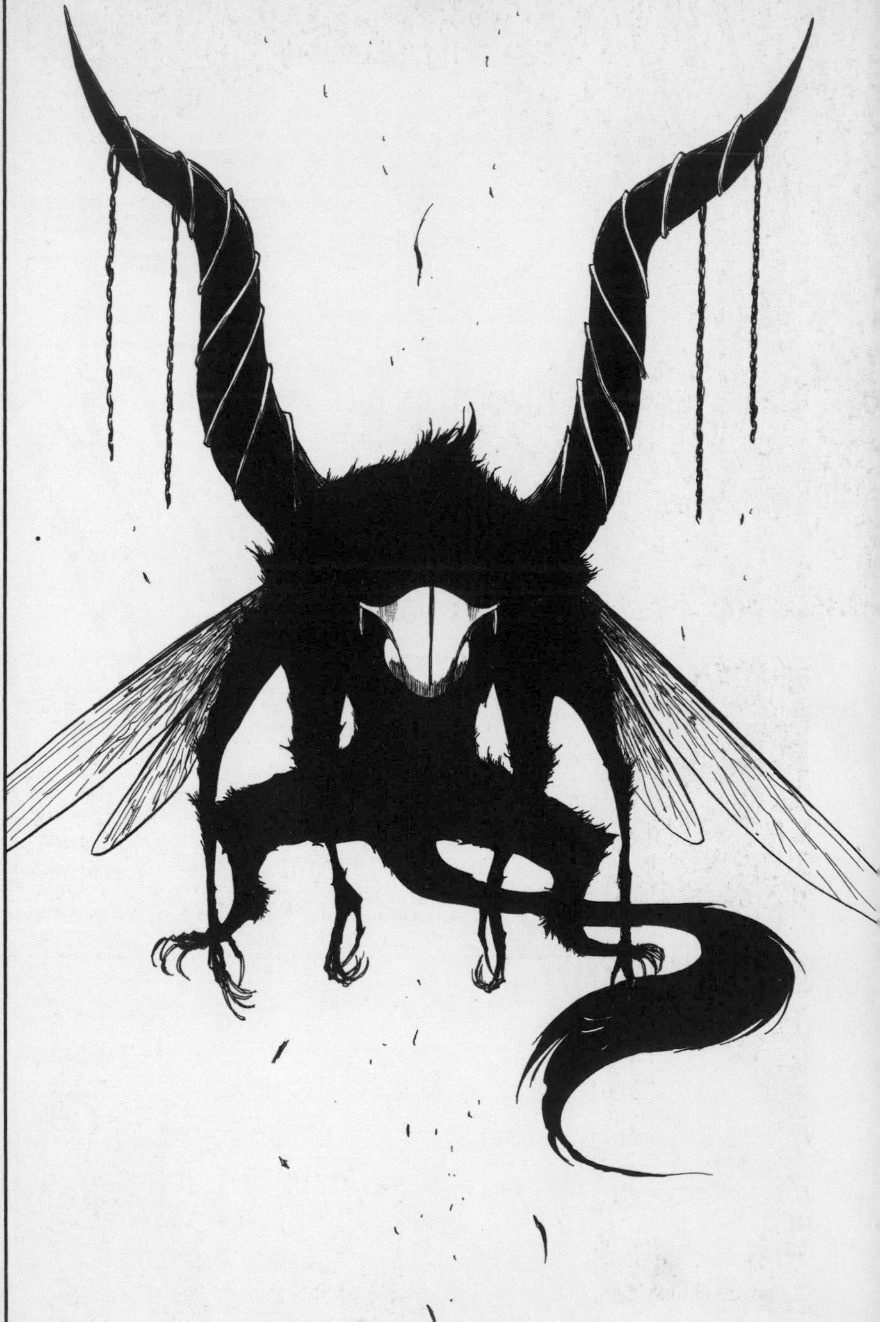

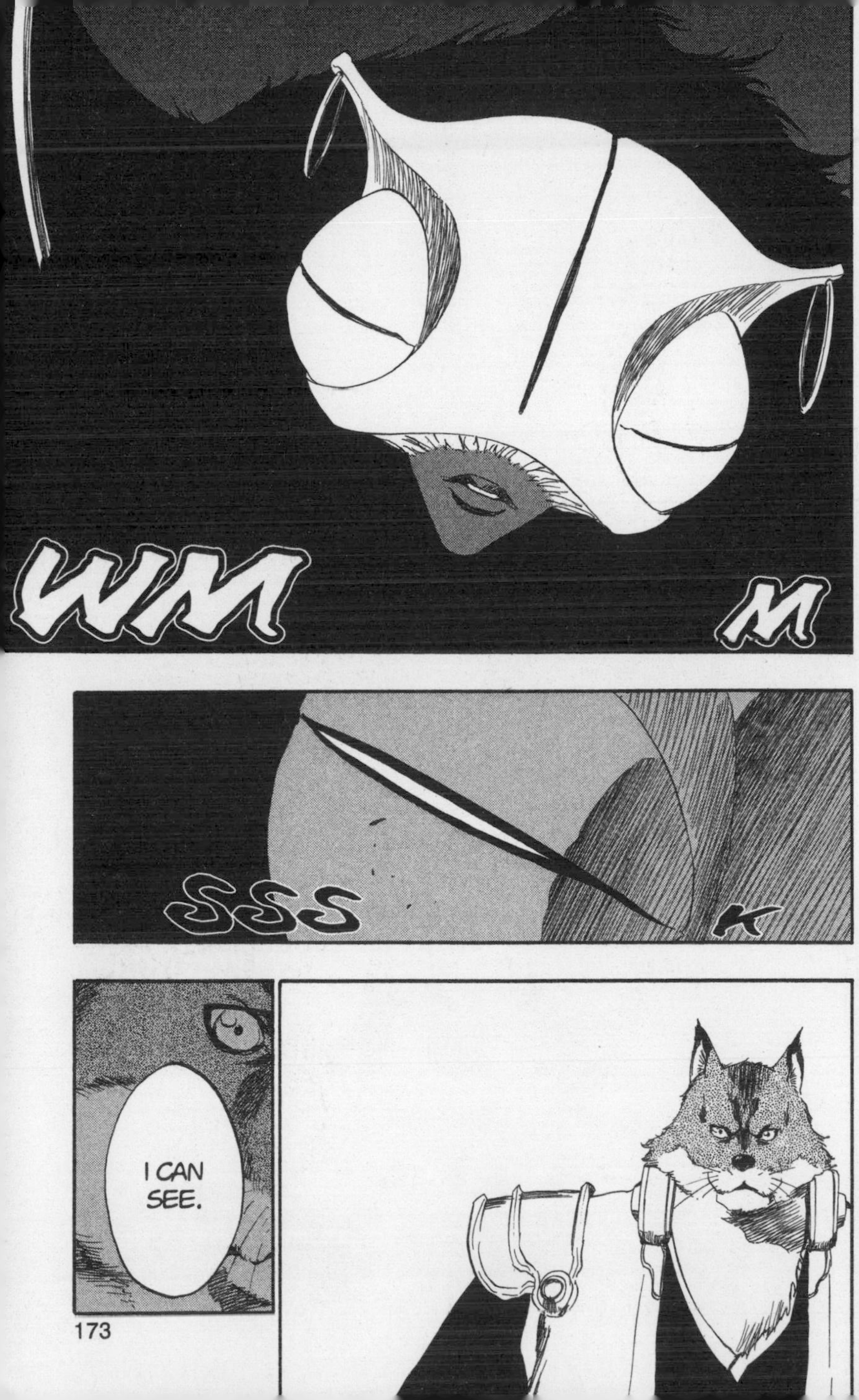
WM
M
SSS
K
I CAN SEE.

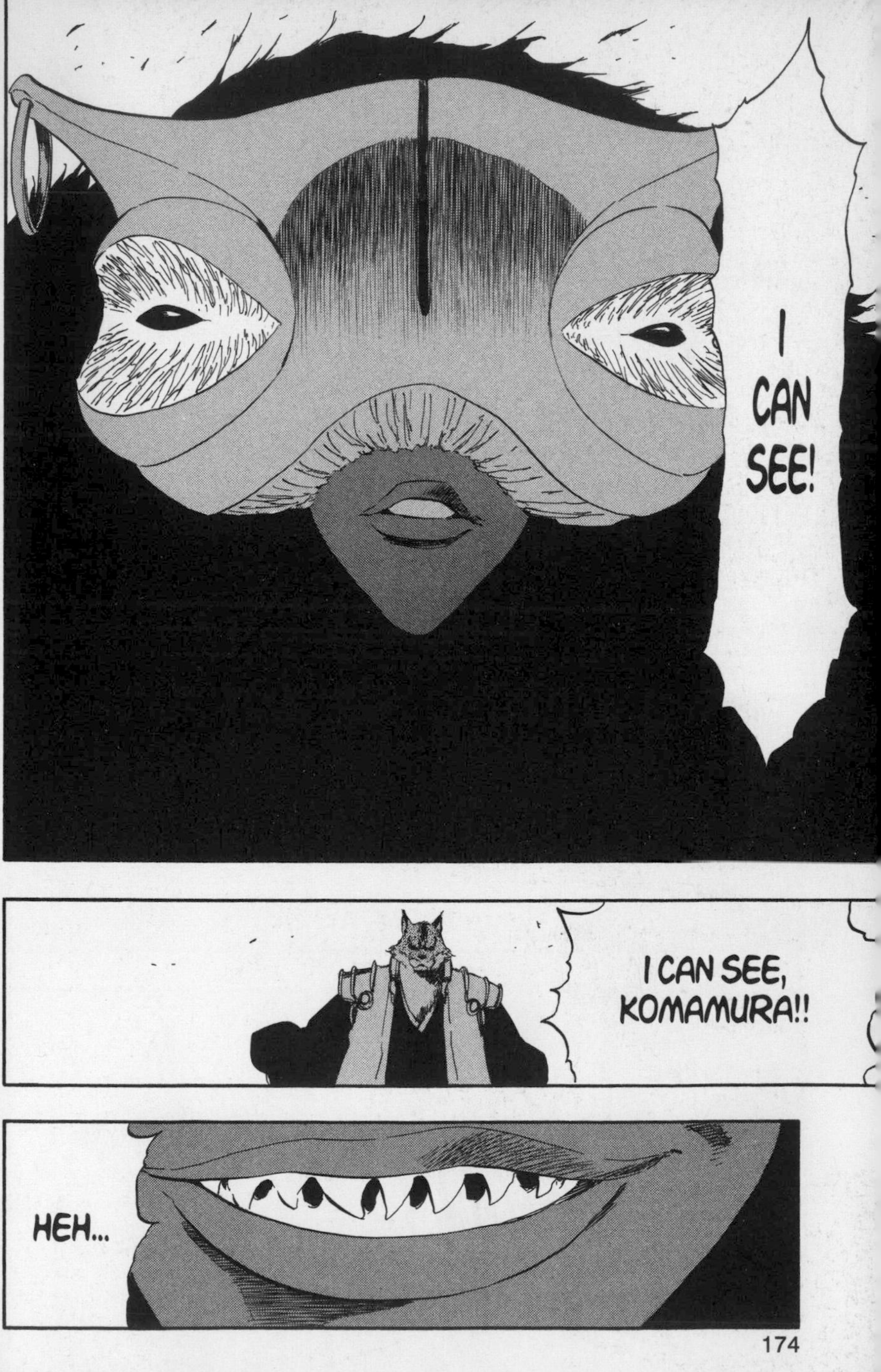
I CAN SEE!
I CAN SEE, KOMAMURA!!
HEH...

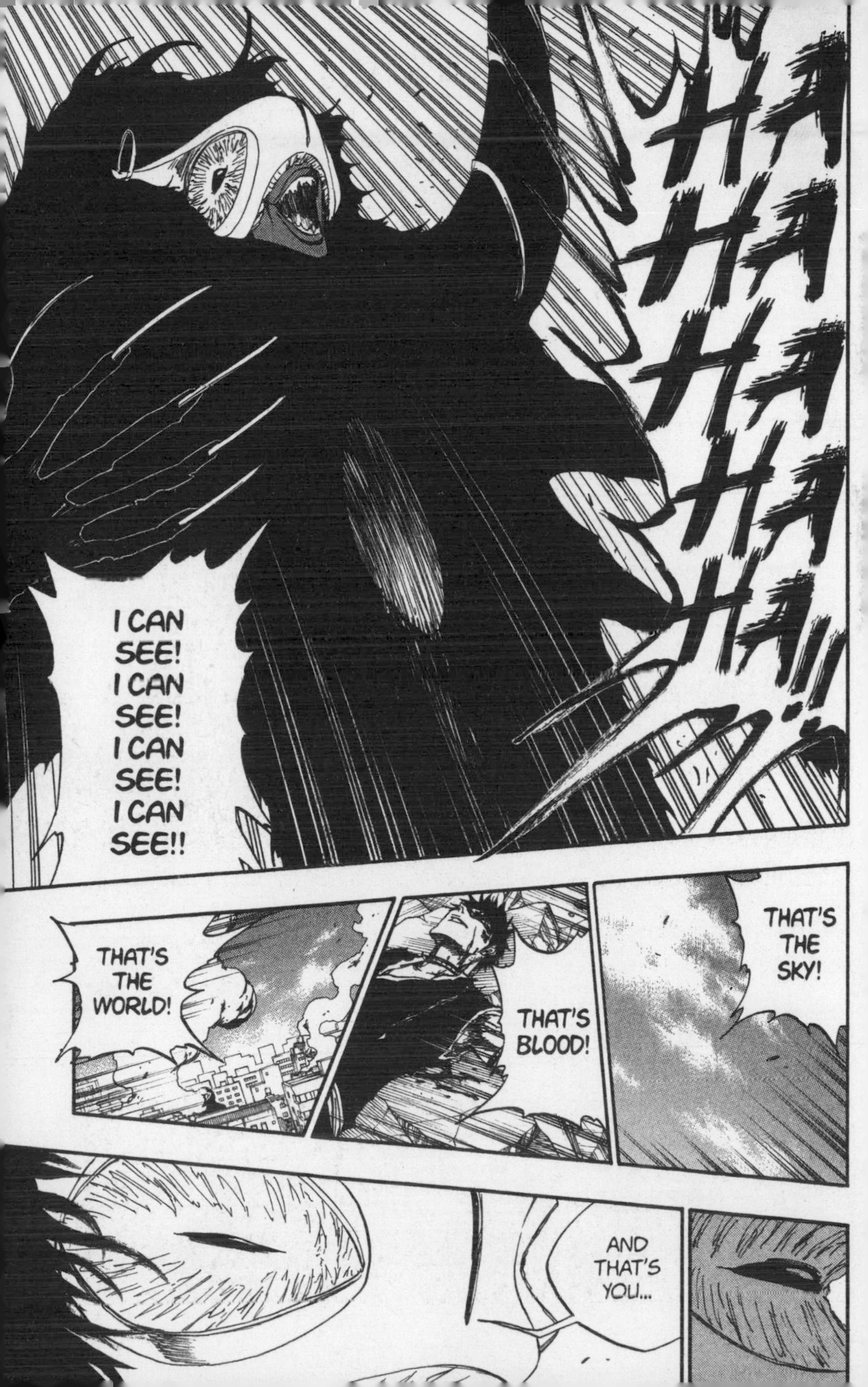
I CAN SEE! I CAN SEE! I CAN SEE! I CAN SEE!!
THAT'S THE SKY!
THAT'S BLOOD!
THAT'S THE WORLD!
AND THAT'S YOU...

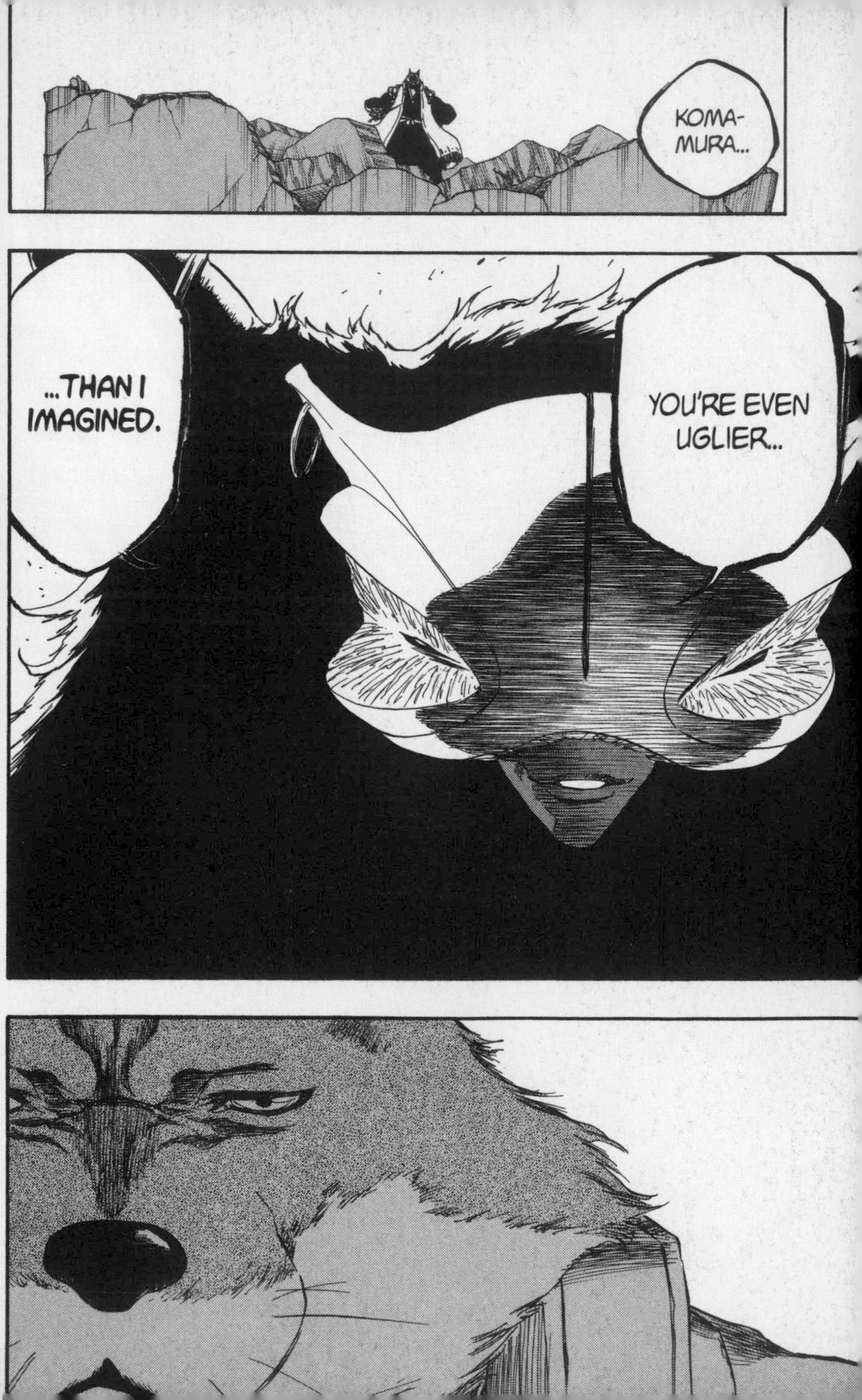
KOMA-MURA...
YOU'RE EVEN UGLIER...
...THAN I IMAGINED.

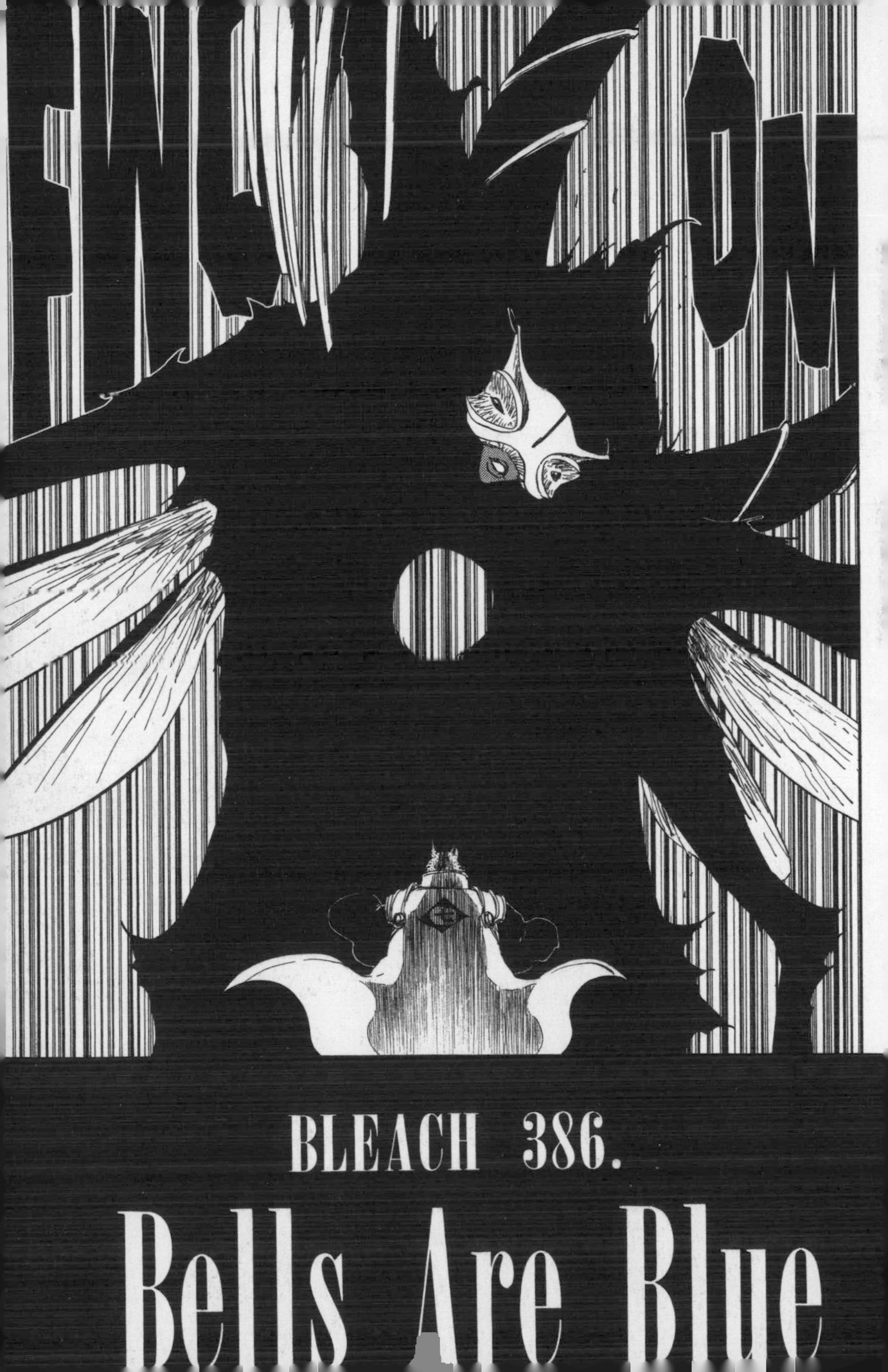

BLEACH 386.

Bells Are Blue

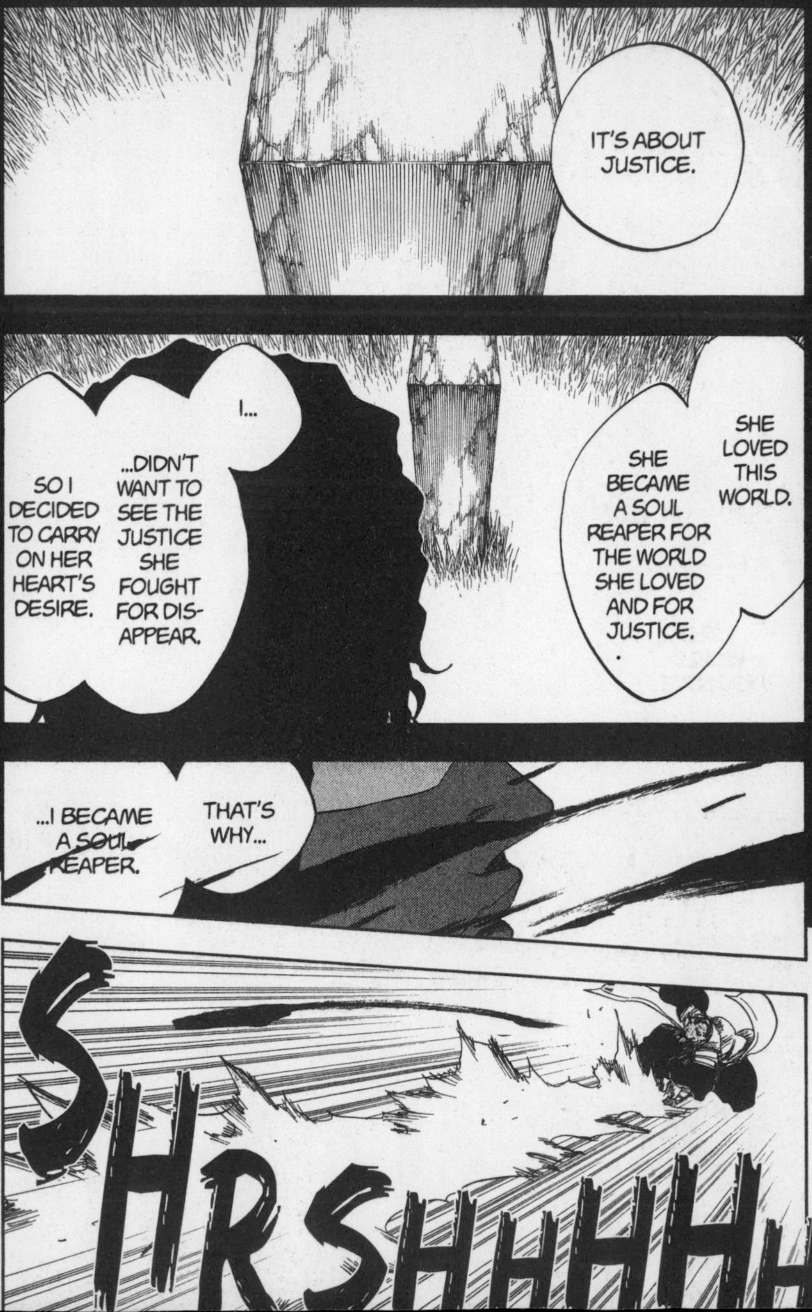
IT'S ABOUT JUSTICE.
SHE LOVED THIS WORLD.
SHE BECAME A SOUL REAPER FOR THE WORLD SHE LOVED AND FOR JUSTICE.
I...
...DIDN'T WANT TO SEE THE JUSTICE SHE FOUGHT FOR DIS-APPEAR.
SO I DECIDED TO CARRY ON HER HEART'S DESIRE.
THAT'S WHY...
...I BECAME A SOUL REAPER.
SHRSHHHHH

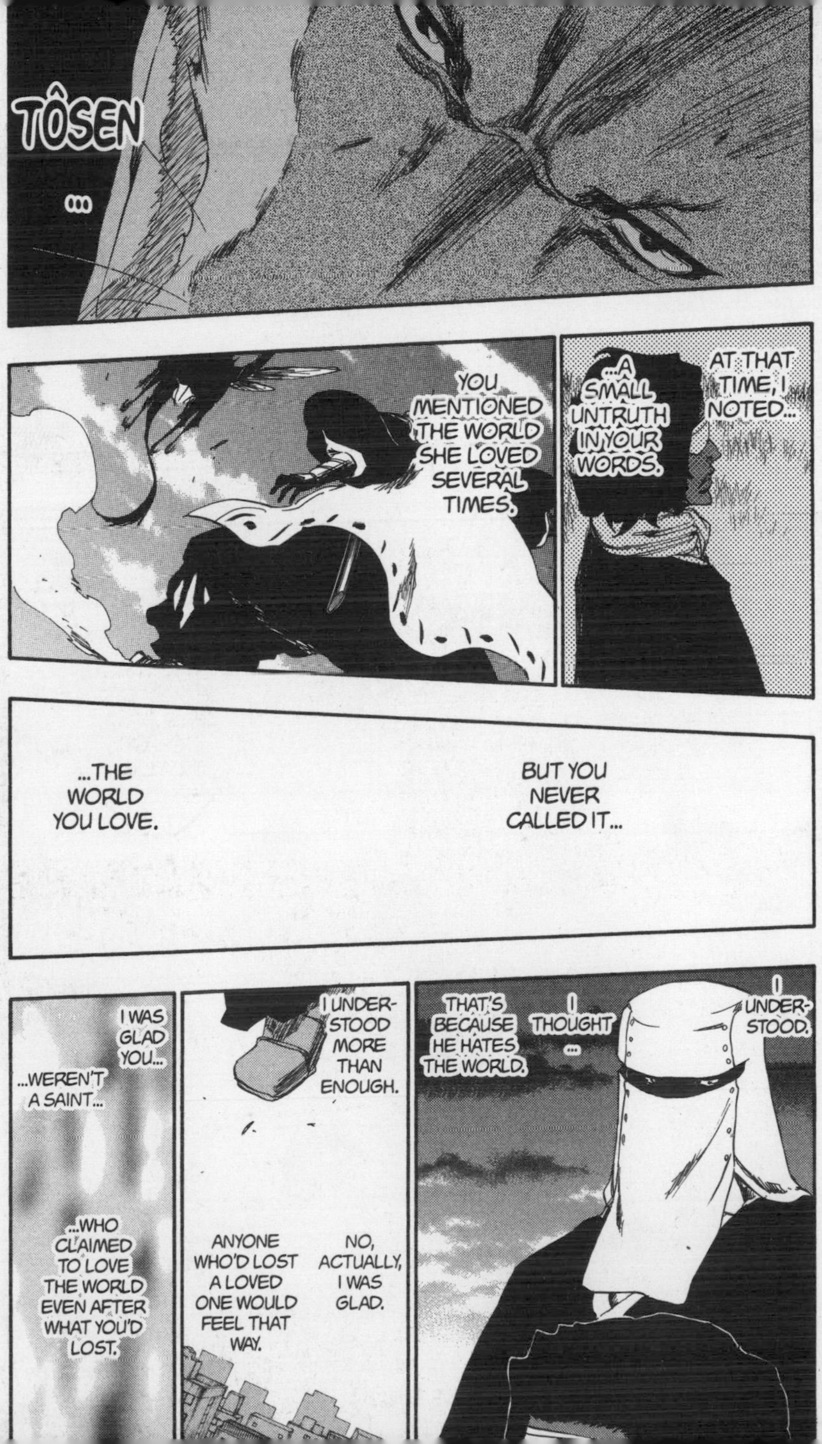
TÔSEN
...
AT THAT TIME, I NOTED...
...A SMALL UNTRUTH IN YOUR WORDS.
YOU MENTIONED THE WORLD SHE LOVED SEVERAL TIMES.
BUT YOU NEVER CALLED IT...
...THE WORLD YOU LOVE.
I UNDER-STOOD.
I THOUGHT...
THAT'S BECAUSE HE HATES THE WORLD.
I UNDER-STOOD MORE THAN ENOUGH.
NO, ACTUALLY, I WAS GLAD.
ANYONE WHO'D LOST A LOVED ONE WOULD FEEL THAT WAY.
I WAS GLAD YOU...
...WEREN'T A SAINT...
...WHO CLAIMED TO LOVE THE WORLD EVEN AFTER WHAT YOU'D LOST.

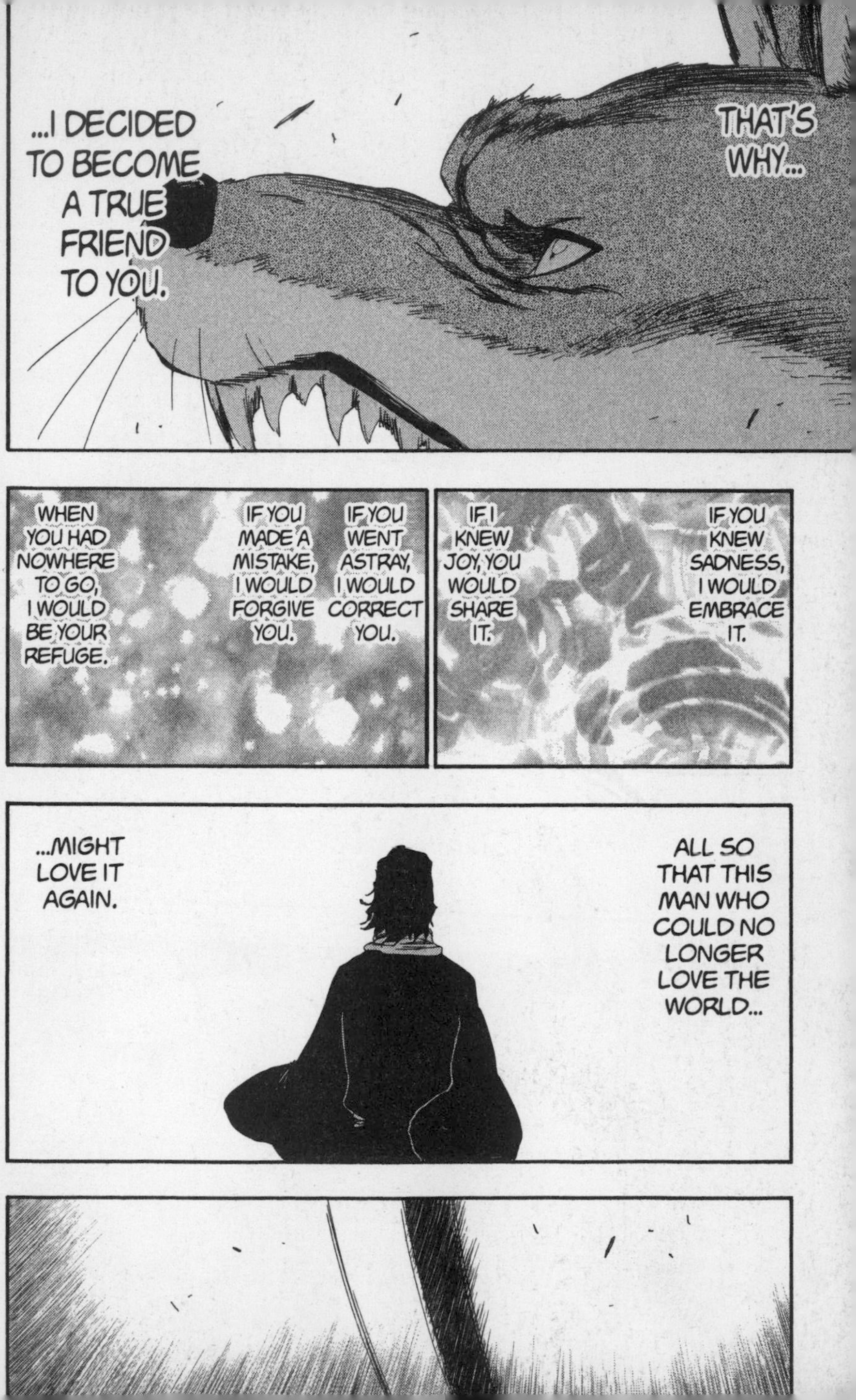
THAT'S WHY...
...I DECIDED TO BECOME A TRUE FRIEND TO YOU.
IF YOU KNEW SADNESS, I WOULD EMBRACE IT.
IF I KNEW JOY, YOU WOULD SHARE IT.
IF YOU WENT ASTRAY, I WOULD CORRECT YOU.
IF YOU MADE A MISTAKE, I WOULD FORGIVE YOU.
WHEN YOU HAD NOWHERE TO GO, I WOULD BE YOUR REFUGE.
ALL SO THAT THIS MAN WHO COULD NO LONGER LOVE THE WORLD...
...MIGHT LOVE IT AGAIN.

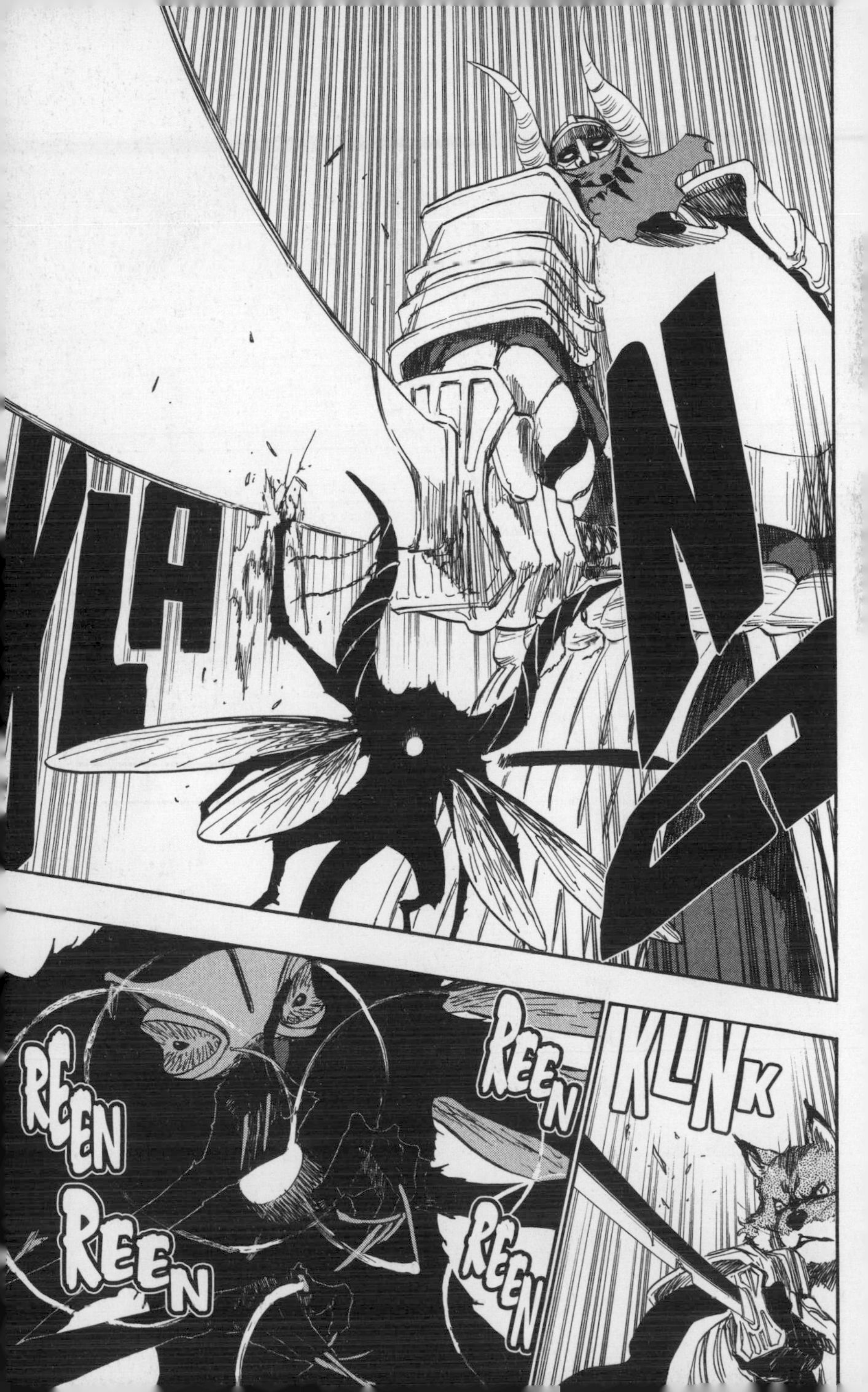
KLINK
REEN
REEN
REEN
REEN

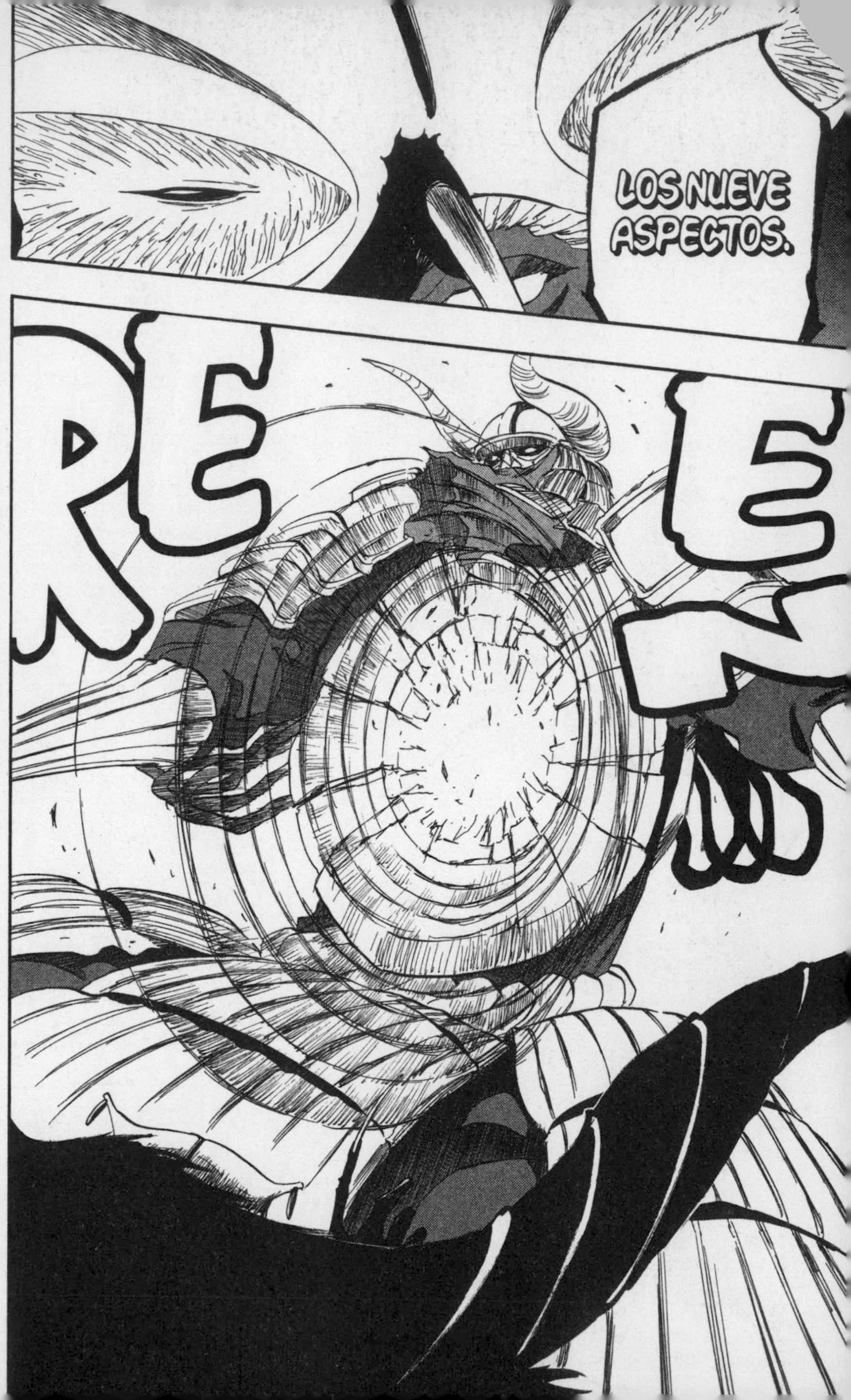
LOS NUEVE ASPECTOS.

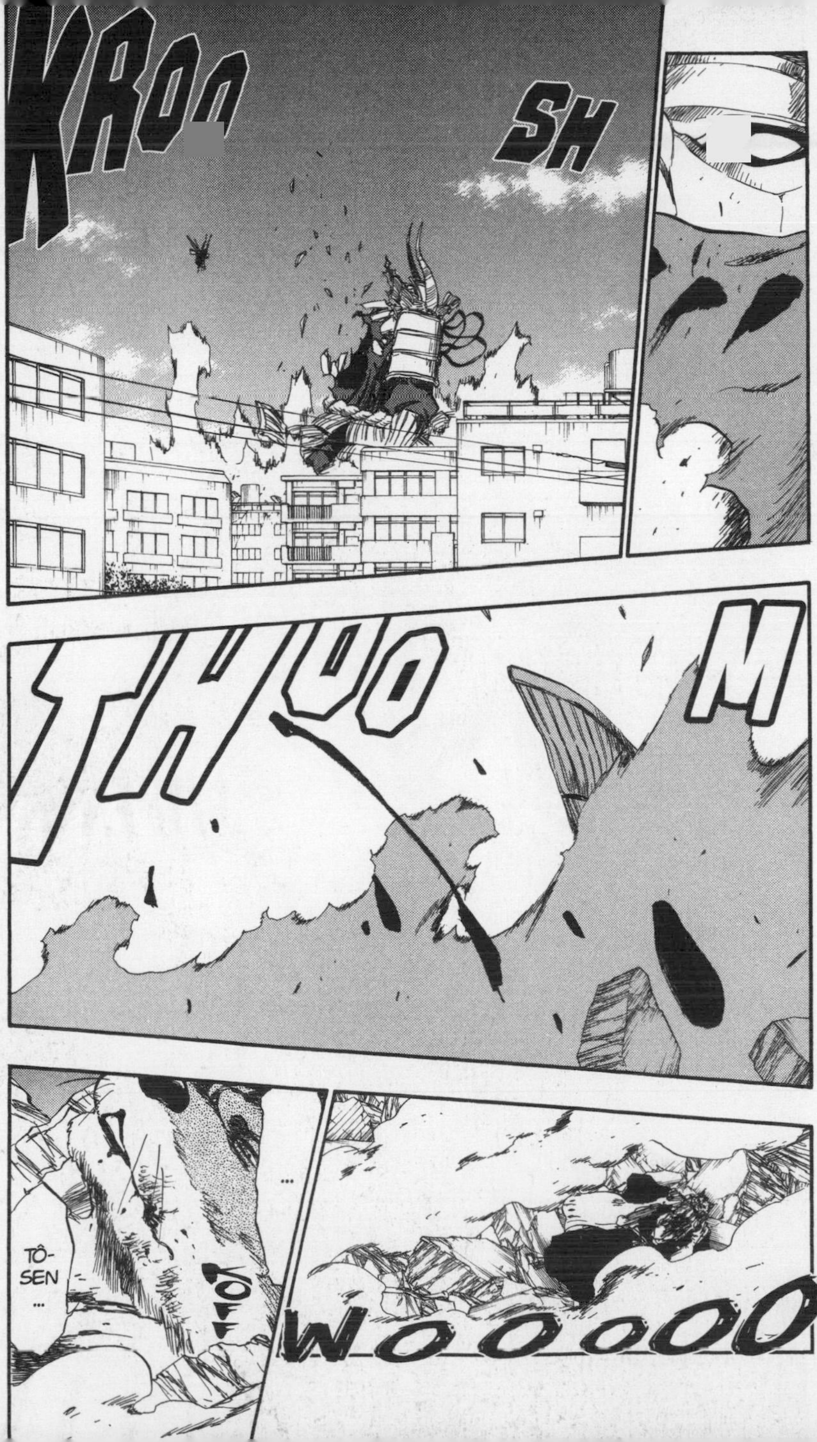
KROO
SH
THOOM
WOOOOOO
...
TÔ-SEN ...

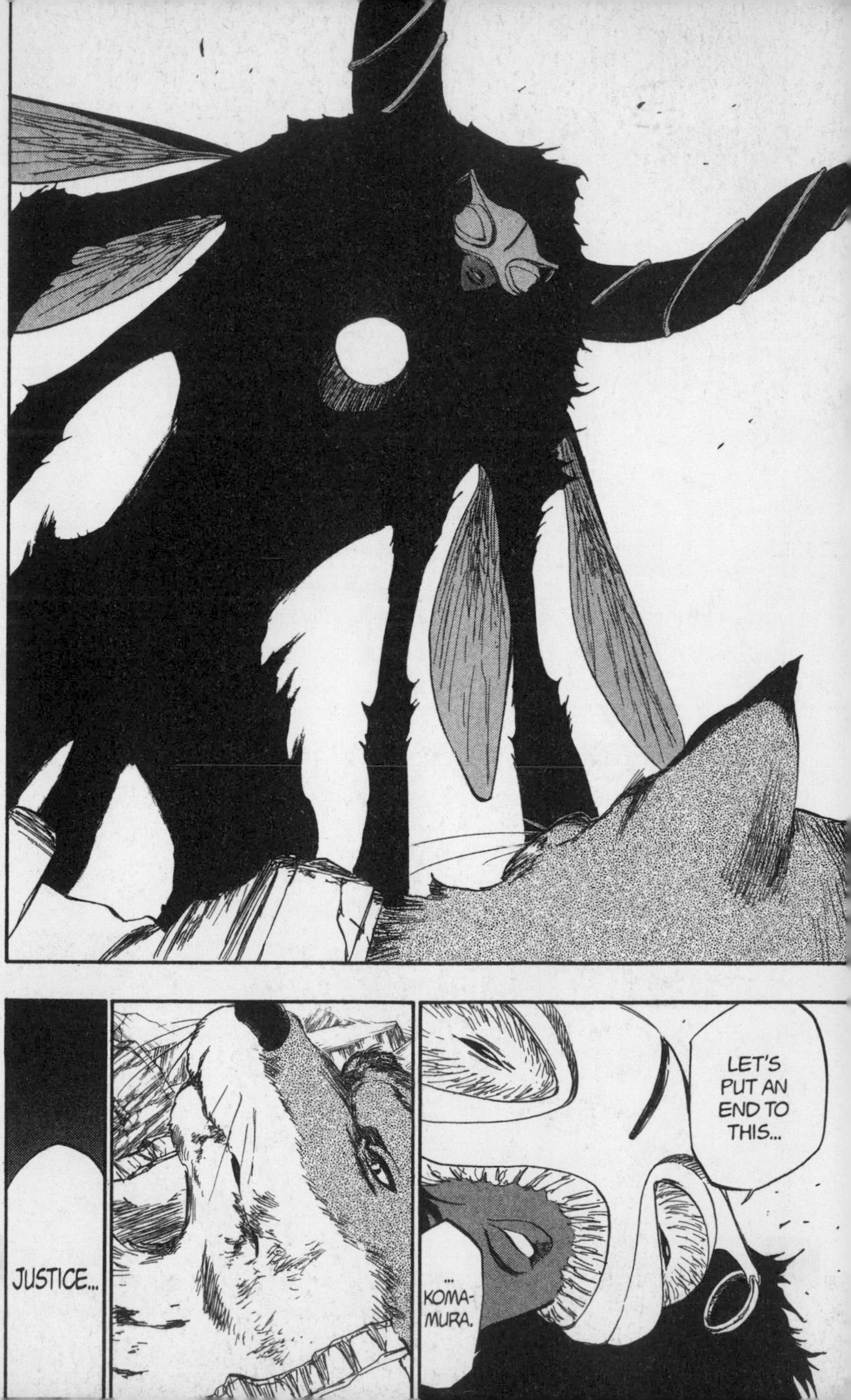
LET'S PUT AN END TO THIS...
...KOMA-MURA.
JUSTICE...

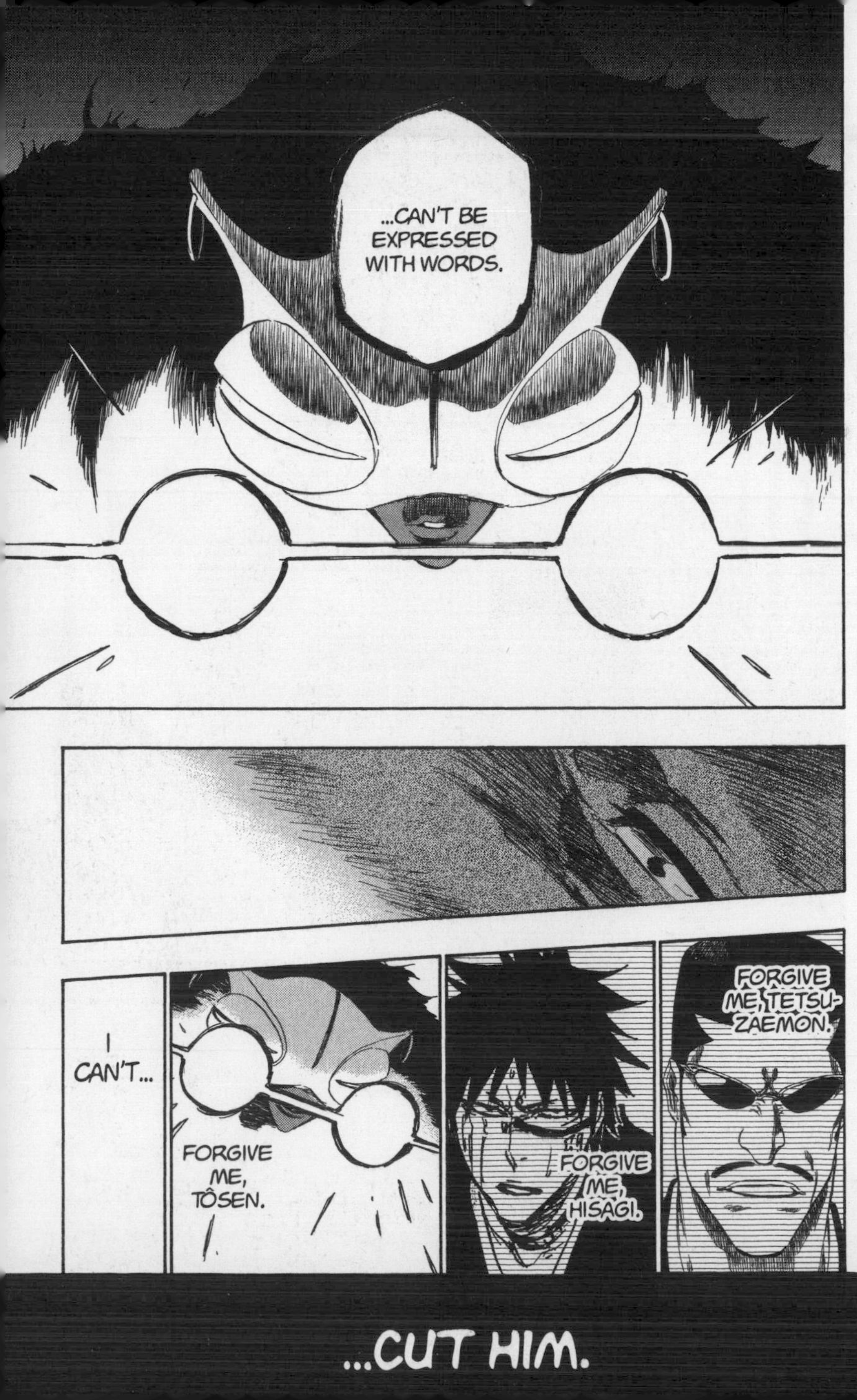
...CAN'T BE EXPRESSED WITH WORDS.
FORGIVE ME, TETSU-ZAEMON.
FORGIVE ME, HISAGI.
FORGIVE ME, TÔSEN.
I CAN'T...
...CUT HIM.

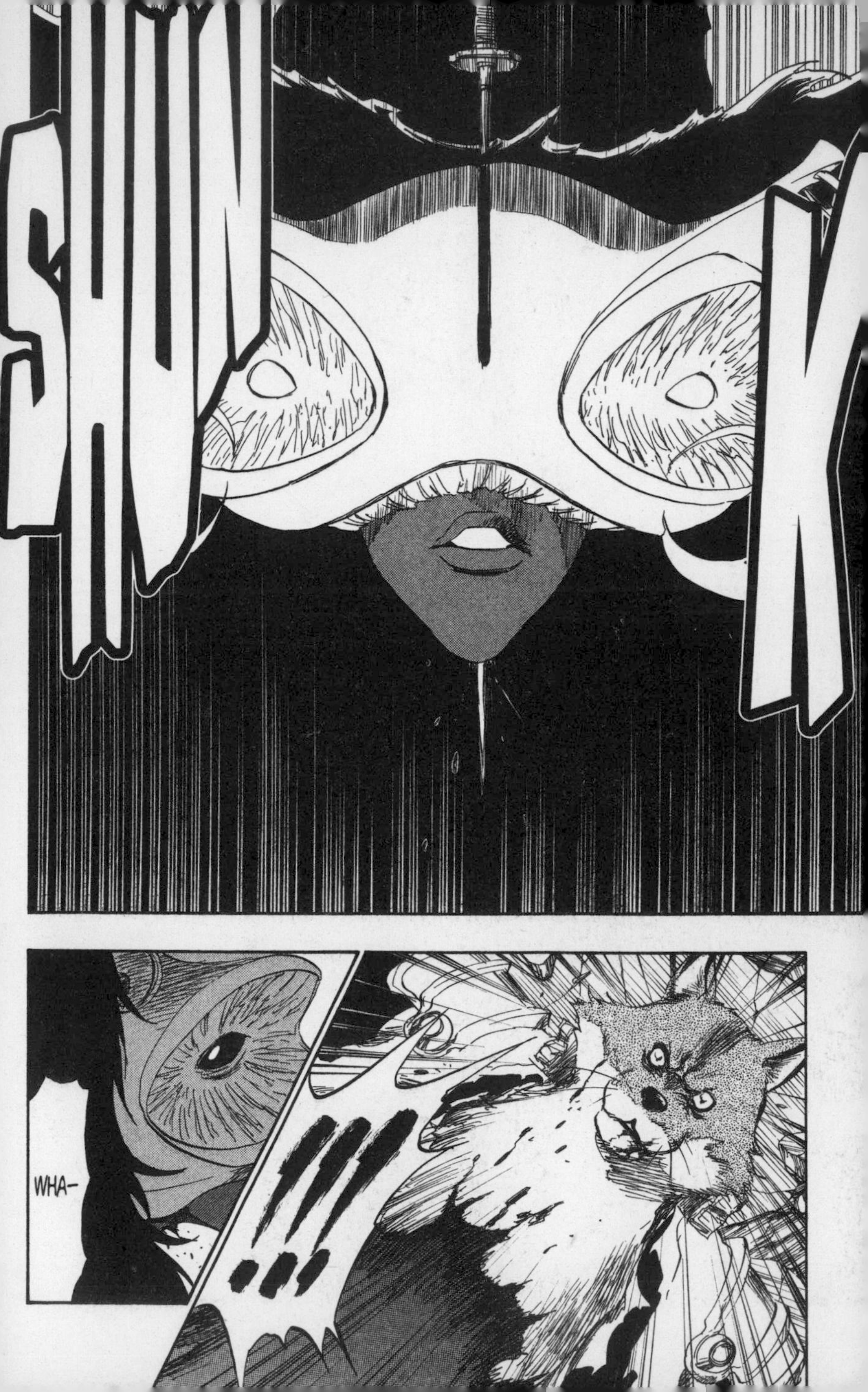
SHUNK
!!...
WHA-

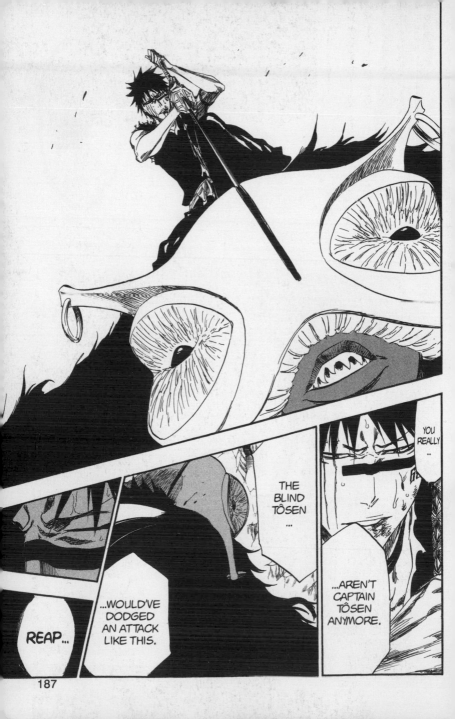

YOU REALLY...

THE BLIND TŌSEN...

...AREN'T CAPTAIN TŌSEN ANYMORE.

...WOULD'VE DODGED AN ATTACK LIKE THIS.

REAP...

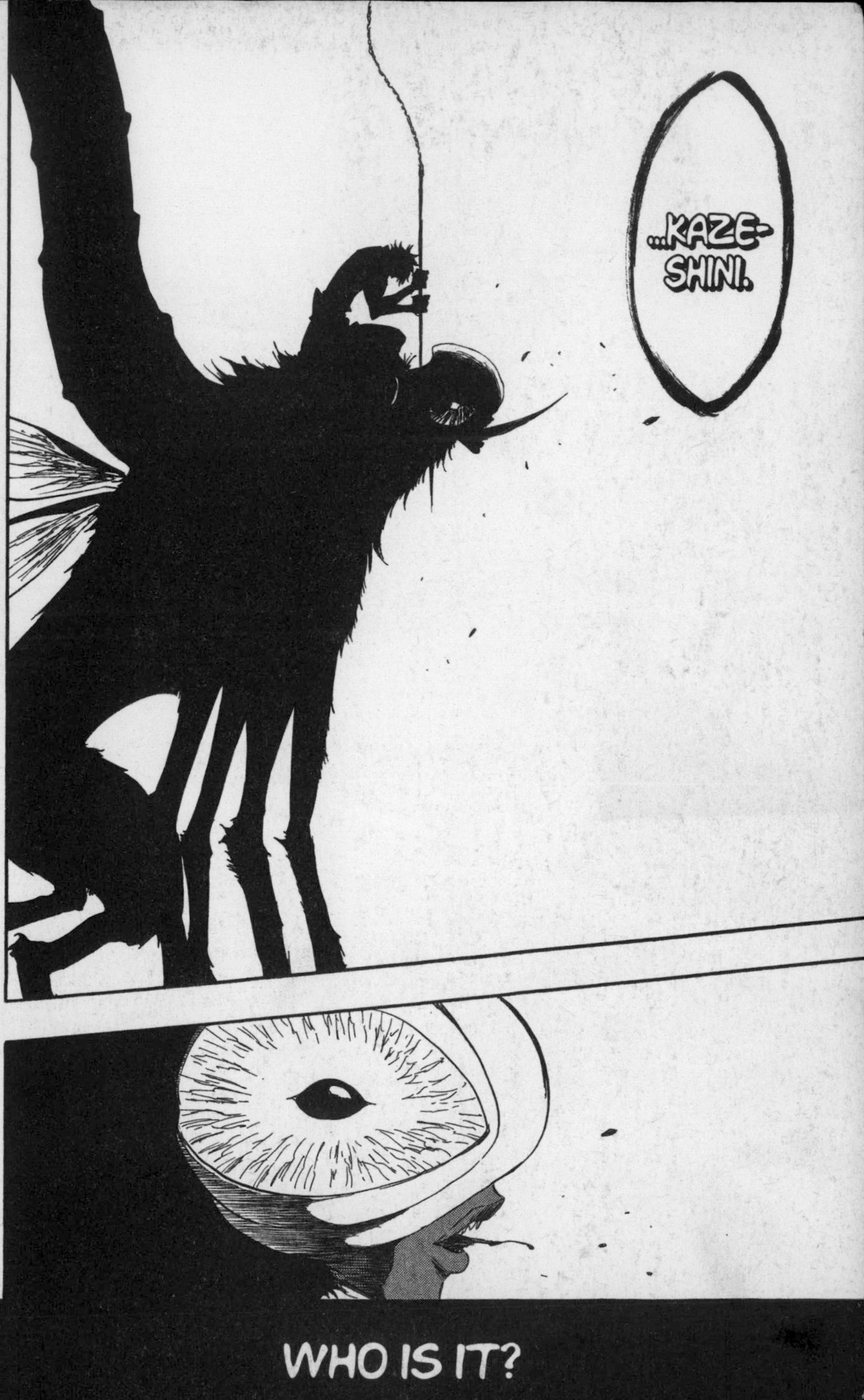
...KAZE-SHINI.
WHO IS IT?

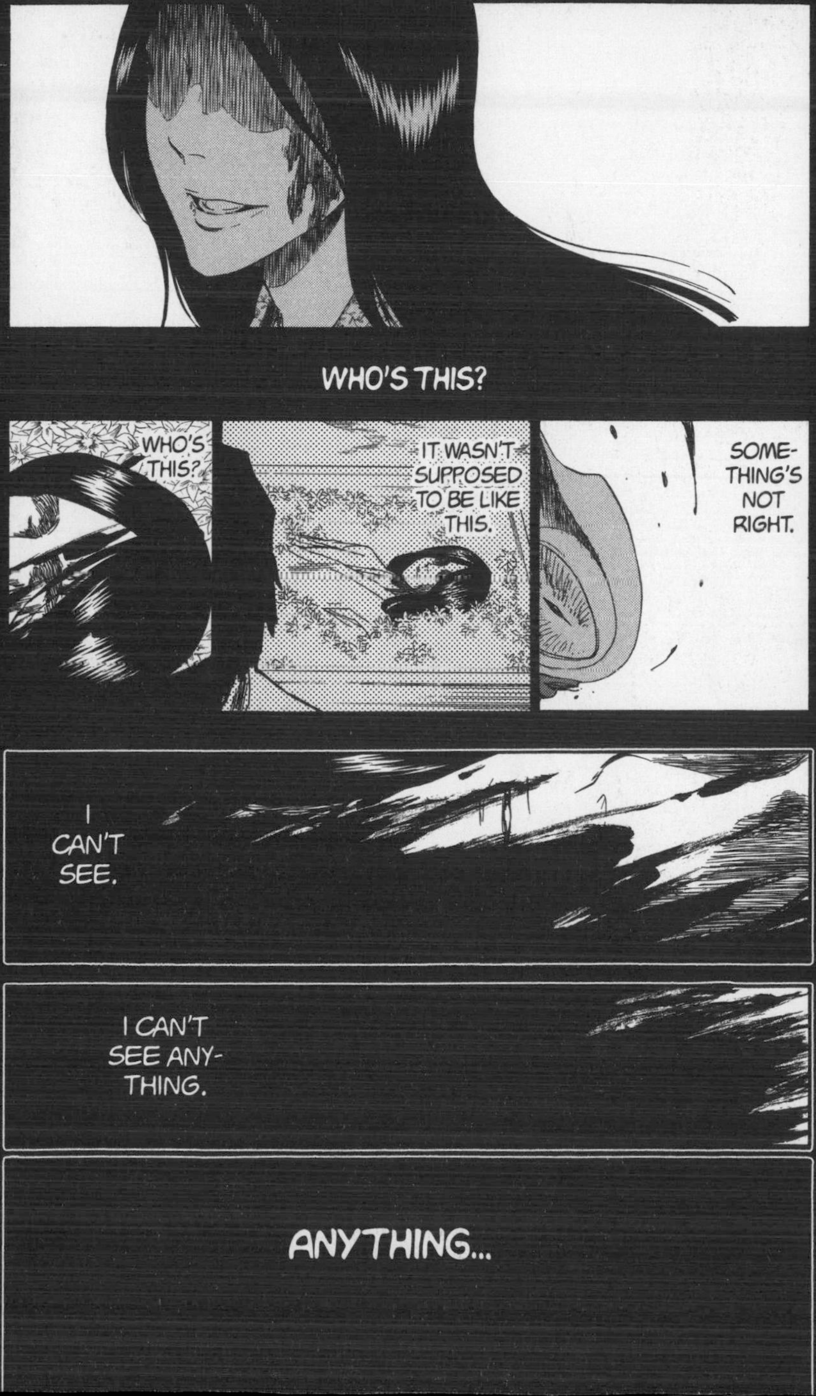
WHO'S THIS?
SOME-THING'S NOT RIGHT.
IT WASN'T SUPPOSED TO BE LIKE THIS.
WHO'S THIS?
I CAN'T SEE.
I CAN'T SEE ANY-THING.
ANYTHING...

CONTI
NUED
IN
BLEACH
45

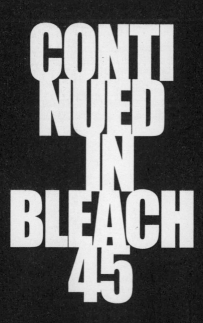

Next Volume Preview

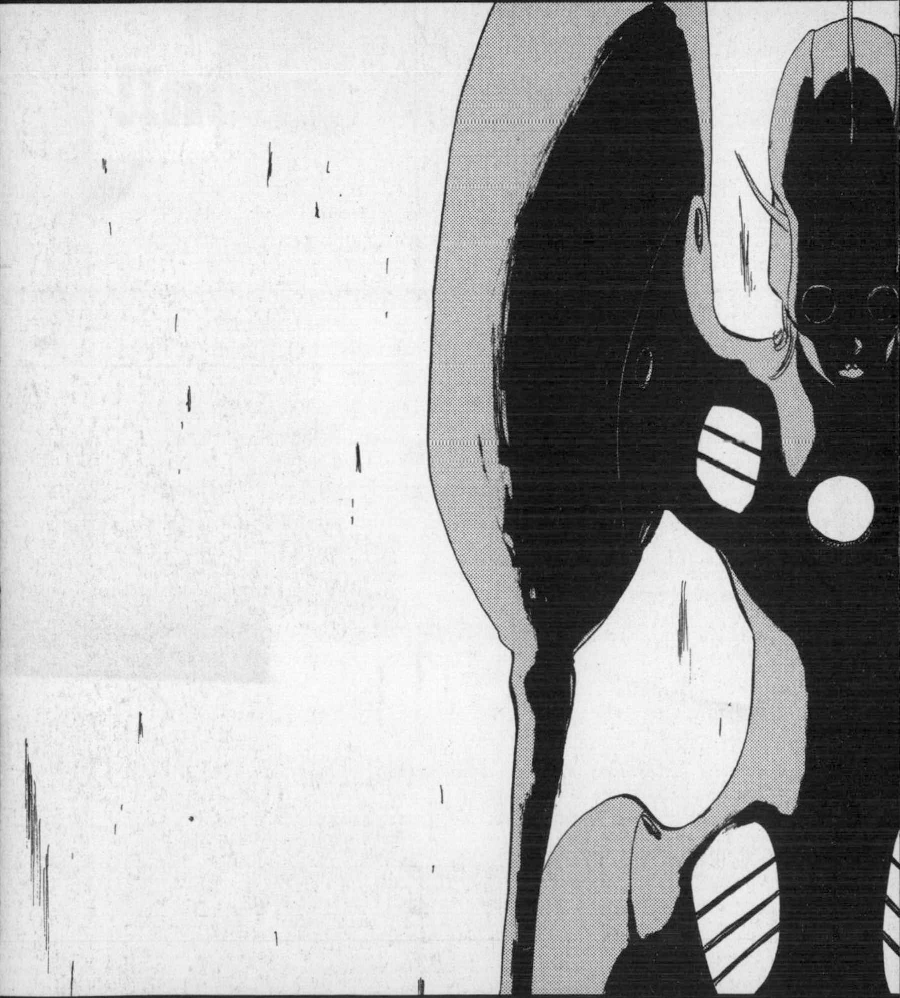

The remaining captains face Aizen as the war heads toward its climax. Has Aizen become invincible, or can Captain General Yamamoto end his reign of terror?! And what role will Ichigo play...?

You're Reading in the Wrong Directio

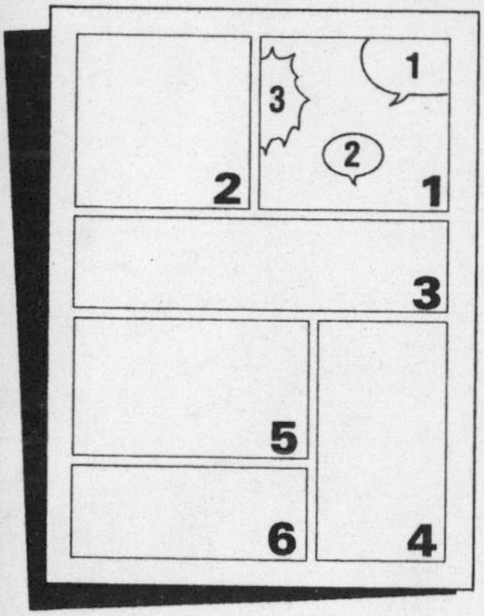
1
2
3
1
2
3
4
5
6

Whoops! Guess what? You're starting at the wrong end of the comic!

...It's true! In keeping with the original Japanese format, **Bleach** is meant to be read from right to left, starting in the upper-right corner.

Unlike English, which is read from left to right, Japanese is read from right to left, meaning that action, sound effects and word-balloon order are completely reversed... something which can make readers unfamiliar with Japanese feel pretty backwards themselves. For this reason, manga or Japanese comics published in the U.S. in English have sometimes been published "flopped"—that is, printed in exact reverse order, as though seen from the other side of a mirror.

By flopping pages, U.S. publishers can avoid confusing readers, but the compromise is not without its downside. For one thing, a character in a flopped manga series who once wore in the original Japanese version a T-shirt emblazoned with "M A Y" (as in "the merry month of") now wears one which reads "Y A M"! Additionally, many manga creators in Japan are themselves unhappy with the process, as some feel the mirror-imaging of their art skews their original intentions.

We are proud to bring you Tite Kubo's **Bleach** in the original unflopped format. For now, though, turn to the other side of the book and let the adventure begin...!

—Editor

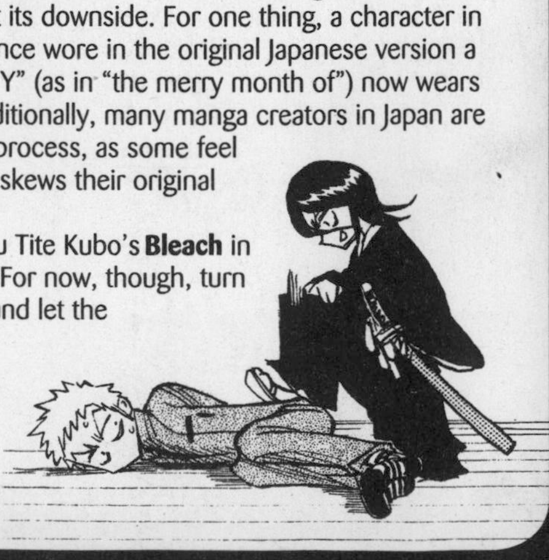